PEARSON EDEXCEL INTERNATIONAL GCSE (9–1)

ENGLISH LANGUAGE A

Student Book

David Grant

Roger Addison
Samantha Brunner
David Foster
Peter Inson
Robert O'Brien
Pam Taylor
Manjari Tennakoon

Published by Pearson Education Limited, 80 Strand, London, WC2R 0RL.

www.pearson.com/international-schools

Copies of official specifications for all Pearson qualifications may be found on the website: https://qualifications.pearson.com

Text © Pearson Education Limited 2022
Edited by Melanie Hoffman and Jane Read
Indexed by Georgina Bowden
Designed by Pearson Education Limited
Typeset by Straive Ltd
Original illustrations © Pearson Education Limited 2022
Cover design @ Pearson Education Limited 2022
Cover photo/illustration © Getty Images: Toby C

The rights of Roger Addison, Samantha Brunner, David Foster, David Grant, Peter Inson, Robert O'Brien, Pam Taylor and Manjari Tennakoon to be identified as authors of this work have been asserted by them in accordance with the Copyright, Designs and Patents Act 1988.

First published 2022

25 24

10 9 8 7 6 5 4

British Library Cataloguing in Publication Data
A catalogue record for this book is available from the British Library

ISBN 978 1 292 44000 2

Printed in the UK by Bell & Bain

Acknowledgements

Images:

(key: b-bottom; c-center; l-left; r-right; t-top)

Inside front cover: [**Shutterstock.com**/Dmitry Lobanov]

123RF: Gilberto Mevi 8, Jozef Polc 47C, Serezniy 52R, Dolgachov 53T, Nico Smit 68, Mikle15 81, Dudlajzov 94, Franck Boston 124, Dizanna 200, Steven Heap 271, Grahof 288, **Alamy Stock Photo:** Nigel Hicks 60, Africa Media Online 62, Pictorial Press Ltd 77, Chris Bull 78, Rodrigo Garrido/Reuters 96, Murray Sanders/Daily Mail/PA Images 103, louise murray 110, Beth Wald/Aurora Photos/Cavan Images 119, Jeff Morgan 16 122, Zahid Hussein/Reuters 132, GL Portrait 141, Kieran Doherty/Reuters 157, Pictorial Press Ltd 158, Archives du 7e Art collection/Photo 12 169, Denis Crawford 210BR, GL Archive 224, Granger Historical Picture Archive 226, IS862/Cultura RM 249, ZUMA Press Inc 247, Granger Historical Picture Archive 254, Photo 12 258, World History Archive 260, Old Paper Studios 262, Konstantin Kirillov 264, Andrew Fox 273, ZUMA Press, Inc. 281TL, Peter Alvey 284TL, Nikolay Tsuguliev 305, Ira Berger 310, Stephen Barnes 323, Photocosma 326BL; **Getty Images:** Matthew Horwood 11, Trudie Davidson/Moment 29, Ittipol Nampochai/EyeEm 47T, 10'000 Hours/DigitalVision 47B, FatCamera/E+ 99, Liyao Xie/Moment 128, Jonathan Saruk/Getty Images News 130, Suzanne Stroeer/Aurora Open 138, WLDavies/E+ 140R, SolStock/E+ 180, Martinedoucet/E+ 183, Zhuyongming/Moment 184, Artem Varnitsin/EyeEm 187, Alexandros Maragos/Moment Open 191, Rawpixel.com 192, Diane Labombarbe/Photodisc 205, Ippei Naoi 213, Tuan Tran 214, Cyndi Monaghan 219, Bachrach 223, Kattiyaearn 234, Susan Vineyard 250, Marco Secchi 267; **Shutterstock:** Evannovostro 40, Monkey Business Images 84, 163, Shutterstock 147, Irina Wilhauk 2, Shunevych Serhii 6, Darren Baker 15, Merla 16, Pablo Caridad 18T, Christopher Ewing 18C, Fabiano Panizzi 18B, ESB Professional 20, Triocean 21, Andrey Vandy-shev 23, Jose HERNANDEZ Camera 51 24, Costazzurra 26L, Ingrid Balabanova 26R, Everett Collection 27, ShulzhenkoElena 32, Anna_Zait-ceva 33, LightField Studios 34, Panitanphoto 37, Shahril KHMD 38L, Tina Bour 38C, Dmitry Galaganov 38R, Hedgehog94 39, BY-_-BY 44, Peter Turner Photography 45, Torsten Pursche 49, Non c 52L, Dan Kos-mayer 53B, Andrey_Popov 54, Neil Roy Johnson 55, Taylor Jackson 56, AsiaTravel 58, Alessia Pierdomenico 61, Spatuletail 65, DisobeyArt 72, Metamorworks 74, Travers Lewis 75, Addkm 80, Terrie L. Zeller 87, Ruta Saulyte-Laurinaviciene 88, Karamysh 98T, Elena Elisseeva 98B, Ponsulak 105, Dotted Yeti 108, Danita Delimont 112, Volodymyr Goinyk 114, Bian-ca L 116, Benemale 117, Wout Kok 136, Mark higgins 140L, Karel Bartik 142, David Brace 145, Mikadun 153, Diego Cervo 154, Chippix 159, Galyna Andrushko 166, Triff 171, Fongbeerredhot 173, Gorodenkoff 174, Ground Picture 176, VasiliyBudarin 179, Rawpixel.com 189, DeymosHR 195, Ink Drop 199, Lamai Prasitsuwan 204, Regien Paassen 206, Vvvita 209, Num Lpphoto 211, Kompass 210BTL, Stockphoto-graf 210BBL, Kreangkrai Pat 210BBR, Tchara 230, Totez 232, RAMNIKLAL MODI 238, Ffolas 239, Archana bhartia 236, Yuzu2020 243, Cdrin 255, IMG Stock Studio 261, Lynne Carpenter 269, Andriy Blokhin 274, Boris Stroujko 275, WICHAI WONGJONGJAIHAN 278, mRGB 279, Paul Aniszewski 281BL, Tammie Sue Teall 284BL, Schankz 285, Benjamin Haas 287, Gorodenkoff 292, Tomertu 295BL, Aris-Tect Group 295BR, SimoneN 295BC, Wit Olszewski 299, Kolomiyets Viktoriya 302, Frame Stock Foot-age 304, Tasha Cherkasova 306, HappyAprilBoy 308, Maria_Petrishina 313, Nataliya Hora 314, Rawpixel.com 319, DKai 321, Liu Zishan 326BC, Camilkuo 326BR; **Pearson Education:** Handan Erek 13.

All other images © Pearson Education

Text:

Excerpt(s) from A WALK IN THE WOODS: REDISCOVERING AMERICA ON THE APPALACHIANTRAIL by Bill Bryson, copyright © 1997 by Bill Bryson. Used by permission of Broadway Books,an imprint of Random House, a division of Penguin Random House LLC. All rights reserved. 6-7, It's over for fossil fuels: IPCC spells out what's needed to avert climate disaster. Copyright Guardian News & Media Ltd 2021 5, 10-11, When it's too windy for wind turbines: the downside of eco-power. © Telegraph Media Group Limited. 11, Lucy Maddox, Myth of the teenager, Does the stroppy adolescent exist?, http://www.prospectmagazine.co.uk/life/teenagers-adolescence-lucy-maddox, March 20, 2013; 14-15, Titanic Voices: 63 Survivors Tell Their Extraordinary Stories, 1e, Amberley Publishing (Holman, H. 2011) 27, This is Just to Say' by William Carlos Williams, from THE COLLECTED POEMS: VOLUME I, 1909-1939, copyright ©1938 by New Directions Publishing Corp. Reprinted by permission of New Directions Publishing Corp, also copyrighted and reprinted here by kind permission of Carcanet Press Limited, Manchester, UK 32, Playing video games can be bad for your health, researchers claim, Used by permisison of The Telegraph 59, "From Taking on the World, by Ellen MacArthur, Michael Joseph (MacArthur, E. 2002), the permission of United Agents LLP on behalf of Ellen MacArthur (Penguin Books 2003) Copyright © Ellen MacArthur, 2003" 59, David Beresford, Nelson Mandela obituary. Copyright Guardian News & Media Ltd 2021 61, I am prepared to die: Nelson Mandela's statement from the dock at the opening of the defence case in the Rivonia Trial, Reprinted by permission of Nelson Mandela

Endorsement Statement

In order to ensure that this resource offers high-quality support for the associated Pearson qualification, it has been through a review process by the awarding body. This process confirms that this resource fully

ABOUT THIS BOOK   VIII

ASSESSMENT OVERVIEW   X

01 READING SKILLS   3

02 WRITING SKILLS   25

03 PAPER 1   57

04 PAPER 2   207

05 PAPER 3   315

EXAM PREPARATION   330

GLOSSARY   334

INDEX   336

3 READING SKILLS

4 TEXT ANALYSIS

- 4 ■ SKIMMING AND SCANNING
- 6 ■ EXPLICIT AND IMPLICIT MEANING
- 8 ■ POINT+EVIDENCE+ EXPLANATION
- 10 ■ EXPLORING A TEXT

16 USE OF LANGUAGE

- 16 ■ WORD CLASSES
- 18 ■ CONNOTATIONS
- 20 ■ DIFFERENT SENTENCE TYPES
- 22 ■ SENTENCES FOR EFFECT

25 WRITING SKILLS

26 VOCABULARY

- 26 ■ CHOOSING THE RIGHT VOCABULARY
- 28 ■ VOCABULARY FOR EFFECT
- 30 ■ LANGUAGE FOR EFFECT
- 32 ■ WHY YOUR CHOICES MATTER

34 SENTENCES

- 34 ■ SENTENCE TYPES
- 36 ■ SENTENCE CONSTRUCTION
- 38 ■ SENTENCES FOR CLARITY
- 40 ■ SENTENCES FOR EFFECT

42 STRUCTURE

- 42 ■ PRINCIPLES OF STRUCTURE
- 44 ■ SEQUENCING IDEAS FOR EFFECT
- 46 ■ LINKING IDEAS

48 PUNCTUATION AND SPELLING

- 48 ■ ENDING A SENTENCE
- 49 ■ COMMAS
- 50 ■ APOSTROPHES
- 51 ■ COLONS, SEMI-COLONS, DASHES, BRACKETS, ELLIPSES
- 52 ■ COMMON SPELLING ERRORS
- 53 ■ IMPROVE YOUR WRITING
- 54 ■ PROOF-READING, CHECKING AND EDITING

57 PAPER 1

58 NON-FICTION TEXTS

- 58 ■ TYPES OF TEXT
- 78 ■ IDENTIFYING THE WRITER'S PERSPECTIVE
- 82 ■ AUDIENCE AND INTENTION
- 84 ■ FACT, OPINION AND EXPERT EVIDENCE
- 86 ■ LANGUAGE FOR DIFFERENT EFFECTS
- 90 ■ THE STRUCTURE OF A TEXT
- 92 ■ UNSEEN TEXTS
- 94 ■ PUTTING IT INTO PRACTICE

96 TEXT ANTHOLOGY: NON-FICTION

- 96 ■ 'THE DANGER OF A SINGLE STORY' – CHIMAMANDA NGOZI ADICHIE
- 103 ■ *A PASSAGE TO AFRICA* – GEORGE ALAGIAH
- 108 ■ *THE EXPLORER'S DAUGHTER* – KARI HERBERT
- 113 ■ 'EXPLORERS OR BOYS MESSING ABOUT' – STEVEN MORRIS
- 117 ■ *BETWEEN A ROCK AND A HARD PLACE* – ARON RALSTON
- 122 ■ 'YOUNG AND DYSLEXIC? YOU'VE GOT IT GOING ON' – BENJAMIN ZEPHANIAH
- 129 ■ *A GAME OF POLO WITH A HEADLESS GOAT* – EMMA LEVINE

134 ■ *BEYOND THE SKY AND THE EARTH: A JOURNEY INTO BHUTAN* – JAMIE ZEPPA

141 ■ *H IS FOR HAWK* – HELEN MACDONALD

147 ■ *CHINESE CINDERELLA* – ADELINE YEN MAH

152 UNSEEN TEXTS

152 ■ IDENTIFYING KEY INFORMATION

154 ■ ANALYSING THE TEXTS

162 COMPARING TEXTS

162 ■ COMPARISONS

168 ■ SELECTING EVIDENCE

170 ■ PUTTING IT INTO PRACTICE

174 TRANSACTIONAL WRITING

174 ■ AN INTRODUCTION TO TRANSACTIONAL WRITING

176 ■ WRITING FOR A PURPOSE: INFORM, EXPLAIN, REVIEW

180 ■ WRITING FOR A PURPOSE: ARGUE, PERSUADE, ADVISE

184 ■ WRITING FOR AN AUDIENCE

188 ■ FORM

194 ■ VOCABULARY FOR EFFECT

198 ■ SENTENCES FOR EFFECT

200 ■ IDEAS AND PLANNING

202 ■ OPENINGS AND CONCLUSIONS

204 ■ PUTTING IT INTO PRACTICE

207 PAPER 2

208 READING SKILLS: FICTION TEXTS

208 ■ TYPES OF TEXT

210 ■ FIGURATIVE LANGUAGE

214 ■ CREATING CHARACTER, ATMOSPHERE AND EMOTION

218 ■ NARRATIVE VOICE

220 ■ STRUCTURE

224 ■ PUTTING IT INTO PRACTICE

226 TEXT ANTHOLOGY: FICTION

226 ■ 'DISABLED' – WILFRED OWEN

230 ■ 'OUT, OUT—' – ROBERT FROST

234 ■ 'AN UNKNOWN GIRL' – MONIZA ALVI

239 ■ 'THE BRIGHT LIGHTS OF SARAJEVO' – TONY HARRISON

247 ■ 'STILL I RISE' – MAYA ANGELOU

254 ■ 'THE STORY OF AN HOUR' – KATE CHOPIN

258 ■ 'THE NECKLACE' – GUY DE MAUPASSANT

267 ■ 'SIGNIFICANT CIGA-RETTES' (FROM *THE ROAD HOME*) – ROSE TREMAIN

273 ■ 'WHISTLE AND I'LL COME TO YOU' (FROM *THE WOMAN IN BLACK*) – SUSAN HILL

281 ■ 'NIGHT' – ALICE MUNRO

292 IMAGINATIVE WRITING

292 ■ AN INTRODUCTION TO IMAGINATIVE WRITING

294 ■ GENERATING IDEAS

296 ■ PLOT

298 ■ OPENINGS

300 ■ NARRATIVE CHOICES

302 ■ CHARACTERS

304 ■ MONOLOGUES AND DIALOGUES

306 ■ DESCRIPTIVE WRITING

308 ■ VOCABULARY FOR EFFECT

310 ■ SENTENCES FOR EFFECT

312 ■ PUTTING IT INTO PRACTICE

315 PAPER 3

316 ■ NON-EXAMINED ASSESSMENT OVERVIEW

318 ■ ASSIGNMENT A: POETRY AND PROSE TEXTS

322 ■ ASSIGNMENT B: IMAGINATIVE WRITING

330 EXAM PREPARATION

334 GLOSSARY

336 INDEX

ABOUT THIS BOOK

This book is written for students following the revised Edexcel International GCSE (9–1) English Language A specification for first teaching September 2022 and covers both years of the course. The specification and sample assessment materials for English Language A can be found on the Pearson Qualifications website.

The course has been structured so that teaching and learning can take place in any order, both in the classroom and in any independent learning. The book contains five chapters: Reading Skills, Writing Skills, Paper 1, Paper 2 and Paper 3.

The Reading Skills and Writing Skills chapters cover fundamental areas of these two key areas of English Language.

Key points
Easy to understand, core points to be taken away from sections or texts.

Exam-style questions
Questions tailored to the Pearson Edexcel specification to allow for practice and development of exam writing technique.

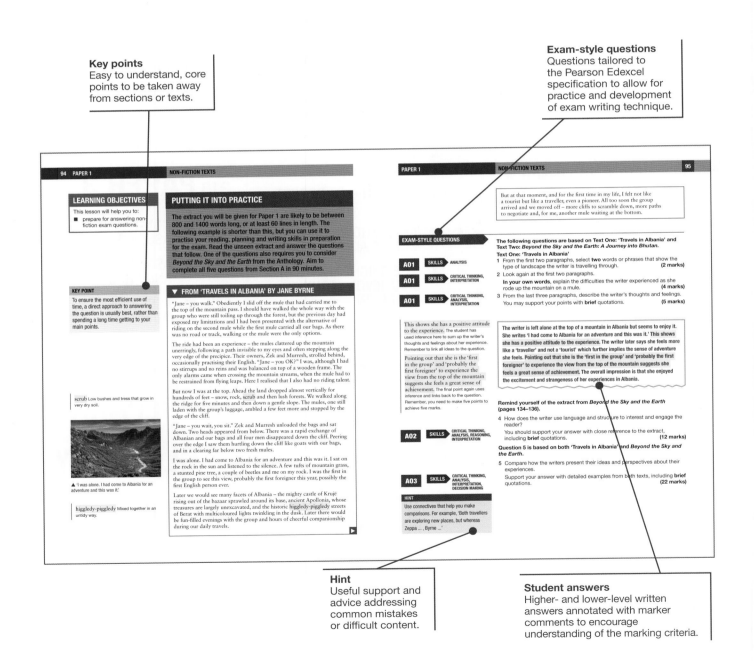

Hint
Useful support and advice addressing common mistakes or difficult content.

Student answers
Higher- and lower-level written answers annotated with marker comments to encourage understanding of the marking criteria.

They build on and reinforce what students already know and develop essential skills that will allow them to succeed on this course. These chapters can be used to teach these reading and writing skills in blocks at the start of the course or integrated into relevant sections of the texts being studied.

The Paper 1 and Paper 2 chapters cover all of the content required by the course, mirroring the two exam papers for those taking this route. The information in the Paper 2 chapter will also help students taking the non-examined assessment route to prepare to complete their assignments. This is also supplemented by the Paper 3 chapter, which gives advice for those taking this non-examined assessment option.

For each section or Anthology text, information is interspersed with activities in order to put learning into practice and exam-style questions to help students prepare and practise for the exam. Other features help to expand students' knowledge and reinforce their learning. All Anthology texts are reproduced in full, with detailed analysis and questions for each text.

You can find more information about the English Language A course, including the Specification and the Sample Assessment Materials, on the Pearson Edexcel website.

Learning objectives
Chapters and Units are carefully tailored to address key assessment objectives central to the course.

Activities
A wide range of varied activities to encourage understanding and embed understanding as an individual, as well as in larger groups to establish cross-peer learning and communication.

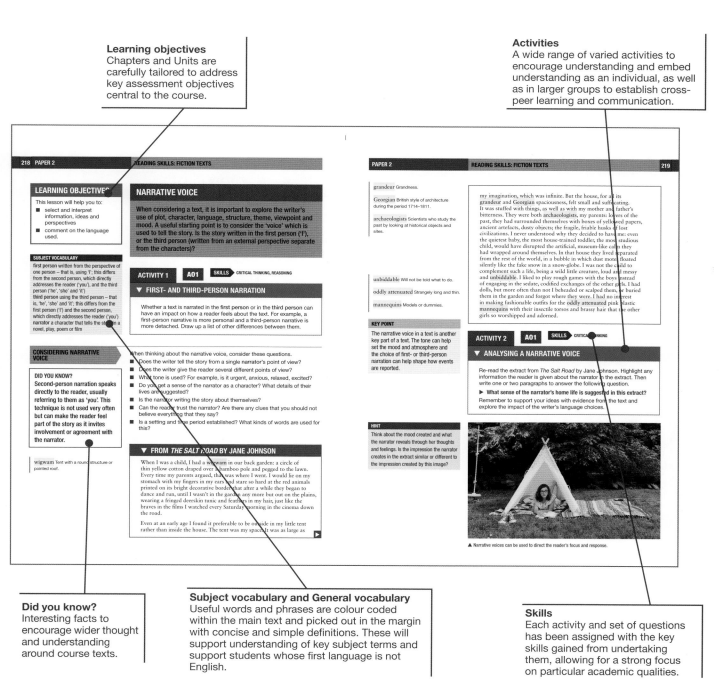

Did you know?
Interesting facts to encourage wider thought and understanding around course texts.

Subject vocabulary and General vocabulary
Useful words and phrases are colour coded within the main text and picked out in the margin with concise and simple definitions. These will support understanding of key subject terms and support students whose first language is not English.

Skills
Each activity and set of questions has been assigned with the key skills gained from undertaking them, allowing for a strong focus on particular academic qualities.

ASSESSMENT OVERVIEW

The following tables give an overview of the assessment for this course. You should study this information closely to help ensure that you are fully prepared for this course and know exactly what to expect in each part of the assessment.

There are two alternative routes that can be taken:

Route 1: 100% written exam papers (Paper 1 and Paper 2).

Route 2: 60% written exam paper and 40% internally assessed non-examined assessment (Paper 1 and Paper 3).

Paper 1 is the compulsory unit for all students taking International GCSE English Language A. Paper 2 is taken by those opting for the 100% exam route (Route 1). Those International GCSE students who opt for the non-examined assessment take Paper 3 instead of Paper 2 (Route 2).

There is also an optional spoken language endorsement for this course. Students must demonstrate their presentation skills in a formal setting, listen and respond to questions and feedback, and use spoken English effectively. For further information about this optional component, please see the International GCSE English Language A specification. It is not reproduced here as the spoken language endorsement is not covered in this book.

ROUTE 1

▼ PAPER 1	▼ PERCENTAGE	▼ MARKS	▼ TIME	▼ AVAILABILITY
NON-FICTION TEXTS AND TRANSACTIONAL WRITING Written exam paper Paper code 4EA1/01 Externally set and assessed by Pearson Edexcel Single tier of entry	60%	90	2 hours 15 minutes	June and November exam series First assessment June 2024

▼ PAPER 2	▼ PERCENTAGE	▼ MARKS	▼ TIME	▼ AVAILABILITY
POETRY AND PROSE TEXTS AND IMAGINATIVE WRITING Written exam paper Paper code 4EA1/02 Externally set and assessed by Pearson Edexcel Single tier of entry	40%	60	1 hour 30 minutes	June and November exam series First assessment June 2024

ROUTE 2

▼ PAPER 1	▼ PERCENTAGE	▼ MARKS	▼ TIME	▼ AVAILABILITY
NON-FICTION AND TRANSACTIONAL WRITING Written exam paper Paper code 4EA1/01 Externally set and assessed by Pearson Edexcel Single tier of entry	60%	90	2 hours 15 minutes	June and November exam series First assessment June 2024

▼ PAPER 3	▼ PERCENTAGE	▼ MARKS	▼ TIME	▼ AVAILABILITY
POETRY AND PROSE TEXTS AND IMAGINATIVE WRITING Non-examined assessment Paper code 4EA1/03 Two teacher-devised assignments, internally set and assessed, and externally moderated by Pearson Edexcel	40%	60	n/a	June and November exam series First assessment June 2024

ASSESSMENT OBJECTIVES AND WEIGHTINGS

▼ SECTION	▼ ASSESSMENT OBJECTIVE	▼ DESCRIPTION	▼ % IN INTERNATIONAL GCSE
READING	**AO1**	Read and understand a variety of texts, selecting and interpreting information, ideas and perspectives	15%
	AO2	Understand and analyse how writers use linguistic and structural devices to achieve their effects	20%
	AO3	Explore links and connections between writers' ideas and perspectives, as well as how these are conveyed	15%
WRITING	**AO4**	Communicate effectively and imaginatively, adapting form, tone and register of writing for specific purposes and audiences	30%
	AO5	Write clearly, using a range of vocabulary and sentence structures, with appropriate paragraphing and accurate spelling, grammar and punctuation	20%

RELATIONSHIP OF ASSESSMENT OBJECTIVES TO UNITS

▼ UNIT NUMBER	▼ ASSESSMENT OBJECTIVE				
	AO1	**AO2**	**AO3**	**AO4**	**AO5**
PAPER 1	7%	8%	15%	18%	12%
PAPER 2 / PAPER 3	8%	12%	0%	12%	8%
TOTAL FOR INTERNATIONAL GCSE	**15%**	**20%**	**15%**	**30%**	**20%**

ASSESSMENT SUMMARY: ROUTE 1

▼ PAPER 1	▼ DESCRIPTION	▼ MARKS	▼ ASSESSMENT OBJECTIVES
	Structure Paper 1 assesses 60% of the total English Language A qualification. There will be two sections on the paper. Students must answer all questions in Section A and one question from a choice of two in Section B.		
NON-FICTION TEXTS AND TRANSACTIONAL WRITING PAPER CODE 4EA1/01	**Section A: Non-fiction Texts** Students will study and analyse a range of contemporary non-fiction texts from the Pearson Edexcel International GCSE English Anthology. One text from the Anthology will be examined. Students must: ■ develop skills to analyse how writers use linguistic and structural devices to achieve their effects ■ explore links and connections between writers' ideas and perspectives.	45	Questions will test the following Assessment Objectives: AO1 – 7% AO2 – 8% AO3 – 15%
	Section B: Transactional Writing Students will explore and develop transactional writing skills. Students must: ■ develop transactional writing skills for a variety of purposes and audiences ■ use spelling, punctuation and grammar accurately.	45	Questions will test the following Assessment Objectives: AO4 – 18% AO5 – 12%
	This is a single-tier exam paper and all questions cover the full ranges of grades from 9–1. The assessment duration is 2 hours 15 minutes. Closed book: texts are not allowed in the exam. However, students will be provided with any relevant extracts in the exam.	The total number of marks available is **90**	

▼ PAPER 2	▼ DESCRIPTION	▼ MARKS	▼ ASSESSMENT OBJECTIVES
	Structure Paper 2 assesses 40% of the total English Language A qualification. There will be two sections on the paper. Students must answer the question in Section A and one question from a choice of three in Section B.		
POETRY AND PROSE TEXTS AND IMAGINATIVE WRITING PAPER CODE 4EA1/02	**Section A: Poetry and Prose Texts** Students will study and analyse a range of fictional poetry and prose texts from the Pearson Edexcel International GCSE English Anthology. The examined texts will be from the Anthology. Students must: ■ develop skills to analyse how writers use linguistic and structural devices to achieve their effects.	30	Questions will test the following Assessment Objectives: AO1 – 8% AO2 – 12%
	Section B: Imaginative Writing Students will explore and develop imaginative writing skills. Students must: ■ develop imaginative writing skills to engage the reader ■ use spelling, punctuation and grammar accurately.	30	Questions will test the following Assessment Objectives: AO4 – 12% AO5 – 8%
	This is a single-tier exam paper and all questions cover the full ranges of grades from 9–1. The assessment duration is 1 hour 30 minutes. Closed book: texts are not allowed in the exam. However, students will be provided with any relevant extracts in the exam.	The total number of marks available is **60**	

ASSESSMENT SUMMARY: ROUTE 2

▼ PAPER 1	▼ DESCRIPTION	▼ MARKS	▼ ASSESSMENT OBJECTIVES
NON-FICTION TEXTS AND TRANSACTIONAL WRITING PAPER CODE 4EA1/01	**Structure** Paper 1 assesses 60% of the total English Language A qualification. There will be two sections on the paper. Students must answer all questions in Section A and one question from a choice of two in Section B.		
	Section A: Non-fiction Texts Students will study and analyse a range of contemporary non-fiction texts from the Pearson Edexcel International GCSE English Anthology. One text from the Anthology will be examined. Students must: ■ develop skills to analyse how writers use linguistic and structural devices to achieve their effects ■ explore links and connections between writers' ideas and perspectives.	45	Questions will test the following Assessment Objectives: AO1 – 7% AO2 – 8% AO3 – 15%
	Section B: Transactional Writing Students will explore and develop transactional writing skills. Students must: ■ develop transactional writing skills for a variety of purposes and audiences ■ use spelling, punctuation and grammar accurately.	45	Questions will test the following Assessment Objectives: AO4 – 18% AO5 – 12%
	This is a single-tier exam paper and all questions cover the full ranges of grades from 9–1. The assessment duration is 2 hours 15 minutes. Closed book: texts are not allowed in the exam. However, students will be provided with any relevant extracts in the exam.	The total number of marks available is **90**	

▼ PAPER 3	▼ DESCRIPTION	▼ MARKS	▼ ASSESSMENT OBJECTIVES
POETRY AND PROSE TEXTS AND IMAGINATIVE WRITING PAPER CODE 4EA1/03	**Structure** Paper 3 non-examined assessment assesses 40% of the total English Language A qualification. The assessment of the component is through two non-examined assessment assignments, internally set and assessed, and externally moderated by Pearson.		
	Section A: Poetry and Prose Texts Students will study and analyse a range of fictional poetry and prose texts from the Pearson Edexcel International GCSE English Anthology. The texts you write about will be from the Anthology. Students must: ■ develop skills to analyse how writers use linguistic and structural devices to achieve their effects.	30	Questions will test the following Assessment Objectives: AO1 – 8% AO2 – 12%
	Section B: Imaginative Writing Students will explore and develop imaginative writing skills. Students must: ■ develop imaginative writing skills to engage the reader ■ use spelling, punctuation and grammar accurately.	30	Questions will test the following Assessment Objectives: AO4 – 12% AO5 – 8%
	This is a single-tier non-examined assessment assignment and will cover the full ranges of grades from 9–1. There is no prescribed word length for the non-examined assessment paper. Typically, the task may be up to 1900 words, but there are no penalties for exceeding this guidance.	The total number of marks available is **60**	

ORANJESTAD 1134 MI
HAVANA 156 MI
LONDON 4565 MI
RIO DE JANEIRO 4171 MI
KINGSTON 488 MI
TURKS + CAICOS 615 MI
BUENOS AIRES 4350 MI
CAPE TOWN 7699 MI
SANTIAGO 4055 MI

READING SKILLS

Assessment Objective 1

Read and understand a variety of texts, selecting and interpreting information, ideas and perspectives

Assessment Objective 2

Understand and analyse how writers use linguistic and structural devices to achieve their effects

Assessment Objective 3

Explore links and connections between writers' ideas and perspectives, as well as how these are conveyed

This chapter focuses on some core reading skills that you can apply to all parts of the English Language A course. Working through these lessons and activities will help you to develop the reading skills that you will need for the exams and non-examined assessment assignments.

The chapter is split into the following sections:
- Text analysis
- Use of language.

In the reading sections of your exams, you will need to be able to meet the Assessment Objectives AO1, AO2 and AO3.

LEARNING OBJECTIVES

This lesson will help you to:
- understand the main ideas that a writer is communicating
- summarise the key points of a text quickly
- build confidence in independent reading.

KEY POINT

Skimming and scanning are important reading techniques. Skimming is reading quickly to get a general sense of a text. Scanning involves looking through a text for specific information.

SKIMMING AND SCANNING

It can be difficult to know where to start when approaching a text for the first time. You need a methodical approach that allows you to understand the main ideas that are being communicated.

Skimming and scanning are two important reading techniques. They are often confused with one another, but they are very different skills. However, both help you to achieve the same aim: to read more quickly and effectively.

SKIMMING

Skimming is useful when you want to quickly get a general idea of what a text is about. When you skim, you read through the text three to four times faster than when you read each word in order to get a sense of the topic, ideas and information being conveyed.

WHEN SHOULD I SKIM?

- When you have a lot to read in a short space of time.
- When revising topics to identify key information.
- When locating an extract in a text.
- When finding relevant material when planning an essay.

SCANNING

Scanning refers to reading through material to find specific information. When you scan, you run your eyes over the information in a text and pull out specific words, phrases or pieces of information. You may not realise that you scan through different texts every day, from television guides to football results.

WHEN SHOULD I SCAN?

- When looking for specific pieces of information quickly.
- When locating a relevant quotation or section in a literature text.

ACTIVITY 1   **SKILLS** ▸ DECISION MAKING

▼ SKIMMING OR SCANNING?

Read the following examples and identify which describes the process of skimming and which describes scanning.

1. You flick through a financial report to find a particular set of data.
2. You quickly go through a 20-page report in a few minutes to determine the overall subject, tone and a few key points.
3. You pick up a newspaper at a coffee shop, look over the first few pages and gather some general information about the events happening in the world.

HINT

To skim effectively, you don't read everything. What you read is more important than what you skip. Try to:
- highlight key points
- rephrase the main point of each paragraph in your own words
- underline any unfamiliar words.

topic sentence the first sentence in a paragraph, often used to explain the key idea

chronologically organised in linear time

flashback when the narrator of a story jumps out of the present in order to describe an event which happened in the past (often in the form of memories)

STRATEGIES FOR SKIMMING

- Read the **topic sentence**. This will give you a good sense of the ideas and structure of the whole text.
- Read the first and last paragraphs.
- Use chapter names, headings and subheadings as a guide.

STRATEGIES FOR SCANNING

- For scanning to be successful, be sure of your purpose. Think about what information you are looking for before you begin to scan the text.
- Consider how the text is structured. Is it arranged alphabetically, by category, **chronologically** or does it use other devices such as **flashback**?
- Use your index finger to help you, such as when scanning a timetable for a train time. Move your finger down the text at the same time as your eyes to help you to maintain focus.

ACTIVITY 2   **SKILLS** ▶ INTERPRETATION

▼ SCANNING AND SUMMARISING INFORMATION

STEP 1	STEP 2	STEP 3	STEP 4	STEP 5
Spend five seconds skim reading the extract below. Write one sentence summarising what this newspaper article is about. Compare your sentence with a partner's. Do you agree?	Now, write three questions about key information in the article. For example: When do greenhouse gas emissions need to start to fall, according to the IPCC?	Swap questions with your partner.	Scan the extract to find the answers to your partner's questions.	Use some or all of the information you have noted in this activity to add one or two further sentences to your summary.

▼ 'IT'S OVER FOR FOSSIL FUELS' FROM *THE GUARDIAN*

Thirty months: that is the very short time the world now has for global greenhouse gas emissions to finally start to fall. If not, we will miss the chance to avoid the worst impacts of the climate crisis.

The conclusion of the world's scientists, collated by the Intergovernmental Panel on Climate Change and approved by all the world's governments, says this reversal requires "immediate and deep" cuts in emissions everywhere.

"It's now or never, if we want to limit global warming to 1.5C," said Prof Jim Skea, a co-chair of the report. "Without immediate and deep emissions reductions across all sectors, it will be impossible."

The implication for the biggest culprit, fossil fuels, is clear: it's over. The IPCC states that existing and currently planned fossil fuel projects are already more than the climate can handle. More projects will lock in even greater emissions and our journey to climate hell.

Responding to the report, the UN secretary general, António Guterres, had a savage assessment of current political and corporate pledges of action: "Some government and business leaders are saying one thing, but doing another. Simply put, they are lying."

"Increasing fossil fuel production will only make matters worse," he said. "It is time to stop burning our planet, and start investing in the abundant renewable energy all around us."

LEARNING OBJECTIVES

This lesson will help you to:

- interpret the information and ideas in a text
- read between the lines to work out what the text implies.

KEY POINT

Explicit meaning is where the writer **ex**plains their ideas.

Implicit meaning is where the writer **im**plies their ideas; you have to infer and **im**agine based on what you know.

SUBJECT VOCABULARY

infer read between the lines

EXPLICIT AND IMPLICIT MEANING

To be a good reader, you need to understand what a text tells you directly, or explicitly, and to infer based on what you think the writer indirectly, or implicitly, suggests in their text. This may be about the writer's views, character or theme.

▲ A couple on their wedding day

EXPLICIT MEANING

The picture shows a woman in a dress holding flowers and standing close to a man in a suit.

IMPLICIT MEANING

You may be able to **infer** that this is a wedding photograph because you have experience of seeing this type of image being related to weddings.

▼ AN EXTRACT FROM *A WALK IN THE WOODS* BY BILL BRYSON

We hiked till five and camped beside a tranquil spring in a small, grassy clearing in the trees just off the trail. Because it was our first day back on the trail, we were flush for food, including perishables like cheese and bread that had to be eaten before they went off or were shaken to bits in our packs, so we rather gorged ourselves, then sat around smoking and chatting idly until persistent and numerous midgelike creatures (no-see-ums, as they are universally known along the trail) drove us into our tents. It was perfect sleeping weather, cool enough to need a bag but warm enough that you could sleep in your underwear, and I was looking forward to a long night's snooze – indeed was enjoying a long night's snooze – when, at some indeterminate dark hour, there was a sound nearby that made my eyes fly open. Normally, I slept through everything – through thunderstorms, through Katz's snoring and noisy midnight pees – so something big enough or distinctive enough to wake me was unusual. There was a sound of undergrowth being disturbed – a click of breaking branches, a weighty pushing through low foliage – and then a kind of large, vaguely irritable snuffling noise.

▶

Bear!

I sat bolt upright. Instantly every neuron in my brain was awake and dashing around frantically, like ants when you disturb their nest. I reached instinctively for my knife, then realized I had left it in my pack, just outside the tent. Nocturnal defense had ceased to be a concern after many successive nights of tranquil woodland repose. There was another noise, quite near.

"Stephen, you awake?" I whispered.

"Yup," he replied in a weary but normal voice.

"What was that?"

"How the hell should I know?"

"It sounded big."

"Everything sounds big in the woods."

This was true. Once a skunk had come plodding through our camp and it had sounded like a stegosaurus.

ACTIVITY 1 | **SKILLS** ▶ CRITICAL THINKING, ANALYSIS, INTERPRETATION

▼ INFERRING FROM A TEXT

Read the extract from *A Walk In the Woods* by Bill Bryson. In pairs, choose a paragraph each and consider the following questions.

▶ **What does the narrator tell you about his thoughts and feelings?**

▶ **Which words and phrases allow you to infer his thoughts and feelings?**

Draw a table with two columns, one for each question, and pick out the key words and phrases from your paragraph which convey explicit and implicit meaning.

KEY VOCABULARY

SUBJECT VOCABULARY

synonyms words that share the same meaning as other words; for example, 'quick' might be a synonym for 'fast'

connotations ideas linked to a word; ideas that have become associated with a word

Writers use a lot of similar phrases to convey meaning. Don't just use 'shows'; using some of these **synonyms** could improve your writing.

- highlights
- suggests
- is redolent of
- has **connotations** of
- exposes
- denotes
- illustrates
- conveys
- introduces
- portrays
- demonstrates
- emphasises
- signifies
- reflects
- implies
- represents
- reveals
- infers
- connotes.

LEARNING OBJECTIVES

This lesson will help you to:
- organise your ideas and structure your writing clearly and with direction.

POINT+EVIDENCE+EXPLANATION

When analysing a text, it is important to express points in a clear and structured way, so you should organise your writing into paragraphs. Each paragraph should be self-contained and make sense on its own. It should be constructed of a group of sentences which all link to the same idea, theme or topic.

MAKING THE PERFECT POINT

HINT

A quotation does not have to be **direct speech**: you can quote evidence from a science journal or a famous play in the same way.

SUBJECT VOCABULARY

quotations words from a text
quotation marks punctuation marks used to indicate where you have quoted
direct speech words spoken by a character in a novel, play or poem

Each paragraph of analysis you write should contain a **Point**, some **Evidence** and an **Explanation**.

1 State your **point** clearly and concisely. Your point should be relevant to the task or question that you have been set.

2 Support your statement with reference to a specific part of the text that you are writing about. **Quotations** can be used as **evidence** to support what you are saying and to help you to make your point. Try to select words or phrases from the text that precisely support your point and keep them as brief as possible. Use inverted commas, also known as **quotation marks**, to indicate where you have used words directly from another text.

3 Use your **explanation** to explain how your quotation supports the point that you have made. You should also aim to explore the writer's use of language in your quotation, going into some detail about the writer's choice of words, language devices or sentence structures.

PERFECT PUNCTUATION

Short quotations of a single line or part of a line should be incorporated within quotation marks as part of the running text of your essay, 'just like this'. Quotations of two or more full lines should be indented from the main body of the text and introduced by a colon, like this:

> 'This is how you would quote a longer piece of text, but make sure that it is all relevant.'

PARAGRAPH SANDWICHES

You can think of your paragraph like a sandwich:

Top slice: the opening topic sentence introduces your main idea.

Fillings: supporting sentences describe and explain your main point, using quotations or textual references to support it.

Bottom slice: a closing sentence to summarise what the writer has done and how and why the writer has done it.

KEY POINT

Follow these four rules for excellent writing:

1 Structure: ideas must be clearly expressed and logically sequenced.
2 Paragraphs: paragraphs should be well constructed and follow on from one another. Quotations should be correctly presented.
3 Vocabulary: use a wide range of key vocabulary with precision.
4 Spelling, punctuation and grammar: maintain accuracy throughout.

SUBJECT VOCABULARY

protagonist the main character

ACTIVITY 1   **SKILLS** ▸ PROBLEM SOLVING, ANALYSIS, REASONING

▼ SUMMARISING WITH POINT, EVIDENCE AND EXPLANATION

Read this paragraph, summarising the novel *Of Mice and Men* by John Steinbeck. Copy the paragraph and colour code or label the Point, Evidence and Explanation. Each one may be more than one sentence.

> Set in the Great Depression of the 1930s, the novel tells of the close friendship between two farm workers, George and Lennie: 'I got you to look after me, and you got me to look after you'. The other men on the ranch are described as 'the loneliest guys in the world' and George and Lennie are proud of the fact that they have each other. The repetition of the second person pronoun 'you' here emphasises the close and reciprocal bond between the men. George and Lennie often repeat this line to one another when they are talking about their dreams for the future and Lennie is always excited when George reaffirms their friendship in this way. Their friendship gives them hope and joy in a desolate world.

ACTIVITY 2   **SKILLS** ▸ CRITICAL THINKING, PROBLEM SOLVING, ANALYSIS, INTERPRETATION

▼ LITERATURE ANALYSIS PARAGRAPHS

Using a text from the English Anthology, write your own question and point–evidence–explanation paragraph about a character or theme. The following questions are examples to help you to construct a question based on your own reading.

▶ **How is the protagonist portrayed in the text?**

▶ **What is the main theme of the text?**

▶ **What is the author trying to convey through the text?**

▶ **How does the opening set the scene for the text?**

Give your question and paragraph to a partner and check each other's work. Consider the following questions and clearly label examples of each within the paragraph.

Does the paragraph include the following?

■ A **point**?

■ Some **evidence**: a quotation or example?

■ An **explanation**: an exploration of the quotation and what it shows? This may include:

    ■ a note on the **language or literary devices** used

    ■ some understanding of the **writer's attitude**

    ■ a **personal response** to the characters or themes of a text.

LEARNING OBJECTIVES

This lesson will help you to:

- approach a non-fiction text critically
- recognise fact and opinion and follow an argument
- build confidence in responding to a text
- understand how writers use language to influence their readers.

EXPLORING A TEXT

This section will help you to prepare for **Paper 1 Section A**, which will test your reading and critical skills. There will be questions on both a prepared and an unprepared non-fiction reading extract. This will be drawn from a range of contemporary non-fiction, including autobiography, travel writing, reportage, media articles, letters, diary entries and opinion pieces. You will find additional information on this section of the exam on pages 58–95.

EXPLORING A TEXT: A GUIDE

SUBJECT VOCABULARY

intention the impact the author wants their writing to have on the reader
rhetorical device using language in a certain way to achieve an effect

Understanding how writers present ideas is key to understanding how texts work. When you read a text, you form an opinion. You need to be aware of a variety of ways in which writers use language to influence their readers.

The devices used tend to be linked to the text's purpose and the writer's intention: the impact they want the text to have on the reader. So a text that tries to persuade a reader of a particular opinion will use rhetorical devices, while a text that describes another country is likely to use a wide range of descriptive and figurative devices to convey a vivid sense of place.

When you read a new piece of non-fiction, you should first try to understand what points are being made.

▼ 'IT'S OVER FOR FOSSIL FUELS' FROM *THE GUARDIAN*

Thirty months: that is the very short time the world now has for global greenhouse gas emissions to finally start to fall. If not, we will miss the chance to avoid the worst impacts of the climate crisis.

The conclusion of the world's scientists, collated by the Intergovernmental Panel on Climate Change and approved by all the world's governments, says this reversal requires "immediate and deep" cuts in emissions everywhere.

"It's now or never, if we want to limit global warming to 1.5C," said Prof Jim Skea, a co-chair of the report. "Without immediate and deep emissions reductions across all sectors, it will be impossible."

The implication for the biggest culprit, fossil fuels, is clear: it's over. The IPCC states that existing and currently planned fossil fuel projects are already more than the climate can handle. More projects will lock in even greater emissions and our journey to climate hell.

Responding to the report, the UN secretary general, António Guterres, had a savage assessment of current political and corporate pledges of action: "Some government and business leaders are saying one thing, but doing another. Simply put, they are lying."

"Increasing fossil fuel production will only make matters worse," he said. "It is time to stop burning our planet, and start investing in the abundant renewable energy all around us."

That is the good news in the new IPCC report. "We know what we need to do and we can do a lot of it already," said Stephen Cornelius of WWF. "But every moment, every policy, every investment, every decision matters to avoid further climate chaos."

The IPCC spells out the huge cost reductions over the last decade in solar and wind power and says that some countries already have electricity grids predominantly powered by renewables. It also strongly highlights the big potential impact from energy-efficient homes, walking and cycling, greener diets and less food waste. All these are popular with people, the IPCC notes.

▶

Protecting and restoring nature can deliver both large-scale cuts in emissions by ending the razing of forests and large-scale removal of CO_2 from the atmosphere through growing trees, the IPCC report says. But it warns this cannot compensate for any delay in cutting fossil fuel burning and must involve Indigenous peoples, who are the best guardians of wild places.

The cost of ending the climate crisis is small, the IPCC concludes. Taking into account the climate damages avoided and the savings in adapting to extreme weather, investing in emissions cuts saves money.

"We must be clear that decisive action on climate is not a 'cost'; it is an investment, not just in our future, but in our survival. It would be the greatest cost-saving of human history," said Steve Trent, at the Environmental Justice Foundation.

ACTIVITY 1   SKILLS ▸ CRITICAL THINKING, ANALYSIS, INTERPRETATION

▼ RECOGNISING FACT AND OPINION

Read the article above taken from *The Guardian* newspaper.

1 What are the writer's purposes and intentions in this text: the impact the writer wants it to have on the reader?
2 Write down two facts and two opinions the writer gives in the article. How do these facts and opinions help the writer to achieve their purpose and intention?

▼ 'WHEN IT'S TOO WINDY FOR WIND TURBINES: THE DOWNSIDE OF ECO-POWER' FROM *THE TELEGRAPH*

On Friday morning, I think for the first time I understood what is meant by the "calm before the storm". The dog and I were walking along an unmade road in an eerie stillness. The sky was pewter with rain, although not a drop had yet fallen. The only sound was the leaves in the trees rustling apprehensively. The whole world felt apprehensive. Waiting. Something wicked this way comes.

Confronted with the blustery conditions, trains were cancelled and schools hastily closed. Some friends in Hertfordshire had to do without power for 24 hours. They managed surprisingly well. A wood-burning stove kept them warm. They cooked on gas.

If the Government continues with its present plans, none of the back-ups that proved so invaluable to my friends will be available. Their idea is to phase out sales of wet wood and house coal. Producing gas is now deemed so environmentally unfriendly that we have to import it instead.

As if to prove how reckless is this rush to reach zero carbon by 2050, after a bit of a storm, a £20 million wind turbine in Wales fell over. They try to keep this quiet, but turbines don't really like winds of more than 50 miles per hour. Nor do they work when there's insufficient breeze. Basically, our entire future electricity supply depends on the Goldilocks theory – not too windy, not too still, just right.

▶

Most people have no idea how crazy this stuff is. I was astonished to learn that when there is too much wind, and not enough electricity demand, wind generators are actually paid by the taxpayer to refrain from producing electricity. Three large wind farms in Scotland received a total of £24.5 million to fail to produce about half of their potential output.

When storms hit in the near future, and the power fails, do be sure to take advantage of your gas cooker and wood or coal fire. If we don't start to fight back against this madness, you won't be allowed to have them for much longer.

ACTIVITY 2

SKILLS REASONING, INTERPRETATION, DECISION MAKING

▼ COMPARING WRITERS' IDEAS

Read the article 'When it's too windy for wind turbines: the downside of eco-power' from *The Telegraph* newspaper.

1 What are the writer's intentions and purposes in this article?

2 Compare the two articles you have been exploring. What similarities and differences in the two writers' purposes and intentions can you identify?

3 What similarities and differences can you identify in the two writers' views on energy?

HOW WRITERS INFLUENCE THEIR READERS

Once you have established the main ideas being communicated in a piece of non-fiction, you should consider whether the article is showing an opinion or **bias**. Look out for the following:

- use of biased language
- use of **emotive language**
- stating of opinion as fact
- use of quotations or the reported views of others
- use of unsupported claims
- the given facts
- an argument.

SUBJECT VOCABULARY

bias not fair; a particular point of view influenced by one's own or someone else's opinions
emotive language dramatic language that stirs emotion in the reader

ACTIVITY 3

SKILLS ANALYSIS, INTERPRETATION, COLLABORATION, INTERPERSONAL SKILLS

▼ RECOGNISING BIAS

Look back at the two articles from *The Guardian* and *The Telegraph* again. In groups, try to find one example of each bullet point above in each of the articles.

▲ 'Kittens need a warm, dry, comfortable place for snoozing'.

SUBJECT VOCABULARY

imperative verbs verbs that give an instruction or command

direct address using second person pronouns 'you' or 'your'

repetition saying the same thing more than once to highlight its importance

triple structure where three words or ideas are linked in order to add emphasis to a key point

hyperbole exaggerating for effect

rhetorical questions questions that are asked to make a point rather than to get an answer

ACTIVITY 4   SKILLS ▸ ANALYSIS

▼ RHETORICAL DEVICES

Rhetorical devices are often used in texts that seek to present a particular point of view or opinion. Match the following rhetorical devices with the correct example sentence.

Emotive language	Kittens need a warm, dry, comfortable place for snoozing.
Imperative verbs	How could anyone leave an animal to suffer like this?
Direct address	These vulnerable, weak kittens need our help.
Repetition	Over 100,000,000 cats need re-homing every week.
Triple structure	You can help us make a difference; all we need is £2 a month.
Hyperbole	Every year the number of cats on the streets increases, every year it is up to us to rescue them.
Rhetorical questions	Donate today!

ACTIVITY 5   SKILLS ▸ PROBLEM SOLVING, ADAPTIVE LEARNING, INNOVATION

▼ WRITING PERSUASIVELY

Write a letter to persuade an organisation to ban the use of animal fur in its products.

Include at least three of the rhetorical devices above in your letter.

Your letter must be at least three paragraphs long and should follow all the conventions of a normal letter.

ACTIVITY 6   SKILLS ▸ CRITICAL THINKING, ANALYSIS, REASONING, INTERPRETATION

▼ ANALYSING IDEAS

Read the following article, 'Myth of the Teenager' by Lucy Maddox, and answer the question.

▸ **How does Lucy Maddox present teenagers in this article?**

Your answer should:

- show a clear understanding of the article and the points that the writer is making
- explore the writer's purposes and intentions: the impact the writer wants to have on the reader
- identify and analyse a variety of the writer's choices of language and rhetorical devices, exploring how they help the writer to achieve their intentions
- use appropriate terminology throughout.

After answering the question, write a one-paragraph summary in which you say how your understanding of the topic has developed or changed as a result of reading this article. What impact has it had on you and why?

GENERAL VOCABULARY

ASBOs court orders used in the UK to restrict anti-social behaviour

hug a hoodie a slogan used to make fun of British politicians who attempt to engage with disaffected young people

stigmatised unfairly discriminated against or disapproved of

vilified discussed or described in a very negative way

SUBJECT VOCABULARY

stereotypes fixed and generalised ideas about particular types of people or groups

syntax the way in which words and phrases are arranged into sentences

'MYTH OF THE TEENAGER' BY LUCY MADDOX

Teenagers often get a bad press. There are easy stories to be mined here: ASBOs, underage drinking, "hug a hoodie," drug use–even, recently, the teenager who drugged her parents to access the internet.

These are not new stereotypes. As a shepherd in Shakespeare's *A Winter's Tale* puts it, "I would there were no age between 10 and three-and-20, or that youth would sleep out the rest; for there is nothing in the between but getting wenches with child, wronging the ancientry, stealing, fighting." Change the syntax, and this description could easily fit in many newspapers today.

Are the stereotypes fair? Is the idea of wild adolescence rooted in evidence? There are two sorts of arguments. On the one hand, neuroscientific evidence seems increasingly to suggest that this is a true developmental phase of its own—teenagers behave differently because their brains are different. On the other, some argue that teenagers behave differently because they are learning to handle so many new situations, and if we hold stereotypical ideas about their behaviour, we risk underestimating them.

Take the latter argument first. Philip Graham, a professor of psychiatry who has written extensively on what he perceives to be a misconception, believes that although hormonal and physical changes are occurring, most teenagers are not risky or moody. Graham sees teenagers as a stigmatised group, often highly competent yet treated as if they were not. He argues that teenagers need to be acknowledged as potentially productive members of society and that the more independence and respect they are given, the more they will rise to the challenge.

"Once young people reach the age of 14, their competence in cognitive tasks and their sexual maturity make it more helpful to think of them as young adults," says Graham. "Media coverage is almost uniformly negative. Adolescence is a word used to describe undesirable behaviour in older adults. Young people of 14, 15 or 16 are thought to be risk-takers… they are people who are experimenting. They are doing things for the first time and they make mistakes. Would you call a toddler who is learning to walk and who falls over all the time a risk-taker? These people are just beginning something."

Graham places less importance on the conclusions of research into risk-taking and on adolescent brain changes – "Not to say there are not a small minority who do take dangerous risks but I think the results have been over-generalised to justify the stereotype."

Instead, Graham argues that the way teenagers make decisions is related to encountering situations they haven't dealt with before. "If they are moving into new types of social situation they do need more help with that." He likens it to learning to drive, something you need expert help with at any age.

However, neuroscientific evidence suggests a basis for the teenage stereotype. Sarah-Jayne Blakemore, a professor at University College London, has specialised in researching the adolescent brain using a variety of techniques, including functional brain scanning. Although also concerned that teenagers can be vilified in the media, Blakemore rejects the idea that adolescence is entirely a social construct: "If you look throughout history at the descriptions of adolescence they are similar, and also in different cultures. Of course this is not to say that all adolescents are the same, but there is quite a lot of evidence that during this period of life there's an increase in risk-taking, peer influence and self-consciousness." Blakemore's research suggests that during the teenage years the brain is still developing the capacity for certain sophisticated skills, including problem-solving, social skills and impulse control.

Blakemore and other researchers describe a gradual development of brain areas related to planning, inhibiting inappropriate behaviour and understanding other points of view. They also suggest a less linear development of the system in the brain that recognises and responds to rewards. "Teenagers tend to be more self-conscious," said Blakemore. "They show more risk-taking when their peers are present." Their social brain is changing and so is their ability to plan, inhibit impulses and make decisions.

"Research by Laurence Steinberg at Temple University in the US has shown that adolescents tend not to take into account future consequences of actions. For example, if you offer them a choice between having £10 now and £100 in six months, whilst adults tend to wait for the larger amount, most adolescents are more likely to go for the lower value now. Life in the future doesn't hold so much importance."

It might make sense, then, that a teenager trying to decide whether to tell a lie in order to go out, or to try an illegal drug, might be influenced more by the reward of the night out or the novel experience, or peer congratulation, than by longer-term negative consequences. "It's not that teenagers don't understand the risks," says Blakemore. "It's just that for some teenagers, in the moment, this understanding goes out of the window."

Despite their different views, both academics conclude that teenagers could benefit from being treated according to their development. Graham suggests friendly advice-giving. It is important to "recognise their desire for autonomy," he says. "They want to do more than they can. We should treat them differently because they are inexperienced… and first experiences are important. A bad experience can put you off something for a long time."

He does not advocate tolerating too much difficult behaviour, though: "Adolescents are influenced by the stereotype as well. If they expect to get away with being 'bolshy' for example… I don't think we should be particularly tolerant of bad behaviour in adolescence."

Blakemore thinks that we should adjust the way we try to motivate teenagers: "Anti-smoking campaigns, for example, might be more effective if they used short-term social negatives like bad breath as a disincentive, rather than longer-term health consequences. And we perhaps expect too much. "We expect them to act like adults but their brains aren't yet completely like an adult brain. Maybe we should be more understanding. Teaching adolescents about how their brains develop might be helpful."

Whether you attribute adolescent differences in decision-making to brain development or lack of experience, educational aims could include the handling of social dilemmas. Parents might be able to help by being explicit about the pros and cons of a situation, considering other people's views or negotiating in a transparent way. We should also bear in mind that teenagers are often uniquely affected by economic and political challenges such as high unemployment levels.

In my view, adolescence is a tricky time, where individuals often struggle to find their own identity in the face of a sometimes hostile outside world, whilst needing peer support. Both Blakemore and Graham are more phlegmatic. "Every time's a tricky time," says Graham. "You try being my age."

▲ Do you think adolescents often struggle to find their own identity?

LEARNING OBJECTIVES

This lesson will help you to:

- identify the main parts of speech
- consolidate your understanding of the function of each part.

WORD CLASSES

Words may be divided into groups called parts of speech:

- verb
- noun
- pronoun
- adjective
- adverb
- preposition
- conjunction
- noun phrase.

PARTS OF SPEECH

SUBJECT VOCABULARY

verb a word that describes actions
noun a word that represents a person, place, object or quality
adjective a word that describes a noun or pronoun
noun phrase a group of words built around a head noun, in which each word adds to the noun's meaning

HINT

Show your knowledge of word classes to make your analysis more precise. For example, comment on:

- the writer's choice of **adjectives** building a vivid picture
- the writer's use of **verbs** creating an impression of rapid movement.

Each part of speech signifies how the word is used, not what a word is. This means that the same word can be a **noun** in one sentence and a **verb** or **adjective** in the next. For example, the word 'book' in the following sentences.

- Books are made of ink, paper and glue.
  (In this case, 'books' is a noun and is the subject of the sentence.)
- Jing waits patiently while Mei books the tickets.
  (In this case, 'books' is a verb and the subject of the sentence is Mei.)

If you were asked to describe the following photograph, you might say, 'The happy lady was laughing'.

▲ The sentence 'The happy lady was laughing' contains a noun, verb and adjective.

This sentence is made up of different parts of speech.

This is a **noun**. It is a **naming word**.

This is a **verb**. It is a word that describes **actions**.

This is a **noun phrase**, built around the **head noun** 'lady'. All the other words in the noun phrase add to its meaning.

The happy lady was laughing.

This is an **adjective**. It is a **describing word**. It tells you more about the **noun**.

ACTIVITY 1   SKILLS ANALYSIS

▼ IDENTIFYING PARTS OF SPEECH

KEY POINT

All words are divided into classes, known as parts of speech.

In the following sentences, circle the adjectives, tick the nouns and underline the verbs.

1 I tripped over the uneven floor.
2 The clumsy boy crashed his new bike.
3 When the old lady reached her house, she sat down.
4 We saw wild horses in the forest.
5 The large crowd cheered as the skilful player scored.
6 The laughing girls annoyed the teacher.
7 A prickly hedgehog snuffled in the dry leaves.
8 The lazy man was sleeping under the tall tree.

PROPER NOUNS

Nouns that name particular things are called proper nouns and begin with capital letters. The names of people and places, days of the week, brand names, company names and titles of films are all proper nouns, e.g. Yara, France, Thursday, Google, Ford, *Avatar.*

PREPOSITIONS

SUBJECT VOCABULARY

preposition a word that is used before a noun or pronoun to show time, place or direction

A **preposition** tells you the position of one thing in relation to another.

Altamash hid **behind** the tree.

You cross **over** a bridge.

ACTIVITY 2   SKILLS ANALYSIS

▼ USING PARTS OF SPEECH

HINT

Many verbs are 'doing' words and are used to describe actions, such as 'the boy **kicked** the ball'. Some verbs are 'being' words: 'The girl **is** muddy.'

Write a suitable word in the gap in each of the following sentences. In the brackets after each sentence, write down what part of speech it is.

1 Sam put the _____ suitcase on the floor. (_____)
2 Athens is the capital of _____. (_____)
3 The mountaineers _____ to the summit.
 (_____)
4 The children sang loudly at the _____. (_____)
5 The cat's _____ was soft and silky. (_____)
6 The helicopter _____ over the motorway.
 (_____)

LEARNING OBJECTIVES

This lesson will help you to:

- explore and develop your interpretations of language
- considering the associations that words hold and how they can be used to create meaning in a text.

SUBJECT VOCABULARY

denotation what something is

KEY POINT

Words and images can have a range of connotations that influence meaning and interpretation.

CONNOTATIONS

Connotations are the associations and ideas which a particular word or image suggests to a reader. It is important to consider the connotations implied by a text in order to explore its effects in detail.

ACTIVITY 1

SKILLS INTERPRETATION

▼ CONNOTATIONS OF IMAGES

Copy and complete the table, writing down the denotation and the connotation for each image. On a piece of paper, draw your own example of a sign or image. Ask a partner to look at your image and identify its denotation and connotation.

▼ IMAGE/SIGN	▼ DENOTATION	▼ CONNOTATION
	Skull and crossbones	Poison, danger

ACTIVITY 2   SKILLS ▶ ANALYSIS, INTERPRETATION

▼ CONNOTATIONS OF WORDS

Your local newspaper runs a weekly column called 'Why I love…', in which a guest writer is asked to write a short article to inform readers of a personal interest. Read the following extract, from a piece called 'Why I love reading', and consider the connotations of the highlighted words, and then answer the question.

> I love reading because I love getting to know new characters. They become friends: I inhabit their lives while I read and when I finish that book, I take a part of them with me. Reading gives me an escape from reality: it's my magic carpet that I can fly on whenever I choose, soaring off on adventures all over the world, from past to present, over the vast terrains of human history. I can see all of the colours of life as I go. They say you never read the same book twice: reading a new book makes me feel slightly new myself because I know something different; I've experienced something more. Reading makes me a bigger, better, smarter version of myself.

▶ **What ideas and attitudes to reading are suggested in the extract?**
Copy and complete the following table, considering the connotations of the highlighted words and phrases used in the extract. Then choose another quotation from the extract and consider its connotation.

▼ PHRASE	▼ CONNOTATION
'new characters… become friends'	By describing characters as 'friends', the writer demonstrates the emotional connection they feel with books and the companionship they get from reading.
'it's my magic carpet'	The metaphor describes reading as a 'magic carpet'. This has connotations of adventure and implies the fantastic experiences that the writer enjoys in reading books. The 'magic carpet' also has connotations of freedom and flight: books give this reader the wings to explore worlds which might otherwise be inaccessible to them.
'all the colours of my life'	

ACTIVITY 3   SKILLS ▶ PROBLEM SOLVING, ADAPTIVE LEARNING

▼ CREATING YOUR OWN CONNOTATIONS

1 Using the extract 'Why I love reading' as a model, write two paragraphs of your own, entitled 'Why I love…' and 'Why I hate…'. Aim to create one positive and one negative description, choosing anything that you will enjoy writing about, from motorbikes to a particular website for example.

2 Identify at least three words or phrases in your writing where you have used connotation to convey your ideas. What are the connotations of the words or phrases you have identified? Write a sentence or two about each one.

LEARNING OBJECTIVES

This lesson will help you to:
- identify the main sentence types.

DIFFERENT SENTENCE TYPES

A sentence is a group of words that are put together in such a way as to mean something. It is a basic component of communication. Clumsy sentence structure leads to writing that is grammatically incorrect and makes it much more difficult for the reader to understand what you are trying to convey. A writer's use of sentence structure in a text adds impact to their ideas. It is important to be able to identify and comment on this in the reading sections of the exam.

TYPES OF SENTENCES

'Friend, car, France holiday' is not a sentence as it doesn't make sense. 'I am driving my friend to France for a holiday' is a sentence. You can understand what it means as it makes complete sense. Sentences come in different forms.

- A **declarative** (or statement) **conveys** information.
  My car is red.

- An **interrogative** (or question) **asks** for information.
  Does it go fast?

- An **imperative** (or command) **tells** someone to do something.
  Get in.

- An **exclamation** shows that someone **feels strongly** about something.
  It's great!

HINT

Remember the **conjunctions** that you can use to create a compound sentence by using the acronym FANBOYS:
For, And, Nor, But, Or, Yet, So.

SUBJECT VOCABULARY

conjunction a word that joins parts of a sentence

ACTIVITY 1

SKILLS ANALYSIS

▼ SENTENCE TYPES

Match the sentences with the sentence types.
1 The door is open.   statement
2 Go and have a wash.   question
3 What a lovely surprise!   command
4 Have you seen my shorts?   exclamation

SIMPLE SENTENCES

SUBJECT VOCABULARY

clause a group of words that make up part of a sentence

A **single** clause **sentence** contains a single subject and a verb, and sometimes an object. It expresses information about one action, event or idea.

The boy ate the chocolate.

PARTS OF A CLAUSE

SUBJECT VOCABULARY

predicate the parts of a sentence that are not the subject, containing the verb and providing information about the subject
pronoun a word that is used instead of a noun

HINT

To determine the subject of a sentence, first isolate the verb and then make a question by placing 'who?' or 'what?' before it. The answer is the subject of the sentence.

A sentence often contains the following elements.

■ The **subject** identifies the topic of a clause or, in other words, what it is about. Every complete sentence contains two parts: a subject and a **predicate**. The subject is what or whom the sentence is about, and the predicate tells you something about the subject. In the following sentence, the predicate is enclosed in brackets ( ), while the subject is in **bold**.

  My hockey teacher and his dog (go running every morning).

■ The **verb** identifies the action of a clause or, in other words, what happens.

  Her boyfriend **gave** her a bunch of flowers.

■ The **object** identifies who or what is directly affected by the action of the verb. This is always a noun, noun phrase or **pronoun**. In the example above, the noun phrase 'a bunch of flowers' is the **direct object**: this is what was given. The pronoun 'her' is an **indirect object**: the flowers were given to her.

Not all verbs are followed by objects:

  Every morning, Mariana **walks** to school.

■ The **adverbials** 'every morning' and 'to school' give additional information about the situation: when, where and how it happened.

▲ 'Last week, Tamika renovated the kitchen.'

ACTIVITY 2   **SKILLS** ANALYSIS

▼ PARTS OF A SENTENCE

Find the subject and verb in the following sentences. Can you find any adverbials as well?
1 Last week, Tamika renovated the kitchen.
2 Did she paint the ceiling?
3 It took a long time.
4 Tamika hates painting.

MULTICLAUSE SENTENCES

A multiclause sentence consists of two or more single clause sentences joined by a **conjunction** such as 'and', 'but', 'when', 'because', 'if', 'although'.

  It was raining. I put up my umbrella. (two sentences)

  It was raining **so** I put up my umbrella. (one sentence with a conjunction)

  I put up my umbrella **because** it was raining. (one sentence with a conjunction)

SUBORDINATE CLAUSES

Subordinate clauses are often present in a sentence. They are called subordinate as they are second to the main action or **main clause** of the sentence but they add further information to it.

  After his Dad gave him some pocket money, Andrew went to the cinema.

'Andrew went to the cinema' is the main clause in this sentence. 'After his Dad gave him some pocket money' is a subordinate clause. 'After' is the **conjunction** that links the subordinate clause to the main clause.

LEARNING OBJECTIVES

This lesson will help you to:

- use a full range of sentence structures
- control and vary sentence structure for effect in your writing.

EDINGLY OPENERS: VARYING SENTENCE STARTERS FOR IMPACT

SUBJECT VOCABULARY

adverb a word that describes a verb or an adjective

HINT

Use a comma after the opener.

SENTENCES FOR EFFECT

Effective use of sentence structure adds significant interest and impact to writing. Learning how to use sentence structure for effect will help you to engage your reader.

In your writing, you need to think about the types of sentence structure you choose to use and the impact they will have on the reader.

EDINGLY openers are ways of opening a sentence with a word ending in -ED (verbs), -ING (verbs) and -LY (adverbs). For example:

exhaust**ed**	panick**ing**	hurried**ly**
terrif**ied**	trembl**ing**	immediate**ly**
shock**ed**	accelerat**ing**	sad**ly**

Positioning one at the beginning of a sentence gives the word and the whole sentence greater impact.

▶ **How could you change these sentences using this technique?**

1 I walked through the dark alley and a hand reached out and grabbed my shoulder.

2 I held my breath as I crept through the deep, dark wood.

3 I was trapped and could not see a way out.

ACTIVITY 1

SKILLS CRITICAL THINKING, ANALYSIS, INTERPRETATION

▼ BUILDING SENTENCES

Sentences can be built up by taking a main clause, for example:

I went back to the house   I looked deep into her eyes

And adding:

- clauses linked with a conjunction, for example:

  and peered through the window   because I knew she was lying

- clauses built around a non-finite *-ing* form verb, for example:

  trembling from head to toe   smiling to myself

- relative clauses, for example:

  which was grimy and cracked   which were cold and unforgiving

- prepositional phrases, for example:

  with fear   in the warm sunshine

1 Build up a sentence using the examples above.
   Choose a main clause.
   i Add another clause, linked with a conjunction.
   ii Add a non-finite clause.
   iii Add a prepositional phrase.
   iv Finally, add a relative clause.

2 Check your sentence makes complete sense. Would it be clearer or more effective if you changed the order in which you have sequenced the different elements of your sentence?

▲ The sentence 'Grasping the handle, she turned it slowly' helps to build tension.

ACTIVITY 2

SKILLS ANALYSIS, INTERPRETATION, DECISION MAKING

▼ CREATING TENSION

Compare the two extracts below and consider how effectively each has created a feeling of tension. The first is written using single clause and shorter multiclause sentences while the second uses only longer multiclause sentences.

1 Which extract creates greater tension?

2 Which extract builds a more vivid picture of the scene?

3 Which sentence types create a greater sense of tension?

4 Which sentence types create a more vivid picture of the scene?

5 Try rewriting the extract, using ideas and sentences from both extracts to achieve both intentions: building tension **and** creating a vivid picture in the reader's mind.

EXTRACT 1

Amelia reached a door. She grabbed the handle and turned it. Pushing the door open, she moved inside. No one was there. She turned and fled.

EXTRACT 2

Amelia stood in the doorway, delaying her decision until the last possible moment. As she plucked up her courage, she studied the door in front of her. It was crafted from an ancient-looking wood, the handle a simple metal ring. Amelia glanced down at her shaking hand as she stretched out to turn the handle. She took two deep breaths, thoughts racing through her mind. Grasping the handle, she turned it slowly; pushing the heavy door in front of her, she stepped into the hallway.

KEY POINT

Clauses can be linked to build longer sentences using:
- conjunctions, such as 'but', 'so', 'because'
- relative pronouns, such as 'which', 'who'
- non-finite -*ing* verbs, such as 'thinking', 'shrugging'
- prepositions, such as 'with', 'next to', 'beside'.

Longer, multiclause sentences can be broken into shorter sentences by separating linked clauses.

ACTIVITY 3

SKILLS INTERPRETATION, ADAPTIVE LEARNING

▼ ADAPTING SENTENCE TYPES FOR EFFECT

Re-write the following extract as three sentences. What is the effect?

Ryan stood as still as stone, listening intently, but the faint rustling continued from inside the bedroom, so putting his good eye to the keyhole, he peered into the dimly lit room.

Re-write the following extract as five sentences. What is the effect?

He squinted through the gloom of the interior, which was quite deserted, with a single candle burning near the altar, thinking that it was sad to see an empty church on Christmas Eve, but, shrugging the thought away, he began a careful inspection of the places where the statue might have been concealed.

THE HINDU

BusinessLine

KOLKATA, LUCKNOW, MUMBAI, NAGPUR, PUNE, VADODARA ● REG.NO. MCS/067/2018 – 20 RNI REGN. N

1.

MARCH 2, 2019

EXPRE

HINDI

W.ECONOMICTIMES.COM

OMIC TIM

WRITING SKILLS

Assessment Objective 4

Communicate effectively and imaginatively, adapting form, tone and register of writing for specific purposes and audiences

Assessment Objective 5

Write clearly, using a range of vocabulary and sentence structures, with appropriate paragraphing and accurate spelling, grammar and punctuation

This chapter focuses on some core writing skills that you can apply to all parts of the English Language A course. Working through these lessons and activities will help you to develop the writing skills that you will need for the exams and non-examination assessment assignments.

The chapter is split into the following sections:
- Vocabulary
- Sentences
- Structure
- Punctuation and spelling.

In the writing sections of your exams, you will need to be able to meet the Assessment Objectives AO4 and AO5.

LEARNING OBJECTIVES

This lesson will help you to:

- appreciate a writer's choice of words
- develop your own choice of words.

CHOOSING THE RIGHT VOCABULARY

Your words need to attract the attention of a reader and keep them engaged so that they will continue to read what you have written. Choosing effective vocabulary is central to achieving this.

Words that engage the senses are particularly effective for this purpose. Look at the following opening sentences.

- It exploded in her face. (**sight**)
- Something was scratching under the door. (**sound**)
- From the kitchen came a waft of the garlic that she loved. (**smell**)
- He pulled a face as if he had swallowed sour milk. (**taste**)
- The wind brushed his skin. (**touch**)

ACTIVITY 1

SKILLS > INNOVATION

▼ ENGAGING THE SENSES

Work with a partner and write an opening sentence for both of the titles below ('The Storm' and 'Disaster in the Kitchen') using at least three of the five senses: sight, sound, smell, taste and touch.

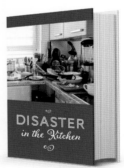

PRECISION

When you write or speak, your choice of words can be very important, especially when you write. When you speak, the person who is listening can ask you to explain yourself if anything you say is not clear. However, when you write, your reader will probably not be able to ask for an explanation so you have to get things right first time.

There are times when you need to be precise in your choice of words. Compare the following sentences, then answer the question.

> Some sort of animal was seen going down the road.

> A thin, scruffy cat was seen hurrying anxiously into the distance down the middle of the road.

▶ **Which of these two sentences is clearer and more precise? Which words and phrases create this clarity and precision?**

Now try this for yourself.

Imagine you have witnessed a crime: a person breaking into a jeweller's shop.

Write one or two sentences describing the criminal and their actions as vaguely as possible. Then write one or two sentences describing the criminal as clearly and precisely as possible.

You could think about:

■ the nouns you choose to focus on in your description

■ the adjectives you choose to add detail and impact to those nouns

■ the verbs you choose to describe the criminal's movements

■ the adverbs you choose to add descriptive detail to those verbs.

Swap your opening sentences with a partner. Which sentence do they feel uses the most engaging vocabulary choices? Ask them to explain their choice.

ACTIVITY 2 SKILLS CRITICAL THINKING, ANALYSIS, INTERPRETATION

▼ PRECISION IN ACTION

In 1912, an enormous ship called the *Titanic* set sail from Britain to the USA carrying over 2000 passengers. It was described as unsinkable. On the fifth day of its voyage, the ship hit an iceberg and sank. More than 1500 people died. This extract is from an account of the disaster, written by one of the survivors. Read the extract carefully, noticing the choice of language used to convey the witness's shock and horror. Then copy and complete the table, selecting key words and phrases that the writer uses to convey what they can see.

In a couple of hours, though, she [the *Titanic*] began to go down more rapidly. Then the fearful sight began. The people in the ship were just beginning to realise how great their danger was. When the forward part of the ship dropped suddenly at a faster rate, so that the upward slope became marked, there was a sudden rush of passengers on all the decks towards the **stern**. It was like a wave. We could see the great black mass of people in the **steerage** sweeping to the rear part of the boat and breaking through into the upper decks. At the distance of about a mile we could distinguish everything through the night, which was perfectly clear. We could make out the increasing excitement on board the boat as the people, rushing to and fro, caused the deck lights to disappear and reappear as they passed in front of them.

▼ KEY WORD OR PHRASE	▼ WHAT IT CONVEYS
Fearful	This word conveys the pitiful state of the panicking passengers who were still on the ship.

▲ Sinking of RMS *Titanic*

GENERAL VOCABULARY

stern rear of a boat
steerage the lower decks where the cheapest accommodation was provided

KEY POINT

The bigger your vocabulary, the more words you have to choose from and the easier it is to express yourself clearly. The best way to improve your vocabulary is by reading and taking an interest in the words that other people use.

LEARNING OBJECTIVES

This lesson will help you to:

■ consider the effect of words and phrases

■ demonstrate an ability to use words and phrases to good effect.

VOCABULARY FOR EFFECT

The words you use come from the vocabulary that you know and can use confidently and comfortably. Some words – *the, some, is, what,* for example – do not have the effect of other words such as *revolting, splendid, monster* and *eliminate.* Here you are going to look at the way writers choose words.

CONNOTATIONS

SUBJECT VOCABULARY

referend the thing or idea to which a word refers

connotations ideas linked to a word; ideas that have become associated with a word

GENERAL VOCABULARY

nauseous feeling sick

A word means more than just its **referend**. For example, the word 'grease' denotes or refers to an oily material often used to lubricate machinery or carry medication. Sometimes, however, the word is used to indicate distaste or revulsion, allowing the word's **connotations**, such as '**nauseous**', 'slimy' and 'sticky', to come into play.

Some words have positive or negative connotations, such as 'success' or 'regrets'.

> They talked all morning about her **success**.

In the first sentence, the use of the word 'success' means that you know that whatever she had done was approved of or appreciated as something positive.

> Now she was left only with her **regrets**.

However, in the second sentence, the use of the word 'regrets' lets you know that the subject now wishes that she had not done something which is seen in a negative light.

ACTIVITY 1

SKILLS ANALYSIS, INTERPRETATION, INNOVATION, COLLABORATION

▼ CHOOSING VOCABULARY IN PRACTICE

1 Work in small groups to write complete sentences using each of the following words and phrases:

> traitor   magic   cool   on the brink   totally helpless

> awesome   readily available   desperate   cruel   adorable

2 Discuss the effect of the words and phrases in each of your sentences.

3 Read the following extract and choose some of the words and phrases in it that have a particular effect on you as a reader. Then copy and complete the table that follows, adding your own ideas. Try to find at least another six examples.

> Once upon a time it was said that three trolls lived in a forest. Local people lived in fear of them and avoided at night the twisting path that wound its way between the trees. From time to time late-night travellers would find themselves lost in the forest, alone and bewildered, and they would imagine the sound of a foot snapping a twig or catch in the corner of their eye something moving in the shadows.
>
> These close encounters with the trolls were reported widely and fed the imaginations of the locals. None of them realised that nobody had ever been harmed in any way by these trolls, but that did not

restrain those people who really enjoyed terrifying their fellow citizens with outrageous tales of a death that could so easily catch up with them in the woods around the town.

The truth of the matter was that the three trolls were very shy. However, they craved the company of other beings and would approach them warily in the forest and then, before they could introduce themselves, their courage would fail and they would scuttle back into the undergrowth, safely out of sight.

▼ WORD OR PHRASE	▼ WHAT EFFECT IT HAS
Once upon a time	This phrase suggests that a fairy tale is about to be told.
Bewildered	This word creates a strong sense of uncertainty.

4 Complete the following sentence stem with six different words or phrases, indicating the effect you are aiming for in each case.

> When it rains we…

SYNONYMS

A synonym is a word that means the same thing or nearly the same thing as another word. It can be used to avoid repeating a word, to echo or widen the reader's understanding or to reinforce an idea.

> The young tree, **the sapling**, was the place chosen by the blackbird to build its nest.

▶ 'Sapling' provides a synonym for 'young tree'. Can you think of any other synonyms?

Here the word 'sapling' provides a synonym for the tree. It helps to develop the referend (tree) by supplying more detail and further connotations.

1 Write down as many synonyms as you can for the underlined word in these sentences.

   i   There was a terrible <u>smell</u> in the room.

   ii I dropped and <u>broke</u> my dad's phone.

   iii I <u>walked</u> through the snow to school.

2 Choose the best synonym to replace each of the underlined words in the sentences above.

3 Write a sentence or two explaining why you chose each synonym and the effect you wanted it to have.

LEARNING OBJECTIVES

This lesson will help you to:

■ appreciate how language can be used to bring about a wide variety of effects.

LANGUAGE FOR EFFECT

In every text, the writer has a purpose and an intention they want to achieve. For example, a writer might have the intention of helping visitors to enjoy their visit to a museum with the purpose of informing them about the things they can see and experience there. Or, a writer might have the intention of highlighting the positive consequences of an activity such as exercise with the purpose of persuading the reader to do more exercise in their daily lives. To achieve this purpose, the writer may use other, secondary, purposes.

ACTIVITY 1
SKILLS PROBLEM SOLVING, ANALYSIS

▼ TYPE OF EFFECT IN WRITING

Look for examples of written material that is informative, transactional, emotive, persuasive, entertaining, inspirational, descriptive, ironic and advisory.

Record the source for each type and be aware that one source may include more than one of these types. You could look on the Internet, in newspapers or magazines, or in a library if you have access to one.

SUBJECT VOCABULARY

transactional non-fiction writing for a purpose: to inform, explain, review, argue, persuade or advise
ironic using words to convey a meaning that is completely opposite to their apparent meaning

ACTIVITY 2
SKILLS CRITICAL THINKING, ANALYSIS, INTERPRETATION, CREATIVITY

▼ IDENTIFYING TYPES OF WRITING IN AN EXTRACT

Read the following extract.

> When you get home after a long day, what is the first thing you want to do? Get something delicious out of the fridge? Watch television? Get on the computer? All of these are fine in moderation – but how often do you go for a walk or a run, or play sport? The food you eat, and the amount of exercise you take, can have a significant impact on your physical and mental health. Ignoring your health can lead to heart problems, diabetes, arthritis and depression. Making healthy choices, on the other hand, can make you happier, fitter and less stressed..
>
> Exercise isn't all about pounding the pavements in the pouring rain. You can visit the gym. Joining a sports team can improve your social life and your health. So why not try it? Your local leisure centre will have all the information you need.

1 Which of the following writing purposes can you identify?

     description   information   explanation   advice

2 Which of the following intentions has the writer tried to achieve?

     humour   shock   fear   sympathy   encouragement

Look at the following sentence.

> Now stop.

Which of the two words in this sentence is emphasised? What is the effect of this?

If the order of the words is altered, something changes.

> Stop now.

Instead of emphasising the action that is to be carried out, to stop, the emphasis is now on the timing of that action – it must be amended now, immediately.

The ordering of words in a sentence is important, particularly at the end of a sentence or before a pause. There is a brief moment before you hear the next word while the sound of the last word continues in your mind. Such a word is emphasised and brought to your attention.

Look at the following sentences. One is the first sentence of the extract in Activity 2, and the other is a re-ordered version. Consider the difference made by re-ordering the words. Which do you think is the more effective? Can you say why?

> When you get home after a long day, what is the first thing you want to do?
> What is the first thing you want to do after a long day when you get home?

It may help you to analyse the phrases further by breaking them down into the following smaller phrases:

- what is the first thing / you want to do / after a long day / when you get home

There are three key ideas: 'when you get home', 'after a long day' and 'the first thing you want to do'. Which of these is the main focus of the sentence? Often writers position the main focus of a sentence at the end to give it added emphasis.

KEY POINT

Your choice of words and phrases, and the way that you arrange and adapt them, is crucial if you want to communicate effectively.

SUBJECT VOCABULARY

rhetorical questions questions that are asked to make a point rather than to get an answer
contrast where two objects, people or ideas are placed next to each other to highlight their differences
repetition saying the same thing more than once to highlight its importance
direct address using second person pronouns 'you' or 'your'
triple structure where three words or ideas are linked in order to add emphasis to a key point
hyperbole exaggerating for effect
alliteration the use of several words together that begin with the same sound or letter
simile a description that says that an object is *like* an image
personification when something which is not human is made to sound human by attributing human qualities to it

ACTIVITY 3

SKILLS INNOVATION, TEAMWORK

▼ OTHER LITERARY DEVICES

Look at the following literary devices. Can you think of an example of each? What effect do they have?

Rhetorical question

Contrast

Repetition

Direct address

Triple structure

Hyperbole

Alliteration

Simile

Personification

LEARNING OBJECTIVES

This lesson will help you to:
- understand the importance of your choices when writing
- see how different choices can change meaning.

GENERAL VOCABULARY

clarity the quality of being expressed clearly

WHY YOUR CHOICES MATTER

You must take care when choosing words, when arranging them and when you incorporate them into speech and writing.

- **Your choice of words** matters because it enables you to write with precision or exactness, **clarity** and an appropriate tone.
- **Your ordering of words** matters because it allows you to express ideas clearly and with impact.
- **Your use of language and literary techniques** matters because it enables you to achieve particular effects with writing.

ACTIVITY 1 **SKILLS** PROBLEM SOLVING, ANALYSIS, INTERPRETATION, CREATIVITY, INNOVATION

▼ HOW ARRANGEMENT OF WORDS AFFECTS MEANING

1 William Carlos Williams was an American poet and doctor. Because his medical work took him into homes where families were facing emergencies, he was able to learn a lot about them. This is one of his most famous poems, 'This is just to say'.

> I have eaten
> the plums
> that were in
> the ice box
>
> and which   5
> you were probably
> saving
> for breakfast.
>
> Forgive me
> they were delicious   10
> so sweet
> and so cold.

It is not difficult to imagine 'This is just to say' as a hasty note of apology scrawled on a sticky note and stuck on a fridge door.

Now look at the words of the poem arranged as ordinary sentences.

> I have eaten the plums that were in the ice box and which you were probably saving for breakfast. Forgive me; they were delicious, so sweet and so cold.

▶

▲ Even relatively simple poems such as 'This is just to say' can create strong images.

Work on your own and pick out key words in the poem which simply present clear facts. What words are left? What are the effects of these other words?

2 Work in a small group and consider the following questions.

▶ **Which words describe the plums? What effect does this description have? Does it simply help you to imagine what the plums were like?**

▶ **What happens to the tone or mood of the poem after the first sentence?**

▶ **Which word is crucial here? What is the effect of the rest of the last sentence: 'they were delicious | so sweet | and so cold'? What would be the effect of describing the plums in the first sentence?**

3 Write a cheeky note of mock apology along the lines of 'This is just to say'. For example, you could write an apology to a particular teacher for failing to do your homework.

4 Remember the different effects of, or purposes for, writing: informative, transactional, emotive, persuasive, entertaining, inspirational, descriptive, ironic and advisory. How many of these can you find in Williams's poem? Explain how these effects are brought about.

KEY POINT

When writing, be clear of your purpose and your intention. Choose vocabulary that helps you achieve them.

ACTIVITY 2   **SKILLS**   **CRITICAL THINKING, ANALYSIS**

▼ CHECKING WRITTEN MATERIAL

When you check your work, look for words or phrases that could be improved. Check for words and phrases that could be revised to:

■ make your writing more appropriately formal or informal

■ make a more significant contribution to your intention.

The writer's intention in this text is to shock the reader with information about how severely criminals were treated in the eighteenth and nineteenth centuries.

> Back in the old days, poor people who stole food just to survive were punished really badly. People as young as six could be hanged just for nicking a loaf of bread. With a choice of death by hunger or death by hanging, loads of people chose to steal to keep themselves alive.

▶ **Find a word or phrase that helps the writer to achieve their intention.**

▶ **Find a word or phrase that is appropriately formal.**

▶ **Find any words or phrases that should be more formal.**

▶ **Identify two words or phrases that could be replaced to help the writer achieve their intention.**

▲ Stealing was often met with extreme forms of punishment, yet some had no choice.

LEARNING OBJECTIVES

This lesson will help you to:

- understand the ways in which sentences can be assembled
- see the way that the meaning of a sentence is made effective.

SENTENCE TYPES

Sentences must be structured for clarity so they can be easily understood. They can also be structured for effect, adding impact to the writer's ideas.

BUILDING SENTENCES

SUBJECT VOCABULARY

clause a group of words that make up part of a sentence

First look at some of the ways in which sentences can be structured. Here is a single clause sentence. It has one main verb, *grabbed*.

> They grabbed their sunglasses.

To this, you can add something more:

> They grabbed their sunglasses and (they) hurried outside.

The original sentence has become a multiclause sentence. Two single **clause** sentences have become joined by a conjunction: *and*. They have become two clauses in a multiclause sentence. Each clause has a verb; in this case, *grabbed* and *hurried*. These two components could also be linked by using one of the verbs in its non-finite (*-ing*) verb form:

> **Grabbing** their sunglasses, they hurried outside.

> They grabbed their sunglasses, **hurrying** outside.

You can develop the sentence further:

> They grabbed their sunglasses and hurried outside although it was raining.

A third clause has been added: *although it was raining*. This clause also contains a verb, *was raining*; however, the clause, *although it was raining*, makes incomplete sense on its own. Without the main clause, you do not know what happened while it was raining.

You could link two of the components in other ways to form multiclause sentences:

> They grabbed their sunglasses although it was raining.

> Although it was raining they grabbed their sunglasses.

Each sentence here has a main clause and a subordinate clause.

▲ 'They grabbed their sunglasses and (they) hurried outside' is a multiclause sentence.

Finally, look at another sentence:

He looked at the menu which was badly written.

A single clause sentence, *He looked at the menu,* has become a main clause to which a relative clause, *which was badly written,* has been added. This relative clause has been linked with a relative pronoun, *which,* to form another multiclause sentence.

MINOR SENTENCES

One type of sentence does not follow the traditional rules of sentence structure. A minor sentence does not contain a verb. It could be just one or two words:

- Good. (A reaction to something.)
- Over here! (Some information.)
- A man. A tall, thin man with bright green eyes. (An element of a story structured as a minor sentence for effect.)

Minor sentences are much more common in speech. However, they can be used in narrative or descriptive writing to create tension, or in argument and persuasive writing for emphasis. It is generally better to avoid minor sentences in more formal, transactional writing.

EXPLORING SENTENCES

KEY POINT

Words and phrases can be built up into different types of sentences. By varying the sentences you use, you help the reader to stay engaged and strengthen the impact of what you write.

ACTIVITY 1

SKILLS ANALYSIS

▼ SPOT THE VERB

1 Copy the sentences below. Underline the verbs. Some sentences may contain several verbs. One of the sentences contains no verbs.

   i   The windows rattled in their frames.

   ii   The wind howled and rain battered the ground.

   iii   Although it was only midday, the sky was black.

   iv   Peering through the window, I noticed a shadow in the trees where the statue had once stood.

   v   Then a sudden silence.

2 Look again at the sentences you copied down. Circle and label the words that link the clauses in each sentence. They could be:

- linked with a conjunction, such as 'and', 'when, 'although'
- linked with a non-finite *-ing* verb, such as 'running', 'hiding', 'looking'
- linked with a relative pronoun, such as 'which', 'who', 'where'.

3 Finally, label each sentence with its sentence type. It could be:

- a single clause sentence
- a multiclause sentence
- a minor sentence.

LEARNING OBJECTIVES

This lesson will help you to:

■ build sentences.

SENTENCE CONSTRUCTION

Sentences can be structured in different ways without changing their meaning. Before you can decide on the most effective sentence structure to express your ideas, you need to be aware of the different structures you could use.

ACTIVITY 1   SKILLS ▷ CRITICAL THINKING, INNOVATION

▼ BREAKING DOWN AND BUILDING UP SENTENCES

1 Look at the sentence below.

Although it was quiet, I knew there was someone in there because I could hear the sound of breathing which was short and shallow as if someone was frightened.

This sentence contains five clauses. Re-write the sentence as five single clause sentences.

2 Now you have tried breaking down a sentence, try building sentences up. Look at the two single clause sentences below.

I walked slowly. I arrived at nine o'clock.

i   Link the sentences using a conjunction to form a multiclause sentence.

ii Link the sentences using a different conjunction to form a multiclause sentence.

iii Link the sentences by making one of the verbs a non-finite *-ing* verb to form a multiclause sentence.

iv Link the sentences by making a different verb a non-finite *-ing* verb to form a multiclause sentence.

v   Look at each of the sentences you have written. In how many sentences can the clauses be swapped without affecting the meaning of the sentence?

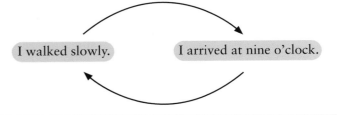

HINT

Some examples of conjunctions are: 'and', 'but', 'so', 'or', 'when', 'because', 'if', 'although'.

KEY POINT

In some multiclause sentences, the sequence of the clauses can be altered without changing the sentence's meaning.

HINT

Some examples of relative pronouns are: 'that', 'which', 'who'.

3 Look at the three single clause sentences below.

> I hurried to the end of the corridor. I looked in the classroom. It was empty.

   i   Link all three clauses using conjunctions to form a multiclause sentence.
   ii Link all three clauses using one conjunction and one non-finite *-ing* verb to form a multiclause sentence.
   iii Link all three clauses using one conjunction and one relative pronoun to form a multiclause sentence.
   iv In how many of the sentences you have written can the clauses be swapped around without affecting the meaning of the sentence?

4 Look at the long multiclause sentence you explored in Question 1:

> Although it was quiet, I knew there was someone in there because I could hear the sound of breathing which was short and shallow as if someone was frightened.

Look again at the version you wrote by breaking this long multiclause sentence down into five single clause sentences.

   i   Re-write the single clause sentences as two or three sentences. You could link some in multiclause sentences, and leave some as single clause sentences. Remember to check that your sentences are clear and make sense.
   ii Try re-writing your sentences again, linking or separating them in a different way, or in a different order. Check that your sentences make clear sense.
   iii Which version do you find more effective?

▲ Changing the order of clauses can create different imagery for a reader as it also changes the emphasis and the order in which information is given.

LEARNING OBJECTIVE

This lesson will help you to:
- write sentences that express your ideas clearly.

SENTENCES FOR CLARITY

The main reason for writing anything is to express your ideas and convey them clearly to the reader. The first thing to consider when structuring sentences for clarity is whether the reader will be able to read and understand them easily.

| ACTIVITY 1 | SKILLS | CRITICAL THINKING, INNOVATION |

▼ MAKING IT CLEAR

Expressing yourself clearly is particularly important when you are giving the reader information. Look at the sentence below.

> Pour a tablespoon of oil into a frying pan and place the frying pan on the stove, then take an egg and crack it open by hitting it sharply on the edge of a bowl or worktop, making sure to tip the contents into a mug or bowl which you can then use to place the egg into the frying pan once the oil is beginning to bubble and sizzle, and leave it there until the egg is cooked to your taste which might be when the yolk is soft and runny or firm and cooked through.

These instructions could be much more clearly expressed.

1 Rewrite the sentence as a series of single clause sentences.
2 Number the sentences so that they are in a logical sequence.
3 Now think about:
- which sentences would be more clearly expressed if you linked them to form multiclause sentences
- which sentences would be more clearly expressed if they remained as single clause sentences.
4 Re-write the information above, using your choice of multiclause and single clause sentences.
5 Ask a partner to read the sentences you have written. Are they more clearly expressed than the original version above?

KEY POINT

Multiclause sentences can be formed using:
- conjunctions
- non-finite verbs
- relative pronouns.

 Instructions need to be clear to be effective.

ACTIVITY 2   **SKILLS** INNOVATION

▼ EXPRESS YOURSELF CLEARLY

1 Write your own instructions and information about a task that you are skilled in. Your main aim is to explain to the reader how to complete that task.

It could be:

- a sporting skill
- a musical skill
- how to play and win a game that you enjoy
- a skill related to a hobby you enjoy.

You could:

- begin by noting all the steps and stages that the task involves
- write an explanation of each step using a single clause or short multiclause sentence
- decide which of your sentences to link using conjunctions, non-finite verb forms or relative pronouns, and which sentences are more effective as shorter sentences.

2 Review the structure of your sentences. Re-write your instructions using different sentence structures to try to make the information you are expressing even clearer and easier to understand.

3 Look at the two versions you have written. Choose the version you think is most clearly expressed. Ask a partner to read that version. Does your partner find your sentences clear and easy to understand?

KEY POINT

When reviewing your sentence structure, look at each clause in each sentence you have written.
Is it linked to the other clauses in the sentence in the most effective way?
Would it be clearer as a single clause sentence?

▶ Write about something you enjoy.

LEARNING OBJECTIVES

This lesson will help you to:

- write sentences for effect to add impact to your ideas.

SENTENCES FOR EFFECT

Different sentence structures can be used to achieve a range of effects in your writing.

ACTIVITY 1

SKILLS ▷ CRITICAL THINKING, ANALYSIS

▼ IDENTIFYING SENTENCE EFFECTS

Each of the sentence types below has been structured to achieve a specific effect.

There is:

- a multiclause sentence building a detailed description to create a vivid picture in the reader's mind
- a multiclause sentence to build tension to a climax in its final clause
- a series of short clauses linked in a multiclause sentence to suggest fast-paced action
- a short sentence to add tension and emphasis to a dramatic moment.

Which sentence is which?

1   The hallway of the house was huge and dark, with long, narrow corridors stretching into the darkness, and every breath reeked of dust and damp.
2   I heard a scratching noise.
3   I turned, and turned again, every muscle tensing, my heart pounding, my mind racing.
4   Then, staring into the gloom of one corridor, through the dust and darkness filling every corner, I could see, heading towards me at a slow and shuffling pace, the shadow of a man.

▶ Multiple clauses give you a chance to create vivid description by evoking different senses.

ACTIVITY 2   SKILLS ▷ CREATIVITY, INNOVATION

▼ BUILDING UP SENTENCES FOR EFFECT

1 Each of the details below could be used to describe a classroom:

   rows of desks   fidgeting students   someone yawning

   a student passing a note to another student

   hands in the air   litter on the floor   a teacher losing her patience

   Use at least three of these details to write a long, multiclause sentence describing a classroom.

2 In the scene you have described, there is going to be a dramatic incident. It could be:

   the teacher bellows at the class   a student loses their temper

   something is thrown across the room

   Write a long, multiclause sentence in which you describe the build-up to this dramatic incident, revealing the incident only at the very end of the sentence.

3 Following this incident, a number of events take place in a very short period of time. They could be:

   a sudden silence   someone laughs   someone storms from the room

   the door slams   someone faints

   Write a multiclause sentence, linking short clauses to suggest fast-paced action.

4 This incident has a dramatic conclusion. It could be:

   the classroom door opens   the headteacher marches in

   the teacher or a student is upset   the teacher makes an announcement

   Write one or two short, dramatic single clause sentences to reveal the dramatic ending to the reader.

ACTIVITY 3   SKILLS ▷ CREATIVITY, INNOVATION

▼ CRAFTING SENTENCES

You are going to write the opening of a story using a range of sentence types for effect. Use the story plan below to help you.

■ Walking in the forest on a stormy day.

■ You hear a loud crack.

■ A tree falls.

■ Your friend is injured.

■ You run for help.

1 Which sentence type will you use in each of the five sections of your story opening? What effect do you want each sentence type to have?

2 Now write your story opening.

LEARNING OBJECTIVES

This lesson will help you to:

■ appreciate how you can structure or organise writing effectively, whether you are providing information, describing something, discussing something or telling a story.

PRINCIPLES OF STRUCTURE

The structure of a piece of writing is essential in engaging the reader and helping them to access the text's ideas and information.

UNDERSTANDING THE PRINCIPLES OF STRUCTURE

One way to think of a text is to divide it into a beginning, middle and end. However, it is more useful to think about what each stage of a text aims to achieve.

Transactional texts can be structured in three stages:

1 **An introduction** to engage the reader and introduce the topic.

2 **A main body** to express the writer's ideas or information.

3 **A conclusion** to sum up the writer's ideas or bring the text to an end, and leave the reader thinking.

Narrative texts can be structured in four stages:

1 **Exposition:** the setting and key characters are introduced.

2 **Conflict:** a problem is introduced.

3 **Climax:** the problem reaches its peak.

4 **Resolution:** the problem is resolved.

SUBJECT VOCABULARY

narrative a story

ACTIVITY 1 **SKILLS** CRITICAL THINKING, ANALYSIS

▼ UNDERSTANDING THE STAGES OF A TEXT

Look at the seven summaries below. Three are summaries of the three stages in a letter to a local newspaper. Four are summaries of the four stages of a well-known story. Which are summaries from a transactional text? Which are summaries from a narrative text?

The boy grows bored and cries 'Wolf! Wolf!'. The villagers rush to protect the sheep but find there is no wolf.	These would give young people something to do and give them pride in where they live.
A boy is given the job of guarding his village's sheep.	There is not enough for young people to do in this village.
The boy and the sheep are eaten by the wolf.	The council should organise a youth club and an outdoor activity park.
The boy grows even more bored and cries 'Wolf! Wolf!'. The villagers ignore him.	

Look again at the summaries above. Sequence them according to the structures below:

Narrative
- Exposition
- Conflict
- Climax
- Resolution

Transactional
- Introduction
- Main body
- Conclusion

STAGES OF WRITING

The principle of stages in writing applies to any piece of writing that you create. Whether it is a brief email, a set of instructions for a gadget, a text book or a novel, it will require an opening, a middle section and an ending.

ACTIVITY 2 **SKILLS** CRITICAL THINKING, ANALYSIS

▼ STAGE TRANSITIONS

1 Work with a partner and identify the three sections in this paragraph:
- the opening setting the scene
- the middle section adding detail
- the ending.

The Turkish teacher met them at the airport and introduced her husband, a company lawyer. Soon they were hurrying along the freeway and then there was a turning off, followed by miles bumping along worn back roads. For a while he wondered just what he had let himself in for and then the car slowed. Away from the road there was a large timber house, set in a large garden. Then he sighed with relief for this was to be his home for the next six weeks.

2 Now identify key words that link the information in the paragraph and show the transition from the opening, to the middle section, to the ending.

KEY POINT

Structure is an essential element of sentences, paragraphs and whole texts.

ACTIVITY 3 **SKILLS** CRITICAL THINKING

▼ BREAKING DOWN STORIES

Look at this summary of *King Lear*, a play by Shakespeare that takes three hours to perform in full!

Exposition: A king of Ancient Britain tries to give control of the kingdom to his daughters.

Conflict: The older daughters accept but the youngest refuses it. The king and his youngest daughter argue and she is sent away.

Climax: The king is treated very cruelly by his older daughters.

Resolution: The king is reconciled with his youngest daughter and dies.

Work with a partner and identify any story that you know and that you think your classmates will know. It could be a television drama, a film or a book you have. Describe the four stages of the story in four sentences.

LEARNING OBJECTIVES

This lesson will help you to:
- sequence ideas and information effectively in your writing.

SEQUENCING IDEAS FOR EFFECT

There are no mechanical rules about the size or length of sentences or paragraphs, nor about the number of lines or words needed in each. The important thing is to ask yourself: How can I best organise sentences and paragraphs so that they are as clear and effective as possible?

ACTIVITY 1

SKILLS CRITICAL THINKING, ANALYSIS, INTERPRETATION

▼ DEVELOPING NARRATIVES

Work with a partner or in groups and read the extract below.

The woman offered him another cup of tea. She had been very friendly since he had stepped into the house. The room seemed all right and now there was another cup of tea. There was something slightly odd about the taste, not enough to worry him and, anyway, he wanted to find out what the rent would be. While she waited for his answer she glanced down at the newspaper and folded it away, hastily, out of sight, behind one of the cushions.

▲ 'The woman offered him another cup of tea.'

There was a knock at the front door. The woman got up and went into the hall to see who it was and he could hear a conversation get under way. From behind the cushion he retrieved the newspaper and read the headline: *Missing students – poisoner suspected*. He took another sip of his tea. This time he screwed up his face and put down the cup. From one side he picked up his coat and stood up.

1 What are your first impressions of the woman in the first three sentences? What creates this impression?

2 How do your impressions of the woman change by the end of the first paragraph? What creates this impression?

3 How have your impressions of the woman changed by the end of the second paragraph? What creates this impression?

ACTIVITY 2   SKILLS ▸ CRITICAL THINKING, ANALYSIS

▼ KEY CONTENT IN PARAGRAPHS

Work with a partner or on your own and identify the key words or ideas in each of the following two paragraphs.

> At the foot of the hill there is a large spread of woodland, pine trees – dark green, that swarm upwards, almost to the top of the hill. Local people love this place, to which they bring their dogs and their children; on most days, you will see them dotted about on the parkland, enjoying this special space.

> Now the local government has announced plans to build a new road through the middle of the parkland, destroying this much loved and valuable local resource. Protests are planned for next week and locals hope that the politicians will be sufficiently embarrassed and re-think their plans.

1 What impression is created of the parkland in the first paragraph? Summarise it in ten words or fewer.

2 What impression is created of the local government in the second paragraph? Summarise it in ten words or fewer.

3 Why might the writer have chosen to position these paragraphs in this order?

▶ A new paragraph can be used to shift tone or ideas.

ACTIVITY 3   SKILLS ▸ ADAPTIVE LEARNING, CREATIVITY

▼ DEVELOPMENT IDEAS

Work with a partner and develop the ideas listed below into a plan for a report in a newspaper.

> a burst water main   a busy road junction
>
> freezing weather conditions   accidents and a busy hospital

1 What will be the intention of your report? Do you want to warn your readers or reassure them? Or something else completely?

2 Note the ideas and information you will include in each paragraph. Remember to arrange the ideas in an order that suits the intention you want your report to achieve.

KEY POINT

As you move from one paragraph to another you should indicate clearly that you are either developing an idea or introducing a new one.

LEARNING OBJECTIVES

This lesson will help you to:
- engage and guide readers by structuring your ideas effectively and signaling how those ideas develop in your writing.

LINKING IDEAS

Good writing is engaging and easy to read. One way effective writers achieve this is by selecting engaging ideas or information and clearly signaling to the reader how one idea or piece of information is linked to the next.

UNDERSTANDING HOW IDEAS LINK TOGETHER

Read this article about the inventor, Nikola Tesla.

Nikola Tesla was born in darkness on July 10th 1856 during a dramatic electrical storm. According to one legend, the midwife declared this to be a bad omen: "He will be a child of darkness!" she warned. "No," his mother replied. "He will be a child of light." [1]

Born to Serbian parents in what is now Croatia, he emigrated to France in 1882 where he worked for the Continental Edison Company, founded by Thomas Edison, the inventor of the modern light bulb. Tesla soon became one of their leading engineers. Already developing ideas for new technologies to harness the power of electricity, Tesla emigrated to the United States where financial backers funded his first company: the Tesla Electric Light Manufacturing Company. Within two years, his backers had lost faith and withdrew their money. Tesla was left penniless. He had to survive for several months working as an electrical repair man and digging ditches. [2]

Word of Tesla's inventions, however, soon reached the Western Union Company. They funded Tesla's experiments with an AC power system which won over all the other systems being developed at the time, and still powers the world today. Tesla went on to work on an invention which has become known as the Tesla Coil, a transformer capable of generating extremely high voltages and high frequencies which became instrumental in the development of fluorescent and neon light, and eventually X rays. It led Tesla to develop a wireless power system, capable of transmitting electrical waves through the air which, in turn, led to the development of radio. Always persuasive, Tesla secured funding for the building of an enormous tower to transmit waves of power. It ran out of money before being completed. [3]

Disappointed and disillusioned, Tesla began to withdraw from the world. He spent the rest of his life living in a New York hotel. Word of further inventions – including rumours of a death ray – occasionally emerged but little of any significance. Nikola Tesla died in 1943. [4]

ACTIVITY 1   **SKILLS** ▸ CRITICAL ANALYSIS, ANALYSIS, REASONING

▼ **IDENTIFYING STRUCTURE**

Read through the article about Nikola Tesla.

Now look at the table below, summarising the structure, intention and content of each section of the text. ▶

▼ STRUCTURE	▼ INTENTION	▼ CONTENT
Introduction	Engaging the reader	An interesting and surprising anecdote
Main body	Detailed information	Growing success and a setback
		Huge success and failure
Conclusion	Ending	The final years

- Which paragraphs contain which content?
- Which paragraphs achieve which intention?

ACTIVITY 2
SKILLS CRITICAL THINKING, CREATIVITY

▼ EXPLORING STRUCTURE

The article about Nikola Tesla is sequenced in chronological order: it begins with his birth and ends with his death. However, the article does not give information about everything that happened in Tesla's life. The writer has carefully selected the ideas he has chosen to include.

1 Look closely at paragraph 2. The writer focuses firstly on Tesla's success at the Continental Edison Company, then on events that followed the forming of the Tesla Electric Light Manufacturing Company.

   i   What links these two pieces of information?

   ii   How are they different?

   iii   What might have been the writer's intention in linking them?

2 Look closely at paragraph 3.

   In what ways is the structure and sequencing of ideas in this paragraph similar to the structure and sequence of ideas in paragraph 2?

3 Now think about how each paragraph is linked to the previous one.

   i   What words or ideas link the second paragraph to the first? Note down a quotation from each that shows this link. For example: Paragraph 1: 'He will be a child of light.' links to Paragraph 2:...

   ii   What words or ideas link the third paragraph back to the second? Note a quotation from each showing this link.

   iii   What words or ideas link the fourth paragraph back to the third? Note a quotation from each showing this link.

ACTIVITY 3
SKILLS CRITICAL THINKING, CREATIVITY

▼ LINKING POINTS AND IDEAS

Find a piece of writing about a topic that interests you. It could be on sport, music, IT, engineering, fashion, cooking, travel or a piece of fiction. Mark or identify each of the main points as they are introduced and make a list of them. Re-order the list if you think the structure of the writing could be improved then re-write the piece in your own words, taking care to link your points.

▲ You could try structuring your writing around these images.

LEARNING OBJECTIVES

This lesson will help you to:
- control sentences accurately so that what is written can be read easily and clearly understood.

ENDING A SENTENCE

The way in which the end of a sentence is punctuated can have a dramatic impact on its purpose and content.

Read this extract aloud.

> there are three ways of ending a sentence this is very important if you do not punctuate sentences accurately they are very difficult to read then the meaning will not be clear do you understand this it is extremely important

Now read this extract aloud.

> There are three ways of ending a sentence. This is very important. If you do not punctuate sentences accurately they are very difficult to read. Then the meaning will not be clear. Do you understand this? It is extremely important!

Three ways of signalling the end of the sentences have been used in the second extract. Unless you use a question mark for a question or an exclamation mark to stress something important or dramatic, you should use a full stop.

KEY POINT

Punctuate the ends of sentences clearly so that they are easily read and easily understood.

ACTIVITY 1   **SKILLS** ▶ **INNOVATION**

▼ CHOOSING CLOSING PUNCTUATION

Work on your own and punctuate the following extract. If you cannot read the extract aloud, try to imagine the sound of your voice as you read it. Remember, each sentence must have at least one main verb.

> it was night over the hill they could see the stars they had been told of the dangers of the area but they had decided to continue anyway soon they reached the first of the houses where the street took a sharp turn to the right soon they would be back home

Questions must be finished with a question mark. They are formed in two ways. They may be formed with auxiliary verbs such as *would*, *should*, *do*, *does*, and so on. For example: *Should we leave?* or *Does he take sugar?*

Another way of forming questions involves the reversal of the subject/verb order in a statement. For example, *Is it theirs?* This form of question may include question words such as *why*, *what*, *where*, *who*, *whom* and *how*. For example, *How do you like your coffee?*

Exclamation marks can be used to represent strong emotions, emphasise points or suggest volume. They should be used sparingly so as not to lessen their impact.

LEARNING OBJECTIVES

This lesson will help you to:
- understand how commas are used.

COMMAS

Commas are essential to guide the reader, showing how a sentence should be read and understood. A single comma can change the entire meaning of a sentence.

Commas do the following:
- indicate the end of a subordinate clause and separate it from a main clause:

   While it was raining, they watched a film.
- separate items in a list:

   For breakfast he ate cereal, toast, baked beans and two apples.
- clarify meaning by separating ideas:

   His friend who had black hair was found with him. (*It was his friend with black hair who was found with him, not one of his other friends.*)

   His friend, who had black hair, was found with him. (*This friend just happened to have black hair.*)

   - Look at this sentence:

      The River Niger rises in the north of Nigeria, which takes its name from the river, to the north of Lake Oguta, and makes its way southwards towards the delta and out into the Gulf of Guinea.

   The first and second commas separate information about the origin of Nigeria's name and the second and third commas separate further information about the place where the river rises. These three commas enclose additional information that does not impede the main point of the sentence. Without this information, the sentence would still make sense.

      The River Niger rises to the north of Lake Oguta and makes its way southwards towards the delta and out into the Gulf of Guinea.
- open and close direct speech (notice how the actual words that are spoken are enclosed in speech marks, or inverted commas):

   'Come in,' said the doctor, 'do sit down.' The patient made himself comfortable and replied, 'Good to see you, doctor.'

   'You know,' said the doctor, 'it's a good job you made this appointment.'

▲ The river Niger is the main river of West Africa.

ACTIVITY 1   **SKILLS** ▷ **INNOVATION**

▼ USING COMMAS

Insert commas where required in the following extract.

It was raining. Slowly very slowly the puddles filled dull and grey under the dull light. Look out! shouted Henry but it was too late. I told you to look where you were going. You never pay attention ever. Further down the road half a kilometre away an old truck started up misfired once or twice and began a struggle up the hill towards them.

KEY POINT

It is easy to read quickly from the start to the end of a sentence, as long as commas are used correctly to make clear the writer's intentions.

LEARNING OBJECTIVES

This lesson will help you to:
- understand how apostrophes are used.

APOSTROPHES

Apostrophes have two functions. They indicate the omission of one or more letters and, usually with the letter *s*, they indicate possession, meaning that something belongs to someone or something else. Like other punctuation marks, if they are used correctly, they help to make clear to the reader what the writer intended.

Read both these sentences aloud.

It's going to be a long night and there's nowhere to go.

It is going to be a long night and there is nowhere to go.

When you read the second sentence, you have to make just a little more effort to read *It is* and *there is.* In speech, people usually prefer to elide the *i* in *is*. That means the sound is suppressed or glided over for the sake of ease and speed. In writing, however, this is often seen as informal in style.

You can do this with other letters and, so long as you use the apostrophe, this will be clear to the reader. Here is another example:

We haven't a penny between us but she's got plenty.

This time the *o* and *ha* sounds have been missed.

When an apostrophe is used to indicate possession, the apostrophe usually appears before the *s* if the subject is singular and afterwards if the subject is plural.

Helen's mother hid all her brothers' bicycles.

With words that end in *s*, or words that do not take an *s* to show the plural, there are two ways to punctuate possession, for example, *Chris' bike* and *the children's clothes*. Alternatively, an additional *'s* can be added to names ending with an *s*: *Chris's bike*. However, ensure that you remain consistent by only following one of these rules.

Finally, you have to remember *its* and *it's: its* is possessive, while *it's* is a contraction of *it is.*

ACTIVITY 1 SKILLS ▶ INNOVATION

USING APOSTROPHES

Insert the nine apostrophes required here.

'Glad youve come,' she said. 'Ive been lookin for you everywhere. I cant imagine whats the matter ere.'

'Troubles comin soon. Wed best go home.'

KEY POINT

Clear use of the apostrophe allows quick reading and clear meaning.

LEARNING OBJECTIVES

This lesson will help you to:
- understand how to use different punctuation marks.

COLONS, SEMI-COLONS, DASHES, BRACKETS, ELLIPSES

There is a range of different punctuation marks, each capable of achieving a particular effect or changing the meaning of a sentence. Being able to use them all will ensure your writing is varied and engaging.

COLONS

Colons are used to introduce evidence or examples.

> They could see what was stopping the car: a brick wedged under the tyre.

▶ **Write three sentences using a colon like this.**

SEMI-COLONS

Semi-colons are used to join closely related sentences or separate long items in a list.

> It was too late; slowly, he raised his hands.

> They were all there: Rishit who had broken his leg last year; Mishka who had rescued him, although she too had been wounded; and the dog.

▶ **Write two sentences following the first example and two following the second example.**

DASHES

Dashes are used to signal clearly the insertion of non-essential material into a sentence. Their purpose could be to add emphasis, to interrupt or to indicate an abrupt change of thought.

> They were all there – two men and a dog – and she realised that the police would have to be called.

▶ **Write two sentences following the pattern of this example.**

BRACKETS

Brackets are used to add additional material about a preceding item. Remember that, unlike dashes, brackets must be used in pairs.

> Tyrell (lead singer) and Isabella were the band's best performers.

▶ **Insert information in brackets about the asterisked words in the following sentence.**

> Their guide* who had joined them at the airport helped two of them* to carry their bags.

ELLIPSES

Ellipses are used where a word is omitted and are made up of three dots (like full stops). They are most useful in direct speech; when you speak, you are more likely to pause or break off in mid-sentence.

> He paused. 'I don't think I'm…' With that he turned away.

> 'If you don't stop that I'll, I'll…' Before she could finish, they had drowned her in laughter.

KEY POINT

Remember that each of these punctuation marks has a distinctive function.

▶ **Work with a partner and construct two dialogues between two or more characters. Each of you should write the first line of a dialogue, then pass it to your partner who should write the second line. Continue like this until you have written at least ten lines.**

LEARNING OBJECTIVES

This lesson will help you to:
- avoid common spelling errors.

COMMON SPELLING ERRORS

It is easy to find lists of commonly misspelt words on the internet. These sites often provide reminders for some spellings and suggest that you make a list of the words that you find difficult to spell.

Correct spelling is something that depends on your visual memory so reading will help. You should also try to find ways of remembering something about the word, for example, *stationary* and *stationery*.

Where *a* is the final vowel, the word *stationary* means *not moving* or *stopped*. Think of *stopped* as **a**rrested, a word which begins with an *a*.

Where *e* is the final vowel, the word *stationery* refers to **e**nvelopes and writing paper.

▲ Stationary/stationery; similar words, very different things.

Another way to help yourself to remember difficult spellings is to look closely at the word, jotted down perhaps on a scrap of paper, and try to memorise it. Then cover up the word while you try to write it down accurately. Repeat this process if necessary. (Here's another difficult word, necessary. Remember, *shirts are nec**e**ss**a**ry* – one **c**ollar and two **s**leeves.)

Words that contain *e* and *i* together are sometimes easier to spell if you remember the following **mnemonic**:

i *before* e, *except after* c, *unless the sound matches weigh.*

So you have: *yield*, *receive*, *sleigh*. There are exceptions such as *seize*.

Particularly important words that you should make an effort to spell correctly include:

SUBJECT VOCABULARY

mnemonic a device used to aid memory – usually in the form of a saying or rhyme

accompany	disguise	lightening	suspicious
agreeable	dumb	lightning	temperature
anxious	engineer	naughty	thorough
applaud	exhibition	neighbour	though
certificate	experiment	niece	thought
civilised	fulfil	occur	tremendous
compliment	government	occurred	vegetable
complement	fatigue	privilege	ventilation
conferred	height	prosperous	
deceitful	immediately	succession	
decision	language	suspicion	

KEY POINT

Avoiding spelling mistakes will make your writing much more effective and engaging.

LEARNING OBJECTIVES

This lesson will help you to:
- start checking your writing automatically.

IMPROVE YOUR WRITING

Like any practical activity, writing will improve with practice. Write regularly, at least ten minutes a day and always check your writing as you go. It's a good idea to check each paragraph as you proceed. That way you will also have a second look at your ideas, your vocabulary and sentence structure choices and an opportunity to consider again how you will lead your ideas into the next paragraph.

The final stage in the writing process is to check your spelling, punctuation and grammar carefully.

TIPS TO REMEMBER

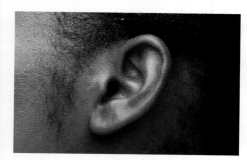

▲ Listening to how your writing reads is almost as important as reading it thoroughly when checking your work.

KEY POINT

Remember that your aim should always be to write clearly, accurately and effectively. As you write, ask yourself: Is this clear? Is this accurate? Will this be effective when someone else reads it?

- Allow your hearing (or the imagined sound of reading) to check grammar and punctuation.
- Allow your sight to check spelling. If you are typing, don't rely on spell checkers.
- When you edit a piece of writing, you have to consider the way words are used and put together so that you can correct errors and improve your choice of vocabulary and sentence structure.

Remember that you must do the following:

- Begin a sentence with a capital letter. A capital letter marks clearly the start of a new sentence. Capital letters must also be used to mark proper nouns and all components of a proper noun, such as Abdul, Singapore and Hong Kong Airport.
- Stop sentences clearly with a full stop, a question mark or an exclamation mark. Use these punctuation marks in direct speech to mark the end of a spoken sentence.
- Use commas in lists and to separate some clauses, as well as for clarifying information and in direct speech. Here the commas indicate the pauses as you read to help indicate the words that are actually spoken.

  Marie uttered the words, 'You fool!' She swallowed hard before continuing. 'What do you think you're doing?' She raised her mobile. 'The police,' she said, 'the police will like this when I send it.'

When you want to include additional information without interrupting the flow of the sentence, you must choose between dashes and brackets:

- Dashes lead the eye to the next word so that the additional information can be easily taken in as you read on. For example, 'It was light – the sort of morning that calls to early risers – so staying in bed seemed sinful.'
- Brackets allow the insertion of shorter, more practical items of information. For example, 'Take out the flour (wholemeal, remember) and weigh out 200 grams.'

LEARNING OBJECTIVES

This lesson will help you to:
- detect items that require correction or that could be improved.

PROOF-READING, CHECKING AND EDITING

There are two important aspects of checking what has been written:
- proof-reading: marking errors in a draft
- editing: looking for opportunities to modify and improve the material.

PROOF-READING: MECHANICAL ACCURACY

When proof-reading, ask yourself the following questions.

▶ **Are words spelt and ordered correctly?**

▶ **Are words changed where necessary so that they work together?**

▶ **Do the words flow when read out loud? If you are unable to read aloud, try imagining reading aloud instead.**

▶ **Have you double checked?**

| ACTIVITY 1 | SKILLS ▷ INNOVATION |

▼ FINDING ERRORS

Work on your own or with a partner and correct the highlighted errors in the first sentence below. Then identify and correct the errors in the second sentence.

There is a hard frost which have been anticipating for some days. Many of the smaler animals had burrow deeply but, fortunately for them, heavy rain then caused the river to bursted it's banks and many of them was drowned.

EDITING

When editing, ask yourself the following questions:

▶ **Is this easy to read?**

▶ **Does it make clear sense?**

▶ **Could more effective words be chosen?**

▶ **Could the structure of any sentences be more effective?**

▶ Proof-reading helps to ensure writing is as powerful as possible.

ACTIVITY 2   SKILLS ▶ ADAPTIVE LEARNING, INNOVATION

▼ EDITING TEXT

Working on your own, read through these sentences and edit them, choosing more effective words where you can and re-ordering them where this will improve the extract.

Across the river at the foot of the mountain, he could see the old railway track. No trains had been seen there for half a century but now a bunch of men from the nearest village, which was about a mile away, had decided to campaign for its restoration. He had heard one of his neighbours, now in his eighties, describing the sound of the whistle from the midday train which was his signal to stop work in the fields and go home for lunch.

KEY POINT

Language is firstly a spoken matter, something understood through hearing before reading or writing. One of the best ways of checking written material is to read it aloud.

When checking your work, you should try to imagine the sound of a voice reading it aloud. Remember that the purpose of writing accurately is to make it easy for someone to read it and understand it with little effort. This is what you should check for when proof-reading and editing a piece of writing, whether it is your own or someone else's.

▲ An old-fashioned steam engine.

Proof-reading and editing are essential to any form of writing. Even the best ideas or most carefully thought-out argument can benefit from these processes, ensuring they are as engaging and effective as possible. Spelling mistakes, grammatical errors or poorly constructed sentences can greatly lessen the impact of a piece of writing, so it is important to carefully check your work and ensure it is of the best possible quality.

PAPER 1: NON-FICTION AND TRANSACTIONAL WRITING

Assessment Objective 1

Read and understand a variety of texts, selecting and interpreting information, ideas and perspectives

Assessment Objective 2

Understand and analyse how writers use linguistic and structural devices to achieve their effects

Assessment Objective 3

Explore links and connections between writers' ideas and perspectives, as well as how these are conveyed

This chapter focuses on Paper 1: Non-fiction and Transactional Writing of the English Language A course. Working through these lessons and activities will help you to develop the reading and writing skills that you will need for the Paper 1 exam.

The chapter is split into the following sections:
- Non-fiction texts
- Text Anthology: Non-fiction
- Unseen texts
- Comparing texts
- Transactional writing.

Paper 1 is worth 60% of the total marks for the course and is split into two sections:
- Section A: Non-fiction
- Section B: Transactional writing.

In Section A of your exam, you will need to be able to meet Assessment Objectives AO1, AO2 and AO3.

In Section B of your exam, you will need to be able to meet Assessment Objectives AO4 and AO5.

Assessment Objective 4

Communicate effectively and imaginatively, adapting form, tone and register of writing for specific purposes and audiences

Assessment Objective 5

Write clearly, using a range of vocabulary and sentence structures, with appropriate paragraphing and accurate spelling, grammar and punctuation

In Paper 1, the assessment objectives are worth the following amounts:
AO1 – 7%
AO2 – 8%
AO3 – 15%
AO4 – 18%
AO5 – 12%

LEARNING OBJECTIVES

This lesson will help you to:

■ understand some of the features of non-fiction texts and prepare you to answer exam questions on them.

TYPES OF TEXT

The types of non-fiction text that may appear in Paper 1 include examples of:

■ biography or autobiography
■ speeches
■ newspaper or magazine articles
■ travel writing
■ diaries or letters
■ reviews
■ reference books.

KEY POINT

All non-fiction writing focuses on real events but the author's views may influence how those events and their version of them are presented.

▲ A library shelf displaying a selection of biographies on Nelson Mandela.

SUBJECT VOCABULARY

objective based on facts, or making a decision that is based on facts rather than on your feelings or beliefs
unbiased fair; not influenced by one's own or someone else's opinions

The texts that you will write about in Paper 1 will be non-fiction. Fiction describes scenes imagined (at least partly) by the writer. Non-fiction writing does the opposite: it is about things that really happened, although you cannot rely on all non-fiction to be accurate.

In an **autobiography**, the writer describes his or her own life. However, some events may not have been remembered accurately, or some events may be exaggerated for effect, perhaps to show the writer as positively as possible. Some autobiographies may be considered more like fiction than non-fiction by their readers because they are not very accurate.

A **biography** is the life story of a famous or interesting person, whether from history or from the present day. Today, there are also 'authorised biographies', in which the subject of the biography gives the writer specific legal permission to produce the biography. The subject can decide which events are included or omitted and how the writer describes them.

Another form of autobiographical writing is the **diary** or **journal**. For example, *The Diary of a Young Girl* by Anne Frank contains important factual material about her daily life during the German occupation of the Netherlands. It is therefore more than just a personal account. However, not all diaries set out to be accurate or truthful. Many diaries have other purposes, such as to entertain, to give personal views and to communicate with friends.

News reports may appear in newspapers or magazines. News is expected to be objective or unbiased and based on clear evidence. As readers, you want to know whether a reporter is trying to present the material in a particular way because of their own opinions on the topic. However, some newspaper and magazine articles are undoubtedly biased. In all forms of non-fiction text, therefore, the question of truth and accuracy really matters. This means that part of the reader's analysis should include looking for any examples of bias or opinion that is not supported by evidence.

Feature articles are usually about a topic of interest to a large number of readers: they can be about almost anything, from family matters to global politics. They are usually based on research. Opinion or comment pieces will contain factual evidence and explanation, but aim to argue a case about a topic of general interest.

ACTIVITY 1   **A01**   SKILLS ▶ CRITICAL THINKING, REASONING, DECISION MAKING

▼ IDENTIFYING TYPES OF NON-FICTION

Which of the types of non-fiction text described on page 58 do you think the following extracts come from? Give reasons for your decision. Which one do you think is more objective? Explain why you think this.

▼ FROM *THE INDEPENDENT* NEWSPAPER

Even the keenest gamers generally suffer nothing more than sore thumbs or tired eyes from their hobby. But scientists looking into the health effects of video game consoles have linked overplaying to dozens of injuries – some even life-threatening. The cases were uncovered after a team of Dutch researchers gathered all reported cases of Nintendo-related injuries, spanning 30 years.

▼ FROM 'SUNRISE IN MOZAMBIQUE' FROM *THE TELEGRAPH* NEWSPAPER

We stepped outside, snapping on our sunglasses as the whitewashed walls blinded us. After trying to coax our tongues around the morning sounds of Portuguese, we walked through the gates on to the dirt-packed road that would soon be bustling.

BIOGRAPHY AND AUTOBIOGRAPHY

Read the following short extract from an autobiography that tells Ellen MacArthur's account of her extraordinary life as a lone yachtswoman. While reading it, think about what MacArthur is writing about and how she has written her account.

▼ FROM *TAKING ON THE WORLD* BY ELLEN MACARTHUR

jib A small sail.

foredeck The deck near the bows of the yacht.

forestay Another sail.

knot A nautical mile per hour.

The wind continued to rise during the first few days, and by the third I was changing down to the storm jib on the foredeck, and was thrown off my feet before cracking my head hard against the inner forestay rod, resulting in an instant lump and a strange nausea. Soon afterwards, the weather front passed, only to bring even stronger 55-knot gusts in a steady 45-knot wind.

It was an unreal, crazy situation: just trying to hang on inside the boat took every ounce of strength. Food was hurled around the cabin along with water containers and spares, while I tried to scrape things up and put them back in the boxes. My hands stung, my eye was swollen, and my wrists were already covered in open sores...

When you first read a text, you need to think about:
■ the genre: this may help you to identify the writer's purpose
■ the writer's purpose: this may help you to identify the writer's intention
■ the writer's intention: this guides the writer's choice of structure, sentence structure and vocabulary.

KEY POINT

Purpose and intention guide the writer's choice of structure, sentence structure and vocabulary. Identifying purpose and intention will help you identify significant choices the writer has made.

HINT

You will need to analyse the techniques used by the writer in order to meet Assessment Objective 2. Think about:

- the story or narrative and what actually happened
- use of precise detail
- frequent use of **personal pronouns**
- first person perspective maintained throughout
- use of emotive language
- use of descriptive language.

SUBJECT VOCABULARY

personal pronoun a word used instead of a noun, such as 'I', 'you' or 'they'

ACTIVITY 2   A01   A02   SKILLS   CRITICAL THINKING, ANALYSIS, INTERPRETATION

▼ EXPLORING PURPOSE AND INTENTION

In the extract from her autobiography, Ellen MacArthur describes a storm she experienced at sea.

1   Think about all the purposes for writing. Which of these purposes is a writer likely to use in an autobiography?

explain   inform   describe   argue   persuade   advise   review

2   Which of these purposes has Ellen MacArthur used in the paragraph that you have read?

3   In almost every text, the writer's intention is to engage the reader: to get and hold their attention. In the paragraph you have just read, which of the following intentions has Ellen MacArthur aimed to achieve in order to engage the reader?

a vivid picture   drama   tension   mystery

fear   humour   anxiety   sympathy

4   Choose one of the intentions you have identified in the extract.

▶   **Look at every word in the extract. Identify one or two words or phrases the writer has chosen to help her achieve that intention.**

▶   **Look at every sentence in the extract. Identify one sentence in which the writer has been particularly successful in achieving your chosen intention. How does the structure of your identified sentence help the writer to achieve their intention? It could be:**

- a short sentence to add emphasis to an idea or key moment
- a long, multiclause sentence to build detailed description
- a long multiclause sentence to suggest a rapid series of events
- a long multiclause sentence listing details to suggest quantity or variety.

▶ Yachtswoman Dame Ellen MacArthur.

OBITUARIES

GENERAL VOCABULARY

broadsheet a newspaper printed on large sheets of paper, especially a serious newspaper

apartheid the former political and social system in South Africa, in which only white people had full political rights and people of other races, especially black people, were forced to go to separate schools, live in separate areas, and so on.

▲ Nelson Mandela

HINT

Obituaries are an interesting form to study but will not appear in the exam.

KEY POINT

The writer of a text may have several intentions: the impact that they want the text to have on the reader. In most texts, one of these intentions is to engage the reader's interest. Other intentions will help them to achieve this.

An obituary is a newspaper article, found most frequently in **broadsheet** newspapers, about a remarkable or well-known person who has died. Its length depends on the fame or significance of the subject but they present a very abbreviated sketch of that person's life. These are usually published in newspapers shortly after the person's death has been announced. Here is a paragraph from one example from *The Guardian* newspaper. After years of imprisonment, Nelson Mandela eventually became president of post-**apartheid** South Africa. Mandela died in 2013.

▼ FROM 'NELSON MANDELA OBITUARY' FROM *THE GUARDIAN*

Mandela greatly enjoyed university, particularly boxing and athletics, and, on the strength of his first-year studies in English, anthropology, politics, native administration and Roman-Dutch law, nursed an ambition to become a civil servant and interpreter – about as high a position as a black man might aspire to in those days. But his ambition seemed to be crushed when, in 1940, in his second year, as a member of the student representative council he was expelled for his part in a rebellion over poor quality food. He returned to Mqhekezweni to find another potential disaster – an arranged marriage was being planned for him.

ACTIVITY 3   A01   A02   SKILLS ▸ CRITICAL THINKING, ANALYSIS, INTERPRETATION

▼ IDENTIFYING INTENTION IN OBITUARIES

The purpose of an obituary is to inform the reader about the life of the person who has died.

1 Note down three pieces of information the text gives you about Nelson Mandela's life.

2 Like most texts, an obituary will always have the intention of engaging the reader's interest. Think about how the writer has tried to engage the reader in the life of Nelson Mandela.

Obituaries may include:

- surprising information
- dramatic events
- significant achievements
- a mystery or cliffhanger making the reader want to keep reading to find out more.

Which of these intentions has the writer achieved in the extract from Nelson Mandela's obituary? Note an example of each one you identify.

ACTIVITY 4   **A01**   **A02**   **SKILLS**   CRITICAL THINKING, ANALYSIS, INTERPRETATION

▼ EXPLORING INTENTION, VOCABULARY AND STRUCTURE

1 Look again at each of the writer's intentions and the examples you identified in Activity 3. Look closely at each word in your examples.

Which of the writer's vocabulary choices help the writer to engage the reader's interest and achieve their intention? Look for vocabulary choices that:

- make the information more surprising
- add drama to the events described
- emphasise the significance of Mandela's achievements
- help to engage the reader's interest in a cliffhanger or mystery.

Note them and write a sentence or two talking about the impact of each one.

2 Now think about how the writer has structured this paragraph from Nelson Mandela's obituary.

  i What does the writer focus on at the beginning of the paragraph?

  ii What does the writer focus on at the end of the paragraph?

  iii Why might the writer have chosen to position these two aspects of Mandela's life in the same paragraph?

KEY POINT

Every choice of vocabulary, sentence structure and text structure that a writer makes should be chosen to help the writer achieve their intention.

SPEECHES

Speeches can be given for many different reasons. Lawyers make speeches in court for the defence or the prosecution. People make speeches in debates or after formal dinners to entertain an audience. However, the most famous speeches are those made by politicians as part of campaigns. The purpose of such speeches is often to rally supporters and give listeners a sense of purpose and inspiration.

For much of his life, Nelson Mandela was a member of the African National Congress (ANC), an organisation dedicated to ending the system of apartheid in South Africa. In 1962, Mandela's activities with the ANC led to his arrest by the South African Government. In 1964, he was back on trial, facing life imprisonment. In this speech that Mandela made to the court, he explains why he opposes apartheid and is so committed to bringing it to an end.

As you read the end of his speech, think about how Mandela shows his listeners that he is fighting for a better and fairer society in South Africa, using techniques such as:

- repetition of key words
- emotive language choices
- highlighting the negative impact of apartheid
- highlighting the benefits of ending apartheid.

▲ Nelson Mandela during his election campaign in 1994.

▼ 'I AM PREPARED TO DIE', BY NELSON MANDELA, PRETORIA SUPREME COURT, SOUTH AFRICA APRIL 1964

endorsed out of Expelled, sent away from.

Africans want to be paid a living wage. Africans want to perform work which they are capable of doing, and not work which the Government declares them to be capable of. Africans want to be allowed to live where they obtain work, and not be endorsed out of an area because they were not born there. Africans want to be allowed to own land in places where they work, and not to be obliged to live in rented houses which they can never call their own. Africans want to be part of the general population, and not confined to living in their own ghettoes. African men want to have their wives and children to live with them where they work, and not be forced into an unnatural existence in men's hostels. African women want to be with their menfolk and not be left permanently widowed in the Reserves. Africans want to be allowed out after eleven o'clock at night and not to be confined to their rooms like little children. Africans want to be allowed to travel in their own country and to seek work where they want to and not where the Labour Bureau tells them to. Africans want a just share in the whole of South Africa; they want security and a stake in society.

Above all, we want equal political rights, because without them our disabilities will be permanent. I know this sounds revolutionary to the whites in this country, because the majority of voters will be Africans. This makes the white man fear democracy.

enfranchisement Given the right to vote. The Black people of South Africa were not given the right to vote in elections until 1994.

But this fear cannot be allowed to stand in the way of the only solution which will guarantee racial harmony and freedom for all. It is not true that the enfranchisement of all will result in racial domination. Political division, based on colour, is entirely artificial and, when it disappears, so will the domination of one colour group by another. The ANC has spent half a century fighting against racialism. When it triumphs it will not change that policy.

This then is what the ANC is fighting. Their struggle is a truly national one. It is a struggle of the African people, inspired by their own suffering and their own experience. It is a struggle for the right to live.

During my lifetime I have dedicated myself to this struggle of the African people. I have fought against white domination, and I have fought against black domination. I have cherished the ideal of a democratic and free society in which all persons live together in harmony and with equal opportunities. It is an ideal which I hope to live for and to achieve. But if needs be, it is an ideal for which I am prepared to die.

KEY POINT

Look at the way an author has used the technical devices of language to persuade the listeners of a certain viewpoint.

SUBJECT VOCABULARY

alliteration the use of several words together that begin with the same sound or letter

onomatopoeia where a word sounds like the noise it makes

simile a description that says that an object is *like* an image

metaphor describing something by comparing it to an image which it resembles, in a way that says the object *is* the image

personification when something which is not human is made to sound human by attributing human qualities to it

emotive language dramatic language that stirs emotion in the reader

The art of speech-making is called **rhetoric**. Rhetorical devices include many techniques used in poetry, since they can add impact to all kinds of writing. These techniques include **alliteration**, **onomatopoeia**, figurative language (**similes**, **metaphors** and **personification**), **emotive language** and word choices.

| ACTIVITY 5 | A01 | A02 | SKILLS | INTERPRETATION, ADAPTIVE LEARNING, CRITICAL THINKING |

▼ EXPLORING IDEAS IN A SPEECH

1 In this speech, Nelson Mandela's purposes are to **explain** his ideas and **argue** his viewpoint. His **intention** is to help his listeners understand his ideas and to influence their viewpoint.

Write two or three sentences summarising Mandela's views. You could note:

- the issues that black people in South Africa face
- the reasons Mandela thinks these issues need to be resolved
- the benefits that resolving these issues will bring
- Mandela and the ANC's determination to resolve these issues.

2 Look again at the bullet points above. How does Mandela's choices of rhetorical devices, vocabulary or sentence structure add impact to them? Write a sentence or two about each one.

| ACTIVITY 6 | A02 | SKILLS | CRITICAL THINKING, ANALYSIS, INTERPRETATION |

▼ APPEALING TO LISTENERS' FEELINGS

Effective speeches will nearly always have a strong appeal to the listeners' feelings. Copy and complete the following table to help you analyse how Nelson Mandela achieves this.

▼ APPEALS TO	▼ QUOTATION	▼ POINT
Sympathy for those who suffer	'African women want to be with their menfolk … Africans want to be allowed out after eleven o'clock at night…'	
The desire for justice and fairness		Emotive language is used to…
Admiration for Mandela's commitment and determination		

DIARIES AND LETTERS

KEY POINT

The most famous published diaries show that the personal viewpoint can be an extremely powerful tool in non-fiction writing.

HINT

As you read the extract, think about:

- the age of the girl who is writing the diary
- signs of her ability to write in an unusually mature way about what she is experiencing
- her explanation as to why she writes the diary.

Many people express their most personal thoughts about their lives in writing that is less planned and more informal than an autobiography. This can be done either in a diary that they write regularly or in a letter to someone close: a friend, a lover or a relative. This means that the perspective of diaries and letters is personal. In fact, many writers of diaries and letters did not originally intend them to be published. The writer's thoughts and feelings can be an important part of a non-fiction text, just like characters' thoughts and feelings play an important part in fiction.

One example is Anne Frank's diary, published as *The Diary of a Young Girl*. Anne was a Dutch teenager who kept a diary over a period of two years during the Second World War. As she and her family were Jewish, they hid from the Nazis in a house in Amsterdam. The diary entries ended when the Frank family was eventually found and arrested. Anne was sent to a concentration camp, where she died. The following extract comes from the early months of Anne's period in hiding.

people Anne personifies the paper.

▼ FROM *THE DIARY OF A YOUNG GIRL* BY ANNE FRANK

'Paper has more patience than people.' I thought of this saying on one of those days when I was feeling a little depressed and was sitting at home with my chin in my hands, bored and listless, wondering whether to stay in or go out. I finally stayed where I was, brooding. Yes, paper does have more patience, and since I'm not planning to let anyone else read this stiff-backed

▲ Anne Frank

notebook grandly referred to as a 'diary', unless I should ever find a real friend, it probably won't make a bit of difference.

Now I'm back to the point that prompted me to keep a diary in the first place: I don't have a friend.

home Is it surprising to find that a diary is preoccupied with home life, family and friends?

time Notice the informal register here.

Let me put it more clearly, since no one will believe that a thirteen-year-old girl is completely alone in the world. And I'm not. I have loving parents and a sixteen-year-old sister, and there are about thirty people I can call friends. I have a throng of admirers who can't keep their adoring eyes off me and who sometimes have to resort to using a broken pocket mirror to try and catch a glimpse of me in the classroom. I have a family, loving aunts and a good home. No, on the surface I seem to have everything, except my one true friend. All I think about when I'm with friends is having a good time. I can't bring myself to talk about anything but ordinary everyday things. We don't seem to be able to get any closer, and that's the problem. Maybe it's my fault that we don't confide in each other. In any case, that's just how things are, and unfortunately they're not liable to change. This is why I've started the diary.

ACTIVITY 7 **A01** **A02** **SKILLS** ▶ CRITICAL THINKING, PROBLEM SOLVING, ANALYSIS, INTERPRETATION

▼ **INTERPRETING WRITING**

The writer's **purpose** in this section of the diary is to **explain** her feelings.

The writer's **intention** is to explore and understand her feelings. Remember, Anne was writing the diary for herself, not for anyone else to read.

1 In the extract, the writer explains why she began writing her diary. What reasons does she give?

2 What can you infer from the extract about the writer's thoughts and feelings at this time in her life?

   i Note down two or three quotations from the extract and identify the feelings the writer is expressing and exploring.

   ii For each quotation you have noted, write one or two sentences identifying the words or phrases from which you made these inferences.

3 Look again at the quotations you have selected.

   i Which one conveys the writer's thoughts and feelings with the greatest impact?

   ii How does the writer's choice of vocabulary or sentence structure add to its impact? Write one or two sentences explaining your ideas.

KEY POINT

Always begin your exploration of a text by identifying the writer's purpose and intentions.

D. H. Lawrence was an English novelist and poet. Born in 1885, his career was focused on writing poetry and fiction; most famously *Lady Chatterley's Lover*. His letters, sent to friends and family, are useful records into his life and history, particularly his traumatic wartime experiences despite not undertaking military service during the First World War on grounds of his personal beliefs and health.

The following extract from a letter that he wrote gives an insight into his feelings at the end of the war.

▼ **FROM 'D. H. LAWRENCE TO LADY CYNTHIA ASQUITH, 30 JANUARY 1915'**

It seems like another life – we *were* happy – four men. Then we came to Barrow in Furness, and saw that the war was declared. And we all went mad. I can remember soldiers kissing on Barrow station, and a woman shouting defiantly to her sweetheart 'When you get at 'em, Clem, let 'em have it', as the train drew off – and in all the tram-cars 'War'. – Messrs Vickers Maxim call in their workmen and the great notices on Vickers' gateways – and the thousands of men streaming over the bridges. Then I went down the coast a few miles. And I think of the amazing sunsets over flat sands and the smoky sea – then of sailing in a fisherman's boat, running in the wind against a heavy sea – and a French onion boat in with her sails set splendidly, in the morning sunshine – and the electric suspense everywhere – and the amazing, vivid, visionary beauty of everything, heightened by the immense pain everywhere.

▶

And since then, since I came back, things have not existed for me. I have spoken to no one, I have touched no one, I have seen no one. All the while, I swear, my soul lay in the tomb – not dead, but with the flat stone over it, a corpse, become corpse cold. And nobody existed because I did not exist myself.

KEY POINT

The strong impact of letters comes from their directness, often written soon after the author's experiences.

KEY POINT

Language analysis is a key skill you will need to demonstrate in a number of questions in your exam.

HINT

Look for sentences that vividly describe what the writer sees or powerfully convey his thoughts and feelings. Which sentences, words or phrases convey the most vivid images or create the most dramatic impression?

Read the extract again and think about:

- the locations that D. H. Lawrence describes
- how he describes his emotions
- the reasons for these feelings.

ACTIVITY 8   **A01**   **A02**   **SKILLS** ▶ CRITICAL THINKING, ANALYSIS, REASONING, DECISION MAKING

▼ ANALYSING LANGUAGE

1 In the extract, the writer refers to things he has seen and things he has felt. What are the writer's two **purposes** in writing this letter?

2 Now think about the impact the writer intended this letter to have on the reader – the person he was writing to. What are the writer's **intentions** in this letter?

3 Focus on the things the writer has seen.
   i Summarise the things the writer sees in two or three sentences.
      - What are the writer's thoughts and feelings as he sees these things?
      - How have the things he has seen affected the writer's thoughts and feelings?
   ii Select quotations that show:
      - what the writer has seen
      - what the writer felt when he saw them
      - the writer's thoughts and feelings at the end of the extract.
   iii For each quotation you have selected, write one or two sentences exploring and analysing the vocabulary or sentence structure choices that add to their impact.

4 Compare the two extracts you have read from Anne Frank's diary and D.H. Lawrence's letter.
   i What similarities can you identify in the writers' purposes and intentions?
   ii Which extract do you feel has the greatest impact? Write a sentence or two explaining your choice.

TRAVEL WRITING

A lot of both fiction and non-fiction writing deals with travel. When it is non-fiction, travel writing is generally autobiographical in form. Travel writers usually try to record their actual experiences. When analysing travel writing, ask yourself the following questions about the writing.

■ What are the writer's purposes? Do they focus on describing in order to create a vivid impression of the people, the place and the way of life there? Do they give information about the place? Do they explain its culture and customs, clothing, food or traditions and bring out how they differ from those you are used to?

■ What are the writer's intentions in telling you about their travels? Is it to make you want to visit the place? To entertain you? To enable you to experience places and people that you may never be able to visit personally?

■ What attitudes does the writer show towards the places visited? Are there feelings of amazement, delight, humour, sympathy, or something else?

The following two extracts are about the writers' experiences in different places: one writes about Mozambique, while the other writes about Somalia.

In 'Sunrise in Mozambique', Harry Kid describes early morning in the town of Mocìmboa da Praia by bringing the scene to life as vividly as he can. As you read the passage, think about:

■ your impressions of the people and the activities described in the text

■ your impressions of the places described in the text

■ your impressions of the writer

■ the way the writer presents a detailed picture.

▲ Two fishermen in a Dhow (a sailing vessel used throughout East Africa, Eastern Arabia, Yemen and South Asia) in Mozambique.

▼ FROM 'SUNRISE IN MOZAMBIQUE' BY HARRY KID

At five o'clock, the dazzling light of sunrise wriggled through the stretched curtain cloth and filled our room, signalling the start of the day.

Before the rays fully took on their ferocious heat, the inhabitants of the coastal town of Mocìmboa da Praia, in Mozambique, were beginning to stir.

In the central yard of the family compound in which we were staying, Mama was banging a clay burner on the floor, removing ash and giving life to the dampened embers from the night before. Her daughter swept away the dust with a hand-held brush made from a thick bundle of reeds. She scolded her brother as he got in her way, coming back from the water tank on the far side of the yard.

We stepped outside, snapping on our sunglasses as the whitewashed walls blinded us. After trying to coax our tongues around the morning sounds of Portuguese, we walked through the gates on to the dirt-packed road that would soon be bustling.

For now, the frames of empty stalls stood like skeletons as their owners ate breakfast. Turning right, we walked a short distance through a hotch-potch of shadows created by the swiftly rising sun until we neared the end of the road and found Selima.

In a patched-together shack, Selima, a Tanzanian of 40, was frying chips glued together with egg on his gas stove – chipsi maiai. We exchanged Swahili greetings, this time with more ease, and ordered two deep-fried eggs. While they bubbled we crossed the street to find a crate of fresh rolls that were offered warm, dusty and chewy from the bake-house. As this fishing town took its first breaths of the day, we feasted and inhaled with it.

Over a cup of tea, we chatted to passers-by in a concoction of Portuguese, French, English and Swahili that somehow was understood, and watched as life flooded the street.

Stalls began to fill with vegetables, clothes and trinkets, shops unbarred their doors and music floated from the record hut. Women walked down the road selling home-made goods, such as boiled cassava, rice cakes and doughnuts from plastic buckets balanced on their heads.

Children scampered around legs, avoiding the motorbikes that wove through the human traffic. We listened to the sounds of life as they rose, blissfully happy on our broken chairs. Now, the business of a morning enveloped this untarmacked road in northern Mozambique.

coax Gently persuade.

hotch-potch A number of things mixed up together.

Swahili A language spoken in eastern and central Africa.

cassava Plant with edible roots.

KEY POINT

In Questions 1–3, you will need to use your scanning and inference skills to identify relevant ideas and information. In Question 4, you will need your language analysis skills.

HINT

To answer exam questions successfully:
- Make sure you answer the question by identifying the key words in it. What exactly is the question asking you to do?
- Identify the relevant part of the text that the question refers to. Look very carefully at each word, phrase and sentence in that section of the text, scanning for useful, relevant information to use in your answer.

ACTIVITY 9   **A01**   **A02**   **SKILLS** ▶ CRITICAL THINKING, ANALYSIS, REASONING, INTERPRETATION

▼ PREPARING FOR EXAM QUESTIONS

1 From paragraphs 1 and 2, identify two words or phrases that show the time of day the text is focusing on.

2 Look again at paragraphs 4–6. **In your own words**, describe the town of Mocìmboa da Praia at this time of day.

3 Look again at the last three paragraphs of the text. In your own words, explain how the town changes as the day goes on.

These three questions are similar to Questions 1–3 in Paper 1.

The following question is similar to Question 4 and is worth 12 marks in the exam.

▶ **How does the writer use language and structure to make this extract entertaining?**

You should support your answer with close reference to the extract, including **brief** quotations.

In your answer you should write about:
- the people, places and details the writer focuses on
- how the writer structures these details
- his choice of vocabulary and sentence structure
- the impact the writer intends his choices to have on the reader.

The following extract is an example of a very different kind of travel writing. While you are reading it, consider the way in which it differs from the previous extract.

▼ FROM *A PASSAGE TO AFRICA* BY GEORGE ALAGIAH

I was in a little hamlet just outside Gufgaduud, a village in the back of beyond... In the ghoulish manner of journalists on the hunt for the most striking pictures, my cameraman and I tramped from one hut to another. What might have appalled us when we'd started our trip just a few days before no longer impressed us much.

There was Amina Abdirahman, who had gone out that morning in search of wild, edible roots, leaving her two young girls lying on the dirt floor of their hut. They had been sick for days, and were reaching the final, enervating stages of terminal hunger. Habiba was ten years old and her sister, Ayaan, was nine. By the time Amina returned, she had only one daughter. Habiba had died. No rage, no whimpering, just a passing away – that simple, frictionless, motionless deliverance from a state of half-life to death itself. It was, as I said at the time in my dispatch, a vision of 'famine away from the headlines, a famine of quiet suffering and lonely death'.

▶

There was the old woman who lay in her hut, abandoned by relations who were too weak to carry her on their journey to find food. It was the smell that drew me to her doorway: the smell of decaying flesh. Where her shinbone should have been there was a festering wound the size of my hand. She'd been shot in the leg as the retreating army of the deposed dictator took revenge on whoever it found in its way. The shattered leg had fused into the gentle V-shape of a boomerang. It was rotting; she was rotting. You could see it in her sick, yellow eyes and smell it in the putrid air she recycled with every struggling breath she took.

ACTIVITY 10 — A03 — SKILLS ▶ CRITICAL THINKING, ANALYSIS, INTERPRETATION, DECISION MAKING

COMPARING TEXTS

This is the type of question you will have to answer when tackling Question 5 of Section A. It carries almost half the marks for the section in the exam (22 marks out of 45).

Compare how the writers of these two travel pieces present their ideas and perspectives on their experiences. Support your answer with detailed examples from both texts including **brief** quotations.

(22 marks)

Read the information in the box in the margin, then copy and complete the table to help you plan your answer.

▼ METHOD/ TECHNIQUE	▼ MOZAMBIQUE	▼ SOMALIA	▼ COMPARISON
The writer's purpose	Describe		
Selection of material	Early morning activities		Very different experiences
The writer's intentions	To convey a vivid impression of the writer's experiences, for example,…	To shock and create sympathy, for example,…	
The writer's attitudes			
Vocabulary or sentence structure choice			

HINT

What particular effects do different writers use to interest the reader? For example, the use of emotive language in *A Passage to Africa* and the use of vivid description in 'Sunrise in Mozambique'. What intentions and purpose do these choices help to achieve?

NEWSPAPER AND MAGAZINE ARTICLES

Reading newspaper or magazine articles regularly, and considering why and how the writer has written them, will improve your reading and writing skills enormously.

Articles can be about anything of interest, from politics and economics to shopping and education. Articles may or may not express strong views or come to definite conclusions about the topic, but they usually inform you of developments, make you aware of things of interest and warn you of dangers. The following articles do express opinions, meaning that they are known as 'opinion pieces'. In opinion pieces, the writer presents an argument: a point of view, supported with evidence. Their intention is to influence the reader's views.

When you read the following extracts, or any newspaper or magazine articles, think about:

- the writer's views
- the writer's intentions in expressing these views
- how the writer's choices of language and structure help to achieve these intentions.

Find some examples from the text as evidence for your points.

▲ Changing social habits are a fertile subject for writers.

▼ 'WEEK-LONG BREAK FROM SOCIAL MEDIA 'LOWERS ANXIETY AND ALLEVIATES DEPRESSION" FROM *THE TELEGRAPH*

Taking a week's holiday from social media sites such as TikTok, Instagram and Twitter improves well-being, lowers anxiety and alleviates depression, a new study suggests.

Researchers at the University of Bath said the results were striking enough that regular breaks could be recommended to help people manage their mental health.

"Many of our participants reported positive effects from being off social media, with improved mood and less anxiety overall," said Dr Jeff Lambert, lead researcher from Bath's Department for Health.

"This suggests that even just a small break can have an impact."

For the research, 154 volunteers aged between 18 and 72, who used social media every day, were asked to either continue their usual routine or take a break for a week. The participants used social media sites for an average of eight hours a week.

For those taking a week off, average wellbeing scores increased 19 per cent, depression scores fell 35 per cent and anxiety scores fell 34 per cent.

"Scrolling social media is so ubiquitous that many of us do it almost without thinking from the moment we wake up to when we close our eyes at night," added Dr Lambert.

"We know that social media usage is huge and that there are increasing concerns about its mental health effects, so with this study, we wanted to see whether simply asking people to take a week's break could yield mental health benefits.

"Of course, social media is a part of life and for many people, it's an indispensable part of who they are and how they interact with others. But if you are spending hours each week scrolling and you feel it is negatively impacting you, it could be worth cutting down on your usage to see if it helps."

The number of people using social media has rapidly increased in recent years. In 2011, around 45 per cent of people said they used sites and apps, but that rose to 71 per cent by 2021.

Among 16 to 44-year-olds, as many as 97 per cent use social media.

HINT

When you are thinking about structure, look at the paragraphs and try to say what the main idea is for each one. For example, in paragraph 1, the writer focuses on the benefits of a week's holiday from social media; in paragraph 2, the focus is on the opinion of health experts from the University of Bath.

| ACTIVITY 11 | A01 | A02 | SKILLS ▶ CRITICAL THINKING, INTERPRETATION |

▼ UNDERSTANDING THE TEXT

KEY POINT

To explore a text's structure, consider the ideas and information the writer has selected and the order in which the writer has sequenced them. How might the reader respond to these ideas in this order?

Before answering the following questions, make sure that you have taken in the key points from the text.

▶ **What is the key viewpoint expressed in the article? Sum it up in one sentence.**

▶ **Which ideas or elements in the text support or develop this viewpoint?**

▶ **Identify three to five vocabulary and sentence structure choices the writer has made to add impact to his view point.**

▶ **Consider the structure of the article: the writer refers to the University of Bath report, gives the views of Dr Jeff Lambert, then gives statistics about the number of people that use social media. What is the effect?**

▼ 'DON'T DEMONISE SOCIAL MEDIA, IT CAN BE A BLESSING FOR TEENS WITH PROBLEMS' FROM *THE GUARDIAN*

I remember my first phone. A sticky-buttoned Nokia, given to me by my mum when I was 11, to be used strictly for communication between myself and her (who else was I going to text?), on the way to and from school. I had to press "7" four times just to type the letter "s".

I'm still in my early twenties, but in the intervening years the world of communication has changed dramatically for kids and teenagers. Almost all have smartphones, and many are so closely attached to them that they check them through the night…

In adolescence, when status and popularity are given such importance, drawing comparisons with others' lives has frequently been linked to low mood. Meanwhile, the pressure to constantly be available, brought on by social media, has been blamed for making young people more anxious and sleep-deprived … And when a child falls victim to bullying at school, social media means that their harassment can continue long into the night…

Yet despite these concerns, statistics around social media and mental health have never rung true for me. I and many young people I know believe that, overall, social media has been a positive force in our lives. Technology raises serious issues for today's young people – but it's not the only problem they face…

A quarter of young people with emotional and behavioural difficulties have a parent with a mental health problem… [W]ith increased exam pressures, … and the shadow of massive tuition fees,… [s]chool days are not what they used to be, for far more reasons than social media.

The benefits of online platforms rarely receive as much airtime as the dangers. For teenagers, the internet can be a space to find like-minded people, especially for those who find it difficult to socialise…

Young people face myriad forces that can have significant impacts on their mental health, and it would be naive to deny that technology is one of them. But it's ultimately a tool that can be utilised in different ways. And the digital world won't be going away anytime … For young people, the natural question shouldn't be "social media: yay or nay", but rather how can we best help them navigate it?

Look again at the articles on pages 72 and 73, comparing:

■ the writers' views on technology

■ how the writers express their views

■ the kinds of evidence that the writers use to support their arguments.

| ACTIVITY 12 | A03 | SKILLS ▶ | CRITICAL THINKING, ANALYSIS, INTERPRETATION, DECISION MAKING |

▼ COMPARATIVE QUESTION

Studying the articles on pages 72–73 together, what do you learn about the writers' views, the language they use to express them, and the evidence that they give to support their views? What is the impact of these elements on you, the reader?

Complete a table like the one below, then write one or two paragraphs comparing the articles.

	▼ VIEWPOINT	▼ EVIDENCE	▼ IMPACT
'Week-long break from social media'			
'Don't demonise social media'			

REVIEWS

Reviews play an important part in the relationship between an artistic product and the public. A series of good reviews can help a book, video game, television series or music album to succeed. A professional review performs several functions, such as:

■ informing the reader about the product and its intended audience

■ engaging the reader with the quality of the writing

■ offering a series of critical judgements on aspects of the product

■ making a recommendation as to whether the work is worth seeing, reading, hearing or buying.

As a reader you will need to consider:

■ the writer's intention: do they present a positive, negative or mixed view?

■ the evidence the writer gives to support their view

■ the language the writer uses to describe or explain the product, and to influence the reader's decision on whether to spend or not spend their money.

▶ Film critics, for example, give people an independent opinion on the quality of a movie.

▼ 'NO TIME TO DIE REVIEW: DANIEL CRAIG'S JAMES BOND SEND-OFF IS EXTRAVAGANT, SATISFYING AND MOVING' FROM *THE TELEGRAPH*

KEY POINT

In order to be trusted by readers, reviewers often try to strike a balance between being too positive and being overly critical.

As the end credits have always promised, James Bond will return. And return he finally has, with Cary Joji Fukunaga's extravagantly satisfying, bulgingly proportioned last chapter to the Craig era, which throws almost everything there is left to throw at 007.

To an extent, No Time to Die is in keeping with its immediate predecessors, 2012's Skyfall and 2015's Spectre. The stakes are simultaneously global and personal, and there are many ideas and images from Bond adventures past. But there are differences, too. For one thing, it's unfashionably colourful. Thank La La Land cinematographer Linus Sandgren for the gorgeous dawns and dusks, plus the rich, sun-blush tones of an early chase scene through the mazy alleys of Matera, the Italian hill town where Bond goes with Dr Madeleine Swann (Léa Seydoux) to lay his grudge against Eva Green's Vesper Lynd to rest.

It's one of the great Bond action sequences. The perilous motorcycle jumps and multiple hair's-breadth brushes with death are all suitably gasp-inducing, but so is the shot of Seydoux's face stricken with sincere terror, and the gradual buckling of the reinforced windows of Bond's Aston Martin as bullets steadily kick at the glass.

Eventually, all roads lead Bond and his successor to Lyutsifer Safin, Rami Malek's robustly vile arch-crook. Safin has no intricate motives: he's simply a creepy psychopath, with nothing more complex than vengeance and world domination on his mind. Even his fortress is a throwback. A concrete castle on an island in the Sea of Okhotsk, it's a classic villain's lair with bulky diagonal columns, hidden trap doors, scuttling minions in hazmat suits, and stolen Monets on the walls.

As for the climax, which sees Bond expertly operate a huge, unwieldy 1950s-built hunk of rusting machinery, there might just be a subtext here: however creaky the mechanisms may appear, they still work when it counts.

We've been expecting you, Mr Bond, for quite some time – and what a joy and relief it is to have you back.

► How does this review make you feel about the film?

ACTIVITY 13   A01   SKILLS ▶ CRITICAL THINKING, ANALYSIS, INTERPRETATION

▼ LANGUAGE USED IN REVIEWS

Copy and complete the following table, identifying two things the writer expresses a positive opinion about, and two things the writer expresses a negative opinion about. Note examples of language the writer uses to express them. Then, using your examples, answer the questions.

▼ POSITIVE THOUGHTS ABOUT…	▼ NEGATIVE THOUGHTS ABOUT…	▼ EXAMPLES FROM THE TEXT

▶ Explain one aspect of the film that the writer enjoys.

▶ How does the writer convey their positive feelings about the film?

▶ Explain one aspect of the film that the writer does not enjoy.

▶ How does the writer convey their negative feelings about the film?

REFERENCE BOOKS AND WEBSITES

Reference books and websites are designed to be consulted, not read all the way through. They usually consist of a large number of articles, sometimes on a great variety of topics. Some reference books offer an overview of all knowledge, such as the famous *Encyclopaedia Britannica*. Other reference books have a much more specialised range – there are thousands of reference books covering every academic discipline and field of knowledge.

Read the following extracts from *Encyclopaedia Britannica*, considering how the writing style differs from the other types of non-fiction writing that you have encountered so far.

▲ In binary, numbers are represented by sequences of the binary digits, 1 and 0.

▼ 'ACQUISITION AND RECORDING OF INFORMATION IN DIGITAL FORM' FROM *ENCYCLOPAEDIA BRITANNICA*

The versatility of modern information systems stems from their ability to represent information electronically as digital signals and to manipulate it automatically at exceedingly high speeds. Information is stored in binary devices, which are the basic components of digital technology. Because these devices exist only in one of two states, information is represented in them either as the absence or the presence of energy (electric pulse). The two states of binary devices are conveniently designated by the binary digits, or bits, zero (0) and one (1).

▲ The Sugarhill Gang broke up in 1985 but reunited in the 1990s and are still performing today. The record producer on 'Rapper's Delight', Sylvia Robertson (a singer, record producer and executive), is credited as the driving force behind the landmark track.

KEY POINT

The information that a reference text gives must be accurate, precise and reliable. One way in which the writers of reference texts achieve this is by using complex vocabulary and a very formal **register**.

SUBJECT VOCABULARY

register the type or style of vocabulary used according to the situation

▼ 'RAP' FROM *ENCYCLOPAEDIA BRITANNICA*

Rap, a musical style in which rhythmic and/or rhyming speech is chanted ('rapped') to musical accompaniment. This backing music, which can include digital sampling (music and sounds extracted from other recordings), is also called hip-hop, the name used to refer to a broader cultural movement that includes rap, deejaying (turntable manipulation), graffiti painting, and break dancing. Rap, which originated in African American communities in New York City, came to national prominence with the Sugarhill Gang's 'Rapper's Delight' (1979). Rap's early stars included Grandmaster Flash and the Furious Five, Salt-N-Pepa, Run-D.M.C., Sha Rock, Roxanne Shante, LL Cool J, Lauryn Hill, Public Enemy (who espoused a radical political message), and the Beastie Boys. Later stars include Nicki Minaj, Snoop Dogg, Jay-Z, Cardi B, Missy Elliot, OutKast, Eminem, Megan Thee Stallion and Lil Wayne.

ACTIVITY 14　　**A01**　　SKILLS ▶ CRITICAL THINKING, ANALYSIS, INTERPRETATION

▼ CHARACTERISTICS OF REFERENCE WRITING

Reference writing is quite different to some of the other text types you have explored in this chapter. Choose one other text from this chapter, then copy and complete the table below for the entry for 'rap' from the *Encyclopaedia Britannica* and your chosen text. Remember to add the title of your chosen text.

▼ FEATURES	▼ REFERENCE TEXT: 'RAP' FROM *ENCYCLOPAEDIA BRITANNICA*	▼ ANOTHER TEXT _____
Purpose		
Intention		
Register		
Language choice		

LEARNING OBJECTIVES

This lesson will help you to:
- identify the writer's perspective
- understand how a writer communicates their perspective to a reader.

IDENTIFYING THE WRITER'S PERSPECTIVE

A writer's perspective is their point of view, or the angle from which they see the subject matter. Even the most purely informative articles, which show no personal angle at all, can be said to have a point of view, even if that point of view is objective or unbiased.

Many articles or pieces of writing that claim to be objective are not always unbiased, because everyone brings a personal, societal or national bias to bear on what they write. An article written for an encyclopaedia in the United States of America will be written from an American perspective, which means that the article may be different to one written in China, even though it is apparently unbiased. If the subject of the writing is politics, history or culture, national perspectives will often be very different. For example, in the travel writing extract on page 69, Harry Kid writes from the perspective of a curious British traveller, not from that of a native Mozambican. The account of the scenes he describes might be quite different if written by someone who had had grown up there and saw them every day.

DIFFERENCES IN PERSPECTIVE

Look at the two accounts of the same incident below. Why do you think Dev and Danil had such different perspectives on the incident?

▼ DEV'S ACCOUNT

It was awful. He hit me hard in the face and all his friends laughed at me when I started to cry. I was just walking past and was trying to be helpful by pointing out that the bell had gone. They always laugh at me in the corridor and I thought if I tried to help they would like me more. I don't understand what is going on.

▲ 'They always laugh at me in the corridor...'

▼ DANIL'S ACCOUNT

This has nothing to do with my friends. They didn't even realise what had happened until after I hit him. I think they were laughing at a joke Adesh had made. I did punch him, but that was because he told me I was going to be late with this smirk on his face like he was going to tell the teacher. I have never really seen him before and I thought he was trying to show me up in front of my friends.

ACTIVITY 1 **A01** SKILLS ▶ PROBLEM SOLVING, ANALYSIS, CREATIVITY

▼ THINKING ABOUT PERSPECTIVE

Neither Dev's nor Danil's account of the same incident is untrue, but the writer of each version of events has a different perspective.

1 Describe what happened in the corridor.

2 What might have influenced the two boys to view the events in such different ways? Write down your ideas.

3 Dev's perspective is that he has been bullied by this group for a long time. Write a sentence explaining Danil's perspective on Dev. Why is it important to have heard Danil's perspective?

DIFFERENT ATTITUDES

KEY POINT

Attitude affects language. When you read extracts, think about how the writer uses language to communicate their views to you and what this reveals about the writer's purpose and intention.

Another way of thinking about perspective is to think of the writer in relation to two or more groups of people with different attitudes – one group which shares their views and another group, or other groups, which do not share these views. Ask yourself which groups would agree with a particular idea or argument and which would disagree. For example, one group might be more conservative (resistant to change), while another group might be more progressive (looking for positive change). Another common opposition is that between the authoritarian or restrictive and the liberal or tolerant. Often, the older generation is seen as being authoritarian and young people are considered to be more liberal.

ACTIVITY 2 **A01** SKILLS ▶ PROBLEM SOLVING, INNOVATION, EMPATHY

▼ DIFFERING ATTITUDES

Think of other ways in which people can be divided into groups whose attitudes are often different from each other.

Are these issues strictly defined so a person can only be in one group or the other? Or are some of them more complicated so that there is some overlap between them and some people can be placed more in between the groups?

ACTIVITY 3   A01   SKILLS ▶ CRITICAL THINKING, ANALYSIS, INTERPRETATION

▼ IDENTIFYING A WRITER'S PURPOSE AND INTENTION

Read the following extracts. Identify the writer's purpose and intention in each one, making a note of the language choices that allow you to identify them. Then copy and complete the table, re-reading the extracts to find more examples to back up your ideas.

EXTRACT A

"I have been doing this for 14 years," Andrew Faris half yells down the phone over the rush of noise behind him. Volunteers at his charity are preparing dinners for homeless people – veggie curry and chicken wings. "People ask me: do you ever take a day off? But there's still so much to be done." Faris, who tells me he is in his late 40s, runs a small, London-based charity called Rhythms of Life. The former photographer takes no salary and has put his life savings, about £70,000, into it.

He and his team of 40 volunteers distribute food to homeless people four days a week. Faris collects leftover food from supermarkets most evenings, and spends the following day preparing meals.

"Andrew is the most selfless, dedicated man I have ever met," says volunteer Frazier Stroud. "He has delivered food, support, employment opportunities and care to homeless people across London and, to my knowledge, has never taken a day off."

▲ Rhythms of Life was set up in London in 2008.

the Grand National A famous British horse race over large jumps.

Eagle A British children's comic.

the Mekon A character in Eagle.

EXTRACT B

... If you saw your neighbour whipping a dog, you'd be on the phone to the police immediately, right? Of course, anyone with a shred of decency condemns hurting animals. Yet, inexplicably, some still turn a blind eye to the cruelty to horses during the Grand National, in which riders are required to carry a whip. Nearly every year, racehorses sustain injuries. Many have paid with their lives.

▲ Horse racing is a popular pastime across the world, but is it cruel?

EXTRACT C

Daddy says I have to eat to get well, even if it hurts. The nurse smiles at me when she brings the jam sandwiches. She smiles differently at the other nurses, and when she smiles at sister it is different again. I wish there were bubbles coming out of her head with words, like in Eagle... Thought bubbles would be a useful invention in real life. When you wake in the night there are strange slapping and scraping noises on the marble, and sometimes screams, but I close my eyes, and pretend I'm at home, and think of my presents, and imagine the Mekon in his bubble, and I do not cry, Daddy, I do not, I do not.

	▼ A	▼ B	▼ C
What attitude does the writer express?			
What is the likely age group of the writer?			
Why do you think the writer wrote the piece?			
What other types of people might share the attitude of each writer?			
What have you noticed about the language used in each extract?			

▶ **How is the language of these extracts influenced by the writer's perspective? You could draw another table to help you answer this question, and remember to include examples.**

LEARNING OBJECTIVES

This lesson will help you to:
- identify the text's audience and understand the writer's intention.

AUDIENCE AND INTENTION

It is not always easy to appreciate a text unless you understand who it was written for and the writer's intention: the impact the writer wanted to have on that audience. If you were a child born in Ghana or Jamaica, then the stories of Anansi the spider would be intended for you and there would be no additional context to learn about. However, in other cases, you may need some background knowledge: for example, Nelson Mandela's speech 'I am prepared to die', does not mean all that it should if its reader is ignorant of the history of South Africa. Likewise, the poem, 'The Bright Lights of Sarajevo', means a great deal more if you know something about the Bosnian War of the 1990s.

HINT

Writers do not only write **from** a particular perspective. They also write with a particular '**view**' in front of them, which includes their purpose, intention and audience. Each of these aspects are closely connected.

When you are reading, you should try to bear in mind the audience known as 'the general reader' or 'the general public'. These phrases are used to indicate that all kinds of people may want to read a book about an expedition to the Himalayas or up the River Amazon, and that you do not need to have any particular interests to find the book interesting. However, it would also be reasonable to suggest that such books will appeal to readers interested in adventurous travel. This group will cross boundaries of age, gender, race, and so on, as it is defined by interest only, although it may include more of one section of the population than another.

▶ Do a survey of people you know and find out if, for example, outdoor adventure books such as *Between a Rock and a Hard Place* might appeal more to male readers than female, or more to younger readers than older ones. You could try this on other texts.

ACTIVITY 1 **A01** **SKILLS** ▶ CRITICAL THINKING, ANALYSIS, REASONING

▼ IDENTIFYING AUDIENCE AND INTENTION

As you work through this book, you will read a wide range of texts written for different audiences and for very different reasons. The following table will help you to compare some of the extracts that you have already encountered between pages 58 and 77. Copy and complete it as best you can.

▼ TEXT	▼ AUDIENCE	▼ INTENTION
The Diary of a Young Girl	Herself; perhaps also for others	To confide her thoughts to an imaginary friend
Ellen MacArthur's autobiography	People interested in ocean yachting and racing or in tough sporting exploits	
'Sunrise in Mozambique'		
Nelson Mandela's 'I am prepared to die' speech		

▶

Now complete a similar table for some of the extracts in the Anthology.

▼ TEXT	▼ AUDIENCE	▼ INTENTION
'The Bright Lights of Sarajevo'	Those interested in the Bosnian war; those interested in the poetry of Tony Harrison and similar writers	To communicate something of the way people went on living during the siege of Sarajevo
'Explorers or boys messing about?'	Readers of *The Guardian*; those interested in accounts of endurance and hardship	
Between a Rock and a Hard Place		

AUDIENCE, PURPOSE, INTENTION AND LANGUAGE

Audience is integral to purpose and intention: if the writer intends their writing to have a particular impact on a particular audience, they must choose their purpose, ideas, vocabulary and sentence structure accordingly.

If the writer does not consider their intention or their audience, they cannot make the best choices in their writing. In the same way, if a carpenter does not know what they want to make, or who they are making it for, how can they decide on the design or the materials they will use to make it? If you were writing a story about a crime for a seven-year-old child, you would choose appropriate content and language for the reader, considering their age or level of understanding. Your choices would be very different if you had to write a script for a stand-up comedian.

KEY POINT

Audience and intention are always relevant to a text. Language choice is dictated by the audience and the impact the writer wants to have on them.

ACTIVITY 2   A01   A02   SKILLS ▶ CRITICAL THINKING, ANALYSIS, REASONING

▼ CHOOSING LANGUAGE FOR AN AUDIENCE AND A PURPOSE

Copy and complete the following table with some of the ways in which language is affected by audience and purpose. Add more entries of your own to the table. The more you think about these aspects of a text, the better you will understand them.

▼ TEXT	▼ AUDIENCE	▼ PURPOSE	▼ LANGUAGE
Nelson Mandela's 'I am prepared to die' speech	The people in the court and the South African government		
H is for Hawk (see pages 141–143)	Readers interested in hawks or birds; fans of non-fiction		
A Passage to Africa (see pages 104–105)			
'Young and dyslexic?' (see pages 123–125)			
Chinese Cinderella (see pages 147–149)			

LEARNING OBJECTIVES

This lesson will help you to:
- distinguish facts from opinions.

FACT, OPINION AND EXPERT EVIDENCE

Non-fiction texts all contain facts or opinions or expert evidence. Information texts feature facts only. Reviews feature facts and opinions. Explanation, argument and persuasive texts also feature facts and opinions but the writer may also use expert evidence to support or develop their own views.

| ACTIVITY 1 | A01 | SKILLS | CRITICAL THINKING, ANALYSIS |

▼ TYPES OF FACTUAL WRITING

Look through this book to find examples of a fact, an opinion and expert evidence, then copy and complete the following table.

▼ TYPE	▼ QUOTATION FROM TEXT	▼ PAGE
Fact		
Opinion		
Expert evidence		

HINT

Look for explanation or argument texts featuring quotes. These are likely to be expert evidence used to support the writer's views.

FACTS AND OPINION

As you have already seen, non-fiction texts often include people's opinions and beliefs, even if they may not be factually true. This includes:
- opinions as statements of belief, such as, 'I think football is the best sport in the world'
- opinions stated as fact, such as, 'Football is the best sport in the world'.

Be careful when someone states an opinion or belief as though it is a fact. For example, the second statement about football has the form of a factual statement, but it is still really just a statement of belief about football. Writers often omit phrases such as 'I think…', 'I believe…' or 'In my opinion' before expressing an opinion. Doing this gives the opinion more weight and encourages the reader to accept the writer's views without questioning them. Advertisers frequently state opinion as fact. Washing products may be advertised as making clothes whiter than other brands of washing detergent, but it is unlikely that these statements can be said to be 'facts'.

An argument is an opinion or set of opinions backed up by reasons and evidence. It would be easy to express an opinion that you are the greatest President of the United States in history, but without evidence it would be hard to convince readers without providing facts or expert evidence to support your opinion.

▶ Over a day or two, write down a collection of opinions stated as facts that you hear or see in the media, among your friends and family or in advertisements.

▲ 'The best sport in the world.' Is this a fact or an opinion?

KEY POINT

Look out for writing that states opinions as facts. In your analysis of the text, highlight where the writer has done this and how it adds weight to their viewpoint.

ACTIVITY 2   **A01**   **SKILLS** ▶ PROBLEM SOLVING

▼ FACT OR OPINION?

Read the following extracts, then decide whether they are fact, opinion, or opinion presented as fact.

'It's a fact that boys are stronger than girls.'

'Everyone knows that our school days are the happiest days of our lives.'

'We should eat a more plant-based diet: it does far less harm to the environment and is much better for our health.'

'Space travel is a waste of money. We have so many problems here on Earth, we should be using our money to solve them before we think about spending a fortune on exploring the universe.'

'The human race is more technologically advanced today than ever before, and we have science and scientists to thank for that.'

ADVICE

Non-fiction texts can contain examples of advice. For example, a book review may advise you to read or not to read a particular book. An online article may advise you how to save money, how to prepare for a hot summer, or recommend places to visit. An 'agony aunt' in a magazine could suggest ways of coping with problems in a personal relationship.

Generally speaking, people appreciate advice more if it comes from someone who knows what they are talking about: an expert. Advice is linked to persuasive writing, since it tries to influence the person being advised.

and you certainly won't be the last!
Use of humour.

Don't raise your voice Advice often suggests things you should do – and things you should not do.

Explain... Negotiate... Imperative verbs suggest actions to take.

I'm sure you can An encouraging tone.

Dear Amit

It is clear from your letter that your situation is making you very unhappy. However, you are not the first teenager who feels their parents do not give them enough freedom – and you certainly won't be the last! Perhaps you should try to see the situation from your parents' point of view. I'm sure they only want to be sure you are safe and well.

One way you can make the situation better is by trying to change the way you deal with disagreements when they arise. For example:

- Don't raise your voice or storm off. Stop, take a deep breath and try to understand your parents' point of view.
- Explain why you feel you should be allowed (for example) to stay out a little bit later.
- Negotiate with your parents and try to agree to a compromise. For example, if you wanted to come home at 10 o'clock, and they want you home at 8 o'clock, could you agree on a compromise of 9 o'clock?

If you can talk to your parents, I'm sure you can resolve this issue. Remember: communication is the key to successful relationships throughout our lives.

All the best

Nadiya

LEARNING OBJECTIVES

This lesson will help you to:
- understand how writers use their language skills to create a range of varied effects.

LANGUAGE FOR DIFFERENT EFFECTS

Writers think about their reader when they are writing. You have already looked at **purpose**, **intention** and **perspective**, and now you are going to build on this by considering more of the effects that writers can achieve with their choice of words, phrases and sentences. Some of the examples in this section will be taken from the extracts you have already looked at.

GETTING CLOSE TO THE READER

Some writers want to create a close relationship with their readers, while others are more distant and formal. In autobiographies, writers may share very private thoughts and deal with difficult emotions. They can use chatty or colloquial speech if they feel that that is the best way to engage with their readers. Diaries can be good examples of this, whether their authors are writing only for themselves or for others.

EMOTIVE LANGUAGE

In *A Passage to Africa*, George Alagiah's intention is to shock the reader and to communicate the suffering that he sees in the villages that he visits. He wants you to see in your mind's eye the things he writes about.

Of the writers that you have read so far, which other writers have used emotive language?

ACTIVITY 1   **AO2**   **SKILLS** CRITICAL THINKING, ANALYSIS

▼ THINKING ABOUT INTENTION AND EFFECT

1 Read the following short extract taken from *A Passage to Africa* by George Alagiah (page 71).

> There was the old woman who lay in her hut, abandoned by relations who were too weak to carry her on their journey to find food. It was the smell that drew me to her doorway: the smell of decaying flesh. Where her shinbone should have been there was a festering wound the size of my hand.

Use the questions below to help you write two or three sentences about some of the writer's key vocabulary choices in the extract.

- How would you describe the highlighted vocabulary choices in the short extract?

  vividly descriptive   emotive   colloquial   technical   simple and blunt   complex and sophisticated

- Which of these intentions do the highlighted vocabulary choices help the writer to achieve?

  humour   shock   revulsion   sympathy   drama   tension   mystery   fear   anxiety

  ▶

2 Now look at another short extract.

> If you saw your neighbour whipping a dog, you'd be on the phone to the police immediately, right? Of course, anyone with a shred of decency condemns hurting animals. Yet, inexplicably, some still turn a blind eye to the cruelty to horses during the Grand National, in which riders are required to carry a whip. Nearly every year, racehorses sustain injuries. Many have paid with their lives.

Use the questions on page 86 to help you write two or three sentences about some of the writer's key vocabulary choices in this extract.

▲ The writer's intention is the impact the writer wants to have on the reader. This could include creating humour, or creating tension.

ACTIVITY 2   **A02**   **SKILLS** ▶ CRITICAL THINKING, ANALYSIS, INTERPRETATION

▼ THINKING ABOUT EFFECT AND LANGUAGE

Now think about this the other way around. What effect does the writer want to achieve with their choice of language? Copy and complete the following table, looking through extracts in this book for examples of each intention.

▼ INTENTION	▼ LANGUAGE	▼ EXAMPLE	▼ EFFECT
To create a vivid picture	Vividly descriptive	*A Passage to Africa*, lines…	You imagine the scene or person described
To direct the reader's emotions	Emotive, using the language of the emotions		
To be friendly to the reader	Colloquial, chatty		
To show expert, reliable knowledge			
To create humour			
To worry or alarm the reader			
To influence the reader's opinions			
To create tension			

KEY POINT

The skilled writer can create a wide range of effects on the reader because they have an excellent command of the language.

LANGUAGE TECHNIQUES

Writers can use a range of language techniques to create the impact they want to achieve. When writing about language techniques, you need to identify and name them, then comment on their effect.

ACTIVITY 3   **A02**   **SKILLS**   CRITICAL THINKING, ANALYSIS, INTERPRETATION

▼ COMMENTING ON LANGUAGE TECHNIQUES

Look at the list of different language techniques below. Copy and complete the table by identifying examples of as many techniques as you can from Extracts A, B and C on pages 80–81 and noting the effect of the language technique.

	▼ LANGUAGE TECHNIQUE	▼ EXTRACT	▼ EXAMPLE	▼ EFFECT
C	Contrast	A	The writer contrasts our attitudes to dogs with our attitudes to racehorses.	To highlight the difference between those two attitudes and encourage the reader to think differently about the treatment of racehorses
L	Lists			
E	Exaggeration (hyperbole)			
A	Alliteration and assonance			
R	Repetition			
E	Emotive language			
R	Register			
F	Figurative language			
R	Rhetorical questions			
O	Onomatopoeia			
S	Short sentences or paragraphs			
T	Triple structure			

HINT

Some people find acronyms helpful in remembering lists of terms. We've suggested 'CLEARER FROST' for the language techniques, but try to think of your own if you can.

COMMENTING ON LANGUAGE

Many students find it difficult to describe the effects of language and its contribution to the writer's intention. Avoid overusing words like 'descriptive' when it is not strictly accurate, or relying on vague phrases such as 'draws the reader in' or 'helps it flow'. Try using some of the following alternatives.

KEY POINT

Learning the terminology for language features will allow you to express yourself more precisely in your analysis of writing.

Alliteration and assonance	Makes language more emphatic/more rhythmic/more memorable
Onomatopoeia	Makes phrases more vivid and powerful
Emotive language	Adds power/strength/emphasis to an image or idea
Verbs of motion and action	Make the language more dynamic and energetic
Hyperbole or exaggeration	Creates humour, a light-hearted or ironic tone
Rhetorical questions	Engages the reader, prompts the reader to respond to the question or ideas in the text
Repetition	Adds emphasis to a particular point or word
List	Highlights the range or variety of events/actions/objects

Choose a text you have read in this book. Identify examples of one or two of these techniques in your chosen text. Write one or two sentences about each of your examples, using some of the ideas above to comment on how the writer's language choice helps them to achieve their intention.

COMMENTING ON THE EFFECT OF SENTENCE STRUCTURE

When you analyse a text, you do not need to comment on the structure of every sentence. Look out for sentences that have a significant impact on you – and think about how each sentence's structure adds to its impact.

Short single clause sentence	Adds dramatic emphasis to or highlights a key moment/event
Long, multiclause sentence listing ideas, objects or events	Highlights the range and variety of ideas/objects/events
Long multiclause sentence linking a series of actions	Suggests fast-paced, frantic action
Long multiclause sentence, linking descriptive details	Builds a vivid picture of the scene/character/event
Long multiclause sentence in which key information is delayed to the end of the sentence	Adds emphasis to or highlights a key moment/idea/action
Minor sentence	Adds tension or drama to the action

HINT

Look again at pages 34–35 to remind yourself about different sentence structures.

Look again at the text you chose to explore above. Identify two or three sentences that you feel have a significant impact. Write one or two sentences about each of your examples, using some of the ideas above to comment on how the writer's choice of sentence structure helps them to achieve their intention.

LEARNING OBJECTIVES

This lesson will help you to:
- understand what structure in writing is and how you can write about it.

THE STRUCTURE OF A TEXT

The structure of a text depends upon two things: the ideas or information that the writer has chosen to include in the text and the order in which the writer has chosen to sequence them.

When you explore the structure of a text, you need to think about how the selection of ideas or information and the order in which they are presented contribute to the writer's intentions. For example, if the writer's intention is to build tension or to shock the reader, how does the text's structure help them to achieve it?

HINT

Look also at the relative sizes of the paragraphs. If they vary quite noticeably then there is probably a good reason for it. A short paragraph can add drama, tension or emphasis to a key idea or event.

ACTIVITY 1   A02   SKILLS ▶ CRITICAL THINKING, ANALYSIS

▼ STRUCTURE AND INTENTION

Look at some structural decisions one student made when writing an account of his encounter with a savage dog:
- Walking home from cricket practice through the park at night.
- Describe darkness, moon, wind in trees.
- Two dogs: one huge, one small. The huge dog ran up to me, barking and snarling. It lunged at me, baring its razor sharp teeth.
- I ran. It chased me. I fell.
- I got up and escaped. Mum gave me a plaster for my cut knee.

The writer's intentions are to build tension and to describe a dramatic incident. Think about the structural choices the writer has made to achieve these intentions: the information they have chosen to include and the order in which they sequenced them. Use your ideas to answer these questions:

▶ **Why does the writer begin by explaining the situation?**

▶ **Why does the writer describe the park?**

▶ **Why does the writer focus only on one of the dogs?**

▶ **Why does the writer delay revealing how seriously he was injured to the very end of the account?**

ACTIVITY 2   A01   A02   SKILLS ▶ CRITICAL THINKING, ANALYSIS, INTERPRETATION, CREATIVITY

▼ IDENTIFYING AN EXTRACT'S STRUCTURE

Read the following extract, thinking about the ideas and information the writer has included, and the order in which they are sequenced.

▼ FROM *CIDER WITH ROSIE* BY LAURIE LEE

I was set down from the carrier's cart at the age of three; and there with a sense of bewilderment and terror my life in the village began.

The June grass, amongst which I stood, was taller than I was, and I wept. I had never been so close to grass before. It towered above me and all around me, each blade tattooed with tiger-skins of sunlight. It was knife-edged, dark, and a wicked green, thick as a forest and alive with grasshoppers that chirped and chattered and leapt through the air like monkeys.

▶

I was lost and didn't know where to move. A tropic heat oozed up from the ground, rank with sharp odours of roots and nettles. Snow-clouds of elder-blossom banked in the sky, showering upon me the fumes and flakes of their sweet and giddy suffocation. High overhead ran frenzied larks, screaming, as though the sky were tearing apart.

For the first time in my life I was out of the sight of humans. For the first time in my life I was alone in a world whose behaviour I could neither predict nor fathom: a world of birds that squealed, of plants that stank, of insects that sprang about without warning. I was lost and I did not expect to be found again. I put back my head and howled, and the sun hit me smartly on the face, like a bully.

▶ **Sum up, in three sentences, the beginning (paragraph 1), middle (paragraphs 2 and 3) and end (paragraph 4) of the extract. Use the third person ('he') in your summary. How is the first paragraph different from the others? Can you see a reason for this?**

▶ **Look again at the four paragraphs from *Cider with Rosie* and write a line about the intention or effect of each paragraph. Then explain why you think Lee chose to put the content in that order.**

▶ **Write two or three sentences analysing the structure of the extract. Use some or all of the words and phrases below to help you.**

the writer structures the text to	show the narrator's growing feelings of	building up to
until finally, the narrator	create tension	create sympathy for

---

HINT

Try to bring together your analytical and writing skills – think about how and why you would structure a piece of your own writing.

KEY POINT

When people talk about the structure of a piece, they are not normally referring to sentence structure, which is usually regarded as a linguistic feature. However, there are two points worth bearing in mind.

1 You might notice that a piece ends or begins with a very short sentence. In which case, the writer is using sentence structure as a deliberate part of the larger structure.

2 Sentence structure is still an important point to consider. If you can make a good point about sentence structure, then you should include it in your answer.

One way to identify the structure of a text is to identify and explore the different writing purposes that the writing is using, such as description, narrative and so on. For example, an extract with some description of the setting or a character, followed by some narrative in which something happens. As soon as you notice these different types of writing, you should be able to say something about why they are there in the extract. Many students do not consciously register when a writer is using dialogue or telling them a character's thoughts, so if you do notice these things, you will give yourself an immediate advantage.

ACTIVITY 3   **A02**   **SKILLS** ▶ CRITICAL THINKING, INTERPRETATION

▼ **IDENTIFYING DIFFERENT WRITING PURPOSES**

Copy and complete the following table, using the analysis you have just made to identify and analyse the writing purpose Lee uses in each paragraph.

	▼ WRITING PURPOSE	▼ QUOTATION	▼ EFFECT (OR INTENTION)
1	Narrative		
2	Descriptive		
3			
4			

LEARNING OBJECTIVES

This lesson will help you to:
■ understand how to tackle Questions 1–3 on an unseen text.

UNSEEN TEXTS

The questions in Paper 1 Section A will be based on two non-fiction extracts: one from the Anthology, with which you will be familiar, and another extract that you will not have seen before. Understanding and analysing this unseen text is critical to your success in this part of the exam.

READING UNSEEN TEXTS

The first thing to do when faced with an unseen text is to read it and start thinking about what it is saying. Try not to be scared by the fact that you have never seen it before. Using the skills that you have learned by studying other texts, you should have all the tools you need to understand it and analyse it effectively.

When you have read the text, use the following questions to help you think about what you have read.

■ What sort of text is it?
■ What is the text about?
■ Who is the intended audience for the text?
■ What is the writer's intention?
■ What literary and linguistic techniques does the writer use?
■ What effects do these techniques have?
■ How does the text make you feel personally?

Simply by answering these questions, you will find that you are able to say a lot about the unseen text. You should spend a short time reading the text and getting a good understanding of it. This will then allow you to focus on answering the specifics in the exam questions.

For this section, you will use the extract from *Cider with Rosie* on pages 90–91 as the unseen text.

ACTIVITY 1 | A01 | A02 | SKILLS ▸ CRITICAL THINKING, ANALYSIS, INTERPRETATION

▼ UNDERSTANDING THE UNSEEN TEXT

Read the extract from *Cider with Rosie*. Spend five minutes quickly answering the questions from the list above. Discuss your answers with a partner.

QUESTION 1

Question 1 assesses your understanding of the unseen text. It will ask you to find information from the text and to give two examples of this. You only need to provide two examples; there are no extra marks for providing more.

EXAM-STYLE QUESTION

A01 SKILLS ▸ ANALYSIS

From lines 3–9, select **two** words or phrases that describe the setting.

(2 marks)

QUESTION 2

HINT

When answering, it is always better to explain a few techniques in detail rather than to list points without explaining them properly.

Question 2 asks you to explain or describe information that the writer clearly states or implies in the extract – for example, the writer's thoughts and feelings. In this example, you would need to think about how you know what the writer is thinking and feeling, looking carefully for words and phrases that give this information explicitly or implicitly. You do not need to support your points with evidence: the question asks you to **use your own words**.

ACTIVITY 2   **A01**   **SKILLS** ADAPTIVE LEARNING, INNOVATION

▼ THOUGHTS AND FEELINGS

SUBJECT VOCABULARY

synonyms words that share the same meaning as other words; for example, 'quick' might be a synonym for 'fast'

Thinking about the extract from *Cider with Rosie*, list all of the things that the author says about how he feels. In the exam, you will be asked to use your own words to explain this, so write a list of **synonyms** for the words the author uses.

EXAM-STYLE QUESTION

A01   **SKILLS** CRITICAL THINKING, INTERPRETATION

Look again at lines 7–13.

In your own words, explain what the writer's thoughts and feelings are of finding himself in a strange new place.

(4 marks)

QUESTION 3

HINT

For Question 3, rather than simply repeating the question, it might be better to find a way straight into the answer, such as 'At first the writer is not at all impressed with what he finds…'

Question 3 also asks you to describe or explain information found in the text. You need to be clear what the text is about and what the writer is saying. You should look to support ideas you have inferred from the text with short quotations as evidence to back them up. Identifying explicit information, or implied information supported with evidence, is an effective method of structuring your answer to this question.

ACTIVITY 3   **A01**   **SKILLS** CRITICAL THINKING, ANALYSIS, INTERPRETATION

▼ USING QUOTATIONS

KEY POINT

Question 2 will ask you to answer using **your own words**. Question 3 will suggest you support your answer with **brief quotations**.

Looking at the extract from *Cider with Rosie*, complete the table below to list what the writer thinks and feels about the village. Give examples from the text to support your ideas.

▼ FEELING	▼ EVIDENCE
The writer feels upset and overwhelmed.	'I put my head back and howled'

EXAM-STYLE QUESTION

A01   **SKILLS** CRITICAL THINKING, ANALYSIS, INTERPRETATION

From lines 1–15, describe the writer's first impressions of the village.

You may support your points with **brief** quotations.

(5 marks)

LEARNING OBJECTIVES

This lesson will help you to:
- prepare for answering non-fiction exam questions.

KEY POINT

To ensure the most efficient use of time, a direct approach to answering the question is usually best, rather than spending a long time getting to your main points.

scrub Low bushes and tress that grow in very dry soil.

▲ 'I was alone. I had come to Albania for an adventure and this was it.'

higgledy-piggledy Mixed together in an untidy way.

PUTTING IT INTO PRACTICE

The extract you will be given for Paper 1 are likely to be between 800 and 1400 words long, or at least 60 lines in length. The following example is shorter than this, but you can use it to practise your reading, planning and writing skills in preparation for the exam. Read the unseen extract and answer the questions that follow. One of the questions also requires you to consider *Beyond the Sky and the Earth* from the Anthology. Aim to complete all five questions from Section A in 90 minutes.

▼ FROM 'TRAVELS IN ALBANIA' BY JANE BYRNE

"Jane – you walk." Obediently I slid off the mule that had carried me to the top of the mountain pass. I should have walked the whole way with the group who were still toiling up through the forest, but the previous day had exposed my limitations and I had been presented with the alternative of riding on the second mule while the first mule carried all our bags. As there was no road or track, walking or the mule were the only options.

The ride had been an experience – the mules clattered up the mountain unerringly, following a path invisible to my eyes and often stepping along the very edge of the precipice. Their owners, Zek and Murresh, strolled behind, occasionally practising their English. "Jane – you OK?" I was, although I had no stirrups and no reins and was balanced on top of a wooden frame. The only alarms came when crossing the mountain streams, when the mule had to be restrained from flying leaps. Here I realised that I also had no riding talent.

But now I was at the top. Ahead the land dropped almost vertically for hundreds of feet – snow, rock, scrub and then lush forests. We walked along the ridge for five minutes and then down a gentle slope. The mules, one still laden with the group's luggage, ambled a few feet more and stopped by the edge of the cliff.

"Jane – you wait, you sit." Zek and Murresh unloaded the bags and sat down. Two heads appeared from below. There was a rapid exchange of Albanian and our bags and all four men disappeared down the cliff. Peering over the edge I saw them hurtling down the cliff like goats with our bags, and in a clearing far below two fresh mules.

I was alone. I had come to Albania for an adventure and this was it. I sat on the rock in the sun and listened to the silence. A few tufts of mountain grass, a stunted pine tree, a couple of beetles and me on my rock. I was the first in the group to see this view, probably the first foreigner this year, possibly the first English person ever.

Later we would see many facets of Albania – the mighty castle of Krujë rising out of the bazaar sprawled around its base, ancient Apollonia, whose treasures are largely unexcavated, and the historic higgledy-piggledy streets of Berat with multicoloured lights twinkling in the dusk. Later there would be fun-filled evenings with the group and hours of cheerful companionship during our daily travels.

▶

But at that moment, and for the first time in my life, I felt not like a tourist but like a traveller, even a pioneer. All too soon the group arrived and we moved off – more cliffs to scramble down, more paths to negotiate and, for me, another mule waiting at the bottom.

EXAM-STYLE QUESTIONS

The following questions are based on Text One: 'Travels in Albania' and Text Two: *Beyond the Sky and the Earth: A Journey into Bhutan.*

Text One: 'Travels in Albania'

A01 SKILLS ANALYSIS

1 From the first two paragraphs, select **two** words or phrases that show the type of landscape the writer is travelling through. **(2 marks)**

A01 SKILLS CRITICAL THINKING, INTERPRETATION

2 Look again at the first two paragraphs.

In your own words, explain the difficulties the writer experienced as she rode up the mountain on a mule. **(4 marks)**

A01 SKILLS CRITICAL THINKING, ANALYSIS, INTERPRETATION

3 From the last three paragraphs, describe the writer's thoughts and feelings.

You may support your points with **brief** quotations. **(5 marks)**

This shows she has a positive attitude to the experience. The student has used inference here to sum up the writer's thoughts and feelings about her experience. Remember to link all ideas to the question.

Pointing out that she is the 'first in the group' and 'probably the first foreigner' to experience the view from the top of the mountain suggests she feels a great sense of achievement. The final point again uses inference and links back to the question. Remember, you need to make five points to achieve five marks.

The writer is left alone at the top of a mountain in Albania but seems to enjoy it. She writes 'I had come to Albania for an adventure and this was it.' This shows she has a positive attitude to the experience. The writer later says she feels more like a 'traveller' and not a 'tourist' which further implies the sense of adventure she feels. Pointing out that she is the 'first in the group' and 'probably the first foreigner' to experience the view from the top of the mountain suggests she feels a great sense of achievement. The overall impression is that she enjoyed the excitement and strangeness of her experiences in Albania.

Remind yourself of the extract from *Beyond the Sky and the Earth* (pages 134–136).

A02 SKILLS CRITICAL THINKING, ANALYSIS, REASONING, INTERPRETATION

4 How does the writer use language and structure to interest and engage the reader?

You should support your answer with close reference to the extract, including **brief** quotations. **(12 marks)**

Question 5 is based on both 'Travels in Albania' and *Beyond the Sky and the Earth*.

A03 SKILLS CRITICAL THINKING, ANALYSIS, INTERPRETATION, DECISION MAKING

5 Compare how the writers present their ideas and perspectives about their experiences.

Support your answer with detailed examples from both texts, including **brief** quotations. **(22 marks)**

HINT

Use connectives that help you make comparisons. For example, 'Both travellers are exploring new places, but whereas Zeppa ... , Byrne ...'

▲ Nigerian poet and novelist Chimamanda Ngozi Adichie.

'THE DANGER OF A SINGLE STORY' CHIMAMANDA NGOZI ADICHIE

BACKGROUND AND CONTEXT

Chimamanda Ngozi Adichie was born the fifth of six children in the town of Nsukka in south-eastern Nigeria, where the University of Nigeria is situated. Her father was a professor of statistics at the university and her mother was the first woman to be in charge of the university's administration department.

Adichie studied medicine and pharmacy at the University of Nigeria for a year and a half. Then she left Nigeria to study communications and political science in the USA. Now she divides her time between Nigeria, where she teaches writing workshops, and the United States.

She has published poetry and fiction and her novels have won several awards. For example, her first novel, *Purple Hibiscus* (2003), was awarded the Commonwealth Writers' Prize for Best First Book (2005). Adichie says of feminism and writing, 'I think of myself as a storyteller, but I would not mind at all if someone were to think of me as a feminist writer... I'm very feminist in the way I look at the world, and that world view must somehow be part of my work.'

BEFORE YOU START READING

1   Think of an ethnic group about which you have a few ideas but about which you know very few actual facts. Write down your honest views of the stereotype of that ethnic group.
2   Find out as much about this group as you can. Write down some new things that surprise you.
3   Do you think others see you in a stereotyped way? Write down some of the stereotypes they might have.

▼ FROM 'THE DANGER OF A SINGLE STORY' BY CHIMAMANDA NGOZI ADICHIE

TED A nonprofit organisation devoted to spreading ideas, usually in the form of short, powerful talks (18 minutes or less); TED stands for Technology, Entertainment and Design.

campus The complex of buildings that make up a university.

Adichie, a successful novelist, delivered this speech at a TED conference. She speaks about the power of storytelling and the danger of a single view.

I'm a storyteller. And I would like to tell you a few personal stories about what I like to call "the danger of the single story." I grew up on a university campus in eastern Nigeria. My mother says that I started reading at the age of two, although I think four is probably close to the truth. So I was an early reader, and what I read were British and American children's books.

▶

I was also an early writer, and when I began to write, at about the age of seven, stories in pencil with crayon illustrations that my poor mother was obligated to read, I wrote exactly the kinds of stories I was reading: all my characters were white and blue-eyed, they played in the snow, they ate apples, and they talked a lot about the weather, how lovely it was that the sun had come out.

Now, this despite the fact that I lived in Nigeria. I had never been outside Nigeria. We didn't have snow, we ate mangoes, and we never talked about the weather, because there was no need to. …

What this demonstrates, I think, is how impressionable and vulnerable we are in the face of a story, particularly as children. Because all I had read were books in which characters were foreign, I had become convinced that books by their very nature had to have foreigners in them and had to be about things with which I could not personally identify. Now, things changed when I discovered African books. There weren't many of them available, and they weren't quite as easy to find as the foreign books.

But because of writers like Chinua Achebe and Camara Laye, I went through a mental shift in my perception of literature. I realized that people like me, girls with skin the colour of chocolate, whose kinky hair could not form ponytails, could also exist in literature. I started to write about things I recognized.

Now, I loved those American and British books I read. They stirred my imagination. They opened up new worlds for me. But the unintended consequence was that I did not know that people like me could exist in literature. So what the discovery of African writers did for me was this: it saved me from having a single story of what books are.

I come from a conventional, middle-class Nigerian family. My father was a professor. My mother was an administrator. And so we had, as was the norm, live-in domestic help, who would often come from nearby rural villages. So, the year I turned eight, we got a new house boy. His name was Fide. The only thing my mother told us about him was that his family was very poor. My mother sent yams and rice, and our old clothes, to his family. And when I didn't finish my dinner, my mother would say, "Finish your food! Don't you know? People like Fide's family have nothing." So I felt enormous pity for Fide's family.

Then one Saturday, we went to his village to visit, and his mother showed us a beautifully patterned basket made of dyed raffia that his brother had made. I was startled. It had not occurred to me that anybody in his family could actually make something. All I had heard about them was how poor they were, so that it had become impossible for me to see them as anything else but poor. Their poverty was my single story of them.

Years later, I thought about this when I left Nigeria to go to university in the United States. I was 19. My American roommate was shocked by me. She asked where I had learned to speak English so well, and was confused when I said that Nigeria happened to have English as its official language. She asked if she could listen to what she called my "tribal music", and was consequently very disappointed when I produced my tape of Mariah Carey.

impressionable Easily influenced.

Chinua Achebe and Camara Laye Prominent and pioneering Nigerian authors in the second half of the 20th century.

raffia Dry palm leaves.

Mariah Carey Popular American singer.

▶

stove What do you notice about this paragraph?

AIDS Auto-immune Deficiency Syndrome, a threat to life in some African countries.

fleecing Exploiting someone financially; robbing someone of their money

Guadalajara City in Mexico popular with tourists.

Alice Walker 20th-century African-American writer.

▲ Guadalajara is the capital of the state of Jalisco in Western Mexico.

She assumed that I did not know how to use a stove.

What struck me was this: she had felt sorry for me even before she saw me. Her default position toward me, as an African, was a kind of patronising, well-meaning pity. My roommate had a single story of Africa: a single story of catastrophe. In this single story, there was no possibility of Africans being similar to her in any way, no possibility of feelings more complex than pity, no possibility of a connection as human equals. …

So, after I had spent some years in the U.S. as an African, I began to understand my roommate's response to me. If I had not grown up in Nigeria, and if all I knew about Africa were from popular images, I too would think that Africa was a place of beautiful landscapes, beautiful animals, and incomprehensible people, fighting senseless wars, dying of poverty and AIDS, unable to speak for themselves and waiting to be saved by a kind, white foreigner. I would see Africans in the same way that I, as a child, had seen Fide's family. …

But I must quickly add that I too am just as guilty in the question of the single story. A few years ago, I visited Mexico from the U.S. The political climate in the U.S. at the time was tense, and there were debates going on about immigration. And, as often happens in America, immigration became synonymous with Mexicans. There were endless stories of Mexicans as people who were fleecing the healthcare system, sneaking across the border, being arrested at the border, that sort of thing.

I remember walking around on my first day in Guadalajara, watching the people going to work, rolling up tortillas in the marketplace, smoking, laughing. I remember first feeling slight surprise. And then, I was overwhelmed with shame. I realised that I had been so immersed in the media coverage of Mexicans that they had become one thing in my mind, the abject immigrant. I had bought into the single story of Mexicans and I could not have been more ashamed of myself.

So that is how to create a single story, show a people as one thing, as only one thing, over and over again, and that is what they become. …

Stories matter. Many stories matter. Stories have been used to dispossess and to malign, but stories can also be used to empower and to humanise. Stories can break the dignity of a people, but stories can also repair that broken dignity.

The American writer Alice Walker wrote this about her Southern relatives who had moved to the North. She introduced them to a book about the Southern life that they had left behind. "They sat around, reading the book themselves, listening to me read the book, and a kind of paradise was regained."

I would like to end with this thought: That when we reject the single story, when we realise that there is never a single story about any place, we regain a kind of paradise.

UNDERSTANDING THE TEXT

This is a speech delivered to a conference with an educational theme. In it, Adichie discusses the power and influence that simple storytelling can have, particularly on the young. She shows from her own experience how stories can cause prejudices and that new stories are then needed to redress the balance.

ACTIVITY 1   **AO1**   **SKILLS** ❯ INTERPRETATION

▼ IDENTIFYING KEY POINTS

> **KEY POINT**
>
> When you first read an argument or explanation text, look at the content of each paragraph and try to identify the key point the writer is using it to make.

Look at each paragraph in the text of Adichie's speech. Note down what each paragraph, or group of paragraphs, is about in a table like the one below. What key point is Adichie using the content of each paragraph to make? Add your ideas to your table.

▼ PARAGRAPHS	▼ CONTENT	▼ KEY POINT
1–4	When she was young, Adichie wrote stories inspired by the books she read, which were all about white people with blue eyes.	Adichie was influenced by the stories she read. They did not reflect her experience or culture.
5–6	Adichie began to read books written by Africans. She realised people like her could appear in, or write, stories.	Stories can reflect the writer's and reader's experience and culture.
7–	A boy from a nearby village came to work for Adichie's family. They went to his village…	

▲ Simple storytelling can have a powerful influence on young children.

ACTIVITY 2   **AO1**   **SKILLS** ❯ CRITICAL THINKING, ANALYSIS, INTERPRETATION

▼ IDENTIFYING KEY THEMES

Copy and complete the following table, identifying the themes of Adichie's speech and adding any examples of your own.

▼ THEME	▼ QUOTATION	▼ POINT
Ignorance	'She… was confused when I said that Nigeria happened to have English as its official language.'	Like other examples in the speech, Adichie's roommate knows nothing about another culture.
Prejudice		
Self-knowledge		
Importance of stories		

> **KEY POINT**
>
> **Themes** are the key ideas that run through, and are explored in, a text.

EXAM-STYLE QUESTION

A02 **SKILLS** CRITICAL THINKING, ANALYSIS, ADAPTIVE LEARNING, CREATIVITY

How does the writer use language and structure to explore ideas about identity and prejudice?

You should support your answer with close reference to the extract, including **brief** quotations.

(12 marks)

EXPLORING LANGUAGE

When you tackle an exam-style question like this, first identify the key words in the question: the words that tell you what the focus of your answer should be.

The exam-style question above focuses on:

■ 'identity': the qualities or culture that make a person who they are

■ 'prejudice': an unfair opinion formed without knowledge or understanding.

The next step is to identify relevant parts of the text to focus on.

ACTIVITY 3 **A01** **SKILLS** CRITICAL THINKING, ANALYSIS, INTERPRETATION

▼ **IDENTIFYING RELEVANT PARTS OF THE TEXT**

Look through the extract again, noting down key ideas the writer uses to explore identity and prejudice.

■ Characters in books that Adichie read

■ Fide's family

■

■

ACTIVITY 4 **A02** **SKILLS** CRITICAL THINKING, ANALYSIS, INTERPRETATION

▼ **IDENTIFYING SIGNIFICANT LANGUAGE CHOICES**

Look again at each of the relevant parts of the text you identified in Activity 3.

For each one:

▶ Identify **one** sentence that shows the writer exploring ideas about identity or prejudice. Choose sentences that you feel have significant impact.

▶ Identify the writer's intention in your chosen sentence. What impact does the writer want it to have on the reader?

▶ Identify **one** significant language choice that helps the writer to achieve her intention in your chosen sentence. It could be a word, a phrase, a rhetorical device, or the structure of your chosen sentence.

▶ Write one or two sentences exploring the impact of the writer's language choice in your chosen sentence: how does it help the writer to achieve her intention?

STRUCTURE

KEY POINT

Persuasion is not only achieved through language choice; structure also plays a significant part in building an argument to influence the reader's or listener's views.

SUBJECT VOCABULARY

persuasive able to make other people believe something or do what you ask

HINT

Notice that only one of the key points focuses on the beliefs and prejudice of others. Three focus on Adichie's own beliefs and prejudices.

An effective **persuasive** speech should have a clear structure with each point clearly linked to allow the audience to follow the writer's argument.

ACTIVITY 5   A01   SKILLS ▶ CRITICAL THINKING, ANALYSIS, ADAPTIVE LEARNING, CREATIVITY

▼ EXPLORING STRUCTURE

Remember: the structure of a text is created by:

- the ideas the writer chooses to include
- the order in which they are sequenced.

Look again at the summary you noted in Activity 1, noting the key points the writer makes in each section of the text.

> 1 Adichie was surprised to learn that stories do not have to be about white people.

> 2 Adiche was surprised that Fide's family did not live a miserable life.

> 3 Adiche's roommate was surprised that she could speak English, could use a stove and didn't listen to 'tribal music'.

> 4 Adiche was surprised to find that Mexicans were not 'abject immigrants'.

1 What is the writer's intention in selecting each of these key points?
2 What is the writer's intention in sequencing them in this order?

ACTIVITY 6   A02   SKILLS ▶ PROBLEM SOLVING, ADAPTIVE LEARNING, CREATIVITY, INNOVATION

▼ ASSESSING RESPONSES

Look again at the exam-style question you saw on page 100 and the paragraphs from two students' responses to it on page 102.

EXAM-STYLE QUESTION

A02   SKILLS ▶ CRITICAL THINKING, ANALYSIS, ADAPTIVE LEARNING, CREATIVITY

How does the writer use language and structure to explore ideas about identity and prejudice?

You should support your answer with close reference to the extract, including **brief** quotations.

(12 marks)

STUDENT A

> Adichie writes about her own prejudice when she went to Mexico. She expected Mexicans to be like the stories she had read and seen. She was surprised when she found them "rolling up tortillas… smoking, laughing." Adichie lists all these harmless things in a long sentence, building a vivid picture of the people she saw, then follows it with two short sentences saying how ashamed she was: "And then I was overwhelmed with shame." The verb 'overwhelmed' suggests she could feel nothing but this powerful emotion. The short sentence structure adds dramatic emphasis to this.

STUDENT B

> Adichie begins her speech talking about when she was young and she read books about white people. She didn't realise that books could be about Africans and people like her. She is trying to show that stories can have a big effect on people and the way they see themselves and other people. She uses lots of good words to show this. For example, she talks about the people in her stories being white with blue eyes playing in the snow. She says this was nothing like where she lived.

1 Which paragraph do you find more successful: Student A's or Student B's?

2 A successful response to a language and structure question needs some key elements. Assess both the sample answers, using the questions below to identify elements each student has included:

▶ Does each student make a **clear point** in their paragraph, stating the writer's intention?

▶ Does each student support their ideas with **evidence** from the text?

▶ Does each student identify significant language or structure choices the writer has made?

▶ Does each student identify the impact of specific language or structure choices the writer has made and how it has helped the writer to achieve their intention?

3 Student B's answer makes relevant points. Rewrite their answer, aiming to include all of the key elements for a successful response. Think about:

■ **contrast:** the writer compares the stories she read with the place where she lived

■ **sentence structure:** the writer **lists** all the things she read about in stories, then **lists** all the ways in which they did not reflect her own experience.

ACTIVITY 7   **A04**   **A05**   **SKILLS** ▶ PROBLEM SOLVING, ADAPTIVE LEARNING, CREATIVITY, INNOVATION

▼ WRITING TASK

> Write about a time when you have been surprised by someone's views or realised that your own views were wrong.
>
> Your response could be real or imagined.

A PASSAGE TO AFRICA
GEORGE ALAGIAH

BACKGROUND AND CONTEXT

George Alagiah was born in Sri Lanka, but when he was five years old his family moved to live in West Africa. He now lives in the United Kingdom and has worked as a newscaster for the BBC for over ten years.

This extract comes from his book *A Passage to Africa.* In this autobiography, he writes about his life and experiences as a TV reporter working mainly across Africa. In this extract, he writes about a report he made when he was covering the civil war in Somalia for the BBC.

▲ BBC newscaster George Alagiah.

BEFORE YOU START READING

1 Find some information about George Alagiah. You can look at the BBC website.

2 Find out something about the civil war in Somalia, which began in the 1990s.

3 In a small group or with a partner, share your ideas on the following questions.

▶ **Why do you think people watch news on television? Do you watch it? If you don't, why not?**

▶ **Have you ever watched a news programme reporting a war or a humanitarian crisis, such as a famine or an earthquake? What do you remember about it and the effect it had on you?**

▶ **Does television reporting of terrible events, such as floods or famines, help the people who are suffering?**

▼ FROM *A PASSAGE TO AFRICA* BY GEORGE ALAGIAH

Alagiah writes about his experiences as a television reporter during the war in Somalia, Africa in the 1990s. He won a special award for his report on the incidents described in this extract.

I saw a thousand hungry, lean, scared and betrayed faces as I criss-crossed Somalia between the end of 1991 and December 1992, but there is one I will never forget.

I was in a little hamlet just outside Gufgaduud, a village in the back of beyond, a place the aid agencies had yet to reach. In my notebook I had jotted down instructions on how to get there. 'Take the Badale Road for a few kilometres til the end of the tarmac, turn right on to a dirt track, stay on it for about forty-five minutes – Gufgaduud. Go another fifteen minutes approx. – like a ghost village.'…

In the ghoulish manner of journalists on the hunt for the most striking pictures, my cameraman … and I tramped from one hut to another. What might have appalled us when we'd started our trip just a few days before no longer impressed us much. The search for the shocking is like the craving for a drug: you require heavier and more frequent doses the longer you're at it. Pictures that stun the editors one day are written off as the same old stuff the next. This sounds callous, but it is just a fact of life. It's how we collect and compile the images that so move people in the comfort of their sitting rooms back home.

There was Amina Abdirahman, who had gone out that morning in search of wild, edible roots, leaving her two young girls lying on the dirt floor of their hut. They had been sick for days, and were reaching the final, enervating stages of terminal hunger. Habiba was ten years old and her sister, Ayaan, was nine. By the time Amina returned, she had only one daughter. Habiba had died. No rage, no whimpering, just a passing away – that simple, frictionless, motionless deliverance from a state of half-life to death itself. It was, as I said at the time in my dispatch, a vision of 'famine away from the headlines, a famine of quiet suffering and lonely death'.

There was the old woman who lay in her hut, abandoned by relations who were too weak to carry her on their journey to find food. It was the smell that drew me to her doorway: the smell of decaying flesh. Where her shinbone should have been there was a festering wound the size of my hand. She'd been shot in the leg as the retreating army of the deposed dictator took revenge on whoever it found in its way. The shattered leg had fused into the gentle V-shape of a boomerang. It was rotting; she was rotting. You could see it in her sick, yellow eyes and smell it in the putrid air she recycled with every struggling breath she took.

And then there was the face I will never forget.

My reaction to everyone else I met that day was a mixture of pity and revulsion. Yes, revulsion. The degeneration of the human body, sucked of its natural vitality by the twin evils of hunger and disease, is a disgusting thing. We never say so in our TV reports. It's a taboo that has yet to be breached. To be in a feeding centre is to hear and smell the excretion of fluids by people who are beyond controlling their bodily functions. To be in a feeding centre is surreptitiously to wipe your hands on the back of your trousers after you've held the clammy palm of a mother who has just cleaned vomit from her child's mouth.

ghoulish To gain pleasure from unpleasant things.

revulsion Disgust.

surreptitiously Secretly.

▶

There's pity, too, because even in this state of utter despair they aspire to a dignity that is almost impossible to achieve. An old woman will cover her shrivelled body with a soiled cloth as your gaze turns towards her. Or the old and dying man who keeps his hoe next to the mat with which, one day soon, they will shroud his corpse, as if he means to go out and till the soil once all this is over.

I saw that face for only a few seconds, a fleeting meeting of eyes before the face turned away, as its owner retreated into the darkness of another hut. In those brief moments there had been a smile, not from me, but from the face. It was not a smile of greeting, it was not a smile of joy – how could it be? – but it was a smile nonetheless. It touched me in a way I could not explain. It moved me in a way that went beyond pity or revulsion.

What was it about that smile? I had to find out. I urged my translator to ask the man why he had smiled. He came back with an answer. 'It's just that he was embarrassed to be found in this condition,' the translator explained. And then it clicked. That's what the smile had been about. It was the feeble smile that goes with apology, the kind of smile you might give if you felt you had done something wrong.

Normally inured to stories of suffering, accustomed to the evidence of deprivation, I was unsettled by this one smile in a way I had never been before. There is an unwritten code between the journalist and his subjects in these situations. The journalist observes, the subject is observed. The journalist is active, the subject is passive. But this smile had turned the tables on that tacit agreement. Without uttering a single word, the man had posed a question that cut to the heart of the relationship between me and him, between us and them, between the rich world and the poor world. If he was embarrassed to be found weakened by hunger and ground down by conflict, how should I feel to be standing there so strong and confident?

I resolved there and then that I would write the story of Gufgaduud with all the power and purpose I could muster. It seemed at the time, and still does, the only adequate answer a reporter can give to the man's question.

I have one regret about that brief encounter in Gufgaduud. Having searched through my notes and studied the dispatch that the BBC broadcast, I see that I never found out what the man's name was. Yet meeting him was a seminal moment in the gradual collection of experiences we call context. Facts and figures are the easy part of journalism. Knowing where they sit in the great scheme of things is much harder. So, my nameless friend, if you are still alive, I owe you one.

inured Hardened.

▶ Does this extract make you think differently about the news stories you see?

UNDERSTANDING THE TEXT

George Alagiah's intention is to explore his role as a reporter, giving his thoughts and feelings about a particularly challenging incident. He is also trying to challenge his readers, to make you think about your role.

The questions in the following table will help you approach this aspect of the text. Read the text again and find answers to the questions in the table. Remember, more than one point can be made in answer to each question.

▼ QUESTION	▼ ANSWER AND EVIDENCE
What kinds of pictures and stories do the television news companies want?	1 Powerful images – 'the most striking pictures' 2 3
What do the television news companies **not** want to show or report?	1 Yesterday's news – old pictures are 'written off as the same old stuff' 2 3
What is implied about TV audiences in this extract?	1 2 3

KEY POINT

The author of this extract used the smile as the central focus of the extract to encourage the reader to discover its significance.

ACTIVITY 1   **A01**   **SKILLS** ▶ CRITICAL THINKING

▼ THE MAN'S SMILE

This smile is the key to a full understanding of the extract because it makes such an impact on the writer.

▶ **Look at the following list of statements about the smile and then find a quotation to illustrate each one:**

■ **it reverses roles**

■ **it asks questions**

■ **it stimulates actions**

■ **it affects the writer very powerfully.**

▶ **Now try to put into your own words what you think the importance of the smile is.**

▶ **In the extract from *A Passage to Africa*, can you find any other examples of things that seem to be the opposite of what they should be?**

EXAM-STYLE QUESTION

A02

SKILLS ▶ CRITICAL THINKING, ANALYSIS, ADAPTIVE LEARNING, CREATIVITY

How does the writer use language and structure to describe the people he sees in Somalia?

You should support your answer with close reference to the extract, including **brief** quotations.

(12 marks)

EXPLORING LANGUAGE

In this extract, George Alagiah is writing both as a journalist and about being a journalist. He vividly describes what he saw, but at the same time he gives the reader an insight into the world of journalism, where reporters compete with each other to get the largest audience.

The sentences below are extracts from students' responses to the exam-style question on page 106. Each one is missing a key element or two. Complete the paragraphs making sure each one features:

- a **point**, clearly stating the writer's intention
- **evidence** to support it
- an **analysis** of the writer's language choices.

This paragraph needs **analysis** to complete it.	At the start of the text, the writer highlights the need that reporters have to find new, shocking images to show on the news. He describes it as 'like craving for a drug'.
This analysis needs a **point** and **evidence** to complete it.	The writer uses this emotive language to highlight the suffering of the people he sees. The writer's intention is to shock and disgust the reader by presenting it using the most vivid and detailed descriptive language choices.
This paragraph is missing **evidence** and some **analysis**.	The writer then describes some of the shocking images he saw in Somalia. For example, he describes the woman left alone in her hut as
Add a **point** and some **analysis** to explore this evidence.	The writer contrasts the situation of the man who smiled who was 'embarrassed to be found weakened by hunger and ground down by conflict' with his own situation 'standing there so strong and confident'

ACTIVITY 2   **A04**   **A05**   **SKILLS**   ADAPTIVE LEARNING, INTERPRETATION, CREATIVITY, INNOVATION

▼ WRITING TASKS

1 Imagine that you are a television or radio news reporter.

▶ **Describe a vivid and dramatic scene for a news item. You can either give this account live to the class or write the script for it.**

▶ **Write an entry for a personal diary giving your real thoughts and feelings about what you saw.**

2 In his book, George Alagiah writes, 'In global terms, if you have a roof over your head, food on the table, a doctor who will not charge you when you are ill and a school place that does not depend on your ability to pay, then, my friend, you are rich.' Write an article, giving your views on what makes you rich.

3 Write a short story entitled 'The Smile'.

THE EXPLORER'S DAUGHTER
KARI HERBERT

BACKGROUND AND CONTEXT

Kari Herbert's father was a polar explorer. She lived as a child with her family in northwest Greenland in the Arctic. She was so fascinated by the place that she returned there later as an adult to write about it.

The book from which this extract is taken, first published in 2004, is partly a memoir (a form of autobiography) and partly a travel book. It gives the reader information about the beautiful country, its people and its animals. She found that the way of life of the Inughuit people of Greenland was changing due to the impact of the modern world. However, they still retained aspects of their traditional way of life, such as hunting for food and driving teams of dogs.

A major part of the extract is an account of a hunt for narwhal. Hunting is a very emotive issue and many conservationists argue that whales should be protected. Kari Herbert's feelings on this topic are divided. She sympathises with both the narwhal and the hunters, who face incredible danger. They hunt in kayaks in water so cold that they would die quickly if their kayak overturned.

▲ The Inughuit of the Arctic understand the intelligence of the narwhal.

BEFORE YOU START READING

1 Do some research.

▶ Find some information about Kari Herbert. You can visit her website.

▶ Find out as much as you can about the Inughuit people of Greenland and their way of life.

▶ Find pictures of **narwhal** and information about them.

GENERAL VOCABULARY

narwhal a species of whale, famous for the long single tusk on its head

2 Some people think that hunting animals should be banned. In a small group or with a partner, share your ideas on the following questions.

▶ **What arguments can you think of in favour of hunting animals?**

▶ **What arguments can you think of against hunting animals?**

▶ **Do you think hunting wild animals should be banned?**

▶ **How important is it to protect endangered species?**

▼ FROM *THE EXPLORER'S DAUGHTER* BY KARI HERBERT

As a small child, Herbert lived, with her family, among the Inughuit people in the harsh environment of the Arctic. In 2002, she revisited the area, staying near Thule, a remote settlement in North Greenland. In this extract, she writes about her experience of watching a hunt for the narwhal, a toothed whale, and what she thought and felt about it.

Two hours after the last of the hunters had returned and eaten, narwhal were spotted again, this time very close. Within an hour even those of us on shore could with the naked eye see the plumes of spray from the narwhal catching the light in a spectral play of colour. Two large pods of narwhal circled in the fjord, often looking as if they were going to merge, but always slowly, methodically passing each other by. Scrambling back up to the lookout I looked across the glittering kingdom in front of me and took a sharp intake of breath. The hunters were dotted all around the fjord. The evening light was turning butter-gold, glinting off man and whale and catching the soft billows of smoke from a lone hunter's pipe. From where we sat at the lookout it looked as though the hunters were close enough to touch the narwhal with their bare hands and yet they never moved. Distances are always deceptive in the Arctic, and I fell to wondering if the narwhal existed at all or were instead mischievous tricks of the shifting light…

The narwhal rarely stray from High Arctic waters, escaping only to the slightly more temperate waters towards the Arctic Circle in the dead of winter, but never entering the warmer southern seas. In summer the hunters of Thule are fortunate to witness the annual return of the narwhal to the Inglefield Fjord, on the side of which we now sat.

The narwhal… is an essential contributor to the survival of the hunters in the High Arctic. The mattak or blubber of the whale is rich in necessary minerals and vitamins, and in a place where the climate prohibits the growth of vegetables or fruit, this rich source of vitamin C was the one reason that the Eskimos have never suffered from scurvy… For centuries the blubber of the whales was also the only source of light and heat, and the dark rich meat is still a valuable part of the diet for both man and dogs (a single narwhal can feed a team of dogs for an entire month). Its single ivory tusk, which can grow up to six feet in length, was used for harpoon tips and handles for other hunting implements (although the ivory was found to be brittle and not hugely satisfactory as a weapon), for carving protective tupilaks, and even as a central beam for their small ancient dwellings. Strangely, the tusk seems to have little use for the narwhal itself; they do not use the tusk to break through ice as a breathing hole, nor will they use it to catch or attack prey, but rather the primary use seems to be to disturb the top of the sea bed in order to catch Arctic halibut for which they have a particular predilection. Often the ends of their tusks are worn down or even broken from such usage.

---

pods Small groups of whales.

fjord A long, narrow strip of the sea, between steep mountains.

mattak or blubber The fat of the whale.

scurvy A painful, weakening disease caused by lack of vitamin C.

tupilaks Charms or figures with magical powers.

predilection Liking.

▶

kayak a type of canoe

The women clustered on the knoll of the lookout, binoculars pointing in every direction, each woman focusing on her husband or family member, occasionally spinning round at a small gasp or jump as one of the women saw a hunter near a narwhal… Each wife knew her husband instinctively and watched their progress intently; it was crucial to her that her husband catch a narwhal – it was part of their staple diet, and some of the mattak and meat could be sold to other hunters who hadn't been so lucky, bringing in some much-needed extra income. Every hunter was on the water. It was like watching a vast, waterborne game with the hunters spread like a net around the sound.

The narwhal… are intelligent creatures, their senses are keen and they talk to one another under the water. Their hearing is particularly developed and they can hear the sound of a paddling kayak from a great distance. That was why the hunters had to sit so very still in the water.

One hunter was almost on top of a pair of narwhal, and they were huge. He gently picked up his harpoon and aimed – in that split second my heart leapt for both hunter and narwhal. I urged the man on in my head; he was so close, and so brave to attempt what he was about to do – he was miles from land in a flimsy kayak, and could easily be capsized and drowned. The hunter had no rifle, only one harpoon with two heads and one bladder. It was a foolhardy exercise and one that could only inspire respect. And yet at the same time my heart also urged the narwhal to dive, to leave, to survive.

This dilemma stayed with me the whole time that I was in Greenland. I understand the harshness of life in the Arctic and the needs of the hunters and their families to hunt and live on animals and sea mammals that we demand to be protected because of their beauty. And I know that one cannot afford to be sentimental in the Arctic. 'How can you possibly eat seal?' I have been asked over and over again. True, the images that bombarded us several years ago of men battering seals for their fur hasn't helped the issue of polar hunting, but the Inughuit do not kill seals using this method, nor do they kill for sport. They use every part of the animals they kill, and most of the food in Thule is still brought in by the hunter-gatherers and fishermen. Imported goods can only ever account for part of the food supply; there is still only one annual supply ship that makes it through the ice to Qaanaaq, and the small twice-weekly plane from West Greenland can only carry a certain amount of goods. Hunting is still an absolute necessity in Thule.

▶ Traditional ways of life in the Arctic are under threat.

UNDERSTANDING THE TEXT

Kari Herbert sympathises with both hunter and hunted. The writer's key intentions are to convey her respect for the narwhal but also her respect for the hunters and their needs. You need to examine the different ways in which the writer achieves both of these within the same extract. Copy and complete the following table with answers and evidence from the extract.

▼ QUESTION	▼ ANSWER AND EVIDENCE
Why do the Inughuit hunt the narwhal? Find as many reasons as you can.	1 Narwhal meat provides food – 'a valuable part of the diet for both man and dogs' 2 3
What details show the difficulties and dangers faced by the Inughuit in the hunt?	1 2 3
What details show the writer's respect and sympathy for the narwhal?	1 2 3

EXPLORING LANGUAGE

The extract has many purposes and intentions and the writer uses language in different ways to fulfil these. She uses description to convey the beauty of the setting, gives the reader information about the Inughuit and the narwhal, dramatises the hunt and gives the reader an insight into her own thoughts and feelings. Copy and complete the following table to help you sort out these various strands.

▼ LANGUAGE USE	▼ EVIDENCE
Language to convey the setting	1 A 'glittering kingdom' 2 3
Language to convey her respect for the narwhal	1 2 3
Language to give information: factual, scientific, other specialised language	1 Precise scientific language makes the information more authoritative – for example, '[Its] mattak or blubber... is rich in necessary minerals and vitamins' 2 3
Language to create tension	1 The way the women react suggests their nervousness – for example, 'spinning round at a small gasp' 2 3
Language to show the conflict in the writer's personal feelings and thoughts	1 2 3

Look again at the evidence you have gathered. Check that you have:

- identified significant language choices in each of your quotations
- explained their significance
- analysed how they contribute to the writer's intentions.

ACTIVITY 1   **A04**   **A05**   **SKILLS** REASONING, CREATIVITY, INNOVATION

▼ WRITING TASKS

1 Write about a place you know well, or have recently re-visited, that has changed significantly in the time that you have known it. Analyse the ways in which it has changed, giving your thoughts about these changes.

2 Some people think that not enough is being done to preserve traditions and customs. What aspects of your way of life would you most want to keep and why?

EXAM-STYLE QUESTION

A02

SKILLS CRITICAL THINKING, ANALYSIS, ADAPTIVE LEARNING, CREATIVITY

How does the writer use language and structure to explore the hunters' way of life?

You should support your answer with close reference to the extract, including **brief** quotations.

(12 marks)

▲ The Fjords of Greenland are a challenging place to explore, let alone live.

'EXPLORERS OR BOYS MESSING ABOUT'
STEVEN MORRIS

BACKGROUND AND CONTEXT

This is a newspaper article that tells the story of two men rescued by the Chilean Navy when their helicopter crashed in the sea in the Antarctic.

BEFORE YOU START READING

1 In a small group or with a partner, discuss your ideas on the following questions.

▶ Expeditions to faraway, unknown places can be expensive. Who should pay for explorers to go exploring?

▶ Who should pay for the rescue when an expedition goes wrong?

▼ 'EXPLORERS OR BOYS MESSING ABOUT? EITHER WAY, TAXPAYER GETS RESCUE BILL' BY STEVEN MORRIS

Adapted from an article published in *The Guardian* newspaper, January 28, 2003: Helicopter duo plucked from liferaft after Antarctic crash.

Their last expedition ended in farce when the Russians threatened to send in military planes to intercept them as they tried to cross into Siberia via the icebound Bering Strait.

Yesterday a new adventure undertaken by British explorers Steve Brooks and Quentin Smith almost led to tragedy when their helicopter plunged into the sea off Antarctica.

The men were plucked from the icy water by a Chilean naval ship after a nine-hour rescue which began when Mr Brooks contacted his wife, Jo Vestey, on his satellite phone asking for assistance. The rescue involved the Royal Navy, the RAF and British coastguards.

Last night there was resentment in some quarters that the men's adventure had cost the taxpayers of Britain and Chile tens of thousands of pounds.

Experts questioned the wisdom of taking a small helicopter – the four-seater Robinson R44 has a single engine – into such a hostile environment.

There was also confusion about what exactly the men were trying to achieve. A website set up to promote the Bering Strait expedition claims the team were planning to fly from the north to south pole in their "trusty helicopter".

But Ms Vestey claimed she did not know what the pair were up to, describing them as 'boys messing about with a helicopter'.

RAF Royal Air Force; the UK's air and space force.

Falmouth Coastal town in Cornwall, England.

▲ Sunset over the Antarctic Ocean.

The drama began at around 1am British time when Mr Brooks, 42, and 40-year-old Mr Smith, also known as Q, ditched into the sea 100 miles off Antarctica, about 36 miles north of Smith Island, and scrambled into their liferaft.

Mr Brooks called his wife in London on his satellite phone. She said: 'He said they were both in the liferaft but were okay and could I call the emergency people?'

Meanwhile, distress signals were being beamed from the ditched helicopter and from Mr Brooks' Breitling emergency watch, a wedding present.

The signals from the aircraft were deciphered by Falmouth coastguard and passed on to the rescue coordination centre at RAF Kinloss in Scotland.

The Royal Navy's ice patrol ship, HMS Endurance, which was 180 miles away surveying uncharted waters, began steaming towards the scene and dispatched its two Lynx helicopters.

One was driven back because of poor visibility but the second was on its way when the men were picked up by a Chilean naval vessel at about 10.20 am British time.

Though the pair wore survival suits and the weather at the spot where they ditched was clear, one Antarctic explorer told Mr Brooks' wife it was 'nothing short of a miracle' that they had survived.

Both men are experienced adventurers. Mr Brooks, a property developer from London, has taken part in expeditions to 70 countries in 15 years. He has trekked solo to Everest base camp and walked barefoot for three days in the Himalayas. He has negotiated the white water rapids of the Zambezi river by kayak and survived a charge by a silver back gorilla in the Congo. He is also a qualified mechanical engineer and pilot.

He and his wife spent their honeymoon flying the helicopter from Alaska to Chile. The 16,000-mile trip took three months.

Mr Smith, also from London, claims to have been flying since the age of five. He has twice flown a helicopter around the globe and won the world freestyle helicopter flying championship.

Despite their experience, it is not the first time they have hit the headlines for the wrong reasons.

In April, Mr Brooks and another explorer, Graham Stratford, were poised to become the first to complete a crossing of the 56-mile wide frozen Bering Strait between the US and Russia in an amphibious vehicle, Snowbird VI, which could carve its way through ice floes and float in the water in between.

But they were forced to call a halt after the Russian authorities told them they would scramble military helicopters to lift them off the ice if they crossed the border.

Ironically, one of the aims of the expedition, for which Mr Smith provided air back-up, was to demonstrate how good relations between east and west had become.

▶

The wisdom of the team's latest adventure was questioned by, among others, Günter Endres, editor of *Jane's Helicopter Markets and Systems*, who said: 'I'm surprised they used the R44. I wouldn't use a helicopter like that to go so far over the sea. It sounds as if they were pushing it to the maximum.'

A spokesman for the pair said it was not known what had gone wrong. The flying conditions had been 'excellent'.

The Ministry of Defence said the taxpayer would pick up the bill, as was normal in rescues in the UK and abroad. The spokesperson said it was 'highly unlikely' it would recover any of the money.

Last night the men were on their way to the Chilean naval base Eduardo Frei, where HMS Endurance was to pick them up. Ms Vestey said: 'They have been checked and appear to be well. I don't know what will happen to them once they have been picked up by HMS Endurance – they'll probably have their bottoms kicked and be sent home the long way.'

UNDERSTANDING THE TEXT

On first reading, this may appear to be an information text, as the article explains what happened to the two men and how they were rescued. However, the writer also takes a strongly critical stance suggesting the two explorers were highly irresponsible and incompetent. The key to understanding the article is in recognising how the writer makes his opinions clear.

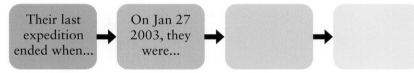

ACTIVITY 1   **A01**   **A02**   **SKILLS** ▶ CRITICAL THINKING, ANALYSIS, INTERPRETATION

▼ IDENTIFYING INFORMATION AND EXPLORING OPINION

1 Write a timeline, noting the key events and information given in the article.

```
Their last          On Jan 27
expedition   →      2003, they    →    [ ]    →    [ ]
ended when...       were...
```

2 Copy and complete the following table, noting evidence and explaining each of the ways in which the writer shows his opinion of the two explorers.

▼ WAYS THE WRITER REVEALS HIS OPINION	▼ EXPLANATION AND EVIDENCE
The explorers' previous expedition	The writer describes it as 'a farce' suggesting that…
Details about this expedition and its dramatic end	
Other people's opinions of the explorers and their adventures	One of the explorers' wives describes them as 'boys messing about'…
Detailed information suggesting they were experienced explorers and adventurers	
The rescue and the money it cost	

▶

3   Write one paragraph summing up the writer's view of these two explorers and their expedition.

4   Look at all of the quotations you have noted from the text. Choose three that most clearly show the writer's view of the two explorers and their expedition. Which words in those three quotations reveal the writer's view most powerfully? Write a sentence or two about each one.

HINT

You could write about something that has happened or a change that has been recently made in your school or college, or in your local area.

ACTIVITY 2   **A04**   **A05**   **SKILLS** CRITICAL THINKING, ANALYSIS, ADAPTIVE LEARNING, CREATIVITY

▼ **OPINION AND FACT**

Think of a recent event or situation of which you have personal experience, and about which you have a critical opinion. Write a short account, including factual details, but use what you have learnt from the extract to find ways to express your opinions as well.

EXAM-STYLE QUESTION

A02   **SKILLS** CRITICAL THINKING, ANALYSIS, ADAPTIVE LEARNING, CREATIVITY

How does the writer use language and structure to describe the two explorers and their adventure in a helicopter?

You should support your answer with close reference to the extract, including **brief** quotations.   **(12 marks)**

▲ A Robinson R44 Helicopter in flight

BETWEEN A ROCK AND A HARD PLACE
ARON RALSTON

BACKGROUND AND CONTEXT

Between a Rock and a Hard Place is an autobiography written by Aron Ralston, an engineer turned outdoorsman and motivational speaker. It relates his experience in 2003 of being trapped for five days and seven hours in Blue John Canyon, in the Utah desert in the southern United States.

His right arm was trapped by a boulder and, unable to free himself, he amputated his arm using a blunt pocketknife. He then had to return through the canyon and climb down a 20-metre slope before he could reach safety and receive medical care.

BEFORE YOU START READING

1 Read about Aron Ralston and his experience. If you are able to, watch *127 Hours*, the 2010 film on the same subject.

2 Think about what attracts people to potentially dangerous outdoor activities and sports. Is it a love of adventure? A sense of boredom? Or something else entirely?

3 Share any accounts of survival or lucky escapes that you have heard or read about.

▲ Blue John Canyon, Utah, USA

▼ FROM *BETWEEN A ROCK AND A HARD PLACE* BY ARON RALSTON

In this first-hand account, Ralston describes how a boulder crushed his right hand while he was climbing and hiking in a canyon. He had not informed anyone of his hiking plans.

drop-off A sheer downward slope.

chockstone A stone that has become stuck between rocks.

I come to another drop-off. This one is maybe eleven or twelve feet high, a foot higher and of a different geometry than the overhang I descended ten minutes ago. Another refrigerator chockstone is wedged between the walls, ten feet downstream from and at the same height as the ledge. It gives the space below the drop-off the claustrophobic feel of a short tunnel. Instead of the walls widening after the drop-off, or opening into a bowl at the bottom of the canyon, here the slot narrows to a consistent three feet across at the lip of the drop-off and continues at that width for fifty feet down the canyon.

Sometimes in narrow passages like this one, it's possible for me to stem my body across the slot, with my feet and back pushing out in opposite directions against the walls. Controlling this counterpressure by switching my hands and feet on the opposing walls, I can move up or down the shoulder width crevice fairly easily as long as the friction contact stays solid between the walls and my hands, feet, and back. This technique is known as stemming or chimneying; you can imagine using it to climb up the inside of a chimney.

overhang A part of something (in this case, the rock) that extends over something else.

traverse Cross.

teeters Balance unsteadily.

Just below the ledge where I'm standing is a chockstone the size of a large bus tire, stuck fast in the channel between the walls, a few feet out from the lip. If I can step onto it, then I'll have a nine-foot height to descend, less than that of the first overhang. I'll dangle off the chockstone, then take a short fall onto the rounded rocks piled on the canyon floor.

Stemming across the canyon at the lip of the drop-off, with one foot and one hand on each of the walls, I traverse out to the chockstone. I press my back against the south wall and lock my left knee, which pushes my foot tight against the north wall. With my right foot, I kick at the boulder to test how stuck it is. It's jammed tightly enough to hold my weight. I lower myself from the chimneying position and step onto the chockstone. It supports me but teeters slightly. After confirming that I don't want to chimney down from the chockstone's height, I squat and grip the rear of the lodged boulder, turning to face back upcanyon. Sliding my belly over the front edge, I can lower myself and hang from my fully extended arms, akin to climbing down from the roof of a house.

torque Rotating force.

ricochets Bounces off.

As I dangle, I feel the stone respond to my adjusting grip with a scraping quake as my body's weight applies enough torque to disturb it from its position. Instantly, I know this is trouble, and instinctively, I let go of the rotating boulder to land on the round rocks below. When I look up, the backlit chockstone falling toward my head consumes the sky. Fear shoots my hands over my head. I can't move backward or I'll fall over a small ledge. My only hope is to push off the falling rock and get my head out of its way.

The next three seconds play out at a tenth of their normal speed. Time dilates, as if I'm dreaming, and my reactions decelerate. In slow motion: the rock smashes my left hand against the south wall; my eyes register the collision, and I yank my left arm back as the rock ricochets; the boulder then crushes my right hand and ensnares my right arm at the wrist, palm

▶

in, thumb up, fingers extended; the rock slides another foot down the wall with my arm in tow, tearing the skin off the lateral side of my forearm. Then silence.

My disbelief paralyzes me temporarily as I stare at the sight of my arm vanishing into an implausibly small gap between the fallen boulder and the canyon wall. Within moments, my nervous system's pain response overcomes the initial shock. Good God, my hand. The flaring agony throws me into a panic. I grimace and growl... My mind commands my body, 'Get your hand out of there!' I yank my arm three times in a naive attempt to pull it out. But I'm stuck.

Anxiety has my brain tweaking; searing-hot pain shoots from my wrist up my arm. I'm frantic, and I cry out... My desperate brain conjures up a probably apocryphal story in which an adrenaline-stoked mom lifts an overturned car to free her baby. I'd give it even odds that it's made up, but I do know for certain that *right now*, while my body's chemicals are raging at full flood, is the best chance I'll have to free myself with brute force. I shove against the large boulder, heaving against it, pushing with my left hand, lifting with my knees pressed under the rock. I get good leverage with the aid of a twelve-inch shelf in front of my feet. Standing on that, I brace my thighs under the boulder and thrust upward repeatedly, grunting, 'Come on...move!' Nothing.

apocryphal Doubtful, untrue.

UNDERSTANDING THE TEXT

▲ 'Another chockstone is wedged between the walls...'

This extract from *Between a Rock and a Hard Place* describes the place where the accident occurred and the event itself. Aron Ralston describes the events in great detail. He recreates the scene of the accident effectively. As he is writing for a general audience, he explains the terminology related to climbing as well as the reasons behind the different things he does. His clearheaded and analytical thinking pattern is vividly conveyed as well as his ability to react quickly and to take action in the face of an unexpected problem.

As this is an autobiography, it is written in the first person and uses a great deal of factual detail to suggest it is an accurate and authentic account.

ACTIVITY 1   **A01**   **A02**   **SKILLS** ANALYSIS, INTERPRETATION

▼ EXPLORING LANGUAGE CHOICE

1 Look at the first three paragraphs. Select words or phrases that show as many of the language features in the list below as you can find.
   - Descriptive language choices to help the reader picture the scene
   - Precise detail using numbers and technical terms to suggest expertise and knowledge
   - Language choices that suggest he is confident in his ability
   - Dramatic or emotive language choices that suggest the danger or physical demands of rock climbing
   - Dramatic or emotive language choices that express things the writer feels: his emotions or physical sensations.

2 Now look at the last three paragraphs. Select words or phrases that show as many of the language features in the list above as you can find.

3 Compare the results of your searches in Questions 1 and 2. How has the writer's focus and language choice changed from the beginning to the end of the extract?

EXPLORING LANGUAGE

Ralston's style is largely factual and analytical. He is very clear and precise in what he says about the events and his reactions. His use of minute details and his step-by-step narrative style are strong techniques that he uses to make his writing effective and interesting.

ACTIVITY 2 A02 SKILLS ANALYSIS, INTERPRETATION

▼ ANALYSING LANGUAGE CHOICE

1 Look at some of the language techniques the writer uses in the extract: each one is shown in the quotations beneath. Which choices are shown in which quotation?

technical terminology	emotive language	vivid descriptive language choice	precise detail using numbers	the present tense: I am	the future tense: I will	simile and comparison

'I'll dangle off the chockstone, then take a short fall onto the rounded rocks piled on the canyon floor.'	'I yank my left arm back as the rock ricochets; the boulder then crushes my right hand and ensnares my right arm at the wrist'	'a chockstone the size of a large bus tire'	'Another refrigerator chockstone is wedged between the walls, ten feet downstream from and at the same height as the ledge'

2 Look at each of the language techniques in each quotation above. What effect does each technique have? Match them to the analytical points below.

shows the writer's confidence and knowledge	creates a sense of drama	builds the reader's expectation of what will happen next, creating shock and surprise when disaster strikes	conveys the writer's extreme pain	creates a feeling of urgency and immediacy, as though the writer is narrating what is happening now, as you read it	helps the reader understand and visualise the scene

ACTIVITY 3 A02 SKILLS ANALYSIS, INTERPRETATION

▼ ANALYSING SENTENCE STRUCTURE CHOICE

Ralston uses a range of sentence structures for effect. Copy the table below, adding one example of each sentence structure, and the impact that each sentence structure has from the 'Effect' column.

▼ STRUCTURE	▼ EXAMPLE	▼ EFFECT
Minor sentence		Highlights a key moment with dramatic intensity
Short sentence		Builds tension
Long multiclause sentence linking a series of actions or events		Builds a vivid picture in the reader's mind
Long multiclause sentence linking descriptive details		Suggests fast paced action
Long multiclause sentence in which a key dramatic moment or detail is delayed to the end of the sentence		Adds emphasis to a key moment or detail

EXAM-STYLE QUESTION

A02

SKILLS CRITICAL THINKING, ANALYSIS, ADAPTIVE LEARNING, CREATIVITY

How does the writer use language and structure to describe his thoughts and feelings?

You should support your answer with close reference to the extract, including **brief** quotations.

(12 marks)

HOW TO WRITE A SUCCESSFUL ANSWER

The following is a paragraph from a student's answer to the question above, focusing on paragraph 5.

> In paragraph 5 the writer vividly describes the terrifying moment when a rock fell towards him. He describes how 'fear shoots my hands over my head,' the verb 'shoots' suggesting a sudden and dramatic movement, highlighting the power of the fear he feels.

Which of the following features of critical analysis has the student achieved?

- identifies the writer's intention
- evidence
- identifies significant language choice
- analyses the impact of language choice: how it contributes to intention
- identifies significant sentence structure
- analyses impact of sentence structure: how it contributes to intention

Write a paragraph responding to the exam-style question above, focusing on paragraph 7. How many of the features in the list can you achieve?

Using this answer as a guide, write your own answer to the following question.

▶ **In your own words, explain the writer's feelings and reactions in paragraph 7.**

ACTIVITY 4

▼ WRITING TASKS

1 Write a magazine article giving your views on the statement: 'Extreme situations bring out the best in all of us'. In the article, you may include:
   - anecdotal incidents that support this statement
   - the positives and negatives of facing extreme situations
   - any other points you wish to make.

2 In 1910, Robert Scott, an English naval officer and explorer, led an expedition to the South Pole. Three explorers from this group set out in July 1911 to collect emperor penguin eggs to be studied by scientists back home. After 35 days, they managed to return to base camp with three eggs. During this trip, the three explorers faced extreme hardship due to cold and weather. Imagine that you are one of the explorers and write a diary entry detailing one day of the journey.

KEY POINT

First-person narration is often noted for its level of detail. This can enable the writer to write with immediacy and power.

'YOUNG AND DYSLEXIC? YOU'VE GOT IT GOING ON'
BENJAMIN ZEPHANIAH

BACKGROUND AND CONTEXT

Benjamin Zephaniah has earned widespread respect for his ability to overcome spite, prejudice and ridicule. Because of his difficulties with reading, his teachers dismissed him as unintelligent and not worthy of their attention. Rejected by a number of schools, he was unable to read when he left education at the age of 13. Unusually and bravely, he refused to give in to despair, acknowledged his difficulties and joined an adult reading class. Since then, he has taken an imaginative and constructive approach to life's challenges.

In this article from *The Guardian* newspaper, Zephaniah explains how this happened, from his early difficulties in school to his determination to write. He performed some of his early work in church at the age of 11, but found himself with a criminal record two years later. Despite this troubled period, he has gone on to become a successful poet and writer. His publication within a well-regarded national newspaper can be seen as an ironic contrast to his earlier life.

▲ Poet Benjamin Zephaniah.

BEFORE YOU START READING

1 Find out more about the author and his very unusual background before he became a highly regarded poet and author. Find out what you can about borstals, reform schools and life in poor inner-city areas of Britain. Write down your thoughts and highlight what you think makes a typical writer. Is Zephaniah what you would consider to be a 'traditional' writer?

2 Read the following example of Zephaniah's poetry, entitled 'White Comedy'. Look at the way that Zephaniah uses the words 'white' and 'black' and the way that they affect other words. Look at some other examples of his poetry. What common themes can you identify within his poems?

I waz whitemailed

By a white witch,

Wid white magic

An white lies,

Branded by a white sheep

I slaved as a whitesmith

Near a white spot

Where I suffered whitewater fever.

Whitelisted as a whiteleg

I waz in de white book

As a master of white art,

It waz like white death.

People called me white jack

Some hailed me as a white wog,

So I joined de white watch

Trained as a white guard

Lived off the white economy.

Caught and beaten by de

whiteshirts

I waz condemned to a white

mass,

Don't worry,

I shall be writing to de Black

House.

▶

▼ 'YOUNG AND DYSLEXIC? YOU'VE GOT IT GOING ON' BY BENJAMIN ZEPHANIAH

This article was published in *The Guardian*, 2 October 2015, and is adapted from Zephaniah's contribution to *Creative, Successful, Dyslexic* (Jessica Kingsley, 2015).

As a child I suffered, but learned to turn dyslexia to my advantage, to see the world more creatively. We are the architects, we are the designers.

I'm of the generation where teachers didn't know what dyslexia was. The big problem with the education system then was that there was no compassion, no understanding and no humanity. I don't look back and feel angry with the teachers. The ones who wanted to have an individual approach weren't allowed to. The idea of being kind and thoughtful and listening to problems just wasn't done: the past is a different kind of country.

At school my ideas always contradicted the teachers'. I remember one teacher saying that human beings sleep for one-third of their life and I put my hand up and said, "If there's a God isn't that a design fault? If you've built something, you want efficiency. If I was God I would have designed sleep so we could stay awake. Then good people could do one-third more good in the world."

The teacher said, "Shut up, stupid boy. Bad people would do one-third more bad." I thought I'd put in a good idea. I was just being creative. She also had a point, but the thing was she called me stupid for even thinking about it.

I remember a teacher talking about Africa and the 'local savages' and I would say, "Who are you to talk about savages?" She would say, "How dare you challenge me?" – and that would get me into trouble.

Once, when I was finding it difficult to engage with writing and had asked for some help, a teacher said, "It's all right. We can't all be intelligent, but you'll end up being a good sportsperson, so why don't you go outside and play some football?" I thought, "Oh great", but now I realise he was stereotyping me.

I had poems in my head even then, and when I was 10 or 11 my sister wrote some of them down for me. When I was 13 I could read very basically but it would be such hard work that I would give up. I thought that so long as you could read how much the banknote was worth, you knew enough or you could ask a mate.

I got thrown out of a lot of schools, the last one at 13. I was expelled partly because of arguing with teachers on an intellectual level and partly for being a rude boy and fighting. I didn't stab anybody, but I did take revenge on a teacher once. I stole his car and drove it into his front garden. I remember him telling us the Nazis weren't that bad. He could say that in the classroom. When I was in borstal I used to do this thing of looking at people I didn't want to be like. I saw a guy who spent all his time sitting stooped over and I thought, "I don't want to be like that", so I learned to sit with a straight back. Being observant helped me make the right choices.

A high percentage of the prison population are dyslexic, and a high percentage of the architect population. If you look at the statistics, I should

dyslexia A reading disorder characterised by difficulty manipulating language either verbally and/or when reading and spelling despite normal intelligence.

the past is a different kind of country A phrase meaning that life was different in the past.

contradict Challenge what someone has said.

stereotyping Making unwarranted assumptions about someone or something.

borstal A residential training centre for young people who are in trouble.

▶

be in prison: a black man brought up on the wrong side of town whose family fell apart, in trouble with the police when I was a kid, unable to read and write, with no qualifications and, on top of that, dyslexic. But I think staying out of prison is about conquering your fears and finding your path in life.

When I go into prisons to talk to people I see men and women who, in intelligence and other qualities, are the same as me. But opportunities opened for me and they missed theirs, didn't notice them or didn't take them.

I never thought I was stupid. I didn't have that struggle. If I have someone in front of me who doesn't have a problem reading and writing telling me that black people are savages I just think, "I'm not stupid – you're the one who's stupid." I just had self-belief.

For my first book I told my poems to my girlfriend, who wrote them down for me. It really took off, especially within the black community. I wrote "wid luv" for "with love". People didn't think they were dyslexic poems, they just thought I wrote phonetically.

At 21 I went to an adult education class in London to learn to read and write. The teacher told me, "You are dyslexic," and I was like, "Do I need an operation?" She explained to me what it meant and I suddenly thought, "Ah, I get it. I thought I was going crazy."

I wrote more poetry, novels for teenagers, plays, other books and recorded music. I take poetry to people who do not read poetry. Still now, when I'm writing the word "knot", I have to stop and think, "How do I write that?" I have to draw something to let me know what the word is to come back to it later. If I can't spell "question" I just put a question mark and come back to it later.

When I look at a book, the first thing I see is the size of it, and I know that's what it's like for a lot of young people who find reading tough. When Brunel University offered me the job of professor of poetry and creative writing, I knew my students would be officially more educated than me. I tell them, "You can do this course and get the right grade because you have a good memory – but if you don't have passion, creativity, individuality, there's no point." In my life now, I find that people accommodate my dyslexia. I can perform my poetry because it doesn't have to be word perfect, but I never read one of my novels in public. When I go to literary festivals I always get an actor to read it out for me. Otherwise all my energy goes into reading the book and the mood is lost.

If someone can't understand dyslexia it's their problem. In the same way, if someone oppresses me because of my race I don't sit down and think, "How can I become white?" It's not my problem, it's theirs and they are the ones who have to come to terms with it.

If you're dyslexic and you feel there's something holding you back, just remember: it's not you. In many ways being dyslexic is a natural way to be.

What's unnatural is the way we read and write. If you look at a pictorial language like Chinese, you can see the word for a woman because the character looks like a woman. The word for a house looks like a house. It is a strange step to go from that to a squiggle that represents a sound.

So don't be heavy on yourself. And if you are a parent of someone with

▲ Dyslexia tends to be most visible in reading and writing skills, but it is essentially about how brains process information. Many dyslexic people have strong creative, reasoning and visual skills.

accommodate Make adjustments for someone or something.

oppresses Makes someone feel inadequate or worthless and limits their freedom.

defect Something that prevents proper functioning or a problem.

dyslexia don't think of it as a defect. Dyslexia is not a measure of intelligence: you may have a genius on your hands. Having dyslexia can make you creative. If you want to construct a sentence and can't find the word you are searching for, you have to think of a way to write round it. This requires being creative and so your 'creativity muscle' gets bigger.

Kids come up to me and say, "I'm dyslexic too," and I say to them, "Use it to your advantage, see the world differently. Us dyslexic people, we've got it going on – we are the architects. We are the designers." It's like these kids are proud to be like me and if that helps them, that is great. I didn't have that as a child. I say to them, "Bloody nondyslexics … who do they think they are?"

UNDERSTANDING THE TEXT

This newspaper article is drawn from Zephaniah's contribution to a book about how dyslexic people can be successful. He presents himself as someone who has found ways of coping with dyslexia, persuading other dyslexics that they should not regard dyslexia as an obstacle, but as an opportunity to be creative, rather than restricted.

In a relatively short space, Zephaniah introduces a number of important points. Mainly, he does this by using short, tightly-written paragraphs so that in a matter of a few minutes you learn what the author understands as the essential elements of his coping with dyslexia.

ACTIVITY 1   **A01**   **SKILLS** ▸ CRITICAL THINKING

▼ ANALYSING THE ARTICLE

Copy and complete the following table, analysing the point the writer is making in each of the examples from the article.

▼ EXAMPLE	▼ WHAT THE WRITER IS SAYING
'no compassion, no understanding and no humanity'	These words show Zephaniah's view of his time in school.
'She also had a point'	
'such hard work that I would give up'	
'But opportunities opened for me and they missed theirs'	
'Do I need an operation?'	
'I don't sit down and think, "How can I become white?"'	

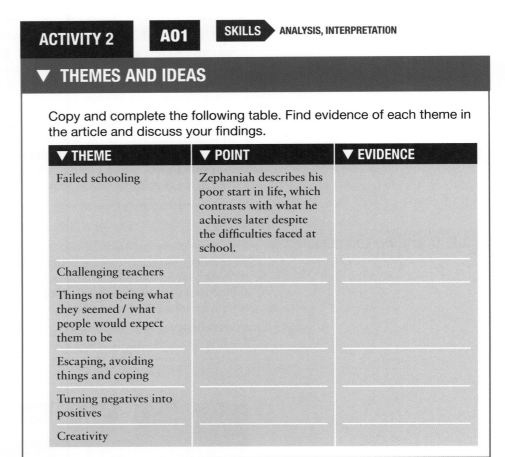

ACTIVITY 2 **AO1** **SKILLS** ANALYSIS, INTERPRETATION

▼ THEMES AND IDEAS

Copy and complete the following table. Find evidence of each theme in the article and discuss your findings.

▼ THEME	▼ POINT	▼ EVIDENCE
Failed schooling	Zephaniah describes his poor start in life, which contrasts with what he achieves later despite the difficulties faced at school.	
Challenging teachers		
Things not being what they seemed / what people would expect them to be		
Escaping, avoiding things and coping		
Turning negatives into positives		
Creativity		

EXPLORING LANGUAGE

An even neutral tone is maintained in the opening paragraphs, despite the fact that Zephaniah is describing events that troubled him at the time. He reports events without reacting to them. In this way, readers are encouraged to draw their own conclusions, and this makes Zephaniah's points more convincing. On two occasions, he simply tells readers what he thought when faced with a teacher whose comments troubled him. Zephaniah shows his self-restraint when provoked.

In his final two paragraphs, Zephaniah provides encouragement and a challenge for any readers who feel disadvantaged by their dyslexia with the striking phrases, 'creativity muscle' and 'Bloody nondyslexics ... who do they think they are?'.

A short, introductory paragraph conveys Zephaniah's conclusion from the outset and engages with the reader: 'We are the architects, we are the designers'. The writing is matter-of-fact and lacks self-pity. From being thrown out of schools to his appointment as a professor of poetry at a university, he presents important events in his life in chronological order to show how he came to see beyond his troubles as a teenager and turned them into something positive, from which both he and the reader can learn.

KEY POINT

Sometimes, non-fiction writers withhold from giving their full reaction to events, allowing the reader to form their own response.

ACTIVITY 3   **A02**   **SKILLS** ANALYSIS

▼ STRUCTURE

Look at the summary below of the key points and ideas Zephaniah makes in the article. Answer the questions alongside.

Paragraph 1	Overcoming dyslexia	Why does the writer begin with this short paragraph?
Paragraphs 2–8	Negative experiences at school	Why does the writer focus so heavily on these two aspects of his life?
Paragraphs 9–13	A summary of his early life and how he overcame its challenges	
Paragraphs 14–16	Success but still overcoming dyslexia	Why does the writer conclude with these points?
Paragraphs 17–20	Positive encouragement for dyslexics	

ACTIVITY 4   **A02**   **SKILLS** ANALYSIS

▼ LANGUAGE CHOICE

1 Look closely at paragraph 2 of the article.

   i   What impression does Zephaniah give of his teachers?

   ii Which of the language and structure features below does Zephaniah use to help him create this impression?

   iii Write one or two sentences analysing how the writer uses one of these language features in this paragraph.

metaphor	simile	triple structure	lists	emotive vocabulary	short sentence for emphasis

2 Look closely at paragraph 9 of the article.

   i   What impression does Zephaniah give of his early life?

   ii Which of the language and structure features above does Zephaniah use to help him create this impression?

   iii Write one or two sentences analysing how the writer uses one of these language features in this paragraph.

3 Look closely at paragraphs 19–20, the final two paragraphs of the article.

   i   What encouragement does Zephaniah give the reader in these paragraphs?

   ii Which of the language and structure features above does Zephaniah use to add impact to this encouragement?

   iii Write one or two sentences analysing the impact of one of these language features in these paragraphs.

ACTIVITY 5   **A04**   **A05**   **SKILLS** ▶ CREATIVITY, INNOVATION

▼ WRITING TASKS

1 A friend has been told that they are dyslexic. Write about what you would do to help and encourage them.

2 Someone in your class is being treated badly by a teacher. Write a story in which this classmate deals with the problem, not by becoming angry, but by thinking creatively.

EXAM-STYLE QUESTIONS ▶

A02

SKILLS ▶ CRITICAL THINKING, ANALYSIS, ADAPTIVE LEARNING, CREATIVITY

1 How does the writer explore his early life and relationship with reading?

You should support your answer with close reference to the extract, including **brief** quotations.

(12 marks)

2 How does the writer use language and structure to encourage the reader to accept and overcome challenges?

You should support your answer with close reference to the extract, including **brief** quotations.

(12 marks)

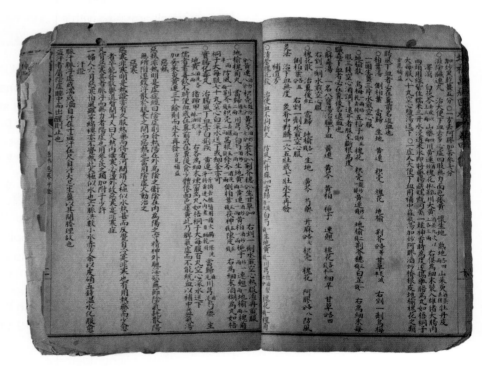

▲ Language systems vary greatly from region to region.

A GAME OF POLO WITH A HEADLESS GOAT
EMMA LEVINE

BACKGROUND AND CONTEXT
This extract comes from a book which was written as a spin-off from Emma Levine's television series about strange and unusual sports. It is a travelogue (a book that describes a travel experience) in which she describes these sports, the people involved and her experiences of filming them. In doing so, she gives an insight not just into the sports themselves, but into the lives and culture of the people who take part in and watch them.

BEFORE YOU START READING
1 Do some research.
- Find some information about Emma Levine. You can visit her website by searching for her name.
- Find a newspaper report on a motor race, perhaps a Formula 1 Grand Prix, and make some notes about the way in which it has been written.
- What is the strangest sport or game you know or can find information about?

2 In a small group or with a partner, share your ideas on the following questions.
- Do you prefer to take part in sport or watch it?
- How important is sport in your life?
- Do you think the involvement of money in sport (for example, gambling or excessive pay for sportspeople) ruins sport?

▼ FROM *A GAME OF POLO WITH A HEADLESS GOAT* BY EMMA LEVINE

Levine travelled throughout Asia researching and filming unusual sports. In this extract, she writes about a donkey race in Karachi, Pakistan.

We drove off to find the best viewing spot, which turned out to be the crest of the hill so we could see the approaching race. I asked the lads if we could join in the 'Wacky Races' and follow the donkeys, and they loved the idea. 'We'll open the car boot, you climb inside and point your camera towards the race. As the donkeys overtake us, we'll join the cars.' 'But will you try and get to the front?' 'Oh yes, that's no problem.'

The two lads who had never been interested in this Karachi sport were suddenly fired up with enthusiasm. We waited for eternity on the brow of the hill, me perched in the boot with a zoom lens pointing out. Nearly one hour later I was beginning to feel rather silly when the only action was a villager on a wobbly bicycle, who nearly fell off as he cycled past and gazed around at us.

Several vehicles went past, and some donkey-carts carrying spectators. 'Are they coming?' we called out to them. 'Coming, coming,' came the reply. I was beginning to lose faith in its happening, but the lads remained confident.

Wacky Races American cartoon featuring racing cars.

▶

Just as I was assuming that the race had been cancelled, we spotted two approaching donkey-carts in front of a cloud of fumes and dust created by some fifty vehicles roaring up in their wake. As they drew nearer, Yaqoob revved up the engine and began to inch the car out of the lay-by. The two donkeys were almost dwarfed by their entourage; but there was no denying their speed – the Kibla donkey is said to achieve speeds of up to 40 kph, and this looked close. The two were neck-and-neck, their jockeys perched on top of the tiny carts using their whips energetically, although not cruelly.

The noise of the approaching vehicles grew; horns tooting, bells ringing, and the special rattles used just for this purpose (like maracas, a metal container filled with dried beans). Men standing on top of their cars and vans, hanging out of taxis and perched on lorries, all cheered and shouted, while the vehicles jostled to get to the front of the convoy.

Yaqoob chose exactly the right moment to edge out of the road and swerve in front of the nearest car, finding the perfect place to see the two donkeys and at the front of the vehicles. This was Formula One without rules, or a city-centre rush hour gone anarchic; a complete flouting of every type of traffic rule and common sense.

Our young driver relished this unusual test of driving skills. It was survival of the fittest, and depended upon the ability to cut in front of a vehicle with a sharp flick of the steering wheel (no lane discipline here); quick reflexes to

anarchic Lawless.

flouting Breaking.

▲ Emma Levine writes about the ancient sports of Asia.

spot a gap in the traffic for a couple of seconds; nerves of steel, and an effective horn. There were two races – the motorized spectators at the back; in front, the two donkeys, still running close and amazingly not put off by the uproar just behind them. Ahead of the donkeys, oncoming traffic – for it was a main road – had to dive into the ditch and wait there until we had passed. Yaqoob loved it. We stayed near to the front, his hand permanently on the horn and his language growing more colourful with every vehicle that tried to cut in front.

The road straightened and levelled, and everyone picked up speed as we neared the end of the race. But just as they were reaching the finishing line, the hospital gate, there was a near pile-up as the leading donkey swerved, lost his footing and he and the cart tumbled over. The race was over.

And then the trouble began. I assumed the winner was the one who completed the race but it was not seen that way by everyone. Apart from the two jockeys and 'officials' (who, it turned out, were actually monitoring the race) there were over a hundred punters who had all staked money on the race, and therefore had strong opinions. Some were claiming that the donkey had fallen because the other one had been ridden too close to him. Voices were raised, fists were out and tempers rising. Everyone gathered around one jockey and official, while the bookmakers were trying to insist that the race should be re-run.

Yaqoob and Iqbal were nervous of hanging around a volatile situation. They agreed to find out for me what was happening, ordering me to stay inside the car as they were swallowed up by the crowd. They emerged sometime later. 'It's still not resolved,' said Iqbal, 'but it's starting to get nasty. I think we should leave.' As we drove away, Yaqoob reflected on his driving skills. 'I really enjoyed that,' he said as we drove off at a more sedate pace. 'But I don't even have my licence yet because I'm underage!'

They both found this hilarious, but I was glad he hadn't told me before; an inexperienced, underage driver causing a massive pile-up in the middle of the high-stakes donkey race could have caused problems.

UNDERSTANDING THE TEXT

The purpose of Emma Levine's book is to describe and inform. Her intention, though, is to do achieve these in as interesting, engaging and entertaining way as possible. As you study this text, you need to think about how she does this.

ACTIVITY 1　　A01　　SKILLS ▶ CRITICAL THINKING, ANALYSIS

▼ THREE RACES

The extract seems a straightforward description and narrative of the race, but it isn't. First of all, there is not just one race happening, but three:

- the donkey race
- the spectators' race
- the writer's, Yaqoob's and Iqbal's race to stay ahead of the donkeys and get the best pictures.

1 Find three short quotations that show these three races taking place.

2 What is the writer's main focus in the text: the race, or the people involved in it? Find some evidence to support your point of view.

ACTIVITY 2   A01   SKILLS ▸ ANALYSIS, INTERPRETATION

▼ TYPES OF WRITING

1 Copy and complete the following table, finding two examples of each of the different kinds of writing used in the extract.

▼ TYPE OF WRITING	▼ EXAMPLES
Description	
Dialogue	
Information	
Narrative	

2 Look at each of the examples you have identified. What intention is the writer aiming to achieve in each one?

humour   excitement   tension   drama   mystery

a vivid picture in the reader's mind   shock   surprise or amazement   sympathy

3 Like much sports journalism and travel writing, one purpose of Emma Levine's writing is to give the reader information. Note down three pieces of information that the writer explicitly states or that can be inferred about:

■ donkey racing
■ Karachi and the people who live there.

KEY POINT

The best travel writing informs **and** entertains the reader. Which do you feel Emma Levine achieves most successfully in this extract?

▲ The Kibla donkey is said to achieve speeds of up to 40 kph.

KEY POINT

Sport, which essentially shows adults playing games, is a fertile subject for writers.

ACTIVITY 3   A02   SKILLS ANALYSIS

▼ LANGUAGE FOR EFFECT

Look at the intentions below, and the quotations from the extract beneath them.

| humour | excitement | tension | drama | mystery |

| a vivid picture in the reader's mind | shock | surprise or amazement | sympathy |

'we spotted two approaching donkey-carts in front of a cloud of fumes and dust created by some fifty vehicles roaring up in their wake.'

'Men standing on top of their cars and vans, hanging out of taxis and perched on lorries, all cheered and shouted, while the vehicles jostled to get to the front of the convoy.'

'there was a near pile-up as the leading donkey swerved, lost his footing and he and the cart tumbled over.'

'Yaqoob and Iqbal were nervous of hanging around a volatile situation.'

'an inexperienced, underage driver causing a massive pile-up in the middle of the high-stakes donkey race could have caused problems.'

1 Identify one intention that the writer is aiming to achieve in each quotation.
2 Identify any words, phrases or language techniques in each quotation that help the writer to achieve that intention. In some of the quotations, a word or phrase has been highlighted to help you.
3 Write one or two sentences about each quotation, explaining the impact that your chosen word or phrase has and how it helps the writer to achieve their intention.

ACTIVITY 4   A04   A05   SKILLS REASONING, CREATIVITY, INNOVATION

▼ WRITING TASKS

1 Write a short story about a race or a hunt.
2 Write a newspaper report on a game involving a team sport, such as football, cricket or basketball.
3 'Taking part in sport is more important than winning'. Argue either in favour of this statement or against it.

EXAM-STYLE QUESTION

A02   SKILLS CRITICAL THINKING, ANALYSIS, ADAPTIVE LEARNING, CREATIVITY

How does the writer use language and structure to create excitement and interest?

You should support your answer with close reference to the extract, including **brief** quotations.

(12 marks)

BEYOND THE SKY AND THE EARTH: A JOURNEY INTO BHUTAN
JAMIE ZEPPA

BACKGROUND AND CONTEXT

Jamie Zeppa is a Canadian writer and college professor. *Beyond the Sky and Earth: A Journey into Bhutan* is an autobiography that recounts her experiences on a two-year assignment as an English lecturer in the 1980s in the mountainous kingdom of Bhutan. It is a memoir, but it should also be classed as travel writing. It is a record of the culture and life of a Himalayan village and her initial reactions and growing attachment to this remote and unexplored part of the world.

Bhutan is a landlocked country in South Asia and was not exposed to western influences until the second half of the 20th century, which enabled it to retain much of its identity and culture. It is a country that has been named the happiest in Asia and the eighth happiest in the world.

BEFORE YOU START READING

1 Do some research about the history and geography of Bhutan.

2 In groups, talk about what makes your own culture different from that of other countries. Are there many differences, or only a few? Talk about the different things that make up your culture, such as language, clothing and traditions.

3 Would you like to travel and work abroad? What would be the advantages and disadvantages? Discuss them in a group or with your class.

▼ FROM *BEYOND THE SKY AND THE EARTH: A JOURNEY INTO BHUTAN* BY JAMIE ZEPPA

SUBJECT VOCABULARY
memoir a form of autobiography

Paro A valley in Bhutan that contains the country's only international airport.

When Zeppa was 24 years old, she left Canada to teach in Bhutan. This memoir grew out of an essay she wrote about her early days in the country.

Mountains all around, climbing up to peaks, rolling into valleys, again and again. Bhutan is all and only mountains. I know the technical explanation for the landscape, landmass meeting landmass, the Indian subcontinent colliding into Asia thirty or forty million years ago, but I cannot imagine it. It is easier to picture a giant child gathering earth in great armfuls, piling up rock, pinching mud into ridges and sharp peaks, knuckling out little valleys and gorges, poking holes for water to fall through.

It is my first night in Thimphu, the capital, a ninety-minute drive from the airport in Paro. It took five different flights over four days to get there, from Toronto to Montreal to Amsterdam to New Delhi to Calcutta to Paro. I am exhausted but I cannot sleep. From my simple, pine-panelled room at the

▶

flavorless Zeppa uses American English spellings.

Saskatchewan A province in Canada known for its harsh winters.

British Columbia A Canadian province on the west coast, containing the city of Vancouver.

impish Mischievous; the term comes from the name of a mythological creature, 'imp', believed to cause trouble.

WUSC World University Service of Canada, a non-profit organisation that works with local bodies to strengthen educational systems and economic opportunities.

Willie Nelson A well-known American musician of country music whose career was at its height in the 1970s.

Rambo The American main character from the Rambo films.

dzong A type of fortress found in the present and former Tibetan Buddhist kingdoms of the Himalayas, particularly Bhutan and south Tibet.

emissary A diplomat or representative for a country.

George Bogle A Scottish traveller and diplomat who was the first to establish diplomatic relations with Tibet.

Druk Sherig hotel, I watch mountains rise to meet the moon. I used to wonder what was on the other side of mountains, how the landscape resolved itself beyond the immediate wall in front of you. Flying in from the baked-brown plains of India this morning, I found out: on the other side of mountains are mountains, more mountains and mountains again. The entire earth below us was a convulsion of crests and gorges and wind sharpened pinnacles. Just past Everest, I caught a glimpse of the Tibetan plateau, the edge of a frozen desert 4,500 meters above sea level. Thimphu's altitude is about half of that but even here, the winter air is thin and dry and very cold.

The next morning, I share breakfast of instant coffee, powdered milk, plasticky white bread and flavorless red jam in the hotel with two other Canadians who have signed on to teach in Bhutan for two years. Lorna has golden brown hair, freckles and a no nonsense, home-on-the-farm demeanour that is frequently shattered by her ringing laughter and stories of wild characters that populate her life in Saskatchewan. Sasha from British Columbia is slight and dark, with an impish smile. After breakfast, we have a brief meeting with Gordon, the field director of the WUSC program in Bhutan, and then walk along the main road of Thimpu. Both Lorna and Sasha have traveled extensively; Lorna trekked all over Europe and northern Africa and Sasha worked for a year in an orphanage in Bombay. They are both ecstatic about Bhutan so far, and I stay close to them, hoping to pick up some of their enthusiasm.

Although Thimphu's official population is 20,000, it seems even smaller. It doesn't even have traffic lights. Blue-suited policemen stationed at two intersections along the main street direct the occasional truck or land cruiser using incomprehensible but graceful hand gestures. The buildings all have the same pitched roof, trefoil windows and heavy beams painted with lotus flowers, jewels and clouds. One-storied shops with wooden-shuttered windows open onto the street. They seem to be selling the same things: onions, rice, milk powder, dried fish, plastic buckets and metal plates, quilts and packages of stale, soft cookies from India – Bourbon Biscuits, Coconut Crunchies and the hideously colored Orange Cream Biscuits. There are more signs of the outside world than I had expected: teenagers in acid washed jeans, Willie Nelson's greatest hits after the news in English on the Bhutan Broadcasting Service, a Rambo poster in a bar. Overall, these signs of cultural infiltration are few, but they are startling against the Bhutanese-ness of everything else.

The town itself looks very old, with cracked sidewalks and faded paintwork but Gordon told us that it didn't exist thirty-odd years ago. Before the sixties, when the third king decided to make it the capital, it was nothing but rice paddies, a few farm houses, and a dzong – one of the fortresses that are scattered throughout the country. Thimphu is actually new. "Thimphu will look like New York to you when you come back after a year in the east," he said.

At the end of the main road is Tashichho Dzong, the seat of the Royal Government of Bhutan, a grand, whitewashed, red-roofed, golden-tipped fortress, built in the traditional way, without blueprints or nails. Beyond, hamlets are connected by footpaths, and terraced fields, barren now, climb steadily from the river and merge into forest. Thimphu will never look like New York to me, I think.

The Bhutanese are a very handsome people, 'the best built race of men I ever saw,' wrote emissary George Bogle on his way to Tibet in 1774, and I find I

▶

▲ Wangdi, Bhutan; monks prepare for a traditional dance at a festival to honour Guru Rinpoche, who brought Buddhism to Bhutan.

Padmasambhava An Indian Buddhist master.

shamanistic religion A religion that has a belief in natural phenomenon and in powerful spirits that can be influenced by shamans (a person who acts as an intermediary between natural and supernatural worlds).

lama A Buddhist monk from Tibet or Mongolia.

Sandalwood A tree grown for its fragrant wood and oil in the Indian subcontinent.

felicitously Pleasingly or well-chosen.

Sanskrit An ancient Indian language.

Jesuits Members of a Roman Catholic order devoted to missionary work.

cordial Friendly and polite.

Ashley Eden An official and diplomat in India under British rule.

Great Game The economic and political conflict between the British Empire and the Russian Empire for supremacy in Central Asia in the 19th century.

agree. Of medium height and sturdily built, they have beautiful aristocratic faces with dark, almond-shaped eyes, high cheekbones and gentle smiles. Both men and women wear their black hair short. The women wear a *kira*, a brightly striped, ankle-length dress and the men a *gho*, a knee-length robe that resembles a kimono, except the top part is exceptionally voluminous. The Bhutanese of Nepali origin tend to be taller, with sharper features and darker complexions. They too wear the gho and kira. People look at us curiously, but they do not seem surprised at our presence. Although we see few other foreigners in town, we know they are here. Gordon said something this morning about Thimphu's small but friendly 'ex-pat' community.

When we stop and ask for directions at a hotel, the young man behind the counter walks with us to the street, pointing out the way, explaining politely in impeccable English. I search for the right word to describe the people, for the quality that impresses me most – dignity, unselfconsciousness, good humor, grace – but can find no single word to hold all of my impressions.

In Thimpu, we attended a week-long orientation session with twelve other Irish, British, Australian and New Zealand teachers new to Bhutan. Our first lessons, in Bhutanese history, are the most interesting. Historical records show that waves of Tibetan immigrants settled in Bhutan sometime before the tenth century, but the area is thought to have been inhabited long before that. In the eighth century, the Indian saint Padmasambhava brought Buddhism to the area, where it absorbed many elements of Bon, the indigenous shamanistic religion. The new religion took hold but was not a unifying force. The area remained a collection of isolated valleys, each ruled by its own king. When the Tibetan lama Ngawang Namgyel arrived in 1616, he set about unifying the valleys under one central authority and gave the country the name Druk Yul, meaning Land of the Thunder Dragon. Earlier names for Bhutan are just as beautiful – the Tibetans knew the country as the Southern Land of Medicinal Herbs and the South Sandalwood Country. Districts within Bhutan were even more felicitously-named: Rainbow District of Desires, Lotus Grove of the Gods, Blooming Valley of Luxuriant Fruits, the Land of Longing and Silver Pines. Bhutan, the name by which the country became known to the outside world, is thought to be derived from *Bhotanta*, meaning the 'end of Tibet' or from the Sanskrit *Bhu-uttan*, meaning 'highlands'.

While the rest of Asia was being overrun by Europeans of varying hue but similar cry, only a handful of Westerners found their way into Bhutan. Two Portuguese Jesuits came to call in 1627, and six British missions paid brief but cordial visits from the late 1700s until the middle of the next century. Relations with the British took a nasty turn during the disastrous visit of Ashley Eden in 1864. Eden, who had gone to sort out a small problem of the Bhutanese raids on British territory, had his back slapped, his hair pulled, and his face rubbed with wet dough, and was then forced to sign an outrageous treaty that led to a brief war between the British and the Bhutanese. Considering the consolidated British empire in the south, and the Great Game being played out in the north between the colonial powers, Bhutan's preservation of its independence was remarkable. I am full of admiration for this small country that has managed to look after itself so well.

UNDERSTANDING THE TEXT

This extract gives the reader a vivid description of the Canadian writer's first impressions of a land that is new to her. It conveys the way in which the writer's reaction changes from an initial lukewarm attitude to a gradual fascination as she begins to learn about the country's history and observe its culture. Aspects of Zeppa's descriptions of Bhutan, for example, of people with 'beautiful aristocratic faces' may be considered to contain subconscious biases.

Travel writing gives personal accounts of explorations and travel experiences. Examples of the genre contain many factual details. Terms that are specific to that culture are explained and opinions are conveyed. Like most travel writing, this extract describes a key event and includes background details and research that may have been carried out after the travel experience ended.

ACTIVITY 1 | A01 | SKILLS ANALYSIS

▼ FEATURES OF TRAVEL WRITING

Copy and complete the following table, finding examples of these features of travel writing in the extract.

▼ FEATURE	▼ EXAMPLE
Central event	
Factual details	
Background details	
Terminology and explanation	
Opinions	
Evidence of research	

ACTIVITY 2 | A02 | SKILLS CRITICAL THINKING, ANALYSIS, INTERPRETATION

▼ LANGUAGE FOR EFFECT

Because this is a memoir, the reader learns about Bhutan through the eyes of the Canadian narrator, and it conveys her mixed feelings effectively. While the text is full of information intended to give the reader a sense of place, it is also her personal view of Bhutan and everything that she sees and experiences.

Copy and complete the following table, making a list of the writer's feelings, giving an example and explaining its effect.

▼ FEELING/ATTITUDE	▼ EXAMPLE	▼ ANALYSIS
A sense of being unable to understand the experience	'… but I cannot imagine it'	The writer seems unable to even understand the geography of the area, as if it is so different from what she is used to that she needs to visualise it in different ways.
A lack of enthusiasm for the country		
	'teenagers in acid washed jeans, Willie Nelson's greatest hits after the news in English on the Bhutan Broadcasting Service…'	

EXPLORING LANGUAGE

In this extract, Jamie Zeppa is both an observer and a participant. She is looking at and reflecting on the elements of culture that she sees around her, but she is also beginning to participate by attending the training session as part of her work as a lecturer. These aspects are reflected in the language choices she makes.

The text's main purposes are to describe and inform. If it was too full of facts, the reader might find it boring or dry. However, Zeppa is able to make it lively and capture the reader's attention. One way she does this is by making it very clear she is writing about her own personal experiences, thoughts and feelings. Another is her skilful use of language.

▶ **In the second paragraph, find two phrases that show that the writer is observing her surroundings.**

▶ **Look at paragraph three and explain in your own words what the writer thinks about Thimphu.**

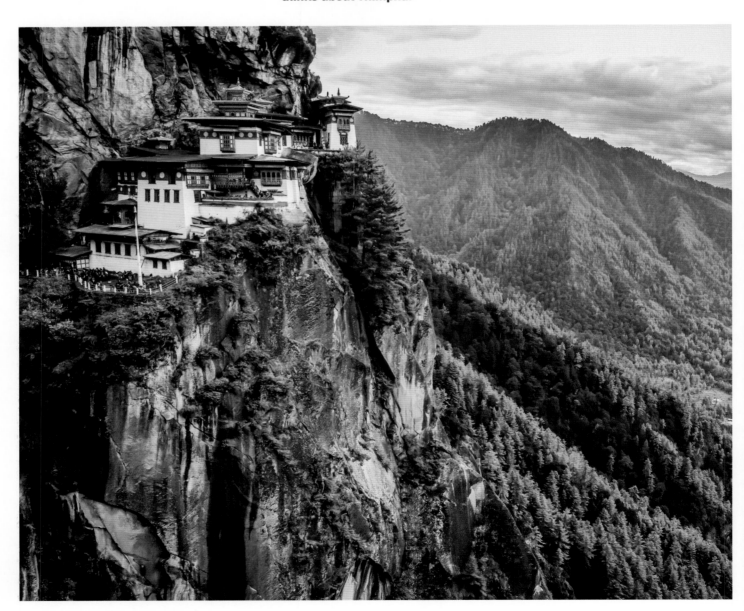

▲ The mountains of the Paro Valley, Bhutan.

ACTIVITY 3   A02   SKILLS ▶ ANALYSIS, INTERPRETATION

▼ TECHNIQUES FOR EFFECT

KEY POINT

When you comment on the writer's use of language, look for significant vocabulary choices and language features.

1 Look closely at the language features and their possible effects listed below.

▼ LANGUAGE FEATURES	▼ EFFECTS
Short sentences	To build a vivid image
Repetition	For emphasis
Hyphenated words	To build an impression of range or variety
Listed nouns or noun phrases	
Listed clauses	

Identify one example of each language feature and its effect in the quotations from the text below.

'Mountains all around, climbing up to peaks, rolling into valleys, again and again.'

'Bhutan is all and only mountains.'

'Flying in from the baked-brown plains of India this morning, I found out: on the other side of mountains are mountains, more mountains and mountains again.'

'I search for the right word to describe the people, for the quality that impresses me most – dignity, unselfconsciousness, good humor, grace – but can find no single word to hold all of my impressions.'

'They seem to be selling the same things: onions, rice, milk powder, dried fish, plastic buckets and metal plates, quilts and packages of stale, soft cookies from India'

2 The extract features a great deal of descriptive language intended to create a vivid impression in the reader's mind. Look at the description quoted below:

'hideously coloured Orange Cream Biscuits'

Look at each word in the description. Which word do you feel has the greatest impact on your impression of these objects? Write a sentence or two explaining your choice.

Now identify three more short descriptions in the text that you find particularly effective. Identify one or two significant vocabulary choices in each, writing a sentence or two explaining the impact that your chosen words have.

ACTIVITY 4   **A04**   **A05**   SKILLS ▶ TEAMWORK, SELF-PRESENTATION

▼ TEN THINGS I NEED ...

1 Give a speech on the topic, 'The ten things I need in order to be happy'. When planning, think of all the little things as well as the important things that you should have in your list. Try to add one item or idea that is really different from other people's, as this can be used to comic effect.

2 In pairs, create the text for a radio commercial advertising an exotic or interesting place to visit, then perform it for the class.

ACTIVITY 5   **A04**   **A05**   SKILLS ▶ PROBLEM SOLVING, CREATIVITY, INNOVATION

▼ WRITING TASKS

1 Write an article for your school newspaper persuading senior students to take a gap year after their final exams. During this year, they should provide some service to the community before beginning their university education. How will you convince them to do so?

2 Look at the following images. Write a narrative beginning with the words, 'I wanted to get away to a place that was different from any that I had known until now'.

▲ 'A place that was different from any that I had known'.

How does the writer use language and structure to convey her growing fascination with Bhutan?

You should support your answer with close reference to the extract, including **brief** quotations.

(12 marks)

H IS FOR HAWK
HELEN MACDONALD

▲ Naturalist and writer Helen Macdonald.

BACKGROUND AND CONTEXT

Helen Macdonald is a very experienced and enthusiastic falconer. When her father died suddenly on a London street, she was devastated. In an attempt to cope with her grief, she decided to buy and train one of the most difficult and aggressive of birds of prey, the goshawk. The experience changed her life, She said: 'The book is a memoir about that year when I lost my father and trained a hawk'.

Macdonald's book, published in 2013, won the Samuel Johnson Prize and Costa Book of the Year Award (both highly prestigious awards in the UK and Ireland). One reviewer, Mark Cocker, said: 'More than any other writer I know, Macdonald is able to summon the mental world of a bird of prey...'. In addition, he praised her writing for its verbal inventiveness and precision.

BEFORE YOU START READING

1　Find out what you can about goshawks and what makes them different from other birds of prey.

2　Find some pictures of hawks on the internet. Try to think of some words or phrases to describe them and their apparent 'personalities'.

3　What is hawking? What do you think might be the rewards of training a goshawk with which to go hawking?

▼ FROM *H IS FOR HAWK* BY HELEN MACDONALD

When Macdonald's father died suddenly of a heart attack, Macdonald was devastated. An experienced falconer, she adopted a goshawk to distract her from her grief. In this extract, Macdonald meets her hawk for the first time.

'We'll check the ring numbers against the Article 10s,' he explained, pulling a sheaf of yellow paper from his rucksack and unfolding two of the official forms that accompany captive-bred rare birds throughout their lives. 'Don't want you going home with the wrong bird.'

We noted the numbers. We stared down at the boxes, at their parcel-tape handles, their doors of thin plywood and hinges of carefully tied string. Then he knelt on the concrete, untied a hinge on the smaller box and squinted into its dark interior. A sudden *thump* of feathered shoulders and the box shook as if someone had punched it, hard, from within. 'She's got her hood off,' he said, and frowned. That light, leather hood was to keep the hawk from fearful sights. Like us.

Another hinge untied. Concentration. Infinite caution. Daylight irrigating the box. Scratching talons, another thump. And another.

Article 10s Certificates required for rare or endangered species sold in the UK.

▶

▲ The hawk, an aggressive bird of prey.

primaries Large feathers at the ends of the wings.

fretful porpentine A defensive porcupine (the phrase is borrowed from Shakespeare's *Hamlet*).

illuminated bestiary A beautifully illustrated medieval book about mythical and real animals.

marionette A puppet worked by strings.

jesses Short leather straps fastened to the legs.

point-source glitter Glitter made up of many points of light.

tautly Tensely, tightly.

hackles Small feathers at the back of the neck.

Thump. The air turned syrupy, slow, flecked with dust. The last few seconds before a battle. And with the last bow pulled free, he reached inside, and amidst a whirring, chaotic clatter of wings and feet and talons and a high-pitched twittering and it's all happening at once, the man pulls an enormous, enormous hawk out of the box and in a strange coincidence of world and deed a great flood of sunlight drenches us and everything is brilliance and fury. The hawk's wings, barred and beating, the sharp fingers of her dark-tipped primaries cutting the air, her feathers raised like the scattered quills of a fretful porpentine. Two enormous eyes. My heart jumps sideways. She is a conjuring trick. A reptile. A fallen angel. A griffon from the pages of an illuminated bestiary. Something bright and distant, like gold falling through water. A broken marionette of wings, legs and light-splashed feathers. She is wearing jesses, and the man holds them. For one awful, long moment she is hanging head-downward, wings open, like a turkey in a butcher's shop, only her head is turned right-way-up and she is seeing more than she has ever seen before in her whole short life. Her world was an aviary no larger than a living room. Then it was a box. But now it is this; and she can see *everything*: the point-source glitter on the waves, a diving cormorant a hundred yards out; pigment flakes under wax on the lines of parked cars; far hills and the heather on them and miles and miles of sky where the sun spreads on dust and water and illegible things moving in it that are white scraps of gulls. Everything startling and new-stamped on her entirely astonished brain.

Through all this the man was perfectly calm. He gathered up the hawk in one practised movement, folding her wings, anchoring her broad feathered back against his chest, gripping her scaled yellow legs in one hand. 'Let's get that hood back on,' he said tautly. There was concern in his face. It was born of care. This hawk had been hatched in an incubator, had broken from a frail bluish eggshell into a humid perspex box, and for the first few days of her life this man had fed her with scraps of meat held in a pair of tweezers, waiting patiently for the lumpen, fluffy chick to notice the food and eat, her new neck wobbling with the effort of keeping her head in the air. All at once I loved this man, and fiercely. I grabbed the hood from the box and turned to the hawk. Her beak was open, her hackles raised; her wild eyes were the colour of sun on white paper, and they stared because the whole world had fallen into them at once. One, two, three. I tucked the hood over her head. There was a brief intimation of a thin, angular skull under her feathers, of an alien brain fizzing and fusing with terror, then I drew the braces closed. We checked the ring numbers against the form.

It was the wrong bird. This was the younger one. The smaller one. This was not my hawk.

Oh.

So we put her back and opened the other box, which was meant to hold the larger, older bird. And dear God, it did. Everything about this second hawk was different. She came out like a Victorian melodrama: a sort of madwoman in the attack. She was smokier and darker and much, much bigger, and instead of twittering, she wailed; great, awful gouts of sound like a thing in pain, and the sound was unbearable. *This is my hawk*, I was telling myself and it was all I could do to breathe. She too was bareheaded, and I grabbed the hood from the box as before. But as I brought it up to her face I looked into her eyes and saw

▶

something blank and crazy in her stare. Some madness from a distant country. I didn't recognise her. *This isn't my hawk*. The hood was on, the ring numbers checked, the bird back in the box, the yellow form folded, the money exchanged, and all I could think was, *But this isn't my hawk*. Slow panic. I knew what I had to say, and it was a monstrous breach of etiquette. 'This is really awkward,' I began. 'But I really liked the first one. Do you think there's any chance I could take that one instead… ?' I tailed off. His eyebrows were raised. I started again, saying stupider things: 'I'm sure the other falconer would like the larger bird? She's more beautiful than the first one, isn't she? I know this is out of order, but I… Could I? Would it be all right, do you think?' And on and on, a desperate, crazy barrage of incoherent appeals.

I'm sure nothing I said persuaded him more than the look on my face as I said it. A tall, white-faced woman with wind-wrecked hair and exhausted eyes was pleading with him on a quayside, hands held out as if she were in a seaside production of Medea. Looking at me he must have sensed that my stuttered request wasn't a simple one. That there was something behind it that was very important. There was a moment of total silence.

Medea Greek revenge tragedy about a woman with magical powers.

UNDERSTANDING THE TEXT

This extract from the book describes the moment when Macdonald first meets the hawk she has decided to train. It is a moment of great significance – the relationship that she builds with this bird is the main topic of the book and is the method that she adopts for dealing with her grief for her father.

Although the second hawk that is pulled out is the one that she has reserved for herself, Macdonald makes a very quick decision on instinct. There is something she does not like about the larger bird and she decides to ask for the one that the man brought out first. She describes both birds in detail.

This kind of writing is sometimes called 'creative non-fiction'. This is because, although it is factual, it is also imaginative and highly-crafted writing. When you re-read the extract, look out for the same kinds of writing that you get in fiction – description, narrative, dialogue, thoughts and feelings, as well as more fact-based explanation.

KEY POINT

Non-fiction can incorporate elements more associated with fiction, such as creative use of narrative.

ACTIVITY 1   A01   SKILLS   ANALYSIS

▼ THEMES

Copy and complete the following table, thinking carefully about the themes of the extract. Add some more themes that you noticed in the extract.

▼ THEME	▼ EXAMPLE	▼ ANALYSIS
Beauty of the bird	Lines 24–26: 'She is a conjuring trick… a fallen angel… like gold…'	Macdonald is completely fascinated, almost overwhelmed, by the bird.
Fierce personality of the bird		
Emotional reaction		

ACTIVITY 2　A01　SKILLS ▷ ANALYSIS

▼ EXAMINING THE DETAIL

Much of the success of creative non-fiction is in the detail and what can be inferred from it. Copy and complete the following table, noting what you can infer from the quotation and the word or phrase that helped you infer it.

▼ LINES	▼ DETAILS	▼ WHAT DOES THIS TELL THE READER?
9–11	'a sudden thump… as if someone had punched it, hard, from within'	The words 'thump', 'punched' and 'hard' suggest the bird is powerful and aggressive.
43–45	'…in one practised movement, folding her wings, anchoring her broad feathered back against his chest…'	
53–55	'Her beak was open, her hackles raised; her wild eyes were the colour of sun on white paper…'	

EXPLORING LANGUAGE

The language of this extract is inventive and intense.

Mark Cocker wrote that Macdonald 'combines a **lexicographer's** pleasure in words as carefully **curated objects** with an inventive passion for words or for ways of releasing fresh effects from the old stock'. Can you see why he said this?

GENERAL VOCABULARY
lexicographer writer of dictionaries
curated objects objects in a museum

ACTIVITY 3　A02　SKILLS ▷ CRITICAL THINKING, ANALYSIS, INTERPRETATION

▼ LANGUAGE FOR EFFECT

1　Look closely at paragraph 3 of the extract, beginning: 'Another hinge untied…'.

How many of these language techniques can you spot? For each one, note a quotation.

| simile | metaphor | repetition | onomatopoeia |

| alliteration | a list | short, minor sentences | long multiclause sentences |

2　Look again at the quotations you have noted. What is the effect of the language technique you have identified?

| emphasis | a series of short vivid snapshots building a striking impression |

| a strong visual picture | suggesting range and variety | something else |

STRUCTURE

To understand the structure of a text, look at the content of each paragraph or break it down into sections.

ACTIVITY 4　　A02　　SKILLS　CRITICAL THINKING

▼ EXPLORING STRUCTURE

The extract is structured to achieve the writer's intentions of creating tension and surprise.

Look at this summary of the structure of the text:

1. The birds are trying to escape.
2. The man takes the bird out. The writer describes it.
3. The writer realises it's the wrong bird.
4. The man takes the right bird out of the box. The writer describes it.
5. The writer panics as she realises she would rather have the first bird.
6. The writer plucks up courage to ask if she can take the first bird. Silence.

1 Which of these six structural elements of the text create or build tension? How?
2 Which elements create surprise? How?
3 Look again at the tensions you have identified in the extract. Which tensions are released or resolved in the extract? How? Which are not?

EXAM-STYLE QUESTIONS

A02

SKILLS　CRITICAL THINKING, ANALYSIS, ADAPTIVE LEARNING, CREATIVITY

1 How does the writer use language and structure to portray the birds and setting?

You should support your answer with close reference to the extract, including **brief** quotations. **(12 marks)**

2 How does the writer create a sense of excitement?

You should support your answer with close reference to the extract, including **brief** quotations.

(12 marks)

▲ '...a whirring, chaotic clatter of wings and feet and talons...'

Look at two students' responses to exam-style Question 2 on page 145.

EXAMPLE STUDENT ANSWER A

> Macdonald is excited about seeing the hawk. You can tell this by the way she repeats that the hawk is 'enormous, enormous'.

EXAMPLE STUDENT ANSWER B

> Macdonald creates excitement using emotive and figurative language to create a forceful effect. For example, in the lines beginning, 'the man pulls an enormous, enormous hawk…', the words 'brilliance and fury' powerfully express her strong feelings while the repetition of 'enormous' shows her shocked surprise.

HINT

Which response do you find more effective?

One of these responses is less successful and would justify the following comments:

- Some understanding of and comment on language and structure and how these are used by writers to achieve effects, including use of vocabulary.
- The selection of references is valid, but not developed.

The other response is more successful and would justify this comment:

- Clear understanding and explanation of language and how it is used to achieve effects, including use of vocabulary and sentence structure.

Which response is more successful?

Note down what the more successful response has done that the less successful response has not.

ACTIVITY 5 **A04** **A05** **SKILLS** CRITICAL THINKING, ANALYSIS, REASONING, INTERPRETATION

▼ WRITING TASKS

1 'If people tried harder to understand and respect every creature that lives on Earth, human beings would stop destroying their planet.' Write a magazine article giving your views on this statement. The article may include:

- the ways in which human beings are damaging the environment
- the ways in which human beings could try to understand and respect other creatures
- any other points you wish to make.

Your response will be marked for the accurate and appropriate use of vocabulary, as well as accuracy of spelling and grammar.

2 How does the writer present the character of the hawks in the extract from *H is for Hawk*?

You should write about:

- the description of their appearance
- the way they behave
- the writer's use of language and techniques to convey these.

You should refer closely to the text to support your answer and use **brief** quotations.

CHINESE CINDERELLA
ADELINE YEN MAH

BACKGROUND AND CONTEXT
Chinese Cinderella is an autobiography by Adeline Yen Mah in which she describes growing up in a wealthy family in Hong Kong in the 1950s. She is rejected by her stepmother and her father is a distant, though powerful, character. She spends much of her time at boarding school.

▲ Chinese-American author and physician Adeline Yen Mah.

typhoon A storm in the Indian or Western Pacific Oceans.

BEFORE YOU START READING
Do some research.
■ Look up Adeline Yen Mah on the internet.
■ Can you find other examples of childhood autobiographies?

▼ FROM *CHINESE CINDERELLA* BY ADELINE YEN MAH

Growing up in a wealthy family in 1950s Hong Kong, Mah should have had an enviable childhood, but she was rejected by her dominating stepmother and despised by her brothers and sisters. She was sent to a boarding school and left there. In this extract from her autobiography, she relates one of the few occasions when she went home.

Time went by relentlessly and it was Saturday again. Eight weeks more and it would be the end of term … in my case perhaps the end of school forever.

Four of us were playing Monopoly. My heart was not in it and I was losing steadily. Outside it was hot and there was a warm wind blowing. The radio warned of a possible typhoon the next day. It was my turn and I threw the dice. As I played, the thought of leaving school throbbed at the back of my mind like a persistent toothache.

'Adeline!' Ma-mien Valentino was calling.

'You can't go now,' Mary protested. 'For once I'm winning. One, two, three, four. Good! You've landed on my property. Thirty-five dollars, please. Oh, good afternoon, Mother Valentino!'

We all stood up and greeted her.

'Adeline, didn't you hear me call you? Hurry up downstairs! Your chauffeur is waiting to take you home!'

Full of foreboding, I ran downstairs as in a nightmare, wondering who had died this time. Father's chauffeur assured me everyone was healthy.

'Then why are you taking me home?' I asked.

'How should *I* know?' he answered defensively, shrugging his shoulders. 'Your guess is as good as mine. They give the orders and I carry them out.'

During the short drive home, my heart was full of dread and I wondered what I had done wrong. Our car stopped at an elegant villa at mid-level, halfway up the hill between the peak and the harbour.

'Where are we?' I asked foolishly.

▶

bridge A card game played with four people.

'Don't you know anything?' the chauffeur replied rudely. 'This is your new home. Your parents moved here a few months ago.'

'I had forgotten,' I said as I got out.

Ah Gum opened the door. Inside, it was quiet and cool.

'Where is everyone?'

'Your mother is out playing bridge. Your two brothers and Little Sister are sunbathing by the swimming pool. Your father is in his room and wants to see you as soon as you get home.'

'See me in his room?' I was overwhelmed by the thought that I had been summoned by Father to enter the Holy of Holies – a place to which I had never been invited. Why? …

Timidly, I knocked on the door. Father was alone, looking relaxed in his slippers and bathrobe, reading a newspaper. He smiled as I entered and I saw he was in a happy mood. I breathed a small sigh of relief at first but became uneasy when I wondered why he was being so nice, thinking, Is this a giant ruse on his part to trick me? Dare I let my guard down?

'Sit down! Sit down!' He pointed to a chair. 'Don't look so scared. Here, take a look at this! They're writing about someone we both know, I think.'

He handed me the day's newspaper and there, in one corner, I saw my name ADELINE YEN in capital letters prominently displayed.

'It was announced today that 14-year-old Hong Kong schoolgirl ADELINE JUN-LING YEN of Sacred Heart Canossian School, Caine Road, Hong Kong, has won first prize in the International Play-writing Competition held in London, England, for the 1951–1952 school year. It is the first time that any local Chinese student from Hong Kong has won such a prestigious event. Besides a medal, the prize comes with a cash reward of FIFTY ENGLISH POUNDS. Our sincere congratulations, ADELINE YEN, for bringing honour to Hong Kong. We are proud of you.'

Is it possible? Am I dreaming? Me, the winner?

'I was going up the lift this morning with my friend C.Y. Tung when he showed me this article and asked me, "Is the winner Adeline Jun-ling Yen related to you? The two of you have the same uncommon last name." Now C.Y. himself has a few children about your age but so far none of them has won an international literary prize, as far as I know. So I was quite pleased to tell him you are my daughter. Well done!'

He looked radiant. For once, he was proud of me. In front of his revered colleague, C.Y. Tung, a prominent fellow businessman also from Shanghai, I had given him face. I thought, Is this the big moment I have been waiting for? My whole being vibrated with all the joy in the world. I only had to stretch out my hand to reach the stars.

'Tell me, how did you do it?' he continued. 'How come *you* won?'

'Well, the rules and regulations were so very complicated. One really has to be dedicated just to understand what they want. Perhaps I was the only one determined enough to enter and there were no other competitors!'

He laughed approvingly. 'I doubt it very much but that's a good answer.'

'Please, Father,' I asked boldly, thinking it was now or never. 'May I go to university in England too, just like my brothers?'

face In this context, a positive successful appearance in the eyes of other people.

▶

'I do believe you have potential. Tell me, what would you study?'

My heart gave a giant lurch as it dawned on me that he was agreeing to let me go. How marvellous it was simply to be alive! Study? I thought. Going to England is like entering heaven. Does it matter what you do after you get to heaven?

But Father was expecting an answer. What about creative writing? After all, I had just won first prize in an international writing competition!

'I plan to study literature. I'll be a writer.'

'Writer!' he scoffed. 'You are going to starve! What language are you going to write in and who is going to read your writing? Though you may think you're an expert in both Chinese and English, your Chinese is actually rather elementary. As for your English, don't you think the native English speakers can write better than you?'

I waited in silence. I did not wish to contradict him.

'You will go to England with Third Brother this summer and you will go to medical school. After you graduate, you will specialise in obstetrics. Women will always be having babies. Women patients prefer women doctors. You will learn to deliver their babies. That's a foolproof profession for you. Don't you agree?'

Agree? Of course I agreed. Apparently, he had it all planned out. As long as he let me go to university in England, I would study anything he wished. How did that line go in Wordsworth's poem? *Bliss was it in that dawn to be alive.*

'Father, I shall go to medical school in England and become a doctor. Thank you very, very much.'

---

obstetrics Caring for women who are having babies.

Wordsworth A Romantic poet who wrote during the 18th and 19th centuries.

ACTIVITY 1   **A01**   **SKILLS** REASONING, CREATIVITY, INTERPERSONAL SKILLS

▼ EXPLORING THE SETTING

Think about the setting and situation shown in the extract: the background to the events that the writer recounts in this section of her autobiography.

1 How would you describe her family's financial situation? Note down two or three details that show this.

2 How would you describe the relationship between the writer and her family. Note down two or three details from the extract that show this.

UNDERSTANDING THE TEXT

Adeline Yen Mah writes to inform, explain and describe. Using these writing purposes, she conveys a powerful impression of events, of her family, and of her relationship with them.

The key to understanding and effectively analysing the piece is to understand the writer's thoughts and feelings about boarding school, about her family, her father in particular, and her future.

ACTIVITY 2 | A01 | SKILLS ▸ CRITICAL THINKING

▼ TRACKING STRUCTURE AND EMOTION

The extract has clear sections as it progresses from one setting to another, and as events unfold.

The structure of the extract could be summarised as:

1. At school
2. Being driven by the chauffeur
3. Coming home
4. Going to see father and hearing about the competition
5. Future plans

1 Look closely at each of the five sections listed above, thinking about the emotions the writer describes or that can be inferred.

Which of these emotions does she feel in each of the five stages of the extract? Select a short quotation showing each of the emotions in each section.

2 Compare the emotions the writer shows or expresses as the events in the extract unfold. Track them in a table like the one below.

Positive					
Neutral					
Negative					
Section	1	2	3	4	5

3 Writers may contrast emotions to exaggerate them. For example, a writer might focus on a happy and joyful event that ends in disaster: the initial happiness gives the disaster greater impact.

Look at the table you have drawn, tracking the emotions shown in the extract. How has Adeline Yen Mah used this technique?

KEY POINT

Writers sometimes explicitly state their emotions: 'I was happy'. More often, the reader must infer them: 'I smiled'.

EXPLORING LANGUAGE

Throughout the extract, the writer uses language choice to achieve her intentions: the response she wants you, the reader, to have to the story she tells.

Look again at the five sections of the extract listed above. Which of the following intentions does the writer aim to achieve in each section?

| humour | excitement | tension | drama | mystery |

| a vivid picture in the reader's mind | shock | surprise or amazement | sympathy |

KEY POINT

Be sure you understand the difference between the emotions a writer expresses in a text and the emotion the writer intends the reader to experience as they read.

For each of the writer's intentions you have noted, select a quotation to show where the writer is trying to achieve it.

In each of the quotations you have selected, identify one or two language choices or techniques the writer has used to help her achieve her intention. Write one or two sentences explaining your choice.

▼ SECTION	▼ INTENTION	▼ QUOTATION	▼ LANGUAGE CHOICE
1	Tension and mystery	'Full of foreboding, I ran downstairs as in a nightmare'	'nightmare' suggests the writer's fear at what might have happened

---

ACTIVITY 3   A04   A05   SKILLS ▶ REASONING, CREATIVITY, INNOVATION

▼ WRITING TASKS

1 Consider the following two statements. Write an argument in favour of one of these statements.

   'Boarding schools teach young people to become confident and well-rounded adults.'

   'Sending young children away to boarding school is cruel and unnatural.'

2 Describe your hopes and dreams for your future and how you would feel if someone made your dreams come true.

EXAM-STYLE QUESTION

A02

SKILLS ▶ CRITICAL THINKING, ANALYSIS, ADAPTIVE LEARNING, CREATIVITY

How does the writer use language and structure to convey her emotions?

You should support your answer with close reference to the extract, including **brief** quotations.

(12 marks)

LEARNING OBJECTIVES

This lesson will help you to:
- read and interpret non-fiction texts.

KEY POINT

In the exam, you will have to compare an unseen text with a text from the Anthology. When you have read the unseen text, check which Anthology text you are being asked to compare it with. What connections can you make between the two texts?

IDENTIFYING KEY INFORMATION

In Paper 1, the extracts will be non-fiction and one of the extracts will be an 'unseen text' which will be unfamiliar to you. Give yourself plenty of time to read the unseen text carefully. However, you won't have time to read and re-read it lots of times so try to apply some of the following active reading strategies.

- Before you read the extract, read the title carefully and think about what it suggests. Based on the title, what do you think the extract may be about?
- If there are a few lines of introduction, read and consider these carefully.
- Read the extract to get a sense of the purpose, intention and content.
- Read the extract again. While you read, use your pen or highlighter to circle key information, ideas, words and phrases to help you answer the questions.

TIP IT!

When you read an unseen text for the first time you should **TIP** it!

- **T**ype: What type of text is it?
- **I**ntention: What impact does the writer intend to have on the reader? To create tension, a sense of mystery, humour or ... ?
- **P**urpose: What is the purpose of this extract? Is it informing you, explaining to you or persuading you?

TYPE OF TEXT

You should be able to establish the type of text that you are reading very quickly. There are three things that will help you here: the content, the layout and the perspective.

- **Content**: What is the text about?
- **Layout**: What does the text look like? News articles usually have headlines, for example.
- **Perspective**: Is it written in the first or third person? Autobiography and travel writing are usually written in the first person. News articles are usually written in the third person.

GENERAL VOCABULARY

conventions features normally associated with something

ACTIVITY 1   **A01**   **SKILLS** ▶ CRITICAL THINKING

▼ TYPES OF NON-FICTION TEXT

Cover the list below with your hand or a piece of paper, then see how many different types of non-fiction text you can name.

news article	autobiography	interview	advertorial feature
magazine article	biography	report	newspaper column
travel writing	text book	journal	

▶ Select one of the types of non-fiction above. What does it look like? Add any conventions of this type of text that you think are important.

AUDIENCE

KEY POINT

Clues as to the writer's intended audience include the level of difficulty of the language and the assumed knowledge contained in the text.

A writer will usually have a particular audience in mind when they write. Look for any clues that might tell you about the intended reader, for example.

- **Age**: Is the subject matter aimed at a particular age group? Does the difficulty of the language suggest a certain readership?
- **Knowledge**: What do you need to know to make sense of the extract?
- **Tone**: What kind of tone is the piece written in? Is the language used formal or informal?

PURPOSE

The main difference between fiction and non-fiction is that non-fiction is usually written for one or more practical purposes, whereas fiction is usually written to entertain. You will need to identify the writer's intention in order to establish the purpose of a non-fiction text. It may help you to think of these 'writing triplets' in order to give you a system for thinking about purpose.

- **Inform, explain, describe**: Is the writer writing to make something clear or to give information?
- **Argue, persuade, advise**: Is the writer writing to discuss an issue or persuade someone to share their views?
- **Explore, imagine, entertain**: Is the writer writing with no other purpose than to entertain the reader?

ACTIVITY 2   **A01**   **SKILLS**   CRITICAL THINKING, PROBLEM SOLVING, INTERPRETATION

▼ TEXT TYPE, AUDIENCE AND PURPOSE

1 Read the extract from *Touching The Void* on pages 163–164 and TIP it. What is the type, intention and purpose of the text? Remember that texts can have a combination of several purposes. Use highlighters to colour code any evidence of different purposes.

EXAMPLE STUDENT ANSWER

> **Type**: First person account.
>
> **Intention**: To create drama, tension and sympathy: the text is about two people in a difficult situation. To create mystery: the reader is encouraged to wonder how they can escape this situation.
>
> **Purpose**: To engage and inform.

2 Summarise briefly in your own words:
- what happened to Joe
- what choices face Simon.

EXAMPLE STUDENT ANSWER

> *Touching the Void* is a book by Joe Simpson. It is a true story of how he and his climbing partner, Simon Yates, set out to become the first people to climb Siula Grande in Peru. They were nearing the end of their climb in the Peruvian Andes when a disastrous accident occurred in which Joe broke his leg. Simon, who was tied to Joe with a rope, felt that if he did not break free, they would both die. As a result, he cut the rope supporting Joe and returned down the mountain, believing Joe to be dead. Although his leg was broken, Joe crawled his way back down the mountain and was eventually rescued.

▲ Siula Grande, Peru.

LEARNING OBJECTIVES

This lesson will help you to:

■ look at unseen texts in detail, considering language and structure.

ANALYSING THE TEXTS

Once you have read the unseen extract and used the TIP technique to begin analysing it, you are ready to explore the writer's choices. How has the writer used language and sentence structure to influence the reader's response?

COPING WITH UNSEEN TEXTS

■ Before you read the unseen extract, read the title carefully. What does it suggest the extract may be about? What can you infer and predict from the title?

■ Consider the beginning and ending of the extract carefully.

■ Read the text in full.

■ As you read, check your understanding. If you find you are losing understanding, go back to a point in the text where you felt confident and read again. What is getting in the way of your understanding? Is it:

  ■ a word you don't recognise? Look at the rest of the sentence in which the word is used. Can you guess the unknown word's meaning?

  ■ complex ideas or information? Stop and re-read the whole paragraph.

■ As you keep reading and your understanding develops, underline any words or phrases that you feel are important – you may choose to come back and comment on these.

■ What type of text is it? A first-person autobiographical narrative, for example? Travel writing? A news article? Or something else?

■ What is the writer's intention? What impact does the text have on you?

■ What is the purpose of the extract? Is it informing you, explaining to you or persuading you?

■ How has the writer used language and sentence structure to create effect?

▶ What do you think the writer's intentions are?

WRITER'S TECHNIQUE

Once you are clear about what the piece is about and what the writer is trying to achieve, you will be able to consider the writer's choices: how has the writer used them to achieve their **intentions** and **purposes**? A useful way to identify and understand writers' choices is to consider the different levels at which they are made:

■ at word level: the vocabulary choices the writer has made

■ at sentence level: the sentence structure choices the writer has made

■ at whole text level: the structural choices the writer has made.

ACTIVITY 1 | A02 | SKILLS ANALYSIS

▼ FEATURES AT WORD LEVEL

Read the following short lines of text. What do you notice about the language used? Can you identify which of the techniques in the Hint box are being used in each?

> Nine out of ten dogs would recommend Doggibix.

> Best Ever Mega Monday Amazing 200% Discount Sale!

> Work, work, work? Get the laughs back in your life this Thursday at the Comedy Club.

> Sunshine Spas: simply the best!

> This film was fast, funny and full of surprises! ★★★★★

> Is your girlfriend terrified of your mother?

HINT

It may help you if you think about these specific devices:

- emotive language
- hyperbole
- facts and statistics
- allliteration
- triple structure
- superlative
- repetition.

ACTIVITY 2 | A01 | SKILLS CRITICAL THINKING, ANALYSIS, INTERPRETATION

▼ *TOUCHING THE VOID*

Imagine that the extract from *Touching the Void* on pages 163–164 is the unseen extract. What words or phrases in Joe's account most vividly shows:

- the pain he suffers as a result of his injuries
- his thoughts and feelings?

STRUCTURING YOUR RESPONSE

Copy and complete the following table, adding your own examples of word level choices to comment on. Review the section, 'Use of Language' (pages 16–23), if you need help thinking about language features in more detail.

▼ WORD LEVEL FEATURE	▼ EXAMPLE	▼ EFFECT
Simple language	'He would leave me. He had no choice.'	Joe's simple language bluntly and dramatically conveys the stark choices Simon faces and how life-threatening Joe's injury really is.
Vividly descriptive vocabulary choice	'The impact catapulted me over backwards and down the slope'	Careful vocabulary choices build a vivid impression of setting and action.

ACTIVITY 3   A02   SKILLS   CRITICAL THINKING, ANALYSIS, INTERPRETATION

▼ FEATURES AT SENTENCE LEVEL

The way in which a writer combines words, phrases and clauses to build sentences is important. Look again at the extract from *Touching the Void*, considering it as a typical unseen extract. Look at the example in the table below, then find two more examples of sentence level choices that you could talk about. Go back to the section, 'Use of Language' (pages 16–23), if you need a reminder of sentence structure features.

▼ SENTENCE LEVEL FEATURE	▼ EXAMPLE	▼ EFFECT
Minor sentences	'My leg!… My leg!'	Joe's account uses a number of short, exclamatory minor sentences that show the sudden urgent horror of the situation. Here, the two exclamation marks and ellipsis convey the pain and panic he is feeling.

HINT

The grammatical construction of a sentence is called its syntax. This includes both punctuation and sentence type. For example: 'Robbed!' The syntax of this exclamatory, one-word minor sentence evokes a sense of emotion and drama. The message is conveyed quickly and emotively to the reader.

ACTIVITY 4   A02   SKILLS   CRITICAL THINKING, ANALYSIS, INTERPRETATION

▼ FEATURES AT TEXT LEVEL

The writer's selection of ideas and the order in which they are sequenced can make a significant contribution to the writer achieving their intentions. Identify and track the development of events and information shown in the extract from *Touching the Void*. What is the impact of the writer's structural choices? Copy and complete the following table, adding another structural choice the writer has made and explaining its impact.

▼ TEXT LEVEL FEATURE	▼ EXAMPLE	▼ EFFECT
Two different perspectives	'I hit the slope…' 'Joe had disappeared…'	Using two different perspectives, the writer can convey both the victim's and his friend's thoughts and feelings in this dramatic event, It adds to the suspense and discomfort as the reader is forced to live through the experience twice, first engaging with Joe's pain then with Simon's grief as he believes his friend is dead.

HINT

Your aim is not simply to identify techniques, but to explain the **effects** of the author's craft. A weak answer simply re-tells the events of the extract; a strong answer comments on the way in which language is used to create meaning and prompt reader response.

| ACTIVITY 5 | A02 | SKILLS | CRITICAL THINKING, ANALYSIS, INTERPRETATION |

▼ CONSIDERING LANGUAGE

Refer back to the extract from Ellen MacArthur's autobiography on page 59. It deals with an emergency she faced on the 44th day of the Vendée Globe yacht race when she had to replace an essential sail. Read the notes below to help you consider how MacArthur's choices as a writer in this extract help to convey the situation, and her thoughts and feelings, as she sails alone in a race around the world.

INDICATIVE CONTENT

KEY POINT

When you analyse a text, first aim to identify the writer's intention and how their selection of ideas and information helps them to achieve it. You can then 'zoom in' on the ways in which the writer's choices at word and sentence level add to the text's impact on the reader.

KEY POINT

Although Ellen MacArthur is a yachtswoman not a writer, her writing is highly effective: she successfully achieves her intentions of conveying the drama and pain of sailing solo.

MacArthur's style is clear and powerful. This short extract highlights the enormous physical challenges in sailing alone in heavy seas. Because the narrative focuses on the physical effects of the bad weather, it makes the fact that MacArthur finds the strength to continue seem even more extraordinary. Remember, MacArthur is alone on this boat in the middle of the ocean. If she is to win the race, or even survive the ordeal, she must tackle all the dangers and threats she faces. To achieve her intention of conveying these, consider the choices she makes at:

Text level:

■ MacArthur's selection of information focuses on the storm and her pain.

■ As the extract progresses, both the storm and the pain grow worse.

■ The absence of speech highlights the fact that MacArthur is all alone.

Word level:

■ Use of technical details ('the storm jib', 'the inner forestay rod') gives the reader a sense of the challenge of sailing and MacArthur's expertise.

■ Plenty of active verbs ('continued', 'thrown', 'hurled') give the reader a sense of immediacy and action.

■ Straightforward, direct language: the lack of figurative language and limited use of adjectives and adverbs adds pace, focusing the reader on the action, not description.

■ Emotive vocabulary choices suggest struggle and pain ('lump', 'nausea', 'hang on', 'swollen', 'sores').

■ Personification of the weather as someone throwing MacArthur's possessions around the yacht ('Food was hurled') suggests that the weather is fighting with her.

▶ Ellen MacArthur's yacht *Kingfisher* competing in the Vendeé Globe race.

Sentence level:

- Long multiclause sentences link sequences of events, suggesting the rapid pace at which they take place: 'The wind continued to rise…'

- Dramatic contrasts are given emphasis by being positioned at the end of multiclause sentences: 'Soon afterwards, the weather front passed, only to bring even stronger 55-knot gusts in a steady 45-knot wind.'

- Shorter clauses, linked with a colon, add emphasis to key information: 'It was an unreal, crazy situation: just trying to hang on inside the boat took every ounce of strength.'

- Listed clauses highlight the number and variety of MacArthur's injuries: 'My hands stung, my eye was swollen…'

TACKLING AN UNSEEN TEXT

Now read the extract below. As you read, consider and try to identify:

- the writer's intentions and purposes: what impact does the writer want to have on the reader?

- structural decisions the writer has made: how does the writer's selection of ideas and information help him to achieve his intention? Why has the writer chosen to sequence them in this way? How might the reader's response develop as they read?

- sentences that have an impact on you: what impact is the writing trying to achieve? Which words, phrases or language techniques help to create that impact? How does the writer's use of sentence structure add to that impact?

▲ George Orwell's other well-known works include *Nineteen Eighty-Four* and *Animal Farm*.

cobbler Someone who makes and repairs shoes.

squalid Dirty and unpleasant.

weazened Thin, weak and old

▼ FROM *HOW THE POOR DIE* BY GEORGE ORWELL

After some days I grew well enough to sit up and study the surrounding patients. The stuffy room, with its narrow beds so close together that you could easily touch your neighbour's hand, had every sort of disease in it except, I suppose, acutely infectious cases. My right-hand neighbour was a little red-haired cobbler with one leg shorter than the other, who used to announce the death of any other patient (this happened a number of times, and my neighbour was always the first to hear of it) by whistling to me, exclaiming 'Numéro 43!' (or whatever it was) and flinging his arms above his head. This man had not much wrong with him, but in most of the other beds within my angle of vision some squalid tragedy or some plain horror was being enacted. In the bed that was foot to foot with mine there lay, until he died (I didn't see him die — they moved him to another bed), a little weazened man who was suffering from I do not know what disease, but something that made his whole body so intensely sensitive that any movement from side to side, sometimes even the weight of the bedclothes, would make him shout out with pain. His worst suffering was when he urinated, which he did with the greatest difficulty. A nurse would bring him the bedbottle and then for a long time stand beside his bed, whistling, as grooms are said to do with horses, until at last with an agonized shriek of 'Je fisse!' he would get started. In the bed next to him the sandy-haired man whom I had seen being cupped used to cough up blood-streaked mucus at all hours. My left-hand neighbour was a tall, flaccid-looking young man who used periodically to have a tube inserted into his back and astonishing quantities of frothy liquid drawn off from some part of his body. In the bed beyond that a veteran of the war of 1870 was dying, a handsome old man with a white imperial, round whose bed, at all hours when visiting was allowed, four elderly female relatives dressed all in black sat exactly like crows, obviously scheming for some pitiful legacy. In the bed opposite me in the farther row was an old bald-headed man with drooping moustaches and greatly swollen face and body, who was suffering from some disease that made him urinate almost incessantly. A huge glass receptacle stood always beside his bed. One day his wife and daughter came to visit him. At sight of them the old man's bloated face lit up with a smile of surprising sweetness, and as his daughter, a pretty girl of about twenty, approached the bed I saw that his hand was slowly working its way from under the bedclothes. I seemed to see in advance the gesture that was coming — the girl kneeling beside the bed, the old man's hand laid on her head in his dying blessing. But no, he merely handed her the bedbottle, which she promptly took from him and emptied into the receptacle.

About a dozen beds away from me was Numéro 57 — I think that was his number — a cirrhosis-of-the-liver case. Everyone in the ward knew him by sight because he was sometimes the subject of a medical lecture. On two afternoons a week the tall, grave doctor would lecture in the ward to a party of students, and on more than one occasion old Numéro 57 was wheeled in on a sort of trolley into the middle of the ward, where the doctor would roll back his nightshirt, dilate with his fingers a huge flabby protuberance on the man's belly — the diseased liver, I suppose — and explain solemnly that this was a disease attributable to alcoholism, commoner in the wine-drinking countries. As usual he neither spoke to his patient nor gave him a smile, a nod or any kind of recognition. While he talked, very grave and upright, he would hold the wasted body beneath his two hands, sometimes giving it a gentle roll to and fro, in just the attitude of a woman handling a rolling-pin. Not that Numéro 57 minded this kind of thing. Obviously he was an old hospital inmate, a regular exhibit at lectures, his liver long since marked down for a bottle in some pathological museum. Utterly uninterested in what was said about him, he would lie with his colourless eyes gazing at nothing, while the doctor showed him off like a piece of antique china. He was a man of about sixty, astonishingly shrunken. His face, pale as vellum, had shrunken away till it seemed no bigger than a doll's.

▶

---

protuberance Something that sticks out.

vellum Material used for covering books or writing on.

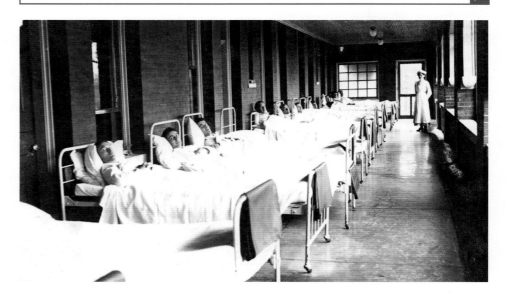

▶ Orwell wrote *How the Poor Die* after being treated at a French hospital in March 1929.

sabots Old-fashioned simple shoes made from wood.

Litany A long Christian prayer.

One morning my cobbler neighbour woke me up plucking at my pillow before the nurses arrived. 'Numéro 57!' — he flung his arms above his head. There was a light in the ward, enough to see by. I could see old Numéro 57 lying crumpled up on his side, his face sticking out over the side of the bed, and towards me. He had died some time during the night, nobody knew when. When the nurses came they received the news of his death indifferently and went about their work. After a long time, an hour or more, two other nurses marched in abreast like soldiers, with a great clumping of sabots, and knotted the corpse up in the sheets, but it was not removed till some time later. Meanwhile, in the better light, I had had time for a good look at Numéro 57. Indeed I lay on my side to look at him. Curiously enough he was the first dead European I had seen. I had seen dead men before, but always Asiatics and usually people who had died violent deaths. Numéro 57's eyes were still open, his mouth also open, his small face contorted into an expression of agony. What most impressed me, however, was the whiteness of his face. It had been pale before, but now it was little darker than die sheets. As I gazed at the tiny, screwed-up face it struck me that this disgusting piece of refuse, waiting to be carted away and dumped on a slab in the dissecting room, was an example of 'natural' death, one of the things you pray for in the Litany. There you are, then, I thought, that's what is waiting for you, twenty, thirty, forty years hence: that is how the lucky ones die, the ones who live to be old. One wants to live, of course, indeed one only stays alive by virtue of the fear of death, but I think now, as I thought then, that it's better to die violently and not too old. People talk about the horrors of war, but what weapon has man invented that even approaches in cruelty some of the commoner diseases? 'Natural' death, almost by definition, means something slow, smelly and painful. Even at that, it makes a difference if you can achieve it in your own home and not in a public institution. This poor old wretch who had just flickered out like a candle-end was not even important enough to have anyone watching by his deathbed. He was merely a number, then a 'subject' for the students' scalpels.

EXAM-STYLE QUESTIONS

A01	SKILLS	ANALYSIS
A01	SKILLS	CRITICAL THINKING, INTERPRETATION
A01	SKILLS	CRITICAL THINKING, ANALYSIS, INTERPRETATION
A02	SKILLS	CRITICAL THINKING, ANALYSIS, REASONING, INTERPRETATION

Re-read the extract from *How the Poor Die*, then answer these questions.

1 Select **two** phrases that the narrator uses to describe his neighbouring patients in the first paragraph. **(2 marks)**

2 Look again at the final paragraph of the text. **In your own words**, explain Orwell's thoughts and feelings at the death of patient Numéro 57. **(4 marks)**

3 Describe the attitudes towards the sick in this hospital. You may support your points with **brief** quotations. **(5 marks)**

4 How does the writer use language and structure to create sympathy for the patients in this extract?

You should support your answer with close reference to the extract, including **brief** quotations. **(12 marks)**

INTERPRETING TEXT

The text below is an extract from a review of a car, the Capybara, when it first went on sale. Read the extract and answer the questions below.

▼ FROM REVIEW OF THE 'CAPYBARA'

First impressions count for a lot, and unfortunately, the first impression of the Capybara isn't great. The styling can at best be described as 'challenging' and at worst 'capable of frightening small children'. Things do get better on climbing through the oddly proportioned door, but the shocked look of passers-by acts as a constant reminder of the styling.

So it's safe to say the exterior is an acquired taste and relocating to the driver's seat is recommended. The interior quality is incredibly strong and suggests the manufacturer's money has been directed here whilst the designers were left to play outside. Beautifully finished equipment and finishes suggest that this is a much more expensive car than it actually is. Anyone sat in the sculpted seats is likely to feel reassured that they are experiencing a quality product and have invested their funds wisely.

Inserting the futuristic key into the central console, you are greeted with a gentle murmur, rather than the expected rasping shout of other cars in this class. This lack of soundtrack continues as you smoothly drive away. Road noise is often an issue for small cars, but there is none here.

The longer you spend in the Capybara, the more you can appreciate its character. This is a happy car, unhampered by its looks and far more focused on transporting you in comfort and luxury. State of the art safety features including laser-guided cruise control, ABS+ and a GPS controlled gearbox cocoon the driver in a relaxed environment that you would expect in luxury cars.

But this isn't a luxury car, this is a relatively cheap, well-engineered small car that does its best to defy the first impressions the exterior styling inspires. If you can look beyond these, you have one of the best small cars on the road.

Remember, first impressions can be misleading – it's what's on the inside that counts.

SUBJECT VOCABULARY

premodified a noun with a description before it, e.g. 'the big blue car'

dynamic verb: a verb that describes actions or events that are happening, e.g. 'I go'

personification when something which is not human is made to sound human by attributing human qualities to it

▶ How does the writer use language to convey information and ideas to the reader? How does this language try to influence the reader's response? Use these questions to help you to identify relevant points.

▶ How does this text address the reader? Why does it do this?

▶ This is a car review, but does it remind you of any other kind of speech or writing? Why might it be trying not to seem too obviously like an advert?

▶ Does the review use many technical terms? Why? Why not?

▶ Identify some of the adjectives and adverbs which are used. What is their purpose here?

▶ Can you identify any nouns which are extensively premodified? Why might adverts tend to use a lot of premodification of nouns?

▶ Can you identify any rhetorical devices which are used to influence the reader?

▶ Can you identify and comment on any dynamic verbs that are used?

▶ Where does the advert use personification? Why does it use this metaphorical device?

LEARNING OBJECTIVES

This lesson will help you to:
- explore links and connections between writers' ideas and perspectives and how these are conveyed.

COMPARISONS

In Paper 1, you will be asked to compare an unseen text with one of the 10 pieces of contemporary non-fiction from the Pearson Edexcel International GCSE Anthology.

- From 'The Danger of a Single Story' by Chimamanda Ngozi Adichie.
- From *A Passage to Africa* by George Alagiah.
- From *The Explorer's Daughter* by Kari Herbert.
- 'Explorers or boys messing about?' by Steven Morris.
- From *Between a Rock and a Hard Place* by Aron Ralston.
- 'Young and dyslexic?' by Benjamin Zephaniah.
- From *A Game of Polo with a Headless Goat* by Emma Levine.
- From *Beyond the Sky and the Earth* by Jamie Zeppa.
- From *H is for Hawk* by Helen Macdonald.
- From *Chinese Cinderella* by Adeline Yen Mah.

QUESTION 5

HINT

The final question is worth approximately half of the marks for the whole section. You should divide your time accordingly.

SUBJECT VOCABULARY

implicit suggested or understood without being stated directly
explicit expressed in a way that is very clear and direct

HINT

Make sure you select information that is relevant to the question.

Question 5 is the final question of Section A. This comparison question is the longest and most complex and represents about half of the marks available in Section A.

5 STEPS TO SUCCESS

STEP 1: Remember that the essay that you write in response to the question will be comparative, based on both Text One and Text Two from the Extracts Booklet. One will be a text from the Anthology, the other will be a text that you have not seen before. The question is likely to focus on:

- the authors' ideas and perspectives on the event, experience or topic they write about
- the authors' use of language and structure.

STEP 2: Make sure that you focus on the question. Begin by stating what the texts are about, both explicitly and implicitly.

STEP 3: Make sure you refer to significant and relevant points of detail, as a very general answer will not be as successful. It is not enough to point things out and 'translate' the text; avoid retelling the story and make sure you explain the impact of the writer's choices. Ask yourself why the author might have used that information, sequence, word, phrase or sentence.

STEP 4: Draw clear links and contrasts between the texts. Depending on which texts you are given, you may also be able to draw contrasts and links within the texts as well. Make sure that you compare and contrast the texts by using words and phrases such as 'similarly', 'in comparison' or 'on the other hand'.

STEP 5: Quote briefly, using a single word or phrase, to support your comments. You may refer to a whole paragraph or long section, but do not copy it out in full. Show that you are quoting by using inverted commas. Because you should only use short quotations, you should integrate them into your sentences and introduce them with a comma or colon. Whenever you quote, always explain in your own words what the quotation means and comment on its effect, with particular focus on language and structure.

STARTING TO COMPARE

Touching the Void is an autobiography by Joe Simpson. Unusually for an autobiography, it is presented from both the perspective of Joe, and of his climbing partner, Simon Yates, in the first person.

Published in 2003, it is a true story of how he and Simon set out to become the first people to climb Siula Grande in Peru. However, the pair are involved in a terrible accident which results in Joe breaking his leg and becoming separated from his partner. Simon is forced to cut the rope connecting the pair as he believes Joe to be dead and this to be his only chance of survival.

Read the following extract that details the accident from both perspectives.

▼ FROM *TOUCHING THE VOID* BY JOE SIMPSON

Joe's account

I hit the slope at the base of the cliff before I saw it coming. I was facing into the slope and both knees locked as I struck it. I felt a shattering blow in my knee, felt bones splitting, and screamed. The impact catapulted me over backwards and down the slope of the East Face. I slid, head-first, on my back. The rushing speed of it confused me. I thought of the drop below but felt nothing. Simon would be ripped off the mountain. He couldn't hold this. I screamed again as I jerked to a sudden violent stop.

Everything was still, silent. My thoughts raced madly. Then pain flooded down my thigh – a fierce burning fire coming down the inside of my thigh, seeming to ball in my groin, building and building until I cried out at it, and my breathing came in ragged gasps. My leg!… My leg!

I hung, head down, on my back, left leg tangled in the rope above me and my right leg hanging slackly to one side. I lifted my head from the snow and stared, up across my chest, at a grotesque distortion in the right knee, twisting the leg into a strange zigzag. I didn't connect it with the pain which burnt my groin. That had nothing to do with my knee. I kicked my left leg free of the rope and swung round until I was hanging against the snow on my chest, feet down. The pain eased. I kicked my left foot into the slope and stood up.

A wave of nausea surged over me. I pressed my face into the snow, and the sharp cold seemed to calm me. Something terrible, something dark with dread occurred to me, and as I thought about it I felt the dark thought break into panic: 'I've broken my leg, that's it. I'm dead. Everyone said it… if there's just two of you a broken ankle could turn into a death sentence… if it's broken… if… It doesn't hurt so much, maybe I've just ripped something.'

I kicked my right leg against the slope, feeling sure it wasn't broken. My knee exploded. Bone grated, and the fireball rushed from groin to knee. I screamed. I looked down at the knee and could see it was broken, yet I tried not to believe what I was seeing. It wasn't just broken, it was ruptured, twisted, crushed, and I could see the kink in the joint and knew what had happened. The impact had driven my lower leg up through the knee joint. …

I dug my axes into the snow, and pounded my good leg deeply into the soft slope until I felt sure it wouldn't slip. The effort brought back the

▲ When climbing at high altitudes in ice and snow, specialised equipment is essential.

▶

Seria Norte A mountain in Peru.

breaking trail The process of making a trail through deep snow.

nausea and I felt my head spin giddily to the point of fainting. I moved and a searing spasm of pain cleared away the faintness. I could see the summit of Seria Norte away to the west. I was not far below it. The sight drove home how desperately things had changed. We were above 19,000 feet, still on the ridge, and very much alone. I looked south at the small rise I had hoped to scale quickly and it seemed to grow with every second that I stared. I would never get over it. Simon would not be able to get me up it. He would leave me. He had no choice. I held my breath, thinking about it. Left here? Alone?… For an age I felt overwhelmed at the notion of being left; I felt like screaming, and I felt like swearing, but stayed silent. If I said a word, I would panic. I could feel myself teetering on the edge of it.

Simon's account

Joe had disappeared behind a rise in the ridge and began moving faster than I could go. I was glad we had put the steep section behind us at last. … I felt tired and was grateful to be able to follow Joe's tracks instead of breaking trail.

I rested a while when I saw that Joe had stopped moving. Obviously he had found an obstacle and I thought I would wait until he started moving again. When the rope moved again I trudged forward after it, slowly.

Suddenly there was a sharp tug as the rope lashed out taut across the slope. I was pulled forward several feet as I pushed my axes into the snow and braced myself for another jerk. Nothing happened. I knew that Joe had fallen, but I couldn't see him, so I stayed put. I waited for about ten minutes until the tautened rope went slack on the snow and I felt sure that Joe had got his weight off me. I began to move along his footsteps cautiously, half expecting something else to happen. I kept tensed up and ready to dig my axes in at the first sign of trouble.

As I crested the rise, I could see down a slope to where the rope disappeared over the edge of a drop. I approached slowly, wondering what had happened. When I reached the top of the drop I saw Joe below me. He had one foot dug in and was leaning against the slope with his face buried in the snow. I asked him what had happened and he looked at me in surprise. I knew he was injured, but the significance didn't hit me at first.

He told me very calmly that he had broken his leg. He looked pathetic, and my immediate thought came without any emotion. … You're dead… no two ways about it! I think he knew it too. I could see it in his face. It was all totally rational. I knew where we were, I took in everything around me instantly, and knew he was dead. It never occurred to me that I might also die. I accepted without question that I could get off the mountain alone. I had no doubt about that.

… Below him I could see thousands of feet of open face falling into the eastern glacier bay. I watched him quite dispassionately. I couldn't help him, and it occurred to me that in all likelihood he would fall to his death. I wasn't disturbed by the thought. In a way I hoped he would fall. I knew I couldn't leave him while he was still fighting for it, but I had no idea how I might help him. I could get down. If I tried to get him down I might die with him. It didn't frighten me. It just seemed a waste. It would be pointless. I kept staring at him, expecting him to fall…

ACTIVITY 1   A03   SKILLS   ANALYSIS, INTERPRETATION

▼ COMPARING JOE AND SIMON'S ACCOUNTS

To help you to develop comparative skills, look back at the *Touching the Void* extract again in order to make comparisons within the text. Look at the notes below, tracking how Joe's account develops. Work with a partner to copy and complete the following table, exploring Simon's account.

▼ HOW DOES JOE DESCRIBE THIS EXPERIENCE?	▼ HOW DOES SIMON DESCRIBE THIS EXPERIENCE?
Joe's account focuses on pain and shock: agony, panic and fear. He is obsessed with pain and the extremity of the damage, using a triple structure of powerful and emotive verbs: 'it was ruptured, twisted, crushed'.	How does Simon describe Joe's injuries?
Joe uses sharp, onomatopoeic language to describe his accident: 'bones splitting' and 'shattering blow'.	How does Simon describe his experience of the moment Joe fell?
Joe uses blunt direct language to show the desperate situation he is facing: 'the impact had driven my lower leg up through the knee joint'; 'we were above 19,000 feet… and very much alone'.	How does Simon describe the situation they are facing?
Joe conveys his thoughts and feelings as he reflects on his situation using vocabulary choices with relentlessly negative connotations: 'something terrible, something dark with dread'; 'I felt the dark thought break into panic'.	What do the language choices in Simon's account suggest about his thoughts and feelings?
At the end of his account, Joe's panic is conveyed in a series of short, single clause and minor sentences, and rhetorical questions, suggesting rapid thought and a sense of growing fear, building tension for the reader.	What does the use of sentence structure suggest about Simon's thoughts and feelings at the end of his account?

EXAM-STYLE QUESTION

A03

SKILLS   CRITICAL THINKING, ANALYSIS, INTERPRETATION, DECISION MAKING

Compare and contrast Joe and Simon's attitudes towards the accident described in the extract from *Touching the Void*. Support your answer with detailed examples, including brief quotations. **(22 marks)**

ACTIVITY 2   A01   A02   A03   SKILLS ▶ CRITICAL THINKING, REASONING, DECISION MAKING

KEY POINT

REMEMBER: This task will help you to develop your comparison skills. In your exam, Question 5 will ask you to compare **two** writers' ideas and perspectives in **two** separate non-fiction texts.

▼ MEETING ASSESSMENT OBJECTIVES

Read the two students' responses to the exam-style question above. How well do you think they meet the following assessment objectives?

■ AO1: showing understanding of the texts, selecting and interpreting significant information, ideas and perspectives

■ AO2: showing understanding and analysis of how writers use language and structure to achieve their effects

■ AO3: exploring links and connections between writers' ideas and perspectives, as well as how these are conveyed

▶

▲ Joe Simpson's is a great story of mountaineering survival.

EXAMPLE STUDENT ANSWER A

Joe's account of the climb is cool and calm and doesn't spare us the grim details of the injury that he sustained earlier in the climb: 'I felt a shattering blow in my knee, felt bones splitting, and screamed'. This shows that he isn't really too badly affected currently by his ordeal. In Simon's account he is also very matter of fact about the experiences of Siula Grande, but the way in which he presents it isn't so horrific. As if he isn't really there and is just doing a commentary on someone else climbing the mountain.

Joe's account of the climb uses a lot more exciting language and a richer vocabulary to keep the reader interested: 'Everything was still, silent. My thoughts raced madly'. Whereas Simon's account only uses very simple language and is more factual rather than exciting: 'I rested a while when I saw that Joe had stopped moving'. I think this suggests that Joe is perhaps more experienced at writing or was more affected by the incident on the Siula Grande.

In conclusion I think that there really aren't that many differences between the two accounts. I think this is because they are both about the same incident and are both written by the two climbers who were involved.

EXAMPLE STUDENT ANSWER B

This extract consists of two first person narratives giving different perspectives on the same event, however the two writers show very different attitudes to the accident.

Although both accounts describe the same event, they have a very different structure and focus. Joe's begins with the accident, creating an explosive and dramatic introduction. It then focuses on his pain and his fear about the situation that he and Simon are in. Simon's account builds up much more slowly to the moment where he realises that Joe is hurt. This creates tension for the reader because we know what Simon is going to see, but he doesn't. The second part of Simon's account focuses much more closely on the situation they are in and the dilemma he is facing.

Joe's account uses much more emotive, dramatic vocabulary choices than Simon's. For example, Joe describes the pain as a 'fierce burning

▶

fire' while Simon simply, clearly and calmly states 'I knew he was injured'. The language choice in the two accounts highlights Joe's pain and suffering and Simon's more analytical thinking about the situation.

Both writers reflect on the difficult situation they are in. Joe's thoughts are conveyed in short, minor and simple sentences, suggesting his panic and confusion. He uses ellipses to suggest his thoughts racing and wandering. Simon also uses ellipses at the end of his accounts: 'I kept staring at him expecting him to fall…'. The ellipsis here has a different effect. It helps to build tension and engages the reader by making them wonder what will happen next.

Joe's account is extremely dramatic whereas Simon aims to achieve more tension as he calmly thinks about the life-and-death choices he must make. The reader is more likely to sympathise with Joe's emotive account and may not feel much sympathy for Simon's cold, calculating approach.

HINT

You must COMPARE and CONTRAST. To do this, use phrases that show you are comparing, such as, 'in comparison', 'in contrast', 'similarly', 'however'.

ACTIVITY 3   **A03**   **SKILLS**   CRITICAL THINKING, ANALYSIS, INTERPRETATION, DECISION MAKING

▼ HOW WRITERS PRESENT THEIR IDEAS

Choose two Anthology texts that are linked in some way. For example:
- 'Explorers or boys messing about?' and *127 Hours* both focus on dramatic accidents.
- 'Young and Dyslexic?' and *Chinese Cinderella* both focus on experiences growing up.

Compare and contrast how the writers present their ideas and perspectives about the experiences described.

You should support your answer with detailed examples from both texts. **(22 marks)**

You should consider the writer's intentions, ideas and attitudes, their choice of structure, language and sentence structure, and its impact on the reader.

KEY POINT

Both the extracts involve the same events but there are differences in perspective and choice of detail that reflect the different priorities of each writer.

LEARNING OBJECTIVES

This lesson will help you to:
- practise and perfect skills to respond effectively to unseen non-fiction in the exam.

SELECTING EVIDENCE

You will need to select quotations in order to support your points quickly, under exam conditions. It is important that the quotations that you use are short and directly relevant to your point.

HINT

The most effective quotations are short, focusing on language choices that you can explore and analyse.

ACTIVITY 1   **A02**   **SKILLS**   CRITICAL THINKING, ANALYSIS

▼ SELECTING SHORT, FOCUSED EVIDENCE

Read the extract from *Touching the Void* on pages 163–164. Look at this short extract from one student's analysis of Joe's account:

> The writer makes the accident feel dramatic: 'The impact catapulted me over backwards and down the slope of the East Face. I slid, head-first, on my back.' The use of the dramatic verb 'catapulted' suggests the speed and force of Joe's fall, creating a powerful image in the reader's mind.

1 How short can you make this student's quotation without making the paragraph any less effective?

2 Effective evidence shows where and how the writer has achieved their intentions. Which of these intentions are achieved in Joe's account? Which are achieved in Simon's account?

- to describe excruciating pain
- to show fear and panic
- to show calm analysis of the situation
- to highlight the danger they are in
- to create tension

3 Now look again at Joe and Simon's accounts. Identify a word, phrase or sentence in which the writer successfully achieves the intentions you have identified. How do the writer's choices of language and structure help them to achieve their intention?

Use your answers to complete tables like the ones below.

Joe's account

▼ INTENTIONS	▼ EVIDENCE	
	Short, relevant quotations	Language or sentence structure choice
To describe pain		Emotive language

Simon's account

▼ INTENTIONS	▼ EVIDENCE	
	Short, relevant quotations	Language or sentence structure choice

ACTIVITY 2　A02　SKILLS ▸ ANALYSIS

▼ BEAT THE CLOCK!

You have three minutes to find an example of each of the following techniques in the *Touching the Void* extract on pages 163–164:

- ellipsis
- exclamation mark
- direct speech
- emotive language
- rhetorical question
- minor sentence.

ACTIVITY 3　A02　SKILLS ▸ CRITICAL THINKING, ANALYSIS, INTERPRETATION

▼ USING EVIDENCE

Look at three short sections from the *Touching the Void* extract below.

> Then pain flooded down my thigh – a fierce burning fire coming down the inside of my thigh, seeming to ball in my groin, building and building until I cried out at it, and my breathing came in ragged gasps. My leg!… My leg!

> I held my breath, thinking about it. Left here? Alone?… For an age I felt overwhelmed at the notion of being left; I felt like screaming, and I felt like swearing, but stayed silent. If I said a word, I would panic.

> I could get down. If I tried to get him down I might die with him. It didn't frighten me. It just seemed a waste. It would be pointless. I kept staring at him, expecting him to fall…

In each section, identify:

- the writer's intention
- any significant features of language or sentence structure choice the writer has made to help them achieve their intention.

Use your ideas to write three paragraphs. In each paragraph, aim to:

- make a clear point stating the writer's intention
- support your point with a short, focused quotation
- analyse the impact of the language or sentence structure choices you have identified.

▲ 'I kept staring at him, expecting him to fall…'

EXAM-STYLE QUESTIONS

A01

SKILLS ▸ ANALYSIS, CRITICAL THINKING, INTERPRETATION

1　Select **two** words or phrases that describe why Simon almost hopes that Joe falls.　**(2 marks)**

2　**In your own words**, explain why Simon is feeling good at the beginning of his account.　**(4 marks)**

LEARNING OBJECTIVES

This lesson will help you to:
- prepare for Section A of the Paper 1 exam.

PUTTING IT INTO PRACTICE

You should prepare for Section A of the Paper 1 exam by answering questions on an unprepared non-fiction reading extract (Text 1) and questions on an extract from the Anthology (Text 2). Text 1 could be drawn from a range of contemporary non-fiction, including autobiography, travel writing, reportage, media articles, letters, diary entries and opinion pieces.

PREPARING FOR THE EXAM: NEED TO KNOW

HINT

Timing is crucial for exam success. As one of the texts will be unfamiliar, you should give Section A more time than Section B, being very careful to leave yourself enough time to complete the paper. It is recommended that you spend 15 minutes reading the extracts, leaving one hour and 15 minutes for Section A and 45 minutes for Section B.

- All questions are compulsory.
- Questions will test reading skills: factual comprehension; inference and an understanding of how writers use language; analysis of how writers use linguistic and structural devices to achieve effect.
- The pattern of questioning consists of short, specific questions on Text 1, followed by a longer question focusing on analysis of the use of language and structure in Text 2, and a comparative question drawing on both texts.
- Questions will be phrased so that they are understandable and clear. The shorter questions will be more factually-based and phrased more directly, for example, 'Select two words or phrases that describe…' or 'Explain what we learn about…'. Questions 4 and 5 are longer and will require more thought and analysis, for example, 'How does the writer use language and structure to describe…'.
- Section A is worth 50% of the total marks for Paper 1.
- Anthologies may not be taken into the exam, but the relevant extract will be reprinted in the Extracts Booklet that you will get with your exam paper.
- Further examples can be found in the Pearson Edexcel exemplar assessment materials.

EXAM-STYLE QUESTIONS

A01	SKILLS	ANALYSIS
A01	SKILLS	CRITICAL THINKING, INTERPRETATION
A01	SKILLS	CRITICAL THINKING, ANALYSIS, INTERPRETATION
A02	SKILLS	CRITICAL THINKING, ANALYSIS, REASONING, INTERPRETATION
A03	SKILLS	CRITICAL THINKING, ANALYSIS, INTERPRETATION, DECISION MAKING

Read the extract from *How the Poor Die* by George Orwell (pages 158–160).

1 Select two words or phrases that describe the patient known as 'Numéro 57'. **(2 marks)**

2 **In your own words**, explain what the writer's thoughts and feelings are towards the other patients. **(4 marks)**

3 Describe what we learn about the writer's character from his thoughts about the other patients and how he describes them. You may support your points with brief quotations. **(5 marks)**

4 Remind yourself of the extract from *A Passage to Africa* (pages 104–105). How does the writer use language and structure to present his views about his experiences as a television reporter in Somalia? You should support your answer with close reference to the extract, including brief quotations. **(12 marks)**

5 [Question 5 is based on both *How the Poor Die* and *A Passage to Africa*.] Compare how the writers present their ideas and perspectives about their experiences. Support your answer with detailed examples from both texts. **(22 marks)**

ANSWERS

1 One mark each for any of the following: 'wasted', 'Utterly uninterested', 'colourless eyes', 'like a piece of antique china', 'about sixty', 'astonishingly shrunken', 'pale as vellum', 'shrunken away', 'his face… seemed no bigger than a doll's'.

2 Marks will be awarded for any reasonable interpretation of the writer's thoughts and feelings, in your own words where possible. One mark each for examples including (up to a maximum of two):

- sadness at the tragedy of the suffering that he sees
- horror at the squalor of the environment and the dehumanising treatment of the patients
- astonishment at his left-hand neighbour's illness
- sympathy towards the old veteran with the apparently scheming relatives.

3 As the question is worth five marks, aim to make five points about the writer's character. You do not have to include quotations, but they may help to support your points. Remember to keep quotations short. Answers may include:

- the writer is a curious person who is interested in everything he sees around him, even things that are morbid or disgusting, which you can see from the detailed descriptions of the other patients' illnesses
- the writer is a sympathetic person who pities Numéro 57 and the way in which he dies ('poor old wretch'/'merely a number')
- the writer is truthful; he would like to be idealistic or romantic about the actions of the patients ('his dying blessing') but reports what actually happens ('But no…')
- the writer is not squeamish or easily upset by horrible sights ('I had time for a good look').

4 Marks awarded for discussion of the writer's presentation of a war-torn country in the autobiographical account, considering how information is conveyed; structure; viewpoint and tone.

Read the following sample student answer and then consider the examiner's comments.

▲ Orwell was fascinated by the other patients at the hospital and wrote eloquently about what he witnessed in *How the Poor Die*.

the way he focuses on particular individuals and their tragedies. This shows an understanding of structure, and the different possibilities of writing about this subject.

He describes the death of the ten year-old Habiba… Here, the student begins to explore language and its effect. Is there anything else you could say about this quotation to show a deeper analysis?

He builds shocking images of the terrible sights he saw… This is an excellent point; sensory description is a key feature of this text.

drawing attention to a particular moment or sight. The student shows insight into structure again here.

George Alagiah has clearly been powerfully affected by what he saw in Somalia. He wants to make his readers see what terrible conditions existed there and how fortunate we are to live in such a different world. He also shows that journalists often just start out by looking for the best stories they can find. But in this case, the stories affected him on a deeply emotional level.

The most powerful effect of Alagiah's writing is the way he focuses on particular individuals and their tragedies. He describes the death of the ten year-old Habiba in a graphic way: 'No rage, no whimpering, just a passing away'. He builds shocking images of the terrible sights he saw but also uses the other senses to convey the horror, as when he writes: 'the smell of decaying flesh'.

One of the striking ways he presents his experiences is by drawing attention to a particular moment or sight. He does this especially when writing about the smile of the unknown man. His translator's explanation that he was 'embarrassed to be found in this condition' disturbed him and he could not get it out of his mind. He also realises that he never even found the man's name, and feels guilty about that, too. He almost seems ashamed of his life as a journalist and the way in which he was normally able to report on such events in a detached way. Overall, Alagiah communicates to the reader the way in which people in that situation lack basic necessities and human respect. However, he also reflects on how he felt to be witnessing and reporting on these events.

EXAMINER'S COMMENTS

This is a well-focused response that makes very thoughtful points about the writer's views and experiences. There are excellent examples focusing on the detail of Alagiah's language.

HINT

Aim for economical and relevant use of quotation in Questions 4 and 5.
Avoid drifting away from the topic or question – for example, by projecting modern ideas about health care onto your reading of the hospital extract.

SUBJECT VOCABULARY

travelogue a book that describes a travel experience

5 Reward responses that compare how the writers present their ideas about their experiences.

Responses may include the following elements or points.

- Both texts describe a memorable experience from a retrospective first-person perspective.

- Both texts describe events seen from an adult's perspective.

- *How the Poor Die* begins with a short narrative sentence about how the writer comes to see the things that he goes on to report to the reader ('After some days…'). The second sentence then focuses on immediate descriptive details ('stuffy room'; 'narrow beds') rather than looking ahead to the deeper reflections that Orwell will discuss later. In comparison, *A Passage to Africa* begins with a list ('hungry, lean, scared and betrayed'), a rhetorical device that emphasises the overwhelmingly difficult conditions of Somalia.

- *How the Poor Die* has a shocking, abrupt title that leads the reader to expect a description of a death and makes the text sound like a matter-of-fact report into the lives of the poor. On the other hand, the title of *A Passage to Africa* makes the reader expect to read a travelogue about a journey to or within Africa, but does not alert the reader to the horror of the writer's journey.

- Orwell uses metaphorical and figurative language in his descriptions to emphasise the points he is making ('as grooms are said to do with horses'; 'in just the attitude of a woman handling a rolling-pin'; 'flickered out like a candle-end'). In comparison, *A Passage to Africa* is written like a piece of journalism and uses careful, predominantly objective descriptions.

- The structure of both texts is quite similar, working slowly through descriptions of a number of characters but creating suspense: in *A Passage to Africa*, as the reader waits for the unforgettable face; in *How the Poor Die*, as the reader waits for a description of the deaths suggested by the title. Similarly, both texts end with searching reflections on humanity and life.

- Neither of the texts uses much direct speech. The only direct speech in *How the Poor Die* is that of the patient who announces the deaths of others ('Numéro 43!' and 'Numéro 57!'), which focuses the reader's attention on seeing and hearing everything through Orwell's eyes and ears, rather than hearing for themselves. Similarly, *A Passage to Africa* only uses direct speech to give directions to the hamlet, which makes it feel immediate, as though the reader could also navigate there using these directions.

ACTIVITY 1   **AO1**   SKILLS ▸ REASONING, COLLABORATION, COOPERATION, EMPATHY, NEGOTIATION

▼ CONSOLIDATING YOUR KNOWLEDGE

Imagine that the Pearson Edexcel exam board have asked a group of students to give them some feedback on their selection of Anthology texts. In groups of five, complete the following tasks.

1 Each of you should choose two or three of the pieces in the Anthology. Using your skimming and scanning skills, summarise what each piece is about.

2 Stage a group discussion to decide which three pieces are the most educational and should definitely stay in the Anthology.

3 Decide as a group which three pieces you would like removed from the Anthology. Make sure you give specific reasons for your choices.

4 Working individually, research and choose one other non-fiction text you would like to be included in the Anthology. Why would you like this to be included? You may wish to include newspaper and magazine articles and autobiographies or biographies.

5 Share your ideas with the rest of your group. Your group of five can only include three new pieces to replace those that you have chosen to remove, which means that you will need to persuade others in your group to choose your suggested piece. Now hold a vote on which three pieces should be included.

6 Debate the following statements, with two of the group arguing for each statement, and three arguing against.

■ 'The Anthology extracts are negative tales of hardship or danger.'

■ 'It is not necessary to give young people a say in what they study; teachers will always make better decisions for them.'

HINT

In every non-fiction text you encounter in the exam, you will need to consider language and structure and how the writers present their ideas. Think about how best to compare these things in the given texts when working under exam conditions.

ACTIVITY 2   **AO1**   **AO2**   **AO3**   SKILLS ▸ CRITICAL THINKING, CREATIVITY

▼ TOP TEN EXAM TIPS

Imagine that you are the teacher in charge of your class. Can you write your own top ten exam tips for Section A?

▲ What are your top ten exam tips?

LEARNING OBJECTIVES

This lesson will help you to:

- understand what is meant by 'transactional writing'.

AN INTRODUCTION TO TRANSACTIONAL WRITING

Transactional writing is non-fiction writing for a purpose: to inform, explain, review, argue, persuade or advise. Each task will require you to write for a primary purpose and one or more secondary purposes. For example, the primary purpose of an information text is to give information, but it could involve explaining the reasons for something and some description. Section B of Paper 1 will give you a choice of one of two transactional writing tasks. You will have about an hour to plan and write it and it is worth half of the total marks for the whole paper. The topic will not require any specialised knowledge. Topics might include aspects of school life, transport and travel, common leisure activities, such as sports, and the internet or aspects of the media.

TYPES OF TRANSACTIONAL WRITING

▲ Gamers need informative texts.

The six types of transactional writing covered in Section B of the paper can be defined as follows:

- To **inform**: to pass on information (this includes descriptive writing)
- To **explain**: to make clear how or why something is as it is
- To **review**: to outline a piece of work, or an event, and comment on it
- To **argue**: to produce a logical sequence of reasons to support a point of view
- To **persuade**: to convince an audience or reader to think or act in a certain way
- To **advise**: to give useful suggestions and ideas to help someone or some people.

ACTIVITY 1   **A01**   **A02**   **A04**   **A05**   **SKILLS** ▷ CRITICAL THINKING, PROBLEM SOLVING, ANALYSIS, ADAPTIVE WRITING

▼ TEXTS WITH DIFFERENT PURPOSES

1 Read the following extracts from texts with different purposes. Identify the language features that are used in each text to help it achieve its purpose.

- **Inform**: A videogame console is an interactive entertainment computer or electronic device that produces a video display signal which can be used with a display device (a television, computer monitor, etc.) to display a videogame.
- **Persuade**: Oculus changes the way you play by maximising the fun and minimising the fuss. The Quest VR headset makes you feel less like a player and more like you're in the game.
- **Explain**: Why do we play videogames? The need for play is a primary component of human development and has been with us since the dawn of intelligence. Even in the brains of animals can be seen the impetus that leads to play. So, before we tackle videogaming, we should assess why we, as a species, need playtime so strongly.

2 Choose a video game, television programme or book that you particularly like. Write three short paragraphs like the paragraphs above. One should inform your reader, one should persuade your reader, and one should explain to your reader.

ACTIVITY 2 **A01** **SKILLS** CRITICAL THINKING

▼ TYPES OF TRANSACTIONAL WRITING

Look back over the following texts from the Anthology, then copy and complete the table. Which types of transactional writing can you find in each text?

	▼ INFORM	▼ EXPLAIN	▼ REVIEW	▼ ARGUE	▼ PERSUADE	▼ ADVISE
From 'The Danger of a Single Story' by Chimamanda Ngozi Adichie						
From *A Passage to Africa* by George Alagiah						
'Explorers or boys messing about?' by Steven Morris						
'Young and dyslexic?' by Benjamin Zephaniah						
From *Chinese Cinderella* by Adeline Yen Mah						

ACTIVITY 3 **A04** **SKILLS** CRITICAL THINKING

▼ PLANNING FOR DIFFERENT PURPOSES

When you plan your response to a transactional writing task, it can be helpful to think about the different purposes you will aim to achieve. For example. the primary purpose of the exam-style question below is to present an **argument**. However, you will almost certainly need to achieve other purposes.

▶ **'Some experts believe that a school uniform creates more problems than it solves and should be abolished in all schools.'**

   Give your views on this topic, arguing either in favour of school uniform or against it. Your argument may include:

   ■ **the advantages and disadvantages of uniforms**

   ■ **the potential problems caused by uniforms**

   ■ **any other points you wish to make.**

You might **describe** a typical school uniform.

You could **explain** why these are advantages or disadvantages.

You might **describe** the kinds of problems they cause.

Look at the exam-style questions below. What is the primary purpose that a response should aim to achieve? What secondary purposes might the response also achieve?

▶ **A young person from another country is coming to spend a term at your school or college. Write to inform them about your school or college and what happens in an ordinary day there.**

▶ **Write an article for your school magazine explaining how you made your decisions about your examination subjects.**

LEARNING OBJECTIVES

This lesson will help you to:

- understand in more detail the features of writing to inform, explain and review, and how you can achieve these writing purposes.

WRITING FOR A PURPOSE: INFORM, EXPLAIN, REVIEW

In many ways, writing to inform is the most straightforward writing task. Its main requirements are that it should be accurate, clear and well organised. Explanation also involves giving information, of course, but there is a greater need to select the information required and organise it so that you explain the topic clearly. A review informs you about a product or event and gives you a reasoned opinion on it.

WRITING TO INFORM

In informative text, it is important to think about your readers and make sure that they will be able to understand what you write.

▲ Informative writing is in some ways the most straightforward writing task, but does have its own challenges.

ACTIVITY 1   A02   SKILLS ▶ ADAPTIVE LEARNING, CREATIVITY

▼ FEATURES OF EFFECTIVE INFORMATIVE WRITING

Read the following question and sample student response.

▶ A young person from another country is coming to spend a term at your school or college. Write to inform them about your school or college and what happens in an ordinary day there.

> Dear Emilja,
>
> Our school is called New City High School. The school has been built on the outskirts of our town and it is quite a new building. The school has 1200 young people from the age of 11 up to 18. The school site has been landscaped and there are lawns and trees on it. There are playgrounds and sports facilities which are very popular.
>
> The day starts at 8.30 am. Most students get there by bus and walk up from the bus turning point outside the school gates. Registration is from 8.30 until 8.45 with your form teacher. All sorts of things go on in registration time. You can hand in notes if you have been off sick, or money if you are paying to go on a school trip. Some days you can go out to the library and return your books. On Tuesday and Friday there is assembly in the hall. This is where we have a speech from the Headteacher and sometimes she gives out prizes and cups to the sports teams that have won. We might have some music if the choir or the school bands have practised something to play to the school.
>
> Following that lesson 1 starts at 8.45 and what you have will depend upon your timetable and what day it is.

> Students are supposed to line up outside classrooms if the teacher is not there. When the teacher arrives you are supposed to: go in quietly; stand behind your chair; wait until the teacher has said 'good morning'; and then you can sit down. Outdoor coats should not be worn in class. Students are supposed to take them off and put them on the back of the chair. There is a cloakroom where they can be left but most students don't because it is not very convenient.
>
> Yours sincerely,
>
> Takuma

Is the information given in this response clear and easy to understand? Which of the features of information writing below help achieve this? Copy the table below, adding examples.

▼ FEATURE	▼ EXAMPLE
An engaging and interesting selection of information	
Each paragraph is focused on one aspect of the topic	
The text has a logical structure, clearly guiding the reader, for example, with time references (e.g. firstly, later, at 1pm) and/or with subheadings	
Precise vocabulary choices	
Sentences structured to express ideas and information clearly, not for effect	
Facts and statistics, not opinions	

Which secondary purposes could the writer have aimed to achieve to make their writing even more effective, interesting and engaging? For example, consider whether the writing would be more engaging and effective if the writer had decided to:

- **explain** some of the reasons why the school does these things
- **describe** aspects of the school day
- **argue** that some aspects of the school needed to be changed
- **persuade** the reader to be on time for school
- **advise** the new student on ways to be organised
- **review** some of the positive and negative aspects of the school.

HINT

The primary purpose of this text is to inform. Which of these secondary purposes would help to inform the reader?

WRITING TO EXPLAIN

Any question that contains the word 'how' or 'why' expects you to do some sort of explanation. Use clear paragraphs to organise your response. In the 45 minutes that you will have in the exam, you will probably have time to include four to six paragraphs. Try to link your paragraphs using signposting words such as 'firstly', 'therefore' and 'in addition'.

ACTIVITY 2   **A04**   **A05**   **SKILLS** ▶ PROBLEM SOLVING, ADAPTIVE LEARNING, CREATIVITY, INNOVATION

▼ EXPLAIN YOURSELF

A magazine is inviting articles for a new column with the title 'Why I enjoy…'. Write an article to send to the magazine, explaining why you enjoy something you like to do.

You could choose:

- playing or watching a sport
- a hobby or interest
- something else.

Aim to give **three** reasons explaining why you enjoy it.

ACTIVITY 3   **A04**   **A05**   **SKILLS** ▶ CRITICAL THINKING, ANALYSIS, INTERPRETATION

▼ FEATURES OF EXPLANATORY WRITING

Look at the response you wrote to Activity 2 above. How many of these features of explanatory writing have you included? Copy and complete the table, adding examples from your writing and noting their effect.

▼ EXPLAIN FEATURES	▼ EXAMPLE	▼ EFFECT
Texts focus on explaining 'how' or 'why'		
Ideas and information are selected to interest and engage the reader		
Texts use features such as paragraphs, bullet points, bold font and subheadings to guide the reader and make meaning clear		
Texts are clearly signposted to guide the reader, (for example, 'firstly')		
Texts use conjunctions to explain cause and effect (for example, 'because')		
Texts may use technical or specialist vocabulary		
Texts may express opinions and be less formal than an information text		

ACTIVITY 4   **A04**   **A05**   **SKILLS** ▶ ADAPTIVE LEARNING, CREATIVITY

▼ ADAPTING YOUR LANGUAGE FOR CHILDREN

Try writing the same piece that you wrote in response to Activity 2 for a group of 11-year-olds. How would you adapt your language for them?

WRITING TO REVIEW

Like any text, reviews need to be well written in order to engage the reader. Since reviews are written for commercial publications, such as newspapers, their register can change depending on the readership: if the readers are teenagers, the language will probably be more colloquial and 'teenager-friendly'.

If you are asked to write a review in Section B, it could be about a book, a film, an event or a video game of your own choice. As part of the review, you should give the positive or negative aspects of the subject that you have chosen and the impact it had on you.

▶ **Look back at the review of *No Time to Die* on page 75 and write a short subheading for each paragraph, summarising what it is about. You could write them as questions. For example, most films reviews will answer questions like:**

- What's it about?
- Is it any good?
- Was it enjoyable to watch?
- Was any part of it surprising or new?

KEY POINT

Although a review gives a personal view, readers need to trust your opinions, so be sure to support them with examples and evidence.

▲ A film reviewer evaluates a film and also offers personal opinions about it.

| ACTIVITY 6 | A04 | **SKILLS** ▷ CRITICAL THINKING, PROBLEM SOLVING |

▼ STRUCTURING A REVIEW

Think of a film that you have enjoyed recently and use the table below to plan a review of it in no more than **five** paragraphs. Look at your subheadings for the *No Time to Die* review for guidance. You could write about the story, the characters, the acting, the visual elements (settings, cinematography, effects), the music and anything else you like or disliked about the film.

Paragraph 1	
Paragraph 2	
Paragraph 3	
Paragraph 4	
Paragraph 5	

Which other purposes will you need to achieve in your writing? In which section? Add them to your plan.

| inform | explain | describe | persuade | advise | argue |

LEARNING OBJECTIVES

This lesson will help you to:
- develop your skills in writing to argue, writing to persuade and writing to advise.

WRITING FOR A PURPOSE: ARGUE, PERSUADE, ADVISE

In each of these types of writing, the aim is to influence the reader using various techniques. There are many kinds of 'argue' question, but they will generally ask you to do one or both of the following:
- present reasons, with evidence, in support of (or against) a viewpoint
- develop a point of view.

WRITING TO ARGUE

A typical 'argue' exam question might be:

'Some experts believe that a school uniform creates more problems than it solves and should be abolished in all schools.'

Give your views on this topic, arguing either in favour of school uniform or against it. Your argument may include:
- the advantages and disadvantages of uniforms
- the potential problems caused by uniforms
- any other points you wish to make.

(45 marks)

Look at the following students' attempts to begin an answer to this question.

EXAMPLE STUDENT ANSWER A

Some experts say school uniform creates more problems than it solves, i am going to tell u my views. My first opinion about school uniform is very clear and I am against the school uniform, School uniforms are horrible, i hate ours. Teachers say that it is smart but i couldn't disagree more. It makes me look fat. And the colour is soo bad it makes u feel ill. There are lots of other reasons why it is rubbish e.g. it is not cheap and it is not good kwality, they say that school uniform makes us look the same so nobody can tell the difference between rich kidz and poor kidz, but u can becos the rich ones still make there uniform look like designer wear always.
School uniform makes us look like zombies.

EXAMPLE STUDENT ANSWER B

School uniform should not be abolished. It makes our school and the students who go to the school look neat and tidy. It shows that we are members of the school community and we are proud to be a part of it. This is important as it helps the local community respect the school and its students.

It could be argued that uniform makes all students look the same and suggests that the school does not treat us as individuals. However, it is what we do at school that makes us individuals: the work we put in, the sports we play and the friends we make. Uniform shows that we are a group of individuals and also part of the school.

▲ Does school uniform create more problems than it solves?

KEY POINT

Whether you agree or disagree with the writer's views, it is the quality of the writer's choices that makes an argument effective.

> Moreover, uniform also has very practical advantages. For instance, we have different ties in our school for prefects and for other students. This is useful when prefects do their duties because they are easily identifiable.

▶ **Which answer is more effective? Why? Note down as many reasons as you can.**

ACTIVITY 1 **AO3** **SKILLS** CRITICAL THINKING, DECISION MAKING

▼ WHAT MAKES AN ARGUMENT EFFECTIVE?

Read the 10 statements given in the following table. Five apply to Answer A and five to Answer B. After reading each statement, put a tick in the correct column depending on whether you think the statement applies to Answer A or Answer B.

▼ STATEMENT	▼ ANSWER A	▼ ANSWER B
Sentences are badly punctuated and there are several spelling mistakes.		
A wide range of words and sentence structures is used to engage the reader.		
Text speak, abbreviations and slang are inappropriately used.		
The first sentence repeats the question and there is a limited range of vocabulary and sentence structures.		
It is clearly and logically structured in paragraphs, each making a relevant point.		
The register is appropriately formal and and ideas are carefully linked by words and phrases.		
The register is too informal and ideas are not linked clearly.		
The structure is unclear and illogical and there are no paragraphs.		
The spelling, punctuation and grammar are correct.		
Points are supported with reasons and evidence is given for them.		

WRITING TO PERSUADE

To persuade means trying to influence someone to:

■ accept a point of view

■ behave in a certain way.

The first type of question might ask you to argue persuasively in favour of a statement in a class debate (for example, 'Mobile phones should be banned in all schools'). The second type of question might ask you to write a letter to persuade one or more people to do something (for example, take part in a charity event).

If you want to persuade someone successfully, you will need to use a strong argument, but you will be even more successful if you use language to make them agree with you.

KEY POINT

You can persuade with the ideas in your argument, but you make your writing more persuasive through your choice of language.

Persuasive writing techniques include:

■ linking your ideas with words that connect and develop them, such as, 'moreover', 'furthermore', 'in addition', 'on the other hand'

■ using words like 'this' or 'these' to link new paragraphs with previous paragraphs

■ emotive language choices to add impact to your views and highlight the reasons the reader needs to change their views or behaviour

■ rhetorical devices to engage and influence the reader.

ACTIVITY 2 | **A02** | **SKILLS** CRITICAL THINKING, INTERPRETATION

▼ ANSWERING A 'PERSUADE' QUESTION

Here is an example of a persuasive speech in answer to the following question.

▶ **Write a speech to persuade the school leaders to redecorate the school.**

> I am here today to tell you that I believe there should be many changes to help students. I know that these ideas will cost a lot of money but I reckon they will greatly improve the facilities and the atmosphere.
>
> First I believe we should redecorate the school. If we made the place look more pleasant then students will be happier and they will work better too. In particular the toilets are in urgent need of refurbishment. It would be a good idea to introduce some new subjects in the curriculum that are more relevant to the students. Teaching methods need to be looked at, so that students can have more modern ways of learning things.
>
> You could also look into methods of making people want to come to school. Perhaps you could give special privileges to students who regularly attend. The school rules need to be looked at as many are out of date. Why not have a special area set aside for smokers, as long as they bring a letter from their parents?

What do you think of this speech? Using the questions below to help you, identify the strengths and weakness of this speech, and make some suggestions on how the writer could improve it.

■ Is the register appropriately formal?

■ Is the opening effective and engaging?

■ Are the ideas clear and logically structured?

■ Are the ideas supported with evidence and further detail?

■ Is the writer's language choice persuasive?

■ Will it influence the school leaders?

■ Is it clearly and accurately written?

WRITING TO ADVISE

People ask for and give advice almost every day. This advice is often personal: *I think you should… I wouldn't if I was you…* Your response to an advise task in your exam will be more structured and more formal. You could be asked to:

■ give helpful opinions, suggestions or information to a specified person or group of people

■ recommend a course of action to someone, perhaps guiding or warning them.

A question may be worded to combine both these possibilities, but the advice will almost always be targeted at a specific audience or reader.

▲ Advising someone involves trying to influence them.

'Writing to advise' is linked to 'writing to argue and persuade'. In each of them, the writer is trying to influence the reader, so viewpoint, persuasion, evidence, and reasoning all play a part.

ACTIVITY 3 **A04** **A05** SKILLS ▶ PROBLEM SOLVING, ADAPTIVE LEARNING, CREATIVITY, INNOVATION

▼ ANSWERING AN 'ADVISE' QUESTION

Imagine you are an expert who gives advice on a website. Write your replies to these questions from a teenager and a parent.

> Hello,
>
> I am being bullied by some people in my form at school. They aren't hitting me, they're just calling me names and I'm fed up with it. What can I do?
> Mohammed

> Hello,
>
> My fourteen-year-old daughter seems to spend all her time on social media. I am really worried about her. I don't understand it. How can I help her?
> Mrs P

ACTIVITY 4 **A02** SKILLS ▶ CRITICAL THINKING

▼ ANALYSING AN ANSWER

Look at this exam-style question and the first part of an example student answer. How good do you think this answer is?

▶ **You have been asked to speak to younger students at your school or college, giving advice on how to cope with exams. Write the talk you would give.**

> To some people, examinations are the most difficult situation to go through. Others find them easy, an opportunity to show off what they have learned. Whichever category you believe that you fall into, it really does not matter. The idea is to realise which category you fall into then understand how to conquer your weaknesses and maximise your strengths. However, what I tell you today will be useful for all of you. The first stage for any examination is to prepare for it. If you fail to prepare, you prepare to fail. It really is as simple as that…

ACTIVITY 5 **A04** **A05** SKILLS ▶ PROBLEM SOLVING, ADAPTIVE LEARNING, CREATIVITY

▼ WRITING A SPEECH

Write your own speech in answer to the question in Activity 4. Your speech should be about 350–400 words long.

LEARNING OBJECTIVES

This lesson will help you to:
- understand how to write for different audiences.

WRITING FOR AN AUDIENCE

Writers need to think carefully about their audience: who will be reading it? As a writer, you need to make decisions about such things as register, style and tone, all of which will depend on your audience.

HINT

It is useful to think about your audience as it will help you make important decisions. However, in the Section B tasks in the exam, a target audience will not be specified and you will be expected to write for a general readership.

▲ 'Certain gases that trap heat are building up in Earth's atmosphere…'

ACTIVITY 1   **A01**   **A02**   **SKILLS** ▷ CRITICAL THINKING, ANALYSIS, INTERPRETATION

▼ **THINKING ABOUT YOUR AUDIENCE**

Consider the following extracts about climate change. What audience do you think each one is written for?

1 Highlight any words or phrases that are particularly suitable for the audience.

2 Circle words and phrases that show the register of the piece of writing.

3 List the decisions that the writer has made to make the writing suitable for the intended audience.

EXTRACT A

Certain gases that trap heat are building up in Earth's atmosphere. The primary culprit is carbon dioxide, released from burning coal, oil and natural gas in power plants, cars, factories etc. (and to a lesser extent when forests are cleared). The second is methane, released from rice paddies, both ends of cows, rotting garbage in landfills, mining operations, and gas pipelines. Third are chlorofluorocarbons (CFCs) and similar chemicals, which are also implicated in the separate problem of ozone depletion … Nitrous oxide (from fertilizers and other chemicals) is fourth…

EXTRACT B

People are seeing change all over the world. Arctic sea ice is melting earlier and forming later. Glaciers are disappearing. Heat waves, storms and floods are becoming more extreme. Insects are emerging sooner and flowers are blooming earlier. In some places, birds are laying eggs before they're expected and bears have stopped hibernating.

EXTRACT C

So what's going on?

For real, all it takes is a couple degrees
Before floods, droughts, and hurricanes are not anomalies
And all these catastrophes become our new realities
Comin' down on the world just like the Sword of Damocles.

We need smarter ideas for sustainable policies
New technologies for a new green economy.
New discoveries, and new questions to ask
'Cuz we can figure out the future by examining the past.

So we sail to the Poles, and sample the extremes,
And drill into the ice, and discover what it means.
So use that brain, and make science a priority
And you can work on stopping global warming with authority.

ACTIVITY 2   A02   SKILLS ▸ ANALYSIS

▼ PERSUADING THE GENERAL PUBLIC

Read the following extract from the Royal Society for the Prevention of Cruelty to Animals (RSPCA), a British charity, which aims to persuade people to give money to the charity. As you read, think about the ways the writer uses language to appeal to the audience and persuade them to donate. When you have read it, copy and complete the table that follows.

Have you ever thought about how the RSPCA is truly amazing?

We've been saving animals from cruelty for nearly 200 years. We lead the world in showing how to live with animals in harmony and respect. And all because enough people in our country care about protecting animals from cruelty. Animals cannot speak out for themselves. So we do.

RSPCA inspectors have always been the most visible part of our work to prevent animals suffering. Today our 370 inspectors and animal welfare officers collect and rescue around 119,000 animals every year. It seems like people are conscious of animals' needs, and they are prepared to bring suffering animals to our attention.

Looking after pitilessly abused and abandoned animals, and finding them new homes is just part of the daily task we face. For instance, our 24-hour cruelty and advice line receives over 3,000 calls on average, every day, that's one call every 29 seconds. And each week our inspectors have to investigate around 2,750 complaints about suspected cruelty to animals. Multiply that by weeks in a month, and then by every month in a year.

The RSPCA could not survive without public support. Thank you for helping to make the RSPCA truly amazing!

HINT

Always think about the purpose of your writing. The words in this charity appeal have been carefully chosen:

- to make you feel the horror of animal cruelty
- to stress the positive effect that the RSPCA has on animal welfare
- to emphasise the importance of donations.

▼ QUESTIONS TO CONSIDER	▼ EXAMPLES FROM THE TEXT
What words in this piece emphasise the cruel way in which some animals are treated?	1 'pitilessly abused' 2 3
What words emphasise the positive aspects of the RSPCA's work?	1 'harmony and respect' 2 3
What words and details emphasise the importance of donations and the people who make them?	1 'enough people in our country care' 2 3

▶ **Find an example of each of the following techniques:**

■ **direct address**

■ **rhetorical questions**

■ **short sentences for dramatic effect**

■ **the use of statistics to prove what is being said**

■ **repetition of words, or use of similar words, for effect.**

HINT

Persuasive and argument texts often use direct address: the pronouns 'you' and 'we' can engage the reader, encouraging them to consider and agree with the writer's views.

ACTIVITY 3 | **A02** | **SKILLS** CRITICAL THINKING, ANALYSIS, INTERPRETATION

▼ PERSUADING A FRIEND

Sometimes the context for advice or persuasion is much more personal. The following extract is by a teenager who has been told by a friend that he is going alone to meet someone he only knows from a social media app. She is writing to persuade her friend not to go. Would you expect her style (or register) to be informal? Why might it use some conversational features?

> Jamali,
>
> Please don't shout at me for writing this, but I doubt if you would let me talk directly to you. I know I am being uptight and intruding on your private life but I am sick with worry, since you told me that you were going to meet this 'girl'. We have always been close friends and you have always trusted me in the past. So listen to me now. What you are doing is plain stupid. Insane, even.

This letter uses different techniques from the RSPCA charity appeal. Link the statements about techniques on the left with the correct explanation for each one on the right.

▶

TECHNIQUE	EXPLANATION
1 The style is very informal and uses conversational language such as 'uptight' and 'plain stupid'.	A This is to make the friend feel guilty and also to reassure him.
2 It uses direct address.	B This is to emphasise what the writer is saying.
3 It uses a variety of sentence structures, including commands and minor sentences.	C This makes the letter more personal and establishes a direct link with the friend.
4 It appeals to the friend on various emotional levels.	D This is appropriate because it is written to a close friend.

▲ Writing to a friend will use a personal style and structure.

ACTIVITY 4   **A04**   **A05**   **SKILLS**   PROBLEM SOLVING, ADAPTIVE LEARNING, CREATIVITY

▼ WRITING IN A SERIOUS STYLE

The extract about the RSPCA in Activity 2 could be easily adapted to be a speech, a leaflet or a part of an article. Write a brief piece in a similarly serious and adult style on a charity of your choice.

LEARNING OBJECTIVES

This lesson will help you to:
- understand how an appreciation of form can help you to write what is needed.

FORM

The form of a text is the set of conventions that distinguish one type of text from another. Think about what makes a letter different from a news article. Form is partly a matter of layout or appearance, partly the approach to the content, and partly the style or the way that the piece is written.

For example, in terms of the content or subject matter, the form of a feature article requires that all the content is clearly relevant to the topic, organised in a logical and clear way. In comparison, the form of a personal letter allows complete freedom to write about anything of interest to both the writer and reader (though there are still certain conventions) and not necessarily in any particular order. In terms of style, a feature article usually needs to be reasonably formal, whereas a personal letter can, of course, be very casual and colloquial.

ACTIVITY 1   **A01**   **SKILLS** ▸ CRITICAL THINKING

▼ IDENTIFYING FORM

Look at the following openings of various pieces of writing.

EXTRACT A

What's in a name?

Names, common as many of them are, are like little codes: they tell people certain things about us, about where we come from.

EXTRACT B

Hi Pierre,

I expect the weather over there in Lyon is loads better than here in Canada. You don't want to be out in the sticks here I can tell you.

EXTRACT C

Dear Sirs,

I write concerning the recent plans for improvements in the local environment.

EXTRACT D

Thrills, spills and a gender twist

If you are a fan of Lian Hearn's books you won't be disappointed by the latest adventure.

▶

Now copy and complete the following table, writing down the things that you notice about the layout and content in extracts A–D.

	▼ TYPE OF FORM	▼ FEATURES OF THE FORM
A		
B		
C		
D		

IDENTIFYING FORM BY ITS PHYSICAL LAYOUT

In many cases, the layout is the most obvious indication of form. However, it is unlikely to be the most important aspect of form.

KEY POINT

Distinguishing one form of writing from another goes beyond the sort of layout differences that one can see at a glance.

▲ Letters to friends can be informal and chatty.

NEWS AND MAGAZINE ARTICLES	■ Short paragraphs ■ Conform to a series of conventional lengths, for example, short articles of 600–800 words; full-length features of around 1,500 or so words ■ Use headlines and subheadings ■ Short introductory summaries
FILM AND BOOK REVIEWS	■ Most commonly around 300–700 words, though can be longer ■ Tend to have a punchy or clever headline and sometimes subheadings
LETTERS	■ If official or business, writer's address top right and date below; addressee's address top left ■ Begin with 'Dear…' ■ Short paragraphs ■ End with 'Yours sincerely', 'All best wishes' or similar, depending on level of familiarity with the reader
SPEECHES	■ Begin with a form of greeting, for example, 'Ladies and gentlemen…' ■ End with a form of farewell, a conclusion suitable to a spoken address rather than a written one: this could take the form of thanks to the audience for listening

IDENTIFYING FORM BY ITS CONTENT

It is the combination of the layout and content that makes forms identifiable. Even without the layout of a letter, the words, 'Dear Luis', at the start of a piece of writing would identify it as a letter. Similarly, when you read a summarising opening sentence such as, 'Yesterday evening, the Prime Minister announced that there would be a referendum…', you recognise it as the start of a news article.

FORM: NEWS ARTICLES

- Headlines tell you what the article is about in a concise, attention-grabbing way. For example, it might use wordplay or alliteration and leave out any words that are not vital to the meaning.
- A standfirst or summary sub-heading gives more detail, engaging the reader further.
- Opening paragraphs introduce the article's focus and often summarise key ideas or information from the piece, which is very different from the opening of short stories or letters.
- The information or opinion given is often supported with statistics or the views of experts.

THE TRUTH ABOUT LYING: IT'S THE HANDS THAT BETRAY YOU, NOT THE EYES

By analysing videos of liars, the team found there was no link between lying and eye movements.

ADAM SHERWIN

It is often claimed that even the most stone-faced liar will be betrayed by an unwitting eye movement.

But new research suggests that 'lying eyes', which no fibber can avoid revealing, are actually a myth.

Verbal hesitations and excessive hand gestures may prove a better guide to whether a person is telling untruths, according to research conducted by Professor Richard Wiseman.

ACTIVITY 2   **A04**   **A05**   **SKILLS**   PROBLEM SOLVING, ADAPTIVE LEARNING, CREATIVITY

▼ WRITING AN ARTICLE

Write a short news article about a new invention. Aim to use all the features listed above.

FORM: FILM AND BOOK REVIEWS

- Titles of reviews aim to engage the reader and indicate the reviewer's opinion.
- A sub-heading gives more details of the reviewer's opinion.
- Ratings give an opinion on how good the book, film or event is.
- The opening paragraph may use figurative language or a rhetorical device to engage the reader's interest.

HAMILTON REVIEW – BROADWAY HIT IS NOW A BREATHTAKING SCREEN SENSATION

Lin-Manuel Miranda's musical is smart, witty, funky and leaves us reflecting on America's past and future

ARIFA AKBAR

Hamilton was hailed as revolutionary theatre in 2015, with its rapping 18th-century statesmen, its funky, feelgood hip-hop and a cast predominantly comprising actors of colour. It went on to conquer Broadway and West End audiences. How does that original Broadway staging fare on the flat screen?

The film keeps all the energy of the stage, from the large-scale war scenes to the political power battles…

▲ What was the last film you enjoyed watching?

ACTIVITY 3 **AO4** **AO5** SKILLS ▸ PROBLEM SOLVING, ADAPTIVE LEARNING, CREATIVITY

▼ WRITING A REVIEW

Write the first two paragraphs of a book or film review, using the features listed on page 190 and appropriate language. You could write the opening of the review you planned on page 179.

FORM: LETTERS

▼ LAYOUT OR PHYSICAL FORM

- Writer's address and the date go in the top right corner
- Addressee's name and address go on the left, lower down
- Start with 'Dear...'
- Can use a subject line to draw the reader's attention to the topic
- End with 'Yours faithfully' if started with 'Dear Sir or Madam'. If started with the addressee's name, end with 'Yours sincerely'. If informal, could end with 'All the best' or 'With love'

▼ CONTENT

- Formal letters normally begin with the reason for writing ('I write concerning the...').
- Informal letters often begin with a thought for the addressee, such as, 'I hope all is well with you'.
- Formal letters contain information and make points. They may also express thanks or make a complaint.
- Informal letters usually contain personal news and plans.
- The last paragraph before signing off usually expresses hopes or good wishes, for example, formally, 'I hope you will give this matter your serious consideration' or, informally, 'all the best until then'.

ACTIVITY 4 **AO4** **AO5** SKILLS ▸ PROBLEM SOLVING, ADAPTIVE LEARNING, CREATIVITY

▼ WRITING A LETTER

KEY POINT

Formal letters have formal rules but there is still scope for your own choices.

Write a letter to the leaders of your school, requesting that they improve the school in two ways that you think are important. In this case, you should use the opening greeting, 'Dear School Leaders'.

FORM: REPORTS

HINT

Reports are an interesting form of conveying information but will not appear in the exam.

A report is a response to a request for detailed information about a place, institution, event or other project. It differs from a news article because it requires extensive research into the background and often then gives a recommendation as to what should happen next. Governments commission numerous reports on all aspects of modern life as the basis for forming policy and making decisions. For example, a town council might need a report on the roads in a part of the town or the way that schools are fulfilling the needs of the community.

ACTIVITY 5 **AO4** **AO5** **SKILLS** PROBLEM SOLVING, ADAPTIVE LEARNING, CREATIVITY

▼ WRITING A REPORT

Write a response to the following question.

▶ **Your school or borough has been allotted a significant amount of extra funding to improve its facilities, which would be enough to pay for some new buildings. You have been asked to write a report on the state of facilities, in either your local community or your school, in one of the following areas:**

■ **sports**

■ **leisure**

■ **arts**

■ **provision for pedestrians and cyclists.**

FORM: BLOGS

A blog, short for 'web log', is a cross between a diary and a personal magazine. They vary from those written and designed by professional journalists and other writers, which resemble online newspapers, to very informal ones written by students or young people. They are found on many sites on the internet.

This is an example of a blog post from a blogger who reviews video games.

> Still only available as an early alpha build on Steam, but already immensely popular, Dean Hall's bleak, utterly unsentimental zombie survival game is unbearably tense and atmospheric. Players are pitched together into a stark landscape, and must survive for as long as possible, ransacking buildings for guns and food and avoiding the undead. But just as in all the best zombie fiction, it's not the rotting monsters you often have to worry about, it's the other survivors. Each server houses up to 40 players, all desperately scavenging for the same meagre supplies. And if you kill another participant, you can take their stuff. There is a clear benefit to adopting a 'shoot first' policy.

ACTIVITY 6 **AO4** **AO5** **SKILLS** PROBLEM SOLVING, ADAPTIVE LEARNING, CREATIVITY

▼ WRITING A BLOG POST

Write a blog post on a hobby or interest that you would like to share with others. Try to use standard English, but you may need to tailor your language to the needs of your audience and use more informal language.

▲ For example, you could write a lifestyle, fashion or travel blog.

FORM: INFORMATION GUIDES

These are leaflets designed to offer the reader a brief guide to a place, a process, a system and so on. Read the following question and think about the information that you might need to include in the guide that you write.

▶ **Write a brief guide to your home town, village or district for new residents or a visitor.**

HINT

Remember that you can introduce a statistic with phrases such as, 'It is believed that...' or 'One expert has said that...'.

As well as providing information, you should organise this information logically using subheadings and bullet points. Include some facts, statistics and opinions, any of which could be quotations. They do not need to be completely accurate; you can invent things. However, remember that this is supposed to be non-fiction, so keep it realistic.

ACTIVITY 7   **A04**   **A05**   **SKILLS** ▶ PROBLEM SOLVING, ADAPTIVE LEARNING, CREATIVITY

▼ WRITING AN INFORMATION LEAFLET

Write an answer to the question on page 192, planning it first using something like the following table.

Introduction	
Paragraph 2	The neighbourhood
Paragraph 3	The wider town or environment
Paragraph 4	Things worth seeing and doing
Conclusion	

You could use a spider diagram to help you gather ideas.

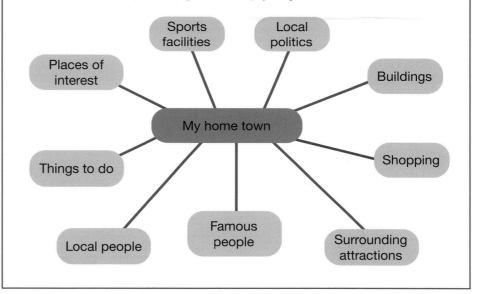

ACTIVITY 8   **A02**   **A04**   **SKILLS** ▶ ANALYSIS, ADAPTIVE LEARNING, CREATIVITY

▼ INFORM AND DESCRIBE

An information guide can include some descriptive writing. The main aim is to bring the topic to life with some vivid phrasing and interesting word choices.

Re-read the information guide that you wrote for Activity 7. Have you included any description? Could you add some now? Look back at some of the extracts in the Anthology to remind yourself of some examples of good descriptive writing.

LEARNING OBJECTIVES

This lesson will help you to:

- select vocabulary to make your writing precise, clear and effective.

VOCABULARY FOR EFFECT

A skilled author's vocabulary choices can make their writing clear and precise, add impact to their ideas and make their writing more engaging for the reader. Vocabulary choice is not a question of using more words, but of selecting the best words to help you achieve your intention. Vocabulary choice improves with reading and practice.

SYNONYMS

SUBJECT VOCABULARY

synonyms words that share the same meaning as other words; for example, 'quick' might be a synonym for 'fast'

KEY POINT

You will not have a thesaurus in your exam. Practise using the thesaurus in your head: you already have a much wider vocabulary than you might think!

Synonyms are words that have the same or a similar meaning. Considering synonyms is a highly effective strategy to improve vocabulary choice, whether you are trying to:

- avoid repeating the same word over and over again
- make your meaning more precise
- achieve your intention more effectively
- add impact to your ideas.

| ACTIVITY 1 | A05 | SKILLS ▷ ANALYSIS, CRITICAL THINKING |

▼ CHOOSING SYNONYMS

The sentences below each express a strong opinion.

- Cricket is an <u>interesting</u> sport.
- It was a <u>terrible</u> game.

For the underlined word in each sentence, build a **synonym bank**: a list of synonyms that you could use to replace the underlined word.

Add impact to each sentence by re-writing it, replacing the underlined word with the most effective synonym from your synonym bank.

If you have access to a thesaurus, look up the underlined words. Can you find any synonyms that you wish you had added to your synonym banks?

| ACTIVITY 2 | A05 | SKILLS ▷ ANALYSIS, CRITICAL THINKING |

▼ BEING PRECISE

The sentences below each contain a two-word phrase that could be made more succinct by replacing it with a one-word synonym:

- I <u>really like</u> vegetables.
- I <u>strongly dislike</u> chocolate.
- The music was <u>extremely loud</u>.

Build a **synonym bank** of words that could replace the underlined phrase in each sentence.

Add precision to each sentence by re-writing it, replacing the underlined phrase with the most effective synonym from your synonym bank.

If you can, use a thesaurus to find other appropriate synonyms.

ACTIVITY 3   A05   SKILLS ANALYSIS, CRITICAL THINKING

▼ REGISTER

The register of a text is its level of formality. For example, if you are messaging a friend, you will use a more informal register than if you are writing a formal letter to the school leaders or headteacher. Vocabulary choice plays a significant part in creating a text's register.

Think about these three very different texts and audiences:

- writing a letter to your headteacher
- giving a speech to the class
- messaging a friend.

How would you end the following sentences for each of the audiences above?

- Homework is a _____ (waste of time / a poor use of time / pointless).
- Junk food is _____ (not nutritious / unhealthy / rubbish).

Now look at the sentence below:

- Mobile phones are really useful when things go wrong.

For which audience is this sentence in an appropriate register? Re-write it in an appropriate register for the other two audiences.

ACTIVITY 4   A05   SKILLS ANALYSIS CRITICAL THINKING

▼ THE RIGHT NUMBER OF WORDS

Adding descriptive language is not always effective. More is sometimes less. Look at the description below:

> The firework quickly travelled into the dark, black, starry, cloudless night sky and loudly exploded in a bright, dazzling, shower of falling white, blue, red and green flashes of colour.

How many of the words could be removed from the sentence without changing its meaning? Make the sentence as short as possible.

How many words **should** be removed from the sentence to make it more powerful? Make the sentence as **short but effective** as possible.

▲ 'The firework ... exploded in a bright dazzling shower...'

ACTIVITY 5   A05   SKILLS ANALYSIS, CRITICAL THINKING

▼ AVOIDING REPETITION

Repetition can be a good rhetorical technique if it is used skilfully, but if it is used badly it can weaken the impact of your writing. Re-write the following text, replacing the words 'point' and 'people' with different synonyms. Try to make the sentences more interesting.

> Social media does have many good points. One is that it helps friends stay in touch; another point is that you can talk to people whenever you like; a third point is that people can introduce friends to other people very easily.

GENERAL VOCABULARY

repetition saying the same thing more than once to highlight its importance

KEY POINT

Always consider your intention when choosing emotive language. Do you want to shock, alarm, reassure or encourage your reader?

ACTIVITY 6 **A05** **SKILLS** ANALYSIS, CRITICAL THINKING

▼ EMOTIVE LANGUAGE

Using emotive language can certainly add impact to your argument. Choosing when and where to use it depends on the intention you want to achieve in your writing.

Compare the synonyms in the pairs of sentences below. What is the writer's intention in each one? Which sentence makes the most effective use of emotive language?

■ If we ignore the harm we are doing to our planet, we will soon be facing a problem.

■ If we ignore the damage we are doing to our planet, we will soon be facing a catastrophe.

■ It is easy to feel lost and alone when you are trying find your way around a new school.

■ It is easy to feel abandoned and isolated when you are trying to find your way around a new school.

ACTIVITY 7 **A05** **SKILLS** ANALYSIS, CRITICAL THINKING

▼ CONNOTATIONS

The connotations of your vocabulary choices can add richness to your writing. Look at the table below. Each of the suggested adjectives could be used to finish the sentences: they have similar meanings but different connotations.

▼ SENTENCE	▼ ADJECTIVE	▼ CONNOTATIONS
'When I finish my homework, I feel…'	sleepy	tired, with associations of boredom
	exhausted	extreme physical fatigue
	drained	emptiness, weakness
'Video games are often…'	vicious	cruel, merciless
	barbaric	uncivilised
	brutal	ruthless, uncaring

Complete the sentences below, choosing synonyms from the suggestions beneath.

Everybody _____ 'likes' on social media.

wants   needs   craves   is desperate for   yearns for

Social media has a _____ influence on our lives.

worrying   startling   alarming   frightening   terrifying

For each sentence you have written, note the connotations you intended to suggest with your vocabulary choice.

ACTIVITY 8 | **AO5** | SKILLS ▷ ANALYSIS, CRITICAL THINKING

▼ CHOOSE YOUR VOCABULARY STRATEGY

As you write, and then review what you have written, think carefully about the words you choose. Consider your purpose, your intention and the impact you want to achieve.

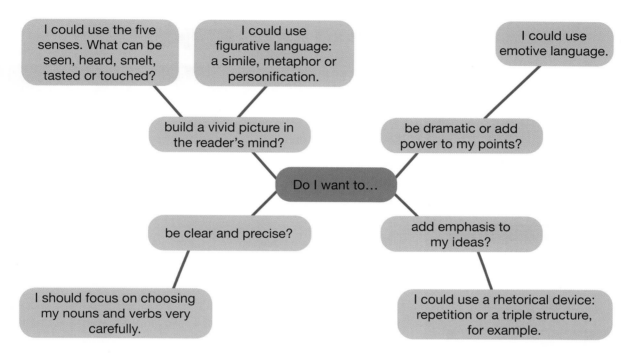

Write an opening paragraph for the following exam-style question, focusing on vocabulary choice.

▶ **The editor of your school newspaper has asked for contributions in response to this topic:**

  'Video games are fun and they are good for you.'

  You can write in favour of the statement or against it.

Aim to:

■ engage and interest your reader: you could describe or explain the role that video games play in some people's lives, or make a strong dramatic statement expressing your views

■ choose vocabulary that will help you achieve your purpose and intention and add impact to your ideas.

ACTIVITY 9 | **AO4** | **AO5** | SKILLS ▷ ANALYSIS, ADAPTIVE LEARNING, CREATIVITY

▼ USING VOCABULARY FOR EFFECT

Re-write the information guide that you wrote in response to Activity 7 on page 193. Aim to improve your writing by focusing closely on vocabulary choice.

LEARNING OBJECTIVES

This lesson will help you to:
- understand how you can control sentences for greater impact.

SENTENCES FOR EFFECT

Consciously structuring your sentences will help your writing to make an impression on readers.

BUILDING SENTENCES

HINT

Conjunctions link ideas and clauses, for example:

when	as	after
before	because	unless
if	unless	although

HINT

Look at pages 34–35 to remind yourself of the different ways in which sentences can be structured.

HINT

You may need to adapt some of the clauses to link them in different ways. Make sure your sentence does not change the meaning of the original sentences

HINT

Adverbials are phrases that have the same function as an adverb; adverbials often begin with a preposition: words such as *in*, *on*, *at*, *with*, *above*, etc.

ACTIVITY 1　　A05　　SKILLS　PROBLEM SOLVING, ADAPTIVE LEARNING

▼ LINKING IDEAS

When you write, think about the choices you have in the building of your sentences. You can:

■ give information in single clause sentences	It might feel like recycling is hard work. It's quick and easy.
■ link information using a conjunction	Although it feels like recycling is hard work, it's quick and easy.
■ link information using a relative pronoun	Recycling, which some may think is hard work, is quick and easy.
■ link information using a non-finite verb	Being quick and easy, recycling is nothing like hard work.

In how many ways can you link the following pieces of information?

We buy far more food than we need. + We put far too much in the bin.

We put our food waste in a recycling bin. + None of it is wasted.

We will drown in our own rubbish. + We will wish we had done more to save the planet.

ACTIVITY 2　　A05　　SKILLS　PROBLEM SOLVING ADAPTING LEARNING

▼ DEVELOPING IDEAS

You can develop your sentences further with adverbs and adverbials. For example:

▼ ADVERBS	▼ ADVERBIALS
actually	every day
finally	at the end of each day
incredibly	in a short while
always	before long
occasionally	after a week
sometimes	with a little effort

Look at the sentences you wrote in Activity 1. Develop them using an adverb or adverbial.

STRUCTURING FOR IMPACT

▲ 'The human race is doomed if we do nothing.'

Now that you have practised building sentences, think about how you can structure them to add impact. You can:

■ use short, single clause sentences to add emphasis

> We must change our ways.

■ list ideas in multiclause sentence to build a picture or create an impression of quantity and variety

> We can recycle our rubbish, walk more, drive less, buy fewer clothes and turn the heating down.

■ link ideas to build a vivid picture

> If we do not act now, the ocean will one day flood the land, islands of plastic waste floating down our streets, while we struggle to breathe the filthy, polluted air.

■ sequence clauses and information for impact. Positioning the ideas or information you want to emphasise at the end of a sentence will give them more impact. Compare the following sentences:

> The human race is doomed if we do nothing.

> If we do nothing, the human race is doomed.

Which version has more impact?

KEY POINT

Think carefully about the structure of your sentences. Their length and the order in which you sequence ideas can add significant impact to your writing.

ACTIVITY 3   **A05**   **SKILLS**   PROBLEM SOLVING, ADAPTIVE LEARNING

▼ EXPERIMENTING WITH SENTENCES

Choose three or more of the ideas below and use them to write a sentence. Experiment with linking the ideas in different ways and changing the order in which you sequence them. Try adding an adverb or adverbial. How does the impact change in each version?

Our lives will change forever.	Our climate will change.
Animals will become extinct.	Temperatures will rise.
The seas will rise.	The world will be very different for our children.

THE IMPORTANCE OF PUNCTUATION

Punctuation errors affect the impact you have on your reader. One of the errors that many students make is using the comma splice: a comma linking ideas where there should be a conjunction to link them or a full stop, semi-colon or colon to separate them.

Look at any commas you have used in the sentences you have written. Are you sure they should be commas? Or should they be full stops?

▼ THE COMMA SPLICE	▼ CORRECT ALTERNATIVES
We watch far too much television, this is why we have no time for anything else.	…too much television. This is why…
	…too much television: this is why…
	…too much television, which is why…

LEARNING OBJECTIVES

This lesson will help you to:

- understand the importance of planning
- improve your planning techniques.

IDEAS AND PLANNING

It is essential to plan before writing. Then, as you write, you can concentrate on the quality of your writing, not what you will write about next. Of the 45 minutes that you have to complete Section B, you should spend 5–10 minutes planning.

PLANNING TECHNIQUES

▲ Spider diagrams can be useful for planning.

You can plan using spider diagrams, thought clouds, lists and so on: it doesn't matter what you use as long as it works for you.

A good idea to start with is to read the task very carefully and note down the **purpose**, the **audience** and the **form** it tells you to use.

Next, think about your **intentions**. This will help you to gather some ideas you can explore in your writing

One way to do this is to think about the ways in which the issue or topic has affected you or people you know or have heard about.

Another is to ask yourself questions, starting with key question words:

| who | what | when | how | why |

ACTIVITY 1 · A04 · SKILLS ▶ PROBLEM SOLVING, REASONING, ADAPTIVE LEARNING, CREATIVITY

▼ STRATEGIES FOR PLANNING

Read the exam-style question below. Note down the purpose, audience and form it tells you to use.

▶ **Write an article for a local or school magazine on the topic: 'Not enough attention is paid to the problem of stress in the lives of modern teenagers'.**

Now think about the intentions you might want to achieve:

| shock the reader | humour | create sympathy for teenagers | alarm or worry the reader | create drama and tension | build a vivid picture in the reader's mind |

Next think of some questions to ask yourself, beginning with key question words:

Who	do I know that feels stressed? makes teenagers stressed?
What	makes us stressed? can we do about it?
When	do we get stressed? did I start feeling teenage stress?
How	can we stop being stressed? can other people help us?
Why	do we get stressed? is stress such a problem?

Note your answers to the questions you have asked yourself. You should now have lots of ideas you can use in your writing.

ACTIVITY 2 | **A04** | **SKILLS** ▶ PROBLEM SOLVING, REASONING, ADAPTIVE LEARNING, CREATIVITY

▼ STRUCTURING YOUR IDEAS

Once you have gathered a range of ideas, you need to think about organising them in a logical structure. Transactional writing texts are almost always structured in three key stages:

Introduction
One paragraph introducing the topic and your view
➡
Main body
Three or more paragraphs explaining and developing your views
➡
Conclusion
One paragraph summing up your views

Look at the exam-style question and the ideas one student gathered in response to it below.

▶ **Your local council wants to improve provisions for teenagers in the neighbourhood. Write a report for the council explaining how, in your view, the local facilities might be improved. In your report, you could consider:**

- **what facilities exist at present**
- **ideas about providing new facilities.**
- **your ideas about how they can be improved**

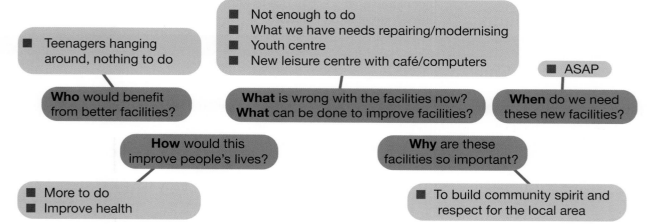

- Teenagers hanging around, nothing to do

- Not enough to do
- What we have needs repairing/modernising
- Youth centre
- New leisure centre with café/computers

- ASAP

Who would benefit from better facilities?

What is wrong with the facilities now?
What can be done to improve facilities?

When do we need these new facilities?

How would this improve people's lives?

Why are these facilities so important?

- More to do
- Improve health

- To build community spirit and respect for the local area

Which three ideas could you use as main points in a response to the question? Which other ideas could you use to support and develop your main points? Note your ideas in a planning table like the one below. Aim to sequence your main points logically.

▼ INTRODUCTION	▼ MAIN BODY		▼ CONCLUSION
	Main points	Supporting points	
	1	1	
	2	2	
	3	3	

HINT

Some exam questions will give bullet points to support you, like this one. They can help you think about the main and secondary purposes for your writing and suggest questions that you can use to help you generate ideas.

ACTIVITY 3 | **A04** | **SKILLS** ▶ PROBLEM SOLVING, REASONING, ADAPTIVE LEARNING, CREATIVITY

▼ PRACTISE YOUR PLANNING

▶ **Write a speech for your class or year group, in which you try to persuade them to participate in the school's extra-curricular activities.**

Plan your response to this question, using the strategies and approaches you have been practising.

LEARNING OBJECTIVES

This lesson will help you to:
- understand how to write effective introductions and conclusions to your writing.

OPENINGS AND CONCLUSIONS

One of the benefits of planning is that you are more likely to write an engaging opening because you have thought about what you are going to write. A mistake that students can make if they have not planned their response is to simply repeat words from the question with a phrase such as, 'In this article I am going to write about…'. Since your reader already knows this, it is a waste of time and unlikely to interest or engage your reader.

OPENINGS

When you read a text, you probably expect the opening to be interesting and to grab your attention in some way. The following table lists some effective techniques that you can use to improve your openings. Which technique you use will depend on the task.

▼ TECHNIQUE	▼ EXAMPLE
A rhetorical question	'How often do you throw something in the bin without even thinking about it?'
An arresting or controversial statement	'It's not children who need educating about recycling – it's the grown-ups who ought to know better.'
A surprising or shocking fact or statistic	'The unreleased energy contained in the average dustbin each year could power a television for 5,000 hours.'
A relevant quotation	'We live in a disposable society. It's easier to throw things out than to fix them.'
A short and relevant anecdote	'I have found it saves money to reuse the plastic containers…'

ACTIVITY 1   A01   A02   SKILLS ▷ CRITICAL THINKING, ANALYSIS

▼ EFFECTIVE OPENINGS

The following extracts are the openings of some of the texts in this book. Read each one and then write down the features that make them effective openings.

EXTRACT A
'I'm a storyteller. And I would like to tell you a few personal stories about what I like to call "the danger of the single story."'

EXTRACT B
'I saw a thousand hungry, lean, scared and betrayed faces as I criss-crossed Somalia between the end of 1991 and December 1992, but there is one I will never forget.'

EXTRACT C
'Paper has more patience than people.'

HINT

Remember that your statistics do not have to be accurate in the exam; they just have to sound plausible. However, if you are writing for homework, you should check that your statistics are correct.

KEY POINT

The pressure of getting started can often lead to a bland opening, written just to get something on the page. It pays to resist this pressure and think carefully about your opening sentence and your opening paragraph.

ACTIVITY 2   **AO4**   **AO5**   **SKILLS** ▶ PROBLEM SOLVING, ADAPTIVE LEARNING, CREATIVITY

▼ USING DIFFERENT KINDS OF OPENING

An introduction has two key functions:

- to introduce the topic you will focus on
- to introduce your views on that topic.

Write two possible introductions to a response to the following question.

▶ **Write an article arguing for or against the proposal that the smacking of children should be made illegal.**

In each of your introductions, aim to use two or three of the techniques from the table on page 202. Make sure both your opening paragraphs achieve the two key functions of an introduction.

CONCLUSIONS

An effective conclusion will leave the reader with a strong impression and should leave them considering your ideas. Different techniques can be used to achieve a strong conclusion, as shown in the following table.

▼ TECHNIQUE	▼ EXAMPLE
The positive consequences of agreeing with your views	'This is surely a recipe for success.'
A warning of the negative consequences of ignoring your views	'If we do not act soon, then it may be too late to save…'
An appeal for action	'We must act now – and act quickly – to save our heritage.'
A question for people to think about	'Couldn't that be the best outcome of them all?'
A vivid image	'Just a single light, shining in the dark.'

ACTIVITY 3   **AO2**   **SKILLS** ▶ ANALYSIS, REASONING

▼ EFFECTIVE CONCLUSIONS

Find three examples of conclusions from extracts in this book and explain why they are effective.

ACTIVITY 4   **AO4**   **AO5**   **SKILLS** ▶ PROBLEM SOLVING, ADAPTIVE LEARNING, CREATIVITY

▼ USING DIFFERENT KINDS OF CONCLUSION

The key functions of a conclusion are:

- to sum up and drive home your views
- to leave the reader thinking about your views.

Look back at the two openings that you wrote in Activity 2. Write two possible conclusions to the pieces. In each of them, aim to use two or three of the techniques from the table above. Make sure both your conclusions achieve the two key functions of a conclusion.

LEARNING OBJECTIVES

This lesson will help you to:
- understand how the methods and techniques discussed in this chapter can combine to make a strong answer.

PUTTING IT INTO PRACTICE

In the exam in Section B, you will have to answer one question from a choice of two. You should aim to spend 45 minutes writing your response to the transactional writing question.

EXAM-STYLE QUESTION

A04   **A05**

SKILLS   CRITICAL THINKING, ANALYSIS, ADAPTIVE LEARNING, CREATIVITY

'Schools have a duty to continually improve conditions for students.'

You have been asked to make a speech to the leaders and teachers of your school or college, giving your views on this statement.

Your speech may include:
- who should have responsibility for improvements
- whether improvements would help students
- any other points you wish to make.

Your response will be marked for the accurate and appropriate use of vocabulary, spelling, punctuation and grammar.   **(45 marks)**

HINT

Think about purpose, audience and form first. Notice that the question asks you to give your views. Your intention should be to influence your audience: to encourage them to consider your views and agree with them.

▲ Consider how swapping paragraphs around changes the tone of the speech.

ACTIVITY 1   **A04**   **SKILLS**   PROBLEM SOLVING, REASONING, ADAPTIVE LEARNING, CREATIVITY

▼ IDEAS AND PLANNING

Using the following table to help you, make your own plan for the exam-style question.

▼ PARAGRAPH PLAN	▼ TECHNIQUES TO USE
■ Intro: describe poor conditions – suggest there is an answer ■ Main body para 1: effect of poor conditions on students and teachers ■ Main body para 2: suggestions for key improvements ■ Main body para 3: benefits of improvements ■ Conclusion: act now for everyone's benefit	■ Rhetorical questions ■ Triple structures ■ Direct address to reader/listener ■ Alliteration – 'crumbling classrooms' ■ Imperatives – short final sentence ■ Long sentences listing benefits/negatives ■ Facts and statistics ■ Emotive language

SAMPLE ANSWER

Triple structure and rhetorical question engages the audience from the start.

Direct address emphasises that this topic is relevant to the audience.

Read through the following answer to the exam-style question and the comments.

INTRODUCTION

For how much longer must students in this school put up with crumbling classrooms, sub-standard social areas and dismal dining rooms? Ambitious and hardworking students in your school deserve better.

Repetition makes these points more powerful.

Emotive language choices with positive connotations add impact to the speaker's views.

Another rhetorical question using direct address to invite the reader or listener to consider their own thoughts and feelings on this topic.

An imperative verb encourages listeners to engage with the topic and allows the writer to introduce a powerfully persuasive description highlighting the benefits of agreeing with their views.

More emotive language choices with positive connotations add impact to the speaker's views.

The pronoun 'us' and the phrase 'it is clear' emphasise the writer's view and encourage the reader/listener to agree.

A short sentence using emotive language is a powerful way to conclude.

MAIN BODY

Perhaps most importantly, a poor quality environment leads to poor quality work. Cramped classrooms, foul toilet facilities and inadequate outdoor space do not motivate students to succeed, or motivate teachers to do their best to help us. A poor environment tells us we are not good enough to deserve better – and we need all the encouragement and support we can get to achieve the qualifications we want and need, and which you want and need us to get.

Your children deserve better: modern, well-equipped classrooms; outdoor space to breathe; appealing eating areas, offering good choice and good value; clean, modern toilets.

Would you want to work somewhere that did not offer these things?

Imagine a school that offered these things. Students would be happy to come to school and enjoy a healthy breakfast in the canteen. They would be happy to go to their lessons, ready to learn, knowing that they would be learning in a comfortable environment with the best facilities to help them. They would feel valued and respected by a school that was prepared to offer them the school they deserve.

CONCLUSION

I do not think that any of us here would suggest the school environment is perfect. It is clear that there is room for improvement. So, the question we must ask ourself is not 'Should these improvements be made?', but 'When will they be made?' Our future depends on it.

KEY POINT

Include a clear and urgent call to action. Imperative verbs can be a highly effective method of making your reader consider your views.

▲ Poor diet and lack of exercise is a problem in the UK.

ACTIVITY 2 | **A04** | **A05** | **SKILLS** PROBLEM SOLVING, ADAPTIVE LEARNING, CREATIVITY

▼ PRACTISE YOUR WRITING

The government is encouraging people to improve their diet and take more exercise. Write a news article to help people get fitter and healthier.

In your article, you could:

- suggest ways in which people could improve their diet and take more exercise
- explain the benefits of a good diet and exercise
- include any other points you wish to make.

PAPER 2: POETRY AND PROSE TEXTS AND IMAGINATIVE WRITING

Assessment Objective 1

Read and understand a variety of texts, selecting and interpreting information, ideas and perspectives

Assessment Objective 2

Understand and analyse how writers use linguistic and structural devices to achieve their effects

This chapter focuses on Paper 2: Poetry and Prose Texts and Imaginative Writing of the English Language A course. Working through these lessons and activities will help you to develop the reading and writing skills that you will need for the Paper 2 exam.

The chapter is split into the following sections:
- Reading skills: Fiction texts
- Text Anthology: Fiction
- Imaginative writing.

Paper 2 is worth 40% of the total marks for the course and is split into two sections:
- Section A: Poetry and prose texts
- Section B: Imaginative writing.

In Section A of your exam, you will need to be able to meet the Assessment Objectives AO1 and AO2.

In Section B of your exam, you will need to be able to meet the Assessment Objectives AO4 and AO5.

Assessment Objective 4

Communicate effectively and imaginatively, adapting form, tone and register of writing for specific purposes and audiences

Assessment Objective 5

Write clearly, using a range of vocabulary and sentence structures, with appropriate paragraphing and accurate spelling, grammar and punctuation

In Paper 2, the assessment objectives are worth the following amounts:
AO1 – 8%
AO2 – 12%
AO4 – 12%
AO5 – 8%

LEARNING OBJECTIVES

This lesson will help you to:
- begin reading and interpreting poetry and prose texts.

TYPES OF TEXT

In the Pearson Edexcel Anthology, you will read a variety of poetry and prose extracts. You will need to analyse and interpret them in order to answer questions in the exam.

APPROACHING PROSE

KEY POINT

It is useful to have a series of questions in your mind when approaching any prose text. These are some examples, but you can think of more.

When you read a prose text, check your understanding by asking yourself the following questions.
- What is it about?
- Where is it set?
- Who is telling it?
- How is the story told?

Next, considering the features of the text will help you to analyse what the writer is doing. These features could include:
- setting
- narrative perspective
- characters
- descriptive techniques
- your response to the characters and events described
- how the plot or characters develop as the story progresses.

APPROACHING POETRY

When you read a poem, you should also start by considering the following questions.
- What is it about?
- How does it make you feel?
- What does it mean to you personally?

Then consider how the poet communicates meaning and feeling. This could be achieved by:
- imagery
- linguistic techniques
- rhythm and rhyme
- structure and form
- possible interpretation or interpretations of the text's implicit meaning.

Read the following poem and then complete Activity 1.

▼ 'PRAISE SONG FOR MY MOTHER' BY GRACE NICHOLS

You were
water to me
deep and bold and fathoming

You were
moon's eye to me
pull and grained and mantling   5

flame tree A species of tree found widely in the Caribbean.

crab's leg, fried plantain Typical Caribbean food.

You were
sunrise to me
rise and warm and streaming

You were   10
the fishes red gill to me
the flame tree's spread to me
the crab's leg/the fried plantain smell
replenishing replenishing

▲ 'You were/sunrise to me'.

ACTIVITY 1   **A01**   **SKILLS** CRITICAL THINKING, ANALYSIS, INTERPRETATION

▼ APPROACHING POETRY

'Praise Song for my Mother' is a poem by Grace Nichols. She was born in Guyana in 1950 and moved to the United Kingdom in 1977. The poem, first published in 1984, celebrates the speaker's gratitude and respect for her mother, using imagery referencing her Caribbean heritage.

Re-read the poem carefully, then answer the following questions.

1 Who is the speaker or narrator in the poem, and what are they like?

2 Who is the speaker or narrator speaking about, and what are they like?

3 What do you think of the poem?

4 Which words or phrases do you particularly like?

5 Why are these words or phrases effective?

6 What do you think the poet's intention was in writing this poem? What impact did Nichols want the poem to have on the reader?

7 Write one paragraph exploring the ways in which the poet achieves her intentions. Remember to support your ideas with evidence from the poem.

LEARNING OBJECTIVES

This lesson will help you to:

■ understand how to identify figurative language

■ consider how figurative language is used for effect in creating character, atmosphere and emotion.

SUBJECT VOCABULARY

simile a description that says that an object is *like* an image

metaphor describing something by comparing it to an image which it resembles, in a way that says the object *is* the image

personification when something which is not human is made to sound human by attributing human qualities to it

FIGURATIVE LANGUAGE

Figurative language is used to create powerful imagery in texts. It can create atmosphere, mood and emotion, or add to readers' understanding and impressions of character or setting.

Figurative language works by making a comparison between one thing and another. The most common figurative techniques are metaphor, simile and personification.

ACTIVITY 1   **A04**   **SKILLS** ANALYSIS, INNOVATION

▼ USING FIGURATIVE LANGUAGE

Look at the photos. Try describing an aspect of each by:

■ using a **simile** to make a comparison:
   'The flames were as hot as...' 'The mushroom looked like...'

■ using a **metaphor** to make a direct comparison:
   'The beach was a...' 'The mountain is a...'

■ using **personification**: use verbs of movement or sound to give human qualities to these non-human objects:
   'The flames ___ed...' 'The sea _____ed...'

FIGURATIVE LANGUAGE IN POETRY

The following poems are excellent examples of how metaphor can be used in poetry.

KEY POINT

Similes and metaphors are sometimes confused. Remember that similes compare using 'like' or 'as', while metaphors make a more direct comparison of one thing to another. For example, 'She's as fierce as a tiger' is a simile, but 'She's a tiger when she's angry' is a metaphor.

▼ 'LOVE IS...' BY ADRIAN HENRI

Love is feeling cold in the back of vans
Love is a fanclub with only two fans
Love is walking holding paintstained hands
Love is.

Love is fish and chips on winter nights   5
Love is blankets full of strange delights
Love is when you don't put out the light
Love is

Love is the presents in Christmas shops
Love is when you're feeling Top of the Pops   10
Love is what happens when the music stops
Love is

Love is white panties lying all forlorn
Love is pink nightdresses still slightly warm
Love is when you have to leave at dawn   15
Love is

Love is you and love is me
Love is prison and love is free
Love's what's there when you are away from me
Love is...   20

▲ 'I give you an onion ... a moon wrapped in brown paper.'

kissogram A humorous greeting.

▼ 'VALENTINE' BY CAROL ANN DUFFY

Not a red rose or a satin heart.

I give you an onion.
It is a moon wrapped in brown paper.
It promises light
like the careful undressing of love.   5

Here.
It will blind you with tears
like a lover.
It will make your reflection
a wobbling photo of grief.   10

I am trying to be truthful.

Not a cute card or a kissogram.

I give you an onion.
Its fierce kiss will stay on your lips,
possessive and faithful   15
as we are,
for as long as we are.

Take it.
Its platinum loops shrink to a wedding-ring,
if you like.   20

Lethal.
Its scent will cling to your fingers,
cling to your knife.

ACTIVITY 2 | A03 | A04 | A05 | SKILLS ▶ ANALYSIS, REASONING, INTERPRETATION, DECISION MAKING, CREATIVITY

▼ USING FIGURATIVE LANGUAGE IN POETRY

1 Re-read 'Love is...' and 'Valentine'. Choose one or two examples from each poem. What does the comparison the poet makes suggest? How does it enrich your understanding of the poet's ideas?

2 In what ways are the two poets' ideas similar and different?

3 Write your own metaphorical poem. Start with the words, 'Life is ...'. Write it in pairs of lines, each pair introducing a metaphor and then explaining its significance. For example:

> Life is a rollercoaster,
> It spins around, its ups and downs…

FIGURATIVE LANGUAGE IN PROSE

In a text, settings can also be used to suggest a mood, ideas or feelings that are important to your wider understanding of that text. Read the following extract carefully, considering the way in which the setting is described.

DID YOU KNOW?

Pathetic fallacy is very similar to personification. It is usually used to make inanimate objects or things reflect what is going on in the scene. For example, if the weather is hot and sunny, it usually represents a 'happy' story. If the weather is dark, cold and stormy, you can usually guess that something bad is going to happen.

▼ FROM *LORD OF THE FLIES* BY WILLIAM GOLDING

Ralph disentangled himself cautiously and stole away through the branches. In a few seconds the fat boy's grunts were behind him and he was hurrying towards the screen that laid between him and the lagoon. He climbed over a broken trunk and was out of the jungle.

The shore was fledged with palm trees. These stood or leaned or reclined against the light and their green feathers were a hundred feet up in the air. The ground beneath them was a bank covered with coarse grass, torn everywhere by the upheavals of fallen trees, scattered with decaying coconuts and palm saplings. Behind this was the darkness of the forest proper and the open space of the scar. Ralph stood, one hand against a grey trunk, and screwed up his eyes against the shimmering water. Out there, perhaps a mile away, the white surf flinked on a coral reef, and beyond that the open sea was a dark blue. Within the irregular arc of the coral lagoon was still as a mountain lake – blue of all the shades a shadowy green and purple. The beach between the palm terrace and the water was a thin bow stave, endless apparently, for to Ralph's left the perspectives of palm and beach and water drew to a point at infinity; and always, almost visible was the heat.

DID YOU KNOW?

A Socratic circle has the following rules:

- Divide your class into two groups.
- The inner circle sits around desks and discusses the question amongst themselves. Only one person may speak at a time. Use an object to indicate who has the power to speak at any given moment.
- The outer circle must remain silent, but should take notes. Whose argument is the most persuasive? Who do you disagree with? Why?
- The inner circle should now be silent. The outer circle may now assess the inner circle's response, praising good points and adding suggestions or extending other points.

SUBJECT VOCABULARY

juxtaposition putting two very different things close together in order to encourage comparison between them

KEY POINT

Use appropriate literary devices to engage your reader in feeling a sense of the place you have chosen.

▲ Golding sets his story on a remote Pacific island.

ACTIVITY 3   **A01**   **A02**   **SKILLS** ▶ CRITICAL THINKING, ANALYSIS, INTERPRETATION

▼ THINKING ABOUT FIGURATIVE LANGUAGE IN PROSE

1 Annotate the extract from *Lord of the Flies*, considering the following two questions.

▶ Note each thing the writer describes: trees, grass, coconuts and so on. Note a word or phrase the writer uses to describe each one. What impression does the writer's language choice create?

▶ How does the way in which the setting is described make the reader feel about the novel?

2 Make a Socratic circle and discuss the following question as a class.

▶ The island is described as 'torn everywhere' by uprooted trees and shadowed by the 'darkness of the forest'. Does Golding's juxtaposition of this with the beautiful 'white surf' and 'coral lagoon' around it forewarn the reader of the events about to unfold?

ACTIVITY 4   **A04**   **A05**   **SKILLS** ▶ CREATIVITY, INNOVATION

▼ A SENSE OF PLACE

Write a short description of a place. Do not name the place, or say where it is. Focus on using language to describe it. Try to create a specific mood: is this a comforting, happy place or a dangerous, worrying place? Swap descriptions with a partner. Can you guess the place that your partner has described?

LEARNING OBJECTIVES

This lesson will help you to:

- understand and analyse how writers introduce characters
- develop fictional characters in your writing
- understand how writers develop and use setting and atmosphere.

▲ The things that you always carry around with you can reveal your character.

CREATING CHARACTER, ATMOSPHERE AND EMOTION

Creating characters is not an easy job. Good writers carefully reveal aspects of a character's personality through a combination of description, behaviour and dialogue.

ACTIVITY 1   **A04**   **A05**   **SKILLS** ▶ CREATIVITY, INNOVATION

▼ WHAT'S IN YOUR POCKET?

The best way to approach character is to put yourself in someone else's shoes or, in this case, pocket!

Create an imaginary character. Think of a few details about them such as their name, age and job. Now imagine five objects they might carry in their pocket or bag. Write down or draw these items. You have now created your character's 'pocket' or 'bag'.

Swap items with a partner. Try to imagine what kind of person would own these things. Share your ideas with your partner.

Imagine this character first thing in the morning: waking and getting up; eating breakfast, going out the front door. Write a short paragraph describing the character's appearance and actions. Use some of the items in their 'pocket' to develop the character.

INTRODUCING A CHARACTER

It is often said that first impressions are the most important, and this is often true of fictional characters. The following extract from Sebastian Sim's novel *Let's Give It Up for Gimme Lao!* introduces the character of Grandma Toh, who looks after the young Gimme when his parents are at work.

▼ FROM *LET'S GIVE IT UP FOR GIMME LAO!* BY SEBASTIAN SIM

GIMME LAO DID not like Grandma Toh at all. He did not like the fact that she made him eat when he wasn't hungry, bathe when he wasn't ready and sleep when he still wanted to play. He hated it when Grandma Toh shovelled piping hot porridge into his mouth with an aluminium spoon so large it stretched his lips till the corners hurt. He disliked the brute strength Grandma Toh employed when she wrapped a hand towel round her palm, ran a damp bar of soap over it and scrubbed his skin with a total absence of mercy till it turned raw and red. And when it came around to the early afternoon soap opera on the radio, he would be made to drop his toys, lie on the sofa and rest his head on her lap. What he detested most was the suffocation he had to fight when Grandma Toh rocked and pressed her ample bosom onto his face. If he fussed, Grandma Toh would shush him fiercely. Nothing must disrupt the story-teller on the radio spinning yet another hypnotic, mesmerising yarn.

▶

KEY POINT

The introduction of a new fictional character is a key moment in a story. The language you choose lays the foundations for filling out the character later.

Gimme Lao was also keenly aware that it was Grandma Toh who tore him wailing and clawing from his mother's arms every morning before his parents disappeared down the corridor. The tearful ritual used to drag on for five minutes or more in the beginning, when Grandma Toh and the young parents restricted their methods to gentle coaxing and persuasion. They soon realised that not only was this ineffective, it often left the mother's blouse stained with snot and tears. Grandma Toh then decided to employ drastic measures. She wrapped one arm around Gimme's waist and pinned his kicking legs to her stomach with the other. As Gimme continued to claw at his mother and wail hysterically, Grandma Toh leaned close to his ears and whispered firmly that he ought to let go at the count of three. She then counted aloud. At the third count she secretly secured one of his toes and pinched it hard with the sharp ends of her nails. Gimme would scream, let go of his mother and swing around to pound his tormentor with his tiny fists. At this point, the young parents were free to scuttle down the corridor and make a run for the bus. Eventually, Gimme learnt to let go before the count of three to spare himself the physical agony. His parents never discovered Grandma Toh's clandestine tactic and would in later years crow over her magical touch in taming the petulant toddler.

KEY POINT

To create characters and guide the reader's impression of them, writers describe their appearance and actions, use direct speech to show what they say and how they say it, and suggest other characters' reactions to them.

ACTIVITY 2 | **AO2** | **SKILLS** CREATIVITY, ANALYSIS, INTERPRETATION

▼ BUILDING A SENSE OF CHARACTER

Read the extract from *Let's Give It Up for Gimme Lao!*

1 Writers use a range of techniques to build characters, conveying:
- their appearance
- their actions
- what they say
- how they say it
- other characters' reactions to them.

2 Which of these techniques does Sebastian Sim **NOT** use in creating the character of Grandma Toh?

3 Why might the writer have decided not to use these techniques? What might their absence suggest about the character of Grandma Toh?

4 Note five things the writer **DOES** show or describe about Grandma Toh to create an impression of her. What impression does each one create of her? Note the language choice that creates this impression. Use your ideas to write at least two paragraphs exploring Sim's use of language in creating the character of Grandma Toh.

HINT

Think very carefully about the connotations and implications of the language you use to describe your character's appearance and movement and how they speak.

ACTIVITY 3 | **AO4** | **AO5** | **SKILLS** ADAPTIVE LEARNING, CREATIVITY, INNOVATION

▼ CHARACTER DEVELOPMENT

Using the techniques that you have considered, write your own short, vivid character description that begins with the description of your character's shoes. You could choose to develop your character based on the character created in Activity 1 or start with a new idea.

CONSIDERING CHARACTER

Consider the following prompts to help extend your understanding of characters. You can apply this to the Anthology texts.

■ **How they appear to others**: What kinds of words are used to describe their features, build and clothing? What does the writer want to suggest to the reader about the character's behaviour, attitude or interests?

■ **What they do**: What can the reader guess about the characters from their actions and behaviour?

■ **What they say**: Does the writer use direct speech? What does this tell you about what the character thinks, feels or is likely to do?

■ **How they say it**: How does the writer make the character speak? Are they always talking about the same thing? Do they have a particular way of talking, e.g. dialect, tone? What is the writer suggesting about their background, feelings or interests?

■ **What other characters say or think about them**: How are you made to see them through other people's eyes? Do other characters like or dislike them, admire or despise them, trust or distrust them? Do you believe what others say about them?

KEY POINT

Understanding character is a critical part of analysing a text. Authors can convey meaning through characters' words and actions and how they interact with each other. Characters can also be used to show how a writer feels about a bigger theme or issue.

| ACTIVITY 4 | A01 | A02 | SKILLS | CRITICAL THINKING, ANALYSIS, REASONING, INTERPRETATION |

▼ CHARACTERS IN POETRY

Character is not unique to prose; poems often present readers with strong, vividly-drawn characters. Read 'In the Middle of Dinner' by Chris Abani and answer the following questions.

1 Note down all the details of the poem's setting. Where is the speaker in the poem? When?

2 What impressions does the poem create of the speaker's mother? Which words help to create these impressions?

3 What impressions does the poem create of the speaker's father? Which words help to create these impressions?

4 What do the final two lines suggest about the speaker's mother?

5 Why do you think Abani wrote this poem?

HINT

Traditionally, a wedding ring is worn on the fourth finger of the left hand. In the poem, the speaker describes his mother removing her wedding ring 'from its groove' on that finger and placing it on her middle finger instead. Some believe that a ring on your middle finger symbolises power. What might this suggest about the speaker's mother?

▲ 'So natural was the move, so tender...'

▼ 'IN THE MIDDLE OF DINNER' BY CHRIS ABANI

my mother put down her knife and fork,

pulled her wedding ring from its groove,

placing it contemplatively on her middle

finger. So natural was the move,

so tender, I almost didn't notice.   5

Five years, she said, five years, once a week,

I wrote a letter to your father. And waited

until time was like ash on my tongue.

Not one letter back, not a single note.

She sighed, smiling, the weight gone. This   10

prime rib is really tender, isn't it? she asked.

SETTING AND ATMOSPHERE

SUBJECT VOCABULARY

setting the place where something is or where something happens, and the general environment
atmosphere the feeling that an event or place gives you

KEY POINT

The setting and the atmosphere it evokes are important devices used by a writer in order to influence readers. Careful choice of language is important in conveying this.

The **setting** of a text helps to create **atmosphere** and may have a significant impact on the reader's response to the text. If a novel is set entirely in one room, it can evoke a tense, claustrophobic feeling. A poem featuring open countryside under clear skies could suggest feelings of freedom and opportunity.

CONSIDERING SETTING AND ATMOSPHERE

When approaching a new text, identify the setting and atmosphere more closely by considering the questions below. Does the writer:

- establish the sense of place, weather, time?
- create a particular atmosphere? For example, is it tense or mysterious?
- give details of the setting? How does this contribute to the atmosphere created?
- choose specific vocabulary to create mood? Can you find examples of nouns, adjectives, verbs or adverbs which do this?
- link setting and mood to the action or characters' feelings? For example, does the setting of a rainy, windy, open space reflect a character's loneliness or sadness?

| ACTIVITY 5 | A02 | SKILLS | CRITICAL THINKING, ANALYSIS, REASONING, INTERPRETATION |

▼ SETTING

Look at the questions in the list above. Answer them in response to one of the fiction texts in the Anthology.

LEARNING OBJECTIVES

This lesson will help you to:

- select and interpret information, ideas and perspectives
- comment on the language used.

SUBJECT VOCABULARY

first person written from the perspective of one person – that is, using 'I'; this differs from the second person, which directly addresses the reader ('you'), and the third person ('he', 'she' and 'it')

third person using the third person – that is, 'he', 'she' and 'it'; this differs from the first person ('I') and the second person, which directly addresses the reader ('you')

narrator a character that tells the story in a novel, play, poem or film

NARRATIVE VOICE

When considering a text, it is important to explore the writer's use of plot, character, language, structure, theme, viewpoint and mood. A useful starting point is to consider the 'voice' which is used to tell the story. Is the story written in the first person ('I'), or the third person (written from an external perspective separate from the characters)?

ACTIVITY 1   **A01**   **SKILLS** ▶ CRITICAL THINKING, REASONING

▼ FIRST- AND THIRD-PERSON NARRATION

Whether a text is narrated in the first person or in the third person can have an impact on how a reader feels about the text. For example, a first-person narrative is more personal and a third-person narrative is more detached. Draw up a list of other differences between them.

CONSIDERING NARRATIVE VOICE

DID YOU KNOW?

Second-person narration speaks directly to the reader, usually referring to them as 'you'. This technique is not used very often but can make the reader feel part of the story as it invites involvement or agreement with the narrator.

wigwam Tent with a round structure or pointed roof.

When thinking about the narrative voice, consider these questions.

- Does the writer tell the story from a single narrator's point of view?
- Does the writer give the reader several different points of view?
- What tone is used? For example, is it urgent, anxious, relaxed, excited?
- Do you get a sense of the narrator as a character? What details of their lives are suggested?
- Is the narrator writing the story about themselves?
- Can the reader trust the narrator? Are there any clues that you should not believe everything that they say?
- Is a setting and time period established? What kinds of words are used for this?

▼ FROM *THE SALT ROAD* BY JANE JOHNSON

When I was a child, I had a wigwam in our back garden: a circle of thin yellow cotton draped over a bamboo pole and pegged to the lawn. Every time my parents argued, that was where I went. I would lie on my stomach with my fingers in my ears and stare so hard at the red animals printed on its bright decorative border that after a while they began to dance and run, until I wasn't in the garden any more but out on the plains, wearing a fringed deerskin tunic and feathers in my hair, just like the braves in the films I watched every Saturday morning in the cinema down the road.

Even at an early age I found it preferable to be outside in my little tent rather than inside the house. The tent was my space. It was as large as ▶

grandeur Grandness.

Georgian British style of architecture during the period 1714–1811.

archaeologists Scientists who study the past by looking at historical objects and sites.

unbiddable Will not be told what to do.

oddly attenuated Strangely long and thin.

mannequins Models or dummies.

my imagination, which was infinite. But the house, for all its grandeur and Georgian spaciousness, felt small and suffocating. It was stuffed with things, as well as with my mother and father's bitterness. They were both archaeologists, my parents: lovers of the past, they had surrounded themselves with boxes of yellowed papers, ancient artefacts, dusty objects; the fragile, friable husks of lost civilizations. I never understood why they decided to have me: even the quietest baby, the most house-trained toddler, the most studious child, would have disrupted the artificial, museum-like calm they had wrapped around themselves. In that house they lived separated from the rest of the world, in a bubble in which dust motes floated silently like the fake snow in a snow-globe. I was not the child to complement such a life, being a wild little creature, loud and messy and unbiddable. I liked to play rough games with the boys instead of engaging in the sedate, codified exchanges of the other girls. I had dolls, but more often than not I beheaded or scalped them, or buried them in the garden and forgot where they were. I had no interest in making fashionable outfits for the oddly attenuated pink plastic mannequins with their insectile torsos and brassy hair that the other girls so worshipped and adorned.

KEY POINT

The narrative voice in a text is another key part of a text. The tone can help set the mood and atmosphere and the choice of first- or third-person narration can help shape how events are reported.

ACTIVITY 2   A01   SKILLS ▶ CRITICAL THINKING

▼ ANALYSING A NARRATIVE VOICE

Re-read the extract from *The Salt Road* by Jane Johnson. Highlight any information the reader is given about the narrator in the extract. Then write one or two paragraphs to answer the following question.

▶ **What sense of the narrator's home life is suggested in this extract?**

Remember to support your ideas with evidence from the text and explore the impact of the writer's language choices.

HINT

Think about the mood created and what the narrator reveals through her thoughts and feelings. Is the impression the narrator creates in the extract similar or different to the impression created by this image?

▲ Narrative voices can be used to direct the reader's focus and response.

LEARNING OBJECTIVES

This lesson will help you to:
- understand how writers organise their work for effect.

STRUCTURE

Writers often use a variety of interesting structural devices to arrange their prose or poems. In the exam, you need to be able to write about how the Anthology texts are organised, considering how structure contributes to your understanding and interpretation of the text.

ANALYSING STRUCTURE

HINT

When analysing the structure of a text as a whole, consider the following questions.
- Is the structure chronological or does it involve **time-shifts**?
- What narrative links are used to suggest a movement in time?
- Is there a contrast in the tone and mood between two parts of a text when time moves?
- How much is revealed about the characters at any one time? What do you learn about the characters when time moves?

SUBJECT VOCABULARY

narrative a story
time-shift moving between different periods of time

The simplest way to tell a story is chronologically, starting at the beginning and going on until you reach the end. When commenting on the structure of narrative, consider the following questions.

BEGINNINGS

- **Is a setting or time established?** What kinds of words are used for this?
- **Is a character (or characters) introduced?** Who are they? What do you learn about them?
- **Is a theme suggested?** What impact does this have on the reader?
- **Is there a narrator?** Do they speak in a commentary (first or third person)? What is their tone of voice like? For example, is it urgent, anxious, relaxed, excited?
- **Is dialogue used?** What effect does it have on the reader? For example, is it entertaining, tense, fast-moving, thoughtful?
- **Is there a prevailing tense (past or present)?** What effect does this have?

MIDDLES

- **Is a problem introduced?** How?
- **Are all the characters behaving in the same way that they did at the beginning?** Which have changed? How? Why?
- **Has the setting changed?** How does it fit in with the plot? Does it give added interest?
- **Are there clear links with the beginning of the story or poem?** What are they? Are they shown through words or actions?
- **Does the writer suggest what is to come?** How?

ENDINGS

- **Does the story or poem come to a definite end?** Does the writer leave the reader to guess what happens?
- **Does the book end as you expected?** Or is it a surprise, or even a shock, ending?
- **Does the end echo the opening?** Does it return to the same theme, setting, characters, for example?
- **Is there a moral or message?** Have the characters learned a lesson? Does the author want to tell the reader something?

DID YOU KNOW?

Some writers create interesting effects by using the technique of time-shift, also known as prolepsis. This allows the reader to make connections between widely separated events. Flashbacks to the past can change the reader's interpretation of events and shifts forward can give you a glimpse of the consequences of a character's choices.

SUBJECT VOCABULARY

prolepsis suggestions of things that will happen, before they do

flashback when the narrator of a story jumps out of the present in order to describe an event which happened in the past (often in the form of memories)

KEY POINT

How a text is structured can influence your understanding of a text and your reaction to it. How and when information is revealed is important to both the plot and character development.

MRS DALLOWAY BY VIRGINA WOOLF

The action of Virginia Woolf's novel, *Mrs Dalloway*, takes place on just one day. At the start, Mrs Dalloway is preparing for the party she will hold at her house that night; the novel ends with the party itself. However, through the characters' thoughts and memories, the writer reveals much more about their lives.

▼ FROM *MRS DALLOWAY* BY VIRGINIA WOOLF

Mrs Dalloway said she would buy the flowers herself. For Lucy had her work cut out for her. The doors would be taken off their hinges; Rumplemayer's men were coming. And then, thought Clarissa Dalloway, what a morning – fresh as if issued to children on a beach.

What a lark! What a plunge! For so it had always seemed to her when, with a squeak of the hinges, which she could hear now, she had burst open the French windows and plunged at Bourton into the open air. How fresh, how calm, stiller than a wave; the kiss of a wave; chill and sharp and yet (for a girl of eighteen as she then was) solemn, feeling as she did, standing there at the open window, that something awful was about to happen; looking at the flowers, at the trees with the smoke winding off them and the rooks rising, falling; standing and – was that it? – "I prefer men to cauliflowers" – was that it? He must have said it at breakfast one morning when she had gone out on to the terrace – Peter Walsh. He would be back from India one of these days, June or July, she forgot which, for his letters were awfully dull; it was his sayings one remembered; his eyes, his pocket-knife, his smile, his grumpiness and, when millions of things had utterly vanished – how strange it was! – a few sayings like this about cabbages.

ACTIVITY 1   **AO1**   **SKILLS**   CRITICAL THINKING, ANALYSIS, INTERPRETATION

▼ ANALYSING STRUCTURE

Mrs Dalloway is a novel with an unusual structure. The technique used is known as stream of consciousness: characters' thoughts, feelings and memories are described as they run through the characters' minds. You can see from this piece how structure and narrative voice are linked.

Re-read the opening of the novel and answer the following questions.

■ What is this extract about? Note down all the different things Mrs Dalloway thinks about.

■ When does each of the things she thinks about take place: in her past, the present or the future?

■ How do you feel about Mrs Dalloway at the end of the extract? Why?

STRUCTURE IN PROSE

'NIGHT' BY ALICE MUNRO

Alice Munro (1931–) is a famous Canadian short story writer. She has won numerous literary awards, including the Nobel Prize in Literature in 2013. She is an innovative writer who made changes to the short story as a genre. Chief among these is the way she uses time shifts and moves the narrative forwards and backwards. Character development and how they are coping with life at different stages is often more important than plot in her stories.

| ACTIVITY 2 | A01 | A02 | SKILLS | CRITICAL THINKING, ANALYSIS, INTERPRETATION |

▼ ANALYSING STRUCTURE

Consider the structure of Alice Munro's short story 'Night' (pages 281–287). Using the series of questions on beginnings, middles and ends on page 220, talk about the story. In particular, think about the ending.

| ACTIVITY 3 | A04 | A05 | SKILLS | ADAPTIVE LEARNING, CREATIVITY, INNOVATION |

▼ AN ALTERNATIVE ENDING

Like many writers, Alice Munro often makes revisions to her stories before they are published. Can you write an alternative ending to 'Night', considering the structural techniques that you have learned about in this chapter?

STRUCTURE IN POETRY

HINT

Reading a poem aloud helps you to hear the impact of line length, line breaks, rhyme and rhythm

Structure is important when analysing poetry too. You should think about the following:

- line length: how do short or long lines affect the pace or tone of the poem?
- line breaks and punctuation: is one image or idea conveyed in each line or does the sense run onto the next line? How does this affect the pace of the poem or add emphasis to key ideas or events?
- rhyme: which ideas or events are highlighted by any rhymes in the poem?
- rhythm: how does the rhythm affect the pace or tone of the poem?

GENERAL VOCABULARY

New England an area in the north-east of the United States of America

'OUT, OUT—' BY ROBERT FROST

Robert Frost (1874–1963) was a popular and critically respected American poet. His poetry often tackles complicated themes about American people and society through the rural settings of New England where he spent most of his life. His work is also influenced by the grief and loss he suffered in his personal life. He won four Pulitzer Prizes for Poetry.

▲ American poet Robert Frost.

ACTIVITY 4　**AO2**　SKILLS ▷ CRITICAL THINKING

▼ LOOKING OUT FOR STRUCTURE

Read 'Out, Out—' (pages 230–231). Make a note of anything that you notice about the structure of the poem. Consider the points in the bullet list on page 222.

'Out, Out—' consists of a single stanza. It is written in 'blank verse', with five stresses to a line, which is known formally as 'iambic pentameter' and which is often used to create a conversational tone. It also lacks a formal rhyme scheme. This form suits the conversational tone. The poem is realistic, shocking and dramatic: consider how the poet uses the structure of the poem to help him achieve these intentions.

The importance of the unusual title is something to be discussed. Particularly, the dash after the repeated word 'Out' in the title indicates an unfinished statement.

ACTIVITY 5　**AO2**　SKILLS ▷ CRITICAL THINKING, ANALYSIS, INTERPRETATION

▼ WRITING ABOUT STRUCTURE IN POETRY

Re-read 'Out, Out—' and look out for significant structural choices the poet has made. Write a paragraph exploring the impact of the poem's structure.

ACTIVITY 6　**AO2**　SKILLS ▷ CRITICAL THINKING, ANALYSIS, REASONING, INTERPRETATION

▼ ANTHOLOGY TEXTS

Review the fiction texts in the Anthology. Which ones are retrospective or use time-shifts? Choose one, then write a paragraph exploring the impact of its structure, considering the following points.

■ How does the writer signal the movement in time to the reader?

■ What is revealed about the characters? How does the writer use the movement of time or other structural features to achieve this?

■ How does the mood change as the story develops? How does the writer create this change? What impact does it have?

LEARNING OBJECTIVES

This lesson will help you to:
- prepare for the Paper 2 exam.

PUTTING IT INTO PRACTICE

The question asked in Paper 2 Section A of the exam tests your reading and analytical skills. It is based on the fiction texts in the Anthology.

UNDERSTANDING THE EXAM CRITERIA

KEY POINT

Exam essays should be fully developed not just in terms of length but in ideas. It is important that you analyse the impact of the writer's choices, rather than just pointing out features or summarising what the text is about.

In order to succeed in answering this question in the exam, you need to:
- show that you have understood what you have read: you can do this by identifying ideas and information from the text that are relevant to the question's focus
- choose relevant, focused evidence from the text to support your ideas
- show that you understand the way in which the writer uses language and structure to create meaning and control the reader's response.

WHAT YOU WILL BE ASKED TO DO

In the exam, you will be asked to respond to **one** of the fiction Anthology texts. There is only one question in Section A of the exam and you must answer it. The question is worth 30 marks.

In this section, you will be presented with an extract from a text and asked to analyse it in the way you will need to do in the exam. This will allow you to practise the skills that you have learned. In the exam, you will only be asked to answer about a text from the Anthology, so this activity is for illustrative purposes only.

FRANKENSTEIN BY MARY WOLLSTONECRAFT SHELLEY

Victor Frankenstein has been building a creature from the body parts of dead people. Now, he is ready to bring the creature to life.

▼ FROM *FRANKENSTEIN* BY MARY WOLLSTONECRAFT SHELLEY

It was on a dreary night of November that I beheld the accomplishment of my toils. With an anxiety that almost amounted to agony, I collected the instruments of life around me, that I might infuse a spark of being into the lifeless thing that lay at my feet. It was already one in the morning; the rain pattered dismally against the panes, and my candle was nearly burnt out, when, by the glimmer of the half-extinguished light, I saw the dull yellow eye of the creature open; it breathed hard, and a convulsive motion agitated its limbs.

How can I describe my emotions at this catastrophe, or how delineate the wretch whom with such infinite pains and care I had endeavoured to form? His limbs were in proportion, and I had selected his features as beautiful. Beautiful! Great God! His yellow skin scarcely covered the work of muscles and arteries beneath; his hair was of a lustrous black, and flowing; his teeth of a pearly whiteness; but these luxuriances only formed a more horrid contrast with his watery eyes, that seemed almost of the same colour as the dun-white sockets in which they were set, his shrivelled complexion and straight black lips.

▲ A portrait of Mary Shelley, completed in 1840.

The different accidents of life are not so changeable as the feelings of human nature. I had worked hard for nearly two years, for the sole purpose of infusing life into an inanimate body. For this I had deprived myself of rest and health. I had desired it with an ardour that far exceeded moderation; but now that I had finished, the beauty of the dream vanished, and breathless horror and disgust filled my heart. Unable to endure the aspect of the being I had created, I rushed out of the room and continued a long time traversing my bedchamber, unable to compose my mind to sleep. At length lassitude succeeded to the tumult I had before endured, and I threw myself on the bed in my clothes, endeavouring to seek a few moments of forgetfulness. But it was in vain; I slept, indeed, but I was disturbed by the wildest dreams. I thought I saw Elizabeth, in the bloom of health, walking in the streets of Ingolstadt. Delighted and surprised, I embraced her, but as I imprinted the first kiss on her lips, they became livid with the hue of death; her features appeared to change, and I thought that I held the corpse of my dead mother in my arms; a shroud enveloped her form, and I saw the grave-worms crawling in the folds of the flannel. I started from my sleep with horror; a cold dew covered my forehead, my teeth chattered, and every limb became convulsed; when, by the dim and yellow light of the moon, as it forced its way through the window shutters, I beheld the wretch— the miserable monster whom I had created.

EXAM-STYLE QUESTION

A01

A02

SKILLS CRITICAL THINKING, ANALYSIS, REASONING, INTERPRETATION

Read the extract from *Frankenstein*.

How does the author convey the narrator's thoughts and feelings?

In your answer, you should write about:

- the setting
- the narrator's reaction to the creature he has created
- the use of language and structure.

You should support your answer with close reference to the extract, including **brief** quotations.

(30 marks)

HINT

Use this paragraph to get you started.

The writer begins by setting the scene and the mood This shows an awareness of tone and structure.

immediately creates connotations of darkness and misery This demonstrates a sound understanding of the effects of the writer's language choices.

adjective 'dreary' and adverb 'dismally' suggesting the narrator's unhappiness This shows a close focus on language choice.

This agony is emphasised by the use of short, sharp exclamations Sentence structure can have a significant impact on the reader. Always look for opportunities to talk about it.

The writer conveys the narrator's mixture of emotions in a range of ways. The writer begins by setting the scene and the mood: 'a dreary night of November' where 'the rain pattered dismally against the panes'. This immediately creates connotations of darkness and misery, in particular the adjective 'dreary' and adverb 'dismally' suggesting the narrator's unhappiness. The writer also uses blunt emotive descriptions to clearly show the narrator's state of mind: 'an anxiety that almost amounted to agony'. This suggests not just worry but a worry so strong it is causing him pain. This agony is emphasised by the use of short, sharp exclamations when he realises what he has done: 'Beautiful! Great God!'.

The student shows a clear understanding of the writer's language choices, such as description of setting, and sentence structures.

'DISABLED'
WILFRED OWEN

BACKGROUND AND CONTEXT

Wilfred Owen is one of the best known of the English poets who wrote about their experiences of the First World War (1914–1918). These experiences had a significant impact on the writers and cost many of them their lives. Owen was strongly influenced by another war poet called Siegfried Sassoon. They met at Craiglockhart Hospital where they had both been sent to recover from shell-shock. Owen twice said that his theme was 'war and the pity of war'. Having returned to his regiment after his time in hospital, he died in battle in November 1918, just seven days before the armistice brought the war to an end on 11th November 1918.

▲ Owen said his writing was about 'war and the pity of war'.

BEFORE YOU START READING

1 You can find out more about Wilfred Owen and his poetry from reference books or on the internet. You could read some more of his poems, which will help you to understand his attitudes to war and how he wrote about it.

2 How would you feel about living with a physical disability such as the loss of a limb? What attitudes to people with disabilities do you find in your society?

3 What can you find out about the kinds of injuries that soldiers suffered in the First World War and the way in which they were treated when they returned from the front?

▼ 'DISABLED' BY WILFRED OWEN

He sat in a wheeled chair, waiting for dark,

And shivered in his ghastly suit of grey,

Legless, sewn short at elbow. Through the park

Voices of boys rang saddening like a hymn,

Voices of play and pleasure after day,   5

Till gathering sleep had mothered them from him.

About this time Town used to swing so gay

When glow-lamps budded in the light blue trees,

And girls glanced lovelier as the air grew dim –

In the old times, before he threw away his knees.   10

Now he will never feel again how slim

▶

Girls' waists are, or how warm their subtle hands;

All of them touch him like some queer disease.

There was an artist silly for his face,

For it was younger than his youth, last year.   15

Now, he is old; his back will never brace;

He's lost his colour very far from here,

Poured it down shell-holes till the veins ran dry,

And half his lifetime lapsed in the hot race,

And leap of purple spurted from his thigh.   20

One time he liked a blood-smear down his leg,

After the matches, carried shoulder-high.

It was after football, when he'd drunk a peg,

He thought he'd better join. – He wonders why.

Someone had said he'd look a god in kilts,   25

That's why; and maybe, too, to please his Meg;

Aye, that was it, to please the giddy jilts

He asked to join. He didn't have to beg;

Smiling they wrote his lie: aged nineteen years.

Germans he scarcely thought of; all their guilt,   30

And Austria's, did not move him. And no fears

Of Fear came yet. He thought of jewelled hilts

For daggers in plaid socks; of smart salutes;

And care of arms; and leave; and pay arrears;

Esprit de corps; and hints for young recruits.   35

And soon, he was drafted out with drums and cheers.

Some cheered him home, but not as crowds cheer Goal.

Only a solemn man who brought him fruits

Thanked him; and then enquired about his soul.

Now, he will spend a few sick years in institutes,   40

Esprit de corps French expression
meaning a feeling of pride.

▶

> And do what things the rules consider wise,
>
> And take whatever pity they may dole.
>
> Tonight he noticed how the women's eyes
>
> Passed from him to the strong men that were whole.
>
> How cold and late it is! Why don't they come   45
>
> And put him into bed? Why don't they come?

UNDERSTANDING THE TEXT

Owen's wounded soldier, who has lost his legs and his arms, sits in a wheelchair in hospital listening to the shouts of boys playing at sunset. He is reminded of the excitement of former early evenings in town before he joined up; 'before he threw away his knees'.

The poem blends the past and present to powerful effect.

- Note down all the details in the soldier's present: his situation, and the things he sees and hears.
- Note down all the things that the soldier remembers from his past.
- Note down the soldier's thoughts about his future.
- What similarities or differences can you identify between the soldier's past, present and future?

Copy and complete the table, noting whether Owen focuses on the soldier's past, present or future in each stanza.

▼ STANZA	▼ PAST?	▼ PRESENT?	▼ FUTURE?
1			
2		✔	
3			
4			
5			
6			
7			

How are the past, present and future linked in the poem? Write one or two sentences how the structure of the poem tracks the wounded soldier's thoughts and feelings about his past, present and future.

EXPLORING LANGUAGE

Look closely at each stanza again. Owen chooses his words very carefully to create a powerful impression of the wounded soldier's thoughts and feelings about his past, present and future.

Note down any significant vocabulary choices you can find in each stanza that suggest his mood. Add them to a table like the one on page 229. What are the implications and connotations of each of the vocabulary choices you have noted?

▼ STANZA	▼ PAST, PRESENT OR FUTURE?	▼ VOCABULARY CHOICE AND IMPLICATIONS AND CONNOTATIONS
1	Present	■ 'shivered' suggests fear, cold, discomfort ■ 'saddening' creates a depressing mood ■
2	Past	■ 'glow' suggests warmth and comfort ■ ■
3		■ ■ ■
4		■ ■ ■
5		■ ■ ■
6		■ ■ ■
7		■ ■ ■

How does the mood of the poem develop as the wounded soldier considers his past, present and future? Write two or three sentences, explaining your ideas and using quotations to show how the writer's vocabulary choices create these different moods.

ACTIVITY 1 **A04** **A05** **SKILLS** CRITICAL THINKING, ANALYSIS, INTERPRETATION, ADAPTIVE LEARNING, CREATIVITY

▼ WRITING TASK

Write an article in which you describe the lives of the wounded soldiers who are being cared for in an institution.

EXAM-STYLE QUESTION

A01

A02

SKILLS CRITICAL THINKING, ANALYSIS, REASONING, INTERPRETATION

How does the writer show a disabled soldier's thoughts and feelings in 'Disabled'?

In your answer, you should write about:

■ the effects of war

■ the present and past attitudes of the disabled soldier

■ the use of contrast

■ the writer's use of words, phrases and language techniques.

You should support your answer with close reference to the extract, including **brief** quotations. **(30 marks)**

'OUT, OUT—'
ROBERT FROST

BACKGROUND

Robert Frost (1874–1963) was one of the major American poets of the 20th century. His poetry was often inspired by the life and scenery of rural New England. 'Out, Out –' was published in the collection *Mountain Interval* in 1916.

The setting of this poem is a farm. The scenery around the farm is beautiful. Life is too hard for it to be enjoyed fully by the family, even by the young son, who has to work all day cutting up wood with a buzz saw. It is believed that Frost based the poem on a real incident that he read about in a newspaper.

BEFORE YOU START READING

1 You can find out more about Robert Frost and his poetry from reference books or on the internet. You could read some more of his poems, which will help you to understand the sort of subjects that he wrote about. These include 'Stopping by Woods on a Snowy Evening', 'Mending Wall', and 'Meeting and Passing'.

2 Think about the way a newspaper would describe this tragic event in comparison with how the poet presents the incident.

▼ 'OUT, OUT—' BY ROBERT FROST

▲ Cutting wood with a saw is dangerous work.

Vermont State in the northeast of the USA.

The buzz saw snarled and rattled in the yard

And made dust and dropped stove-length sticks of wood,

Sweet-scented stuff when the breeze drew across it.

And from there those that lifted eyes could count

Five mountain ranges one behind the other   5

Under the sunset far into Vermont.

And the saw snarled and rattled, snarled and rattled,

As it ran light, or had to bear a load.

And nothing happened: day was all but done.

Call it a day, I wish they might have said   10

To please the boy by giving him the half hour

That a boy counts so much when saved from work.

His sister stood beside them in her apron

To tell them 'Supper.' At the word, the saw,

As if to prove saws knew what supper meant,   15

Leaped out at the boy's hand, or seemed to leap–

He must have given the hand. However it was,

Neither refused the meeting. But the hand!

The boy's first outcry was a rueful laugh,

As he swung toward them holding up the hand,   20

Half in appeal, but half as if to keep

The life from spilling. Then the boy saw all–

Since he was old enough to know, big boy

Doing a man's work, though a child at heart–

He saw all spoiled. "Don't let him cut my hand off–   25

The doctor, when he comes. Don't let him, sister!"

So. But the hand was gone already.

The doctor put him in the dark of ether.

He lay and puffed his lips out with his breath.

And then–the watcher at his pulse took fright.   30

No one believed. They listened at his heart.

Little–less–nothing!–and that ended it.

No more to build on there. And they, since they

Were not the one dead, turned to their affairs.

ether An anaesthetic gas used in the 19th and early 20th centuries.

UNDERSTANDING THE TEXT

The title of the poem is from Shakespeare's *Macbeth*, Act V Scene IV, where Macbeth learns of the death of Lady Macbeth, his wife.

▼ FROM *MACBETH* BY WILLIAM SHAKESPEARE

She should have died hereafter;

There would have been a time for such a word.

To-morrow, and to-morrow, and to-morrow,

Creeps in this petty pace from day to day,

To the last syllable of recorded time;   5

And all our yesterdays have lighted fools

The way to dusty death. Out, out, brief candle!

Life's but a walking shadow, a poor player,

That struts and frets his hour upon the stage,

And then is heard no more. It is a tale   10

Told by an idiot, full of sound and fury,

Signifying nothing.

Think about the way in which Frost makes use of the quotation from *Macbeth* and in particular why the reference to death as life's 'brief candle' going out might apply particularly to the situation that Frost describes in the poem.

Frost generally uses straightforward vocabulary, but 'Out, Out—' contains some difficult phrases. These are listed in the following table. Copy and complete the table with explanations of these difficult phrases to develop your understanding of the poem.

▼ LANGUAGE	▼ EXPLANATION
'stove-length sticks of wood'	Logs the right size to put in a wood-burning stove.
'As it ran light'	When it ran freely because it was not cutting anything difficult.
'As if to prove saws knew what supper meant'	
'Neither refused the meeting'	
'put him in the dark of ether'	
'the watcher at his pulse took fright'	
'No more to build on there'	

▶ Word choice in poetry is often used to create vivid impressions; in this case, 'stove-length sticks of wood'.

EXPLORING LANGUAGE

Although Frost's language choice is simple, he uses it to create a vivid impression of this incident. Look at some of the key quotations from the poem below.

'The buzz saw snarled and rattled'	Onomatopoeia
'Sweet-scented stuff when the breeze drew across it'	Repetition
'The saw… Leaped out at the boy's hand'	Punctuation for effect
'But the hand!'	Personification
Don't let him cut my hand off– The doctor, when he comes. Don't let him, sister!'	Exclamation
'They listened at his heart. Little–less– nothing!–and that ended it.'	Short, blunt sentences
No more to build on there.'	Sensory description

Which language technique has Frost used in each quotation? What effect does it have? Write one or two sentences about each one.

ACTIVITY 1   **A01**   SKILLS ▷ CRITICAL THINKING, ANALYSIS, INTERPRETATION

▼ READING BETWEEN THE LINES

KEY POINT

KEY POINT

Frost creates much of this poem's impact by making the reader infer information and ideas.

Although the boy is shown to be part of a family, he also seems isolated and unloved; there is little evidence of sympathy for him from his family. What does the poem's language show you about:

■ the boy's sister

■ the relationships within the family

■ the family's reactions to the boy's tragic early death?

Copy and complete the table with examples of language referring to the above points, explaining what each example shows you.

▼ LANGUAGE REFERRING TO FAMILY	▼ WHAT DOES THIS SHOW?

ACTIVITY 2   **A01**   SKILLS ▷ TEAMWORK, EMPATHY

▼ EXPLAINING THE ACCIDENT

Work with a partner, imagining that one of you is a police officer and that the other is a member of the family who actually saw the accident, describing the event to the police officer. In your roles, conduct an interview to investigate the circumstances of the accident.

ACTIVITY 3   **A04**   **A05**   SKILLS ▷ CRITICAL THINKING, ANALYSIS, INTERPRETATION, ADAPTIVE LEARNING, CREATIVITY

▼ WRITING TASK

Write an article on the dangers to children of undertaking adult work, persuading people to adhere to health and safety advice.

EXAM-STYLE QUESTION ▷

A01

A02

SKILLS ▷ CRITICAL THINKING, ANALYSIS, REASONING, INTERPRETATION

How does the writer create a sense of horror in 'Out, Out—'?

In your answer, you should write about:

■ the way in which the chainsaw is presented

■ the way in which the seriousness of the situation is gradually revealed

■ the poet's use of words, phrases and language techniques.

You should support your answer with close reference to the extract, including **brief** quotations.

(30 marks)

'AN UNKNOWN GIRL'
MONIZA ALVI

BACKGROUND
Moniza Alvi was born in Lahore, Pakistan. She has a Pakistani father and an English mother. Her father moved the family to England when she was very young, and she did not go back to Pakistan until after her first book of poems had been published. She worked for several years as a teacher in London and is now a freelance writer and tutor.

▲ Henna being used for body decoration.

BEFORE YOU START READING

1 You can find out more about Moniza Alvi and her poetry from reference books or on the internet. You could read some more of her poems, such as 'Presents from my Aunts', which will help you to understand her attitudes toward her Pakistani heritage.

2 Think about what Moniza Alvi says about her background and its links to her poetry:

'Presents from My Aunts' ... was one of the first poems I wrote. When I wrote this poem, I hadn't actually been back to Pakistan. The girl in the poem would be me at about 13. The clothes seem to stick to her in an uncomfortable way, a bit like a kind of false skin and she thinks things aren't straightforward for her.'

I found it was important to write the Pakistan poems because I was getting in touch with my background. And maybe there's a bit of a message behind the poems about something I went through, that I want to maybe open a few doors if possible.

3 If you or your family have moved from one country to another, think about your feelings about the original country. If you have not, talk to someone you know who has moved from one country to another and ask them about how they feel about the place that their family came from, or read about other people's experiences.

▼ 'AN UNKNOWN GIRL' BY MONIZA ALVI

In the evening bazaar

studded with neon

an unknown girl

is hennaing my hand.

She squeezes a wet brown line   5

from a nozzle.

She is icing my hand,

which she steadies with hers

on her satin-peach knee.

In the evening bazaar   10

for a few rupees

an unknown girl

is hennaing my hand.

As a little air catches

my shadow-stitched kameez   15

a peacock spreads its lines

across my palm.

Colours leave the street

float up in balloons.

Dummies in shop-fronts   20

tilt and stare

with their Western perms.

Banners for Miss India 1993,

▶

bazaar A marketplace.

hennaing A method of applying a temporary tattoo using a strong reddish-brown dye (henna).

kameez A loose-fitting tunic.

Miss India The national winner in a Miss World beauty contest.

▲ 'I'll scrape off the dry brown lines before
I sleep...'

for curtain cloth

and sofa cloth   25

canopy me.

I have new brown veins.

In the evening bazaar

very deftly

an unknown girl   30

is hennaing my hand.

I am clinging

to these firm peacock lines

like people who cling

to the sides of a train.   35

Now the furious streets

are hushed.

I'll scrape off

the dry brown lines

before I sleep,   40

reveal soft as a snail trail

the amber bird beneath.

It will fade in a week.

When India appears and reappears

I'll lean across a country   45

with my hands outstretched

longing for the unknown girl

in the neon bazaar.

UNDERSTANDING THE TEXT

This poem describes the poet's visit to India and the time she had her hand hennaed by a girl in the bazaar. It was an experience she never forgot.

India is presented as a vibrant and colourful country of contrasts. Images of Indian tradition and culture are interspersed with images suggesting the influence of western culture: the poet refers to a beauty contest and to Western perms. The lasting impression of India for the poet and the reader is, though, the traditionally Indian henna peacock on the poet's hand.

In her description of the bazaar where she has her hand hennaed, Alvi conveys her thoughts and feelings about India. She depicts the bazaar as a blend of traditional Indian culture and western culture. Compare the two quotations below.

'a little air catches my shadow-stitched kameez a peacock spreads its lines across my palm'	'Dummies in shop-fronts tilt and stare with their Western perms.'

What impression does Alvi give of her thoughts and feelings about Indian culture in these quotations? What impression does Alvi give of her thoughts and feelings about the elements of western culture she sees in the bazaar in these quotations? How do these impressions differ?

Note down anything else in the poem that reveals the poet's thoughts and feelings about India.

EXPLORING IMAGERY

Alvi's language choices are generally straightforward, but she creates some images that take a little thought to visualise.

Look closely at some of the examples of imagery below. Copy and complete the table below, noting:

- the visual impressions each one creates
- key words or phrases that help to create that impression
- any connotations of those key words or phrases that add meaning to those impressions
- any other images that create a significant impression as you read the poem.

▼ IMAGES	▼ YOUR IMPRESSIONS
'She is icing my hand'	A strong visual impression of henna squeezed from a tube; 'icing' has connotations of decorating a cake, suggesting celebration…
'on her satin-peach knee'	
'My shadow-stitched kameez'	
'canopy me'	
'I have new brown veins'	'veins' suggest blood, life…
'curtain cloth and sofa cloth canopy me'	
'I'll lean across a country with my hands outstretched'	

EXPLORING LANGUAGE

▲ The poem creates a vivid impression of India.

KEY POINT

The poem contrasts Indian culture with the influence of western culture.

The poem creates a vivid impression of India. Note down five or more quotations that help to create your impressions. You could start with the quotations below.

| 'studded with neon' |
| 'Now the furious streets are hushed' |
| 'people who cling to the sides of a train' |

For each quotation you have noted, write one or two sentences, explaining your impressions. Which words, phrases or language techniques has the writer used to create your impressions of India?

ACTIVITY 1 **A04** SKILLS ▶ INTELLECTUAL INTEREST, SELF-PRESENTATION

▼ REPORTING ON ANOTHER CULTURE

Imagine you are a television reporter working on a travel programme. Research your chosen destination and prepare a short talk about your impressions.

ACTIVITY 2 **A04** **A05** SKILLS ▶ CRITICAL THINKING, ANALYSIS, INTERPRETATION, ADAPTIVE LEARNING, CREATIVITY

▼ WRITING TASK

Write an article entitled either 'Why I like make-up', or 'Make-up: a waste of time and money'.

EXAM-STYLE QUESTION

A01

A02

SKILLS ▶ CRITICAL THINKING, ANALYSIS, REASONING, INTERPRETATION

How does the writer of 'An Unknown Girl' present her feelings about the country she has visited?

In your answer, you should write about:

- the images of the country
- the way she feels about having her hand painted
- the writer's use of words, phrases and techniques.

You should support your answer with close reference to the extract, including **brief** quotations.

(30 marks)

'THE BRIGHT LIGHTS OF SARAJEVO'
TONY HARRISON

BACKGROUND AND CONTEXT

Tony Harrison was born in Leeds, Yorkshire, in 1937 and is a leading poet and translator. He has often written about social issues and sometimes about international issues. He wrote 'The Bright Lights of Sarajevo' when a national British newspaper sent him to write about Bosnia, a country in south-eastern Europe, in September 1995.

The Bosnian War took place between 1992 and 1995. It was a bitter conflict between parts of the former Yugoslavia, which broke out along old national and cultural boundaries at the beginning of the 1990s. The main division was between Bosnia and Serbia, but the political situation was very complex. The war was motivated by ethnic prejudice and Muslims in the region suffered horrific persecution.

The poem is set in Sarajevo, capital city of Bosnia, during the siege mounted by Serb forces which lasted the entire duration of the war. Thousands of people died in the city during the siege.

GENERAL VOCABULARY

siege a situation in which an army or the police surround a place and try to gain control of it or force someone to come out of it

Yugoslavia a country which separated into several smaller countries in the early 1990s

BEFORE YOU START READING

1 The siege of Sarajevo is the longest siege of a capital city in modern history. Using the internet, do some research into the series of conflicts that broke apart Yugoslavia.

2 One event that captured the attention of the international media and people worldwide was the gunning down of a young couple commonly referred to as 'the Romeo and Juliet of Sarajevo'. Find out about them.

3 Think about how you would feel if your daily routines became restricted and it became too dangerous to even go out to buy a loaf of bread. How would you cope?

▶ 'match-lit flare test'.

prams A pushchair usually used for transporting children, used for a different purpose here.

meagre A very small amount.

grams A small unit of measuring weight. Together, 'meagre' and 'grams' emphasise the scarcity of food during the siege.

shells Explosive missiles or bombs.

bread Serbo-Croatian has several dialects used in Bosnia and Herzegovina. 'Heljeb' (intentionally mis-spelled by Harrison) is the Ljekavian term for bread, while 'hleb' is Ekavian. 'Kruh' is the term for bread in Croatian.

ploys Plans or actions used to gain an advantage of some type.

▼ 'THE BRIGHT LIGHTS OF SARAJEVO' BY TONY HARRISON

After the hours that Sarajevans pass

queuing with empty canisters of gas

to get the refills they wheel home in prams,

or queuing for the precious meagre grams

of bread they're rationed to each day,   5

and often dodging snipers on the way,

or struggling up sometimes eleven flights

of stairs with water, then you'd think the nights

of Sarajevo would be totally devoid

of people walking streets Serb shells destroyed,   10

but tonight in Sarajevo that's just not the case–

The young go walking at a stroller's pace,

black shapes impossible to mark

as Muslim, Serb or Croat in such dark,

in unlit streets you can't distinguish who   15

calls bread *hjleb* or *hleb* or calls it *kruh*.

All takes the evening air with a stroller's stride,

no torches guide them, but they don't collide

except as one of the flirtatious ploys

when a girl's dark shape is fancied by a boy's.   20

Then the tender radar of the tone of voice

shows by its signals she approves his choice.

Then match or lighter to a cigarette

to check in her eyes if he's made progress yet.

And I see a pair who've certainly progressed   25

beyond the tone of voice and match-lit flare test

and he's about, I think, to take her hand

and lead her away from where they stand

▶

1992 On 27th May 1992, a breadline in Sarajevo was attacked with mortar fire, killing many people.

Pleiades An open star cluster of the constellation Taurus, also known as Seven Sisters. In Greek mythology, they were the daughters of Atlas who became stars.

AID flour-sacks Humanitarian aid is provided to conflict sites by international organisations. There is irony here in the fact that the sack is used to create barricades that protect civilians from mortar and sniper fire.

---

on two shell scars, where, in 1992

Serb mortars massacred the breadshop queue   30

and blood-dunked crusts of shredded bread

lay on this pavement with the broken dead.

And at their feet in holes made by the mortar

that caused the massacre, now full of water

from the rain that's poured down half the day,   35

though now even the smallest clouds have cleared away,

leaving the Sarajevo star-filled evening sky

ideally bright and clear for bomber's eye,

in those two rain-full shell-holes the boy sees

fragments of the splintered Pleiades,   40

sprinkled on those death-deep, death-dark wells

splashed on the pavement by Serb mortar shells.

The dark boy-shape leads dark girl-shape away

to share one coffee in a candlelit café

until the curfew, and he holds her hand   45

behind AID flour-sacks refilled with sand.

UNDERSTANDING THE TEXT

KEY POINT

The poet is writing about a complex conflict and it is a great challenge to capture its multiple facets in poetry, but it is also a situation with great literary potential.

The poem is about the devastation and disruption caused by war and the resilience of the human spirit in the face of this. The poem highlights the difficulties faced by the citizens of Sarajevo and contrasts this with young couples whose relationships are slowly progressing in a city that seems to symbolise death. Harrison also uses references to the couples' surroundings to show that, while life will continue in harsh environments, the reality of the situation is inescapable. He also explores the roots of the conflict, by showing that ethnic divides disappear in the shadows of the night.

THEMES

▶ **What are the main themes of the poem?**

The table on page 242 shows some of the themes. Complete the table by finding examples from the text and adding your ideas, analysing how the example illustrates the theme. One quotation illustrating the theme of 'war' has been added for you as an example.

▼ THEME	▼ EXAMPLE	▼ ANALYSIS
War	'and often dodging snipers on the way'	Shows that, even while doing an ordinary task, there is a real risk of being killed. This highlights the reality of living in a war zone.
Deprivation		
Love		

SETTING AND EVENTS

SUBJECT VOCABULARY

paradox a situation (or description) which seems contradictory and unlikely, but is actually true or accurate

The poem shows the **paradoxes** of life in Sarajevo at this time: for example, how ethnic difference is invisible and unimportant at night despite its central significance in the conflict, and how romance can blossom in the midst of violence and destruction.

Look closely at some key quotations from the poem below. Each of these shows the setting and the events described in the poem.

'queuing with empty canisters of gas to get the refills they wheel home in prams'

'queuing for the precious meagre grams of bread they're rationed to each day'

'dodging snipers on the way'

'struggling up sometimes eleven flights of stairs with water'

'The young go walking at a stroller's pace'

'and he's about, I think, to take her hand'

Add to these quotations and, for each one, write one or two sentences explaining what it suggests about life in Sarajevo at the time the poem describes.

Finally, write one or two sentences summing up life in Sarajevo during the Bosnian war.

EXPLORING LANGUAGE ▶

GENERAL VOCABULARY

conversational informal, as though spoken in conversation with someone else

SUBJECT VOCABULARY

rhyme scheme the rhyming pattern used in a poem
rhyming couplet a pair of lines that rhyme
contrast where two objects, people or ideas are placed next to each other to highlight their differences

KEY POINT

Think about the links between some of these contrasting pairs. For example, in what ways could war and love be linked with darkness and light?

STYLE AND RHYME

The simple language choices and the use of very long sentences with very few full stops give the poem a conversational tone.

▶ **Identify one or two words or phrases from the poem that give the impression the poet is talking informally to the reader.**

The rhyme scheme of the poem is similarly simple: it is written in rhyming couplets.

▶ **Think about the effect of the poem's conversational style and rhyme scheme. Does the simple rhyme scheme and style suggest the events the poet is writing about are simple and unimportant? Or does the conversational style contrast with the emotive content of the poem and add impact to the poet's ideas? Write one or two sentences explaining your ideas.**

CONTRAST

Throughout the poem, Harrison contrasts different aspects of life in Sarajevo.

Find quotations from the poem that show any of the below.

	▼ QUOTATION	▼ QUOTATION	
War			Love
Darkness			Light
Poverty			Wealth
Hunger			Plenty
Fear			Calm
Beauty			Ugliness

Look again at all the quotations you have found. Does this poem present a positive view of life in Sarajevo, or a negative view? Write two or three sentences explaining your ideas.

▲ Traces of the war can be seen in bullet holes in this building in Sarajevo.

WORD CHOICE

Many of Harrison's word choices in the poem are simple and descriptive. However, some have a significant impact. Look at each of the quotations below. In each quotation identify:

- at least one word or phrase that highlights the contrasts you have already identified
- the connotations and implications of the word or phrase you have chosen.

'the hours that Sarajevans pass / queuing'

'precious meagre grams of bread'

'a stroller's pace'

'two shell scars, where, in 1992
Serb mortars massacred the breadshop queue'

'blood-dunked crusts of shredded bread
lay on this pavement with the broken dead.'

Can you identify any other word choices Harrison has made that have a significant impact?

ACTIVITY 1 | A04 | A05 | SKILLS ▶ PROBLEM SOLVING, CREATIVITY, INNOVATION, INTELLECTUAL INTEREST

▼ WRITING TASKS

1. Write a story that focuses on surviving and making the best of a very difficult situation.
2. Imagine you are one of the boy-shapes or girl-shapes in the poem. Write an entry in your diary for a day and night during the siege of Sarajevo.

EXAM-STYLE QUESTIONS

A01

A02

SKILLS ▶ CRITICAL THINKING, ANALYSIS, REASONING, INTERPRETATION

1. How does the writer successfully convey the horror of war and the ability of human beings to rise above it? In your answer, you should write about:
   - the ideas about war conveyed in the poem
   - the way the writer uses images and contrast
   - the writer's use of words, phrases and language techniques.

You should support your answer with close reference to the extract, including **brief** quotations. **(30 marks)**

HINT

Remember that the word 'how' means that you are expected to discuss methods or techniques used by the writer to create certain effects. To improve your answers, you need to be able to comment in some detail about particular words and phrases, explaining the impact on the reader or how you think the poet intends the reader to react. It is better to write about a few quotations in detail than to try to fit in a lot of points without explaining them properly.

2 How does the writer present the difficult and dangerous conditions in Sarajevo in 'The Bright Lights of Sarajevo'? In your answer, you should write about:

■ the description of the physical environment

■ the way people are behaving

■ the writer's use of words, phrases and language techniques.

You should support your answer with close reference to the extract, including **brief** quotations. **(30 marks)**

WRITING A SUCCESSFUL ANSWER

Below are two examples of opening paragraphs written in response to Question 2 above. Which do you think is more successful? Look at the criteria for Assessment Objectives 1 and 2 on page 328. Which paragraph achieves these? What improvements would you suggest to make both of these paragraphs more effective?

EXAMPLE STUDENT ANSWER A

'The Bright Lights of Sarajevo' is a poem by Tony Harrison that is set in the background of the Bosnian war. This war went on for many years and resulted in lots of casualties. The writer wants to show that he is against war and uses contrast to do this. The biggest contrast he uses is between love and war. He describes the city in detail as well.

EXAMPLE STUDENT ANSWER B

Set against the Bosnian war, this poem delivers a strong message about the devastation caused by war and the way people are able to rise above it. For this purpose he mainly uses contrast as a technique. Firstly, he describes Sarajevo during the day and then at night. This helps the reader to visualise the difference and understand what it was like to live there during the siege of 1992.

ACTIVITY 2 | A03 | SKILLS ▶ CRITICAL THINKING, ANALYSIS, INTERPRETATION, DECISION MAKING

▼ FINDING SIMILARITIES AND DIFFERENCES

'Corpse' is a poem taken from *Sarajevo Blues*, a collection written by Semezdin Mehmedinovic, who lived in Sarajevo during the siege. Written by a citizen rather than an observer, the ideas and language of this poem have similarities to, as well as differences from, 'The Bright Lights of Sarajevo'. Think about these similarities and differences and write them down in the table that follows. You can look at features such as structure and rhyme scheme, as well as the themes and ideas.

▼ 'CORPSE' BY SEMEZDIN MEHMEDINOVIC

We slowed down at the bridge

to watch some dogs tear a

corpse apart by the river

and then we went on

nothing in me has changed   5

I heard the crunch of snow under tires

like teeth biting into an apple

and felt the wild desire to laugh

at you

because you call this place hell   10

and you flee from here convinced

that death outside Sarajevo does not exist

▼ SIMILARITIES	▼ DIFFERENCES
Both poems give details from daily life, such as 'crunch of snow under the tires', 'empty canisters of gas'.	The titles. 'Bright Lights…' has apparently positive connotations but 'Corpse' creates an immediately negative impression.

▲ Award-winning American writer Maya Angelou.

'STILL I RISE'
MAYA ANGELOU

BACKGROUND
Maya Angelou was an American poet, writer, singer, composer, actor, director, lecturer and civil rights activist. Her illustrious career, which spanned six decades, won her both fame and critical acclaim as well as numerous awards and honorary degrees. Her work centres on such themes as racism, family, women and identity, and she is an important figure in the Black literary tradition.

She has written seven volumes of autobiography, which include *I Know Why the Caged Bird Sings* and *A Song Flung up to Heaven*. Her candid discussion of her life and the range of her writing has made her an inspiration to many.

BEFORE YOU START READING
1 Read about slavery in the United States of America.
2 Everyone wants to be treated fairly and they become angry if treated unfairly. But are you always fair to other people? Talk about situations where you might have behaved unfairly.
3 Percy Bysshe Shelley (1792–1822) was a major Romantic poet who wrote that 'poets are the unacknowledged legislators of the world'. Throughout history, poetry has been used as a medium of protest and a call to social change. Do some research to find examples of poetry of protest. You could also look at the work of modern-day rap and hip hop artists, and at the way in which pop music has become a medium through which social and political issues are addressed.

▼ 'STILL I RISE' BY MAYA ANGELOU

> You may write me down in history
> With your bitter, twisted lies,
> You may trod me in the very dirt
> But still, like dust, I'll rise.
>
> Does my sassiness upset you?   5
> Why are you beset with gloom?
> 'Cause I walk like I've got oil wells
> Pumping in my living room.
>
> Just like moons and like suns,
> With the certainty of tides,   10
> Just like hopes springing high,
> Still I'll rise.
>
> Did you want to see me broken?
> Bowed head and lowered eyes?
> Shoulders falling down like teardrops,   15
> Weakened by my soulful cries?

sassiness Lively spiritedness, sometimes considered cheeky.

oil wells In the 19th and early 20th centuries, the discovery of oil and the rapid growth of the petroleum industry made oil an integral part of the US economy and a symbol of wealth.

haughtiness Being arrogantly superior.

gold mines The discovery of gold in California in 1848 and the period of panning and mining for gold that followed is a significant period in American history.

huts A reference to slave accommodation on plantations.

Does my haughtiness offend you?
Don't you take it awful hard
'Cause I laugh like I've got gold mines
Diggin' in my own backyard.   20

You may shoot me with your words,
You may cut me with your eyes,
You may kill me with your hatefulness,
But still, like air, I'll rise.

Does my sexiness upset you?   25
Does it come as a surprise
That I dance like I've got diamonds
At the meeting of my thighs?

Out of the huts of history's shame
I rise   30
Up from a past that's rooted in pain
I rise
I'm a black ocean, leaping and wide,
Welling and swelling I bear in the tide.

Leaving behind nights of terror and fear   35
I rise
Into a daybreak that's wondrously clear
I rise
Bringing the gifts that my ancestors gave,
I am the dream and the hope of the slave.   40
I rise
I rise
I rise.

UNDERSTANDING THE TEXT

'Still I Rise' is a powerful challenge aimed at the people who have oppressed the speaker and her community. Instead of expressing simple anger at the unfairness of one group oppressing another, she challenges the very foundations of oppression by asserting her pride in who she is. She is proud of herself and her people and implies that this pride is rooted in the strength and resilience of her people. The similes she uses – of oil wells, gold and diamonds – assert that she is of great worth, and that her belief in herself is enough to overcome the attitudes of others.

The speaker's spirit is compared with a force of nature through the use of imagery relating to the natural world. The speaker is like dust: usually seen as worthless but overpowering when it rises like a storm. The speaker is like moons and suns that will always rise, giving light and life.

The poem has several themes:

- racism
- oppression
- pride in oneself and one's background
- feminism
- beauty
- independence.

KEY POINT

The poet uses similes to signify resistance to oppression and the indomitable power of the human spirit.

▲ 'Bringing the gifts that my ancestors gave...'

Copy and complete the following table, finding examples from the poem that relate to these themes and adding your thoughts about how the language illustrates each theme.

▼ THEME	▼ EXAMPLE	▼ ANALYSIS
Racism		
Oppression		
Pride in oneself and one's background	'Bringing the gifts that my ancestors gave'	The speaker sees her background as a source of pride rather than as a disadvantage. The word 'gifts' shows everything she inherited in a positive light.
Feminism		
Beauty		
Independence		

EXPLORING DIRECT ADDRESS

The poem 'Still I Rise' is built around the language technique of direct address: the speaker talks directly to her audience, addressing them as 'you'.

▶ **Who do you think the speaker is talking to?**

▶ **Do you feel the speaker is talking directly to you? What effect does the use of direct address have on you?.**

KEY POINT

Writers make language choices to add impact to their ideas. When you read a text, look for writing with impact, then think about the language choices and techniques the writer has used to create that impact.

RHETORICAL QUESTIONS

One of the clearest ways in which the speaker directly addresses her audience is through the use of rhetorical questions.

Look closely at each of the rhetorical questions in the poem – you can scan the text for question marks to help you identify them.

▶ **How many rhetorical questions can you find?**

▶ **Some of the rhetorical questions are in pairs, some are in threes, and some stand alone. How does this add to their impact?**

▶ **How does the writer's use of rhetorical questions suggest the speaker's tone of voice as she addresses her audience?**

▲ The oil industry grew rapidly in the US in the 19th and early 20th centuries.

THE SPEAKER AND HER AUDIENCE

Both the speaker and the audience being addressed are clearly defined by the language used.

Look carefully at the quotations from the poem below.

'your bitter, twisted lies'
'I walk like I've got oil wells Pumping in my living room'
'Still I'll rise'
'Did you want to see me broken?'
'You may kill me with your hatefulness'
'Up from a past that's rooted in pain I rise'

▶ **Choose two quotations that most clearly show the speaker's view of their audience.**

▶ **Choose two quotations that create a vivid impression of the speaker.**

▶ **What impressions do your chosen quotations create of the speaker and her audience? Write one or two sentences about each of them. You could choose from the vocabulary suggestions below to help you.**

confrontational	challenging	strong	dishonest
manipulative	aggressive	polite	bold
miserable	assertive	abusive	violent
optimistic	pessimistic	self-pitying	sympathetic

EXPLORING LANGUAGE

Angelou's language choices in the poem are rich and powerful.

In addition to direct address and rhetorical questions, she uses a range of other language techniques to add impact to her ideas.

Think about Angelou's use of:

■ repetition

■ colloquial speech

■ alliteration

Find two or more examples of each technique.

Write one or two sentences exploring the impact of each technique in your examples.

HINT

Think about how each technique suggests the speaker's tone of voice. Does it make the speaker sound angry, confident, fearful, determined, or something else?

EXPLORING IMAGERY

The poem's ideas are enriched with a wealth of simile and metaphor. Look, for example, at these similes:

'You may trod me in the very dirt But still, like dust, I'll rise'	'I laugh like I've got gold mines Diggin' in my own backyard'

Think about the connotations and implications of these similes.

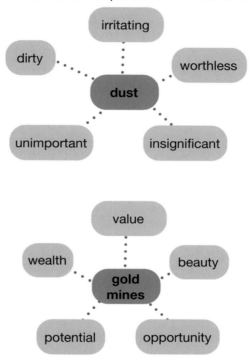

▶ **What does each of these similes add to Maya Angelou's ideas and the reader's response to them?**

▶ **Look through the poem for other similes – scan the poem for the word 'like' to find them. Note their connotations and implications in a spidergram like the ones above, then write one or two sentences exploring what they add to the poet's ideas and the reader's response.**

Now think about the poet's use of metaphor, where the speaker makes direct comparisons. For example:

'I am the dream and hope of the slave'

▶ **What connotations or implications can you identify in this metaphor?**

▶ **Write one or two sentences beginning with the words 'I am…' to explain much more clearly and explicitly what the speaker means.**

▶ **Compare the sentence you have written with the metaphor that Maya Angelou uses to express the same idea. Why do you think Angelou chose to use a metaphor, rather than stating her meaning more explicitly and literally?**

▶ **Find other examples of metaphor in the poem – scan for the words 'I'm' and 'I am' to find them. Note their connotations and implications, then write one or two sentences exploring what they add to the poet's ideas and the reader's response.**

SUBJECT VOCABULARY

implications what is implied or suggested

HINT

Metaphors are comparisons that are directly stated. They are statements that do not make literal sense but create an image and enrich meaning in the reader's mind.

EXPLORING STRUCTURE

INTENTION AND STRUCTURE

Look at some of the key ideas that Angelou expresses in the poem.

The speaker feels oppressed.	The speaker feels strong.
The speaker thinks her audience wants to crush her.	The speaker is unstoppable.

Track how these ideas are presented and how they develop as the poem progresses.

In Stanza 1, the speaker expresses feelings of...

In Stanza 2, the speaker expresses...

RHYME

Rhyme can add emphasis to a word and the idea it conveys.

The second and fourth lines of the first seven stanzas in the poem have a rhyme. Look at all the rhyming words that Angelou places at the end of the second and fourth lines:

- lies / rise
- tides / rise
- eyes / cries
- eyes / rise
- surprise / thighs
- gloom / room
- hard / backyard

Which word, and which idea, is given the greatest emphasis and impact in Angelou's use of rhyme?

A CHANGE IN STRUCTURE

The first seven stanzas of the poem have a regular rhythm and a regular rhyme scheme. However, the rhyme scheme and the poem's rhythm suddenly changes in the final two stanzas of the poem.

Focus on these final two stanzas. Find examples of:
- very short lines
- some longer lines
- rhyme
- repetition.

How does each of these elements add impact to the poet's ideas?

ACTIVITY 1   **A01**   **A04**   **SKILLS** INTERPERSONAL SKILLS, NEGOTIATION

▼ THE IMPORTANCE OF FREEDOM AND RESPECT

Many people believe that the right to be free and to be respected is one of the most important rights that human beings have. Do you agree? Or do you think other things in life are more important? Discuss your reasons why either with a partner or in a group.

HINT

In your writing, you could take on a **persona:** a fictitious character whose life, thoughts and feelings are different to your own.

ACTIVITY 2   **A04**   **A05**   **SKILLS** CRITICAL THINKING, ANALYSIS, INTERPRETATION, ADAPTIVE LEARNING, CREATIVITY

▼ WRITING TASK

In 'Still I Rise', Maya Angelou expresses her thoughts and feelings about how she and her community have been treated in the past and her response to that treatment. Write a poem or letter to a parent or teacher (or any other figure in authority) expressing your thoughts and feelings about:

■ how they have treated you

■ your response to that treatment.

EXAM-STYLE QUESTION

A01

A02

SKILLS CRITICAL THINKING, ANALYSIS, REASONING, INTERPRETATION

How does the poet challenge and triumph over her oppressors? In your answer, you should write about:

■ the ideas about racism and oppression conveyed in the poem

■ the poet's use of comparison and imagery

■ the poet's use of words, phrases and language techniques.

You should support your answer with close reference to the extract, including **brief** quotations   **(30 marks)**

WRITING A SUCCESSFUL ANSWER

Read carefully through the two paragraphs from a student's response to the exam-style question above. Which aspects of the response are successful? What targets for improvement would you suggest for this student?

HINT

Remember: commenting in detail and depth on the impact of the writer's choices makes for a stronger answer.

The poet seems very angry about the way she has been treated by other people in the past. She talks about 'bitter, twisted lies' and how these people 'trod me in the very dirt'. This makes her seem very angry. However, she also seems strong and resilient because, although she has been treated badly, she is not letting it affect her life. Throughout the poem she repeats 'I'll rise' and 'I rise' and 'Still I'll rise'. This is very effective.

Maya uses lots of similes and metaphors as well. She says she walks like she's 'got oil wells' and laughs like she's got 'gold mines / Diggin' in my own backyard.' These are effective because they are interesting and they make you want to keep reading.

▲ Kate Chopin, writing in the late 19th century, was a pioneer of feminist literature.

'THE STORY OF AN HOUR' KATE CHOPIN

BACKGROUND AND CONTEXT

Katherine O'Flaherty, known by her married name Chopin, was an American author of short stories and novels. She is best known for her collection of short stories as well as her novel, *The Awakening*, which was published in 1899.

The roles of men and women were very traditionally defined in the 19th century, and this was common in 19th century writing. However, Chopin's stories were daring rather than traditional and often portrayed women as trapped and unhappy in their marriages. As a result, she was criticised and her books were even banned from libraries. She is now known as an important early feminist writer and admired for her honest depictions of women's lives.

'The Story of an Hour' was first published in *Vogue* in 1894 and is one of her most popular stories. It tells the story of a woman's reaction to being told that her husband has died in an accident.

BEFORE YOU START READING

1 Feminism means supporting women's rights and the equality of the sexes. You can find out more about the history of feminism from reference books or on the internet. You might like to research the following questions:

■ What law in the UK gave women the right to have their own earnings and property for the first time?

■ When were women first allowed to graduate from Oxford University?

■ When were women first allowed to vote in UK parliamentary elections?

2 Kate Chopin's short stories are widely available online and in print. You could read more of her short stories, such as 'Reflections', 'Desiree's Baby' or 'The Storm', which will help you to understand her attitudes towards being a woman in the 19th century. You might like to explore some short stories written by other female authors of the time: Charlotte Perkins Gilman's 'Turned' (1911) presents similarly unconventional female characters for the period.

3 The film *Five Stories of an Hour* presents five dramatisations of the story; each one keeps the brevity of the story, but reads between the lines in a different way. Watch this online and compare these interpretations with one another and with your own reading of the story and the characters.

KEY POINT

Kate Chopin's short stories are notable for their honest portrayal of women's lives in the period.

▼ 'THE STORY OF AN HOUR' BY KATE CHOPIN

Knowing that Mrs. Mallard was afflicted with a heart trouble, great care was taken to break to her as gently as possible the news of her husband's death.

1

It was her sister Josephine who told her, in broken sentences; veiled hints that revealed in half concealing. Her husband's friend Richards

2

▶

▲ 'There stood, facing the open window, a comfortable, roomy armchair.'

repression When someone does not allow themselves to express feelings or desires.

was there, too, near her. It was he who had been in the newspaper office when intelligence of the railroad disaster was received, with Brently Mallard's name leading the list of "killed." He had only taken the time to assure himself of its truth by a second telegram, and had hastened to forestall any less careful, less tender friend in bearing the sad message.

She did not hear the story as many women have heard the same, with a paralyzed inability to accept its significance. She wept at once, with sudden, wild abandonment, in her sister's arms. When the storm of grief had spent itself she went away to her room alone. She would have no one follow her.   3

There stood, facing the open window, a comfortable, roomy armchair. Into this she sank, pressed down by a physical exhaustion that haunted her body and seemed to reach into her soul.   4

She could see in the open square before her house the tops of trees that were all aquiver with the new spring life. The delicious breath of rain was in the air. In the street below a peddler was crying his wares. The notes of a distant song which some one was singing reached her faintly, and countless sparrows were twittering in the eaves.   5

There were patches of blue sky showing here and there through the clouds that had met and piled one above the other in the west facing her window.   6

She sat with her head thrown back upon the cushion of the chair, quite motionless, except when a sob came up into her throat and shook her, as a child who has cried itself to sleep continues to sob in its dreams.   7

She was young, with a fair, calm face, whose lines bespoke repression and even a certain strength. But now there was a dull stare in her eyes, whose gaze was fixed away off yonder on one of those patches of blue sky. It was not a glance of reflection, but rather indicated a suspension of intelligent thought.   8

There was something coming to her and she was waiting for it, fearfully. What was it? She did not know; it was too subtle and elusive to name. But she felt it, creeping out of the sky, reaching toward her through the sounds, the scents, the color that filled the air.   9

Now her bosom rose and fell tumultuously. She was beginning to recognize this thing that was approaching to possess her, and she was striving to beat it back with her will—as powerless as her two white slender hands would have been. When she abandoned herself a little whispered word escaped her slightly parted lips. She said it over and over under her breath: "free, free, free!" The vacant stare and the look of terror that had followed it went from her eyes. They stayed keen and bright. Her pulses beat fast, and the coursing blood warmed and relaxed every inch of her body.   10

She did not stop to ask if it were or were not a monstrous joy that held her. A clear and exalted perception enabled her to dismiss the suggestion as trivial. She knew that she would weep again when she saw the kind, tender hands folded in death; the face that had never looked save with love upon her, fixed and gray and dead. But she saw beyond that bitter moment a long procession of years to come that would belong to her absolutely. And she opened and spread her arms out to them in welcome.   11

▶

There would be no one to live for during those coming years; she would live for herself. There would be no powerful will bending hers in that blind persistence with which men and women believe they have a right to impose a private will upon a fellow-creature. A kind intention or a cruel intention made the act seem no less a crime as she looked upon it in that brief moment of illumination.   12

And yet she had loved him—sometimes. Often she had not. What did it matter! What could love, the unsolved mystery, count for in the face of this possession of self-assertion which she suddenly recognized as the strongest impulse of her being!   13

"Free! Body and soul free!" she kept whispering.   14

Josephine was kneeling before the closed door with her lips to the keyhole, imploring for admission. "Louise, open the door! I beg; open the door—you will make yourself ill. What are you doing, Louise? For heaven's sake open the door."   15

"Go away. I am not making myself ill." No; she was drinking in a very elixir of life through that open window.   16

Her fancy was running riot along those days ahead of her. Spring days, and summer days, and all sorts of days that would be her own. She breathed a quick prayer that life might be long. It was only yesterday she had thought with a shudder that life might be long.   17

She arose at length and opened the door to her sister's importunities. There was a feverish triumph in her eyes, and she carried herself unwittingly like a goddess of Victory. She clasped her sister's waist, and together they descended the stairs. Richards stood waiting for them at the bottom.   18

latchkey A key that for the outside door of a house.

Some one was opening the front door with a latchkey. It was Brently Mallard who entered, a little travel-stained, composedly carrying his grip-sack and umbrella. He had been far from the scene of the accident, and did not even know there had been one. He stood amazed at Josephine's piercing cry; at Richards' quick motion to screen him from the view of his wife.   19

But Richards was too late.   20

When the doctors came they said she had died of heart disease—of the joy that kills.   21

UNDERSTANDING THE TEXT

'The Story of an Hour' is about a woman, Mrs Mallard, who has a heart condition which means that she should not become over-excited. She is told, and briefly believes, that her husband has been killed in a train accident. The story documents the mix of the intense emotions, confusion and sense of freedom that she feels upon hearing this news.

The story focuses on Mrs Mallard's thoughts and feelings about her relationship with her husband:

- his sudden death
- her life of freedom after his death
- his sudden reappearance, causing her death.

Using the table and suggestions below as an example, sum up Mrs Mallard's emotions at each stage in the story, noting which paragraphs focus on which emotion.

Then think about your response at each stage in the story. How do you respond to the character of Mrs Mallard as she goes through this experience?

EXPLORING LANGUAGE

▼ IN PARAGRAPHS	▼ MRS MALLARD FEELS...	▼ THE READER FEELS....
1–3		
4–8		
9–18		
19–21		

sympathy	confusion	shock	joy
happiness	relief	horror	anger
amusement	disappointment	sadness	tension

Which of Mrs Mallard's feelings is given the greatest amount of space and therefore the greatest emphasis in the story? What does this suggest about the writer's intention in the story?

Look again at each of the different emotions Mrs Mallard experiences in the story. For each emotion you have identified, note two short quotations showing them.

Which word or phrase in your chosen quotation shows or suggests this emotion most clearly? Write a sentence or two about each of your chosen words or phrases, exploring its implications or connotations.

For example, 'the storm of grief' – 'grief' suggests a violent, dramatic but short-lived emotion.

EXPLORING STRUCTURE

Consider how Kate Chopin uses contrast to add tension and drama to the story. Look again at the emotions you have identified in the four sections of the story. Which ones show contrast?

Find the two shortest paragraphs in the paragraph. How does their shortness give dramatic emphasis to two of the key moments in the story?

EXAM-STYLE QUESTION

A01

A02

SKILLS CRITICAL THINKING, ANALYSIS, REASONING, INTERPRETATION

How does the writer engage the reader's interest in 'The Story of an Hour'?

In your answer, you should write about:

- Mrs Mallard's reaction to the news
- the writer's use of language
- the writer's use of structure.

You should support your answer with close reference to the extract, including **brief** quotations.   **(30 marks)**

▲ Maupassant's favourite themes include the countryside and daily life, but also pessimism, despair, madness and death.

'THE NECKLACE'
GUY DE MAUPASSANT

BACKGROUND AND CONTEXT

This story is translated from French. It was written by Guy de Maupassant, who lived from 1850 to 1893 and was famous for his short stories. It is set against the background of 19th century Paris in France, where society was divided into strict social classes. Monsieur and Madame Loisel (the main characters) are not poor, but neither are they rich. They depend on the little money Monsieur Loisel earns from his minor job with the government.

BEFORE YOU START READING

1 Find out more about Guy de Maupassant. There are many websites giving information about him. His short stories are also available online, such as 'Vendetta' and 'Boule de Suif'.

2 Think of a time when you made a mistake that had serious consequences. Who or what was to blame? What lessons did you draw from the experience?

▼ 'THE NECKLACE' BY GUY DE MAUPASSANT

She was one of those pretty, delightful girls who, apparently by some error of Fate, get themselves born the daughters of very minor civil servants. She had no dowry, no expectations, no means of meeting some rich, important man who would understand, love, and marry her. So she went along with a proposal made by a junior clerk in the Ministry of Education.

She dressed simply, being unable to afford anything better, but she was every whit as unhappy as any daughter of good family who has come down in the world. Women have neither rank nor class, and their beauty, grace, and charm do service for birthright and connections. Natural guile, instinctive elegance, and adaptability are what determines their place in the hierarchy, and a girl of no birth to speak of may easily be the equal of any society lady.

She was unhappy all the time, for she felt that she was intended for a life of refinement and luxury. She was made unhappy by the run-down apartment they lived in, the peeling walls, the battered chairs, and the ugly curtains. Now all this, which any other woman of her station might never even have noticed, was torture to her and made her very angry. The spectacle of the young Breton peasant girl who did the household chores stirred sad regrets and impossible fancies. She dreamed of silent antechambers hung with oriental tapestries, lit by tall, bronze candelabras, and of two tall footmen in liveried breeches asleep in the huge armchairs, dozing in the heavy heat of a stove. She dreamed of great drawing-rooms dressed with old silk, filled with fine furniture which showed off trinkets beyond price, and of pretty little parlours, filled with perfumes and just made for intimate talk at five in the afternoon with one's closest friends who would be the most famous and sought-after men of the day whose attentions were much coveted and desired by all women.

hierarchy A strict order of importance.

Breton Someone from Brittany, an area of north-western France.

liveried Part of a uniform, usually a servant's uniform.

trinket A small decorative object.

▶

When she sat down to dinner at the round table spread with a three-day-old cloth, facing her husband who always lifted the lid of the soup-tureen and declared delightedly: 'Ah! Stew! Splendid! There's nothing I like better than a nice stew…', she dreamed of elegant dinners, gleaming silverware, and tapestries which peopled the walls with mythical characters and strange birds in enchanted forests; she dreamed of exquisite dishes served on fabulous china plates, of pretty compliments whispered into willing ears and received with Sphinx-like smiles over the pink flesh of a trout or the wings of a hazel hen.

She had no fine dresses, no jewellery, nothing. And that was all she cared about; she felt that God had made her for such things. She would have given anything to be popular, envied, attractive, and in demand.

She had a friend who was rich, a friend from her convent days, on whom she never called now, for she was always so unhappy afterwards. Sometimes, for days on end, she would weep tears of sorrow, regret, despair, and anguish.

One evening her husband came home looking highly pleased with himself. In his hand he brandished a large envelope.

'Look,' he said, 'I've got something for you.'

She tore the paper flap eagerly and extracted a printed card bearing these words:

> 'The Minister of Education and Madame Georges Ramponneau request the pleasure of the company of Monsieur and Madame Loisel at the Ministry Buildings on the evening of 18 January.'

Instead of being delighted as her husband had hoped, she tossed the invitation peevishly onto the table and muttered: 'What earthly use is that to me?'

'But, darling, I thought you'd be happy. You never go anywhere and it's an opportunity, a splendid opportunity! I had the dickens of a job getting hold of an invite. Everybody's after them; they're very much in demand and not many are handed out to us clerks. You'll be able to see all the big nobs there.'

She looked at him irritably and said shortly: 'And what am I supposed to wear if I do go?'

He had not thought of that. He blustered: 'What about the dress you wear for the theatre? It looks all right to me…' The words died in his throat. He was totally disconcerted and dismayed by the sight of his wife who had begun to cry. Two large tears rolled slowly out of the corners of her eyes and down towards the sides of her mouth.

'What's up?' he stammered. 'What's the matter?'

Making a supreme effort, she controlled her sorrows and, wiping her damp cheeks, replied quite calmly: 'Nothing. It's just that I haven't got anything to wear and consequently I shan't be going to any reception. Give the invite to one of your colleagues with a wife who is better off for clothes than I am.'

He was devastated. He went on: 'Oh come on, Mathilde. Look, what could it cost to get something suitable that would do for other occasions, something fairly simple?'

She thought for a few moments, working out her sums but also wondering

    ▶

Sphinx-like Mysterious and difficult to interpret.

Monsieur and Madame Loisel Mr and Mrs Loisel.

peevishly Irritably, crossly.

big nobs Wealthy people of high social status.

francs The former currency of France before the introduction of the euro.

posy A small bunch of flowers.

▲ A 19th century engraving of flower sellers.

Venetian From Venice, in Italy.

how much she could decently ask for without drawing an immediate refusal and pained protests from her husband who was careful with his money. Finally, after some hesitation, she said: 'I can't say precisely, but I daresay I could get by on four hundred francs.'

He turned slightly pale, for he had been setting aside just that amount to buy a gun and finance hunting trips the following summer in the flat landscape around Nanterre with a few friends who went shooting larks there on Sundays. But he said: 'Very well. I'll give you your four hundred francs. But do try and get a decent dress.'

The day of the reception drew near and Madame Loisel appeared sad, worried, anxious. Yet all her clothes were ready. One evening her husband said: 'What's up? You haven't half been acting funny these last few days.'

She replied: 'It vexes me that I haven't got a single piece of jewellery, not one stone, that I can put on. I'll look like a church mouse. I'd almost as soon not go to the reception.'

'Wear a posy,' he said. 'It's all the rage this year. You could get two or three magnificent roses for ten francs.'

She was not convinced. 'No. There's nothing so humiliating as to look poor when you're with women who are rich.'

But her husband exclaimed: 'You aren't half silly! Look, go and see your friend, Madame Forestier, and ask her to lend you some jewellery. You know her well enough for that.'

She gave a delighted cry: 'You're right! I never thought of that!'

The next day she called on her friend and told her all about her problem. Madame Forestier went over to a mirror-fronted wardrobe, took out a large casket, brought it over, unlocked it, and said to Madame Loisel: 'Choose whatever you like.'

At first she saw bracelets, then a rope of pearls and a Venetian cross made of gold and diamonds admirably fashioned. She tried on the necklaces in the mirror, and could hardly bear to take them off and give them back. She kept asking: 'Have you got anything else?'

'Yes, of course. Just look. I can't say what sort of thing you'll like best.'

All of a sudden, in a black satinwood case, she found a magnificent diamond necklace, and her heart began to beat with immoderate desire. Her hands shook as she picked it up. She fastened it around her throat over her high-necked dress and sat looking at herself in rapture. Then, diffidently, apprehensively, she asked: 'Can you lend me this? Nothing else. Just this.'

'But of course.'

She threw her arms around her friend, kissed her extravagantly, and then ran home, taking her treasure with her.

The day of the reception arrived. Madame Loisel was a success. She was the prettiest woman there, elegant, graceful, radiant, and wonderfully happy. All the men looked at her, enquired who she was, and asked to be introduced. All the cabinet secretaries and under-secretaries wanted to waltz with her. She was even noticed by the Minister himself.

▶

homage Respect.

She danced ecstatically, wildly, intoxicated with pleasure, giving no thought to anything else, swept along on her victorious beauty and glorious success, and floating on a cloud of happiness composed of the homage, admiration, and desire she evoked and the kind of complete and utter triumph which is so sweet to a woman's heart.

She left at about four in the morning. Since midnight her husband had been dozing in a small, empty side-room with three other men whose wives were having an enjoyable time.

He helped her on with her coat which he had fetched when it was time to go, a modest, everyday coat, a commonplace coat violently at odds with the elegance of her dress. It brought her down to earth, and she would have preferred to slip away quietly and avoid being noticed by the other women who were being arrayed in rich furs. But Loisel grabbed her by the arm: 'Wait a sec. You'll catch cold outside. I'll go and get a cab.'

But she refused to listen and ran quickly down the stairs. When they were outside in the street, there was no cab in sight. They began looking for one, hailing all the cabbies they saw driving by in the distance.

Seine The river that runs through Paris.

hackney cab An early form of taxi.

They walked down to the Seine in desperation, shivering with cold. There, on the embankment, they at last found one of those aged nocturnal hackney cabs which only emerge in Paris after dusk, as if ashamed to parade their poverty in the full light of day. It bore them back to their front door in the rue des Martyrs, and they walked sadly up to their apartment. For her it was all over, while he was thinking that he would have to be at the Ministry at ten.

Standing in front of the mirror, she took off the coat she had been wearing over her shoulders, to get a last look at herself in all her glory. Suddenly she gave a cry. The necklace was no longer round her throat!

Her husband, who was already half undressed, asked: 'What's up?'

She turned to him in a panic: 'I… I… Madame Forestier's necklace… I haven't got it!'

He straightened up as if thunderstruck: 'What?… But… You can't have lost it!'

They looked in the pleats of her dress, in the folds of her coat, and in her pockets. They looked everywhere. They did not find it.

'Are you sure you still had it when you left the ballroom?' he asked.

'Yes, I remember fingering it in the entrance hall.'

'But if you'd lost it in the street, we'd have heard it fall. So it must be in the cab.'

'That's right. That's probably it. Did you get his number?'

'No. Did you happen to notice it?'

'No.'

They looked at each other in dismay. Finally Loisel got dressed again. 'I'm going to go back the way we came,' he said, 'to see if I can find it.' He went out. She remained as she was, still wearing her evening gown, not having the

▲ '…her heart began to beat with immoderate desire'.

strength to go to bed, sitting disconsolately on a chair by the empty grate, her mind a blank.

Her husband returned at about seven o'clock. He had found nothing.

He went to the police station, called at newspaper offices where he advertised a reward, toured the cab companies, and tried anywhere where the faintest of hopes led him. She waited for him all day long in the same distracted condition, thinking of the appalling catastrophe which had befallen them.

Loisel came back that evening, hollow-cheeked and very pale. He had not come up with anything.

'Look,' he said, 'you'll have to write to your friend and say you broke the catch on her necklace and you are getting it repaired. That'll give us time to work out what we'll have to do.'

She wrote to his dictation.

A week later they had lost all hope.

Loisel, who had aged five years, said: 'We'll have to start thinking about replacing the necklace.'

The next day they took the case in which it had come and called on the jeweller whose name was inside. He looked through his order book.

'It wasn't me that sold the actual necklace. I only supplied the case.'

After this, they trailed round jeweller's shops, looking for a necklace just like the other one, trying to remember it, and both ill with worry and anxiety.

In a shop in the Palais Royal they found a diamond collar which they thought was identical to the one they were looking for. It cost forty thousand francs. The jeweller was prepared to let them have it for thirty-six.

They asked him not to sell it for three days. And they got him to agree to take it back for thirty-four thousand if the one that had been lost turned up before the end of February.

Loisel had eighteen thousand francs which his father had left him. He would have to borrow the rest.

He borrowed the money, a thousand francs here, five hundred there, sometimes a hundred and as little as sixty. He signed notes, agreed to pay exorbitant rates of interest, resorted to usurers and the whole tribe of moneylenders. He mortgaged the rest of his life, signed papers without knowing if he would ever be able to honour his commitments, and then, sick with worry about the future, the grim poverty which stood ready to pounce, and the prospect of all the physical privation and mental torture ahead, he went round to the jeweller's to get the new necklace with the thirty-six thousand francs which he put on the counter.

When Madame Loisel took it round, Madame Forestier said in a huff: 'You ought really to have brought it back sooner. I might have needed it.'

She did not open the case, as her friend had feared she might. If she had noticed the substitution, what would she have thought? What would she have said? Would she not have concluded she was a thief?

▲ A photograph of the Palais Garnier and Place de l'Opera in Paris; taken around the late 19th century.

exorbitant An extremely high value that is much higher than it should be.

▶

sous Coins of very small value.

Champs-Elysées A famous street in Paris.

Then began for Madame Loisel the grindingly horrible life of the very poor. But quickly and heroically, she resigned herself to what she could not alter: their appalling debt would have to be repaid. She was determined to pay. They dismissed the maid. They moved out of their apartment and rented an attic room.

She became used to heavy domestic work and all kinds of ghastly kitchen chores. She washed dishes, wearing down her pink nails on the greasy pots and saucepans. She washed the dirty sheets, shirts, and floorcloths by hand and hung them up to dry on a line; each morning she took the rubbish down to the street and carried the water up, pausing for breath on each landing. And, dressed like any working-class woman, she shopped at the fruiterer's, the grocer's, and the butcher's, with a basket over her arm, haggling, frequently abused and always counting every penny.

Each month they had to settle some accounts, renew others, and bargain for time.

Her husband worked in the evenings doing accounts for a shopkeeper and quite frequently sat up into the early hours doing copying work at five sous a page.

They lived like this for ten years.

By the time ten years had gone by, they had repaid everything, with not a penny outstanding, in spite of the extortionate conditions and including the accumulated interest.

Madame Loisel looked old now. She had turned into the battling, hard, uncouth housewife who rules working-class homes. Her hair was untidy, her skirts were askew, and her hands were red. She spoke in a gruff voice and scrubbed floors on her hands and knees. But sometimes, when her husband had gone to the office, she would sit by the window and think of that evening long ago when she had been so beautiful and so admired.

What might not have happened had she not lost the necklace? Who could tell? Who could possibly tell? Life is so strange, so fickle! How little is needed to make or break us!

One Sunday, needing a break from her heavy working week, she went out for a stroll on the Champs-Elysées. Suddenly she caught sight of a woman pushing a child in a pram. It was Madame Forestier, still young, still beautiful, and still attractive.

Madame Loisel felt apprehensive. Should she speak to her? Yes, why not? Now that she had paid in full, she would tell her everything. Why not? She went up to her.

'Hello, Jeanne.'

The friend did not recognize her and was taken aback at being addressed so familiarly by a common woman in the street. She stammered: 'But... I'm sorry... I don't know... There's some mistake.'

'No mistake. I'm Madame Loisel.'

Her friend gave a cry: 'But my poor Mathilde, how you've changed!'

'Yes, I've been through some hard times since I saw you, very hard times. And it was all on your account.'

▶

Ministry A government department.

'On my account? Whatever do you mean?'

'Do you remember that diamond necklace you lent me to go to the reception at the Ministry?'

'Yes. What about it?'

'Well I lost it.'

'Lost it? But you returned it to me.'

'No, I returned another one just like it. And we've been paying for it these past ten years. You know, it wasn't easy for us. We had nothing… But it's over and done with now, and I'm glad.'

Madame Forestier stopped. 'You mean you bought a diamond necklace to replace mine?'

'Yes. And you never noticed the difference, did you? They were exactly alike.' And she smiled a proud, innocent smile.

Madame Forestier looked very upset and, taking both her hands in hers, said:

'Oh, my poor Mathilde! But it was only an imitation necklace. It couldn't have been worth much more than five hundred francs!…'

UNDERSTANDING THE TEXT

▲ The lost and found glass slipper is the key to Cinderella's happy ending.

The story has something in common with the fairytale 'Cinderella', but the outcome is completely different.

Look at this summary of the story 'Cinderella':

- Cinderella is treated badly by her family.
- She is prevented from going to the Prince's ball as she has no dress to wear.
- A fairy godmother magically appears and provides a carriage, dress and glass slippers for Cinderella.
- Cinderella goes to the ball and meets the Prince. They fall in love, but she must leave early and, in her hurry, loses one of her glass slippers.
- The Prince finds the woman the glass slipper fits and marries her.

In what ways is the story of Madame Loisel in 'The Necklace' similar to the story of Cinderella? In what ways does it differ? Think about:

- Madame Loisel's home life
- how she acquires the outfit she feels she needs in order to go to the party
- events at the party
- events after the party
- the story's ending.

EXPLORING CHARACTER

In the first few sentences of the story, you learn that Madame Loisel is young and attractive, and, whilst not rich, she is certainly not poor. Why then is she 'unhappy all the time'?

Copy and complete the table, making a list of the reasons you can find for her unhappiness, using the first section (up to 'tears of sorrow, regret, despair, and anguish').

Note down five to ten things the reader is told or shown about Madame Loisel in the story. How do you respond to the character of Madame Loisel?

▼ MADAME LOISEL	▼ YOUR RESPONSE
She is 'pretty' and 'delightful' but disappointed with her life.	Is she spoilt and ungrateful? Or should she be pitied?
She is unhappy about the invitation that her husband has struggled to get and was so pleased to show her.	
She cries until her husband agrees to buy her a dress.	

Review all of the ideas you have noted. Do you feel Madame Loisel deserves sympathy for her actions in the story? Or is she to blame for her own unhappiness?

There are two other key characters in the story: Monsieur Loisel and Madame Forestier. Note down three to five things you learn about them and your response to them.

▼ MONSIEUR LOISEL	▼ YOUR RESPONSE
He has worked hard to get an invitation to a party. He proudly presents it to his wife.	
He offers to buy his wife a dress.	

▼ MADAME FORESTIER	▼ YOUR RESPONSE
She offers to lend her jewellery to her friend.	

Which of the three characters that you have explored do you find the most sympathetic or admirable character?

EXPLORING LANGUAGE

Look carefully at the quotations below, comparing the writer's choice of details and ideas in each one.

> 'She dreamed of great drawing-rooms dressed with old silk, filled with fine furniture which showed off trinkets beyond price, and of pretty little parlours, filled with perfumes...'

> 'She had no fine dresses, no jewellery, nothing.'

> 'She danced ecstatically, wildly, intoxicated with pleasure, giving no thought to anything else, swept along on her victorious beauty and glorious success, and floating on a cloud of happiness...'

> 'Her hair was untidy, her skirts were askew, and her hands were red. She spoke in a gruff voice and scrubbed floors on her hands and knees.'

How does the writer select details and use language and sentence structure to show:

■ Madame Loisel's dreams of how her life should be
■ Madame Loisel's disappointment in the reality of her married life
■ the glamour and excitement of the party
■ the life of suffering that Madame Loisel ends up living?

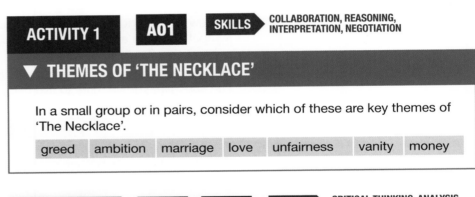

ACTIVITY 1   **A01**   SKILLS ▸ COLLABORATION, REASONING, INTERPRETATION, NEGOTIATION

▼ **THEMES OF 'THE NECKLACE'**

In a small group or in pairs, consider which of these are key themes of 'The Necklace'.

| greed | ambition | marriage | love | unfairness | vanity | money |

ACTIVITY 2   **A04**   **A05**   SKILLS ▸ CRITICAL THINKING, ANALYSIS, INTERPRETATION, ADAPTIVE LEARNING, CREATIVITY

▼ **WRITING TASK**

Plan a story in which a character dreams of a better life which they work hard to achieve. Do their dreams end in triumph or disaster?

EXAM-STYLE QUESTION

A01

A02

SKILLS ▸ CRITICAL THINKING, ANALYSIS, REASONING, INTERPRETATION

How does the writer try to make the character of Madame Loisel interesting for the reader in 'The Necklace'?

In your answer, you should write about:

■ her relationship with her husband
■ her unhappiness before and after the party
■ her happiness when she is at the party
■ the writer's use of language and structure.

You should support your answer with close reference to the extract, including **brief** quotations.   **(30 marks)**

▲ Novelist Rose Tremain has said that she aims to attain a 'new clarity' through her books for both herself and her readers.

'SIGNIFICANT CIGARETTES' (FROM *THE ROAD HOME*) ROSE TREMAIN

BACKGROUND AND CONTEXT

Rose Tremain is an established and highly successful English novelist who seeks out the strange and unfamiliar as subjects for her fiction. 'Significant Cigarettes' is an extract from her novel, *The Road Home*. It tells the story of a journey of an incredibly poor man called Lev. He travels from Eastern Europe to London, where he hopes to make a better life for himself. Before Lev left his own country, his wife had died. In order to make the journey, he has to leave his young daughter behind.

The arrival in Britain of large numbers of migrants who want to find work has caused concern and anger among some people. In 'Significant Cigarettes', Tremain shows the reader something of what it is like to be poor and desperate.

BEFORE YOU START READING

1 What do you think might be difficult about welcoming strangers into your home?
2 How would you try to help a child who was suddenly left in your care by a parent who was fleeing abroad? What considerations would be the most important?
3 Have you ever explored or visited a place that was totally unfamiliar to you? What did you find? What did you learn?

▼ 'SIGNIFICANT CIGARETTES' BY ROSE TREMAIN

On the coach, Lev chose a seat near the back and he sat huddled against the window, staring out at the land he was leaving: at the fields of sunflowers scorched by the dry wind, at the pig farms, at the quarries and rivers and at the wild garlic growing green at the edge of the road.

Lev wore a leather jacket and jeans and a leather cap pulled low over his eyes and his handsome face was grey-toned from his smoking and in his hands he clutched an old red cotton handkerchief and a dented pack of Russian cigarettes. He would soon be forty-three.

After some miles, as the sun came up, Lev took out a cigarette and stuck it between his lips, and the woman sitting next to him, a plump, contained person with moles like splashes of mud on her face, said quickly: 'I'm sorry, but there is no smoking allowed on this bus.'

Lev knew this, had known it in advance, had tried to prepare himself mentally for the long agony of it. But even an unlit cigarette was a companion – something to hold on to, something that had promise in it – and all he could

▶

quarries Places where large amounts of stone or sand are dug out of the ground.

be bothered to do now was to nod, just to show the woman that he'd heard what she'd said, reassure her that he wasn't going to cause trouble; because there they would have to sit for fifty hours or more, side by side with their separate aches and dreams, like a married couple. They would hear each other's snores and sighs, smell the food and drink each had brought with them, note the degree to which each was fearful or unafraid, make short forays into conversation. And then later, when they finally arrived in London, they would probably separate with barely a word or a look, walk out into a rainy morning, each alone and beginning a new life. And Lev thought how all of this was odd but necessary and already told him things about the world he was travelling to, a world in which he would break his back working – if only that work could be found. He would hold himself apart from other people, find corners and shadows in which to sit and smoke, demonstrate that he didn't need to belong, that his heart remained in his own country.

There were two coach-drivers. These men would take turns to drive and to sleep. There was an on-board lavatory, so the only stops the bus would make would be for gas. At gas stations, the passengers would be able to clamber off, walk a few paces, see wild flowers on a verge, soiled paper among bushes, sun or rain on the road. They might stretch up their arms, put on dark glasses against the onrush of nature's light, look for a clover leaf, smoke and stare at the cars rushing by. Then they would be herded back onto the coach, resume their old attitudes, arm themselves for the next hundred miles, for the stink of another industrial zone, or the sudden gleam of a lake, for rain and sunset and the approach of darkness on silent marshes. There would be times when the journey would seem to have no end.

Sleeping upright was not something Lev was practised in. The old seemed to be able to do it, but forty-two was not yet old. Lev's father, Stefan, sometimes used to sleep upright, in summer, on a hard wooden chair in his lunch break at the Baryn sawmill, with the hot sun falling onto the slices of sausage wrapped in paper on his knee and onto his flask of tea. Both Stefan and Lev could sleep lying down on a mound of hay or on the mossy carpet of a forest. Often, Lev had slept on a rag rug beside his daughter's bed, when she was ill or afraid. And when his wife, Marina, was dying, he'd lain for five nights on an area of linoleum flooring no wider than his outstretched arm, between Marina's hospital bed and a curtain patterned with pink and purple daisies, and sleep had come and gone in a mystifying kind of way, painting strange pictures in Lev's brain that had never completely vanished.

Towards evening, after two stops for gas, the mole-flecked woman unwrapped a hard-boiled egg. She peeled it silently. The smell of the egg reminded Lev of the sulphur springs at Jor, where he'd taken Marina, just in case nature could cure what man had given up for lost. Marina had immersed her body obediently in the scummy water, lain there looking at a female stork returning to its high nest, and said to Lev: 'If only we were storks.'

'Why d'you say that?' Lev had asked.

'Because you never see a stork dying. It's as though they didn't die.'

If only we were storks.

On the woman's knee a clean cotton napkin was spread and her white hands smoothed it and she unwrapped rye bread and a twist of salt.

'My name is Lev,' said Lev.

---

linoleum Floor covering made from strong shiny material.

scummy Unpleasant and dirty.

▶

Yarbl Fictional city in an unspecified eastern European country.

Baryn Fictional city in an unspecified eastern European country.

▲ '...in his village, darkness had always arrived in precisely the same way, from the same direction, above the same trees...'

Auror Fictional city in an unspecified eastern European country.

'My name is Lydia,' said the woman. And they shook hands, Lev's hand holding the scrunched-up kerchief, and Lydia's hand rough with salt and smelling of egg, and then Lev asked: 'What are you planning to do in England?' and Lydia said: 'I have some interviews in London for jobs as a translator.'

'That sounds promising.'

'I hope so. I was a teacher of English at School 237 in Yarbl, so my language is very colloquial.'

Lev looked at Lydia. It wasn't difficult to imagine her standing in front of a class and writing words on a blackboard. He said: 'I wonder why you're leaving our country when you had a good job at School 237 in Yarbl?'

'Well,' said Lydia. 'I became very tired of the view from my window. Every day, summer and winter, I looked out at the school yard and the high fence and the apartment block beyond, and I began to imagine I would die seeing these things, and I didn't want this. I expect you understand what I mean?'

Lev took off his leather cap and ran his fingers through his thick grey hair. He saw Lydia turn to him for a moment and look very seriously into his eyes.

He said: 'Yes, I understand.'

Then there was a silence, while Lydia ate her hard-boiled egg. She chewed very quietly. When she'd finished the egg, Lev said: 'My English isn't too bad. I took some classes in Baryn, but my teacher told me my pronunciation wasn't very good. May I say some words and you can tell me if I'm pronouncing them correctly?'

'Yes, of course,' said Lydia.

Lev said: 'Lovely. Sorry. I am legal. How much please. Thank you. May you help me.'

'May I help you,' corrected Lydia. 'May I help you,' repeated Lev.

'Go on,' said Lydia.

'Stork,' said Lev. 'Stork's nest. Rain. I am lost. I wish for an interpreter. Bee-and-bee.'

'Be-and-be?' said Lydia. 'No, no. You mean "to be, or not to be".'

'No,' said Lev. 'Bee-and-bee. Family hotel, quite cheap.'

'Oh, yes, I know. B & B.'

Lev could now see that darkness was falling outside the window and he thought how, in his village, darkness had always arrived in precisely the same way, from the same direction, above the same trees, whether early or late, whether in summer, winter or spring, for the whole of his life. This darkness – particular to that place, Auror – was how, in Lev's heart, darkness would always fall. And so he told Lydia that he came from Auror, had worked in the Baryn sawmill until it closed two years ago, and since then he'd found no work at all and his family – his mother, his five-year-old daughter and he – had lived off the money his mother made selling jewellery manufactured from tin.

'Oh,' said Lydia. 'I think that's very resourceful, to make jewellery from tin.'

'Sure,' said Lev. 'But it isn't enough.'

▶

Tucked into his boot was a small flask of vodka. He extracted the flask and took a long swig. Lydia kept eating her rye bread. Lev wiped his mouth with the red handkerchief and saw his face reflected in the coach window. He looked away. Since the death of Marina, he didn't like to catch sight of his own reflection, because what he always saw in it was his own guilt at still being alive.

'Why did the sawmill at Baryn close?' asked Lydia.

'They ran out of trees,' said Lev.

'Very bad,' said Lydia. 'What other work can you do?'

Lev drank again. Someone had told him that in England vodka was too expensive to drink.

Immigrants made their own alcohol from potatoes and tap water, and when Lev thought about these industrious immigrants, he imagined them sitting by a coal fire in a tall house, talking and laughing, with rain falling outside the window and red buses going past and a television flickering in a corner of the room. He sighed and said: 'I will do any work at all. My daughter Maya needs clothes, shoes, books, toys, everything. England is my hope.'

Towards ten o'clock, red blankets were given out to the coach passengers, some of whom were already sleeping. Lydia put away the remnants of her meal, covered her body with the blanket and switched on a fierce little light above her under the baggage rack and began reading a faded old paperback, printed in English. Lev saw that the title of her book was The Power and the Glory. His longing for a cigarette had grown steadily since he'd drunk the vodka and now it was acute. He could feel the yearning in his lungs and in his blood, and his hands grew fidgety and he felt a tremor in his legs. How long before the next gas stop? It could be four or five hours. Everyone on the bus would be asleep by then, except him and one of the two drivers. Only they would keep a lonely, exhausting vigil, the driver's body tensed to the moods and alarms of the dark, unravelling road; his own aching for the comfort of nicotine or oblivion – and getting neither.

He envied Lydia, immersed in her English book. Lev knew he had to distract himself with something…. In desperation, he took from his wallet a brand new British twenty-pound note and reached up and switched on his own little reading light and began to examine the note. On one side, the frumpy Queen, E II R, with her diadem, her face grey on a purple ground, and on the other, a man, some personage from the past, with a dark drooping moustache and an angel blowing a trumpet above him and all the angel's radiance falling on him in vertical lines. 'The British venerate their history,' Lev had been told in his English class, 'chiefly because they have never been subjected to Occupation. Only intermittently do they see that some of their past deeds were not good.'

The indicated lifespan of the man on the note was 1857–1934. He looked like a banker, but what had he done to be on a twenty-pound note in the twenty-first century? Lev stared at his determined jaw, squinted at his name written out in a scrawl beneath the wing collar, but couldn't read it. He thought that this was a person who would never have known any other system of being alive but Capitalism. He would have heard the names Hitler and Stalin, but not been afraid – would have had no need to be afraid of anything except a little loss of capital in what Americans called the Crash,

The Power and the Glory Novel by the British author Graham Greene.

diadem A circle of jewels worn on the head.

Occupation When land is occupied by a hostile force.

the Crash The Wall Street Crash of 1929, the worst stock market crash in American history.

▶

▲ '...I'm going to their country now and I'm going to make them share it with me: their infernal luck.'

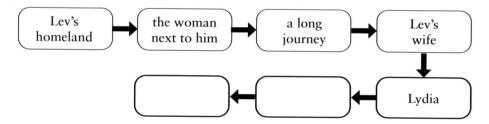

when men in New York had jumped out of windows and off roofs. He would have died safely in his bed before London was bombed to ruins, before Europe was torn apart. Right to the end of his days, the angel's radiance had probably shone on this man's brow and on his fusty clothes, because it was known across the world: the English were lucky. Well, thought Lev, I'm going to their country now and I'm going to make them share it with me: their infernal luck. I've left Auror and that leaving of my home was hard and bitter, but my time is coming.

UNDERSTANDING THE TEXT

'Significant Cigarettes' is an extract from the opening of a novel. This means that you should not simply read it as an account of events but as a piece of writing designed to draw you in to the novel's characters and themes. In this piece, you learn about Lev and Lydia and the things that concern them, themes which may be important in the novel.

KEY POINT

It is important to realise that this is a scene from the early part of a novel and not a text designed to stand alone.

The author provides a contrast between two characters who are travelling side by side, for some days, on a bus. You are told about their lives back home and their reasons for travelling, and you are provided with an insight into their expectations of life when they arrive in London. This information encourages the reader to imagine how they will cope at their journey's end.

Copy and complete the following flowchart, identifying all the different things on which the writer focuses in the extract.

```
Lev's      →   the woman    →    a long     →    Lev's
homeland        next to him       journey          wife
                                                     ↓
   [        ]  ←  [        ]  ←                     Lydia
```

EXPLORING LANGUAGE

Look at some of the key ideas in the extract:

- Lev's thoughts and feelings about his homeland
- Lev's craving for a cigarette
- Lev's relationship with his wife
- Lev's thoughts and feelings about his daughter
- Lev's hopes for the future in Britain.

For each of these key ideas, identify a sentence that clearly shows it and note the impression it creates.

How does the structure of each sentence you have identified add impact to the impression the writer has created?

Which words or phrases in each sentence help to create that impression? Write one or two sentences, exploring their connotations or implications.

EXPLORING DIALOGUE

Much of the extract focuses on Lev's thoughts about his past and his future, but the dialogue between Lev and Lydia is also an important part of the extract. Look at their conversation on page 269. In what ways are Lev and Lydia similar? In what ways are they different?

Look closely at the section of the extract on page 269 in which Lev shows Lydia his English-speaking skills:

'Lovely. Sorry. I am legal. How much please. Thank you. May you help me...'

'I am lost. I wish for an interpreter. Bee-and-bee.'

What does each of these words and phrase suggest about Lev's expectations of his life in Britain?

ACTIVITY 1 **A01** **SKILLS** INTERPERSONAL SKILLS, NEGOTIATION

▼ **FUNCTION OF THE EXTRACT WITHIN THE NOVEL**

Discuss the effect that Lydia has on Lev. Why do you think that their meeting and travelling together is important in this extract and perhaps in the novel as a whole?

ACTIVITY 2 **A04** **A05** **SKILLS** ADAPTIVE LEARNING, CREATIVITY, INNOVATION

▼ **WRITING TASKS**

1 Imagine you are Lev. Write an article for a newspaper giving advice to people who might be considering coming to Britain to find work.

2 Write a description of a long journey to an unfamiliar destination with an unusual companion.

EXAM-STYLE QUESTIONS

A01

A02

SKILLS CRITICAL THINKING, ANALYSIS, REASONING, INTERPRETATION

1 How does the writer present the character of Lev in 'Significant Cigarettes'? In your answer, you should write about:
- Lev's memories and thoughts
- the dialogue between characters
- the writer's use of language and structure.

You should support your answer with close reference to the extract, including **brief** quotations. **(30 marks)**

2 How does the writer show Lev's thoughts and feelings about the future in 'Significant Cigarettes'? In your answer, you should write about:
- the dialogue between Lev and Lydia
- how the writer presents Lev's life at home and the life he expects in Britain
- the writer's use of language and structure.

You should support your answer with close reference to the extract, including **brief** quotations. **(30 marks)**

'WHISTLE AND I'LL COME TO YOU' (FROM *THE WOMAN IN BLACK*)
SUSAN HILL

BACKGROUND AND CONTEXT

Susan Hill is an English writer of literary novels, ghost stories, children's books, detective novels and memoirs. She has won the Whitbread, Somerset Maugham and John Llewellyn Rhys awards and has been shortlisted for the Booker Prize. She is known for writing in the Gothic style with its distinctive creation of suspense through a description of background and atmosphere.

The Woman in Black is probably the most well-known of her ghost stories written in this tradition and its stage production is the second longest running play in London's West End.

The novel is narrated in the first person by Arthur Kipps, a solicitor who has been sent to Eel Marsh House, near the remote village of Crythin Gifford, to organise the papers and finances of the late Mrs Drablow. The huge house has lain empty since her death.

For days, Kipps works alone in the house, increasingly unable to ignore or explain the mysterious noises and strange events he encounters, until finally he comes face to face with the ghostly figure of the Woman in Black.

▲ English writer Susan Hill.

BEFORE YOU START READING

1 Read about the Gothic novel and find out about some of its more famous examples, such as Bram Stoker's *Dracula*, Charlotte Brontë's *Jane Eyre* and Daphne du Maurier's *Rebecca*.

2 There are several movie adaptations of *The Woman in Black*. Try to watch one as a class, paying particular attention to the way in which the story's background is shown and how an atmosphere of eeriness and suspense is created.

3 Do you believe in ghosts and the supernatural? Talk about some of the ghost stories you know from the folklore of your country and culture. What are their common features? Are they similar or different to the typical stories of the Gothic tradition?

▼ 'WHISTLE AND I'LL COME TO YOU' BY SUSAN HILL

casements Windows that are set on hinges and open like doors.

During the night the wind rose. As I had lain reading I had become aware of the stronger gusts that blew every so often against the casements. But when I awoke abruptly in the early hours it had increased greatly in force. The house felt like a ship at sea, battered by the gale that came roaring across the

▶

marsh An area of low-lying land that generally remains flooded all year round.

nook and cranny An idiom pair that means every possible place.

nostalgically Thinking about a pleasure from the past.

banshee In Irish folklore, a female spirit whose wailing warns of an impending death.

anguish Severe mental or physical suffering.

▲ Susan Hill's ghost stories are distinctive for their creation of suspense.

conjecture An opinion formed on the basis of incomplete information.

Mrs. Drablow Owner of Eel Marsh House; it was to sort out the legal matters arising from her death that the narrator had come to Crythin Gifford.

retainer A person attached or owing service to a household; a servant.

open marsh. Windows were rattling everywhere and there was the sound of moaning down all the chimneys of the house and whistling through every nook and cranny.

At first I was alarmed. Then, as I lay still, gathering my wits, I reflected on how long Eel Marsh House had stood here, steady as a lighthouse, quite alone and exposed, bearing the brunt of winter after winter of gales and driving rain and sleet and spray. It was unlikely to blow away tonight. And then, those memories of childhood began to be stirred again and I dwelt nostalgically upon all those nights when I had lain in the warm and snug safety of my bed in the nursery at the top of our family house in Sussex, hearing the wind rage round like a lion, howling at the doors and beating upon the windows but powerless to reach me. I lay back and slipped into that pleasant, trance-like state somewhere between sleeping and waking, recalling the past and all its emotions and impressions vividly, until I felt I was a small boy again.

Then from somewhere, out of that howling darkness, a cry came to my ears, catapulting me back into the present and banishing all tranquility.

I listened hard. Nothing. The tumult of the wind, like a banshee, and the banging and rattling of the window in its old, ill-fitting frame. Then yes, again, a cry, that familiar cry of desperation and anguish, a cry for help from a child somewhere out on the marsh.

There was no child. I knew that. How could there be? Yet how could I lie here and ignore even the crying of some long dead ghost?

'Rest in peace,' I thought, but this poor one did not, could not.

After a few moments I got up. I would go down into the kitchen and make myself a drink, stir up the fire a little and sit beside it trying, trying to shut out that calling voice for which I could do nothing, and no one had been able to do anything for… how many years?

As I went out onto the landing, Spider the dog following me at once, two things happened together. I had the impression of someone who had just that very second before gone past me on their way from the top of the stairs to one of the other rooms, and, as a tremendous blast of wind hit the house so that it all but seemed to rock at the impact, the lights went out. I had not bothered to pick up my torch from the bedside table and now I stood in the pitch blackness, unsure for a moment of my bearings.

And the person who had gone by, and who was now in this house with me? I had seen no one, felt nothing. There had been no movement, no brush of a sleeve against mine, no disturbance of the air, I had not even heard a foot step. I had simply the absolutely certain sense of someone just having passed close to me and gone away down the corridor. Down the short narrow corridor that led to the nursery whose door had been so firmly locked and then, inexplicably, opened.

For a moment, I actually began to conjecture that there was indeed someone – another human being – living here in this house, a person who hid themselves away in that mysterious nursery and came out at night to fetch food and drink and to take the air. Perhaps it was the woman in black? Had Mrs Drablow harboured some reclusive old sister or retainer, had she left behind her a mad friend that no one had known about? My brain span all manner of wild, incoherent fantasies as I tried desperately to provide a

▶

Samuel Daily A prosperous landowner that Kipps had met on the train to Crythin Gifford.

rational explanation for the presence I had been so aware of. But then they ceased. There was no living occupant of Eel Marsh House other than myself and Samuel Daily's dog. Whatever was about, whoever I had seen, and heard rocking, and who had passed me by just now, whoever had opened the locked door was not 'real'. No. But what was 'real'? At that moment I began to doubt my own reality.

The first thing I must have was a light and I groped my way back across to my bed, reached over it and got my hand to the torch at last, took a step back, stumbled over the dog who was at my heels and dropped the torch. It went spinning away across the floor and fell somewhere by the window with a crash and the faint sound of breaking glass. I cursed but managed by crawling about on my hands and knees, to find it again and to press the switch. No light came on. The torch had broken.

For a moment I was as near to weeping tears of despair and fear, frustration and tension, as I had ever been since my childhood. But instead of crying I drummed my fists upon the floorboards, in a burst of violent rage, until they throbbed.

It was Spider who brought me to my sense by scratching a little at my arm and then by licking the hand I stretched out to her. We sat on the floor together and I hugged her warm body to me, glad of her, thoroughly ashamed of myself, calmer and relieved, while the wind boomed and roared without, and again and again I heard that child's terrible cry borne on the gusts towards me.

UNDERSTANDING THE TEXT

'Whistle and I'll Come to You' is the title of the tenth chapter of *The Woman in Black*.

This extract describes a night at Eel Marsh House and the ghostly happenings that trouble the narrator. The text conveys the thoughts and feelings of the narrator as they shift from contemplating the harsh weather and reminiscing about his childhood, to extreme fear as he hears the wailing of the child and begins to strongly feel the presence of someone or something in the house.

The atmosphere of the house is effectively conveyed not only through the vivid description, but also in Arthur Kipps's readiness to believe that there may even be a person hiding there. His willingness to believe in the supernatural creates a similar reaction in the reader, making the extract all the more powerful and evocative.

EXPLORING GENRE

The Gothic novel is a genre of fiction in which adventure, romance and the supernatural combine to engage and chill the reader.

▶ What images does the term 'Gothic' bring to your mind?

Some of the elements that are commonly found in Gothic literature include:

a remote castle or large house	mysteries from the past	inexplicable events	extreme emotions
darkness	storms, thunder, lightning	overbearing, ruthless men	women in distress
danger	unexplained noises	ancient curses	significant dreams
isolation	confinement	escape	violence

The Woman in Black has some, though not all, of the features of the Gothic novel. Which of the elements above can you identify in the extract? Find evidence from the text to support each one.

EXPLORING VOCABULARY

Susan Hill's vocabulary choice in the extract is a vital element of the atmosphere she creates. Look at some of her key choices below.

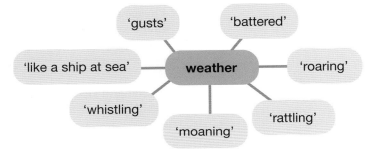

▶ **What class of word does Hill most frequently use to describe the wind: noun, noun phrase, verb, adjective or adverb?**

▶ **Which of these techniques does Hill frequently use to describe the wind: onomatopoeia, personification, simile, alliteration or repetition?**

▶ **What is the impact of these choices? Write one or two sentences explaining your ideas.**

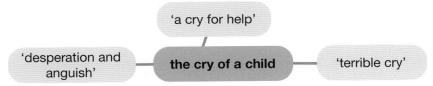

▶ **What impressions of the child's cry does Hill's vocabulary create?**

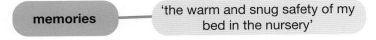

▶ **How do the narrator's memories contrast with the experience he describes at Eel Marsh House?**

▶ **What effect does this contrast have?**

KEY POINT

The writer conveys the narrator's emotions partly through his response to events, but largely through sentence structure.

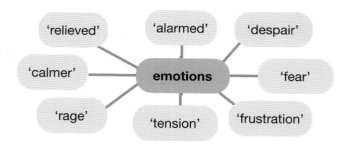

▶ The only explicit reference to emotion in the first twelve paragraphs of the extract is when Kipps says he is 'alarmed'. The remainder of the vocabulary choices above appear in the final two paragraphs. What is the effect of this sudden outburst of emotion at the end of the extract?

EXPLORING SENTENCE STRUCTURE

Susan Hill uses a wide variety of sentence structures for effect in the extract. Look at these sentences from the extract:

> 'There was no child. I knew that.'
>
> 'I listened hard. Nothing.'
>
> 'The first thing I must have was a light and I groped my way back across to my bed, reached over it and got my hand to the torch at last, took a step back, stumbled over the dog who was at my heels and dropped the torch.'
>
> 'There had been no movement, no brush of a sleeve against mine, no disturbance of the air, I had not even heard a foot step.'
>
> 'And the person who had gone by, and who was now in this house with me?'

Which of the following sentence structures and effects can you identify in the sentences above?

A single clause sentence	to create dramatic impact
A minor sentence	
A multiclause sentence in which the most dramatic detail is positioned in the final clause	to suggest fast paced action
A multiclause sentence linking a series of events or actions	to build tension up to a dramatic moment or revelation
A rhetorical question	to suggest the range and variety of details or ideas
A multiclause sentence listing details or ideas	to suggest confusion and uncertainty

HINT

Look at pages 34–35 to remind yourself about different types of sentence structure.

▶ Find one or more further examples of each sentence structure, listed above. Do they have the same effect as the examples you have already explored?

▶ There are several rhetorical questions in the extract. How many can you find? What does this suggest about the narrator's state of mind throughout the extract?

EXPLORING STRUCTURE

The structure of a text depends upon:

■ the ideas and details the writer chooses to include

■ the order in which the writer chooses to sequence them.

Susan Hill has structured the extract to create and build tension.

Look at the sequence of ideas and details in the extract:

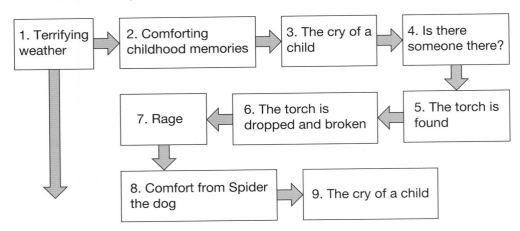

Copy and complete a graph like the one below, charting how the narrator's mood and the atmosphere of the extract changes as it progresses.

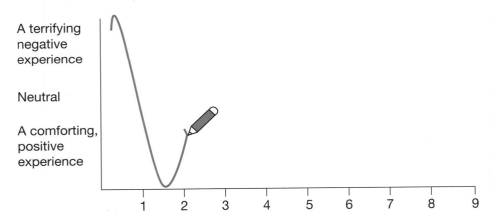

How has Hill structured the text to contrast and exaggerate the terrifying negative experiences with the comforting positive experiences?

▶ By the time the torch is dropped, a sense of tension has clearly been established.

Ann Radcliffe's novel, *The Italian*, is the story of a nobleman called Vivaldi and his attempt to marry Elena, a beautiful orphan. The following extract shows the way in which Radcliffe creates the eerie atmosphere of a chamber in a ruined fortress where Vivaldi and his servant Paulo are trapped for the night.

▼ FROM *THE ITALIAN* (1797) BY ANN RADCLIFFE

Vivaldi again examined the walls, and as unsuccessfully as before; but in one corner of the vault lay an object, which seemed to tell the fate of one who had been confined here, and to hint his own: it was a garment covered with blood. Vivaldi and his servant discovered it at the same instant; and a dreadful foreboding of their own destiny fixed them, for some moments, to the spot. Vivaldi first recovered himself, when instead of yielding to despondency, all his faculties were aroused to devise some means for escaping; but Paulo's hopes seemed buried beneath the dreadful vestments upon which he still gazed. 'Ah, my Signor!' said he, at length, in a faltering accent, 'who shall dare to raise that garment? What if it should conceal the mangled body whose blood has stained it!'

Vivaldi, shudderingly, turned to look on it again.

'It moves!' exclaimed Paulo; 'I see it move!' as he said which, he started to the opposite side of the chamber. Vivaldi stepped a few paces back, and as quickly returned; when, determined to know the event at once, he raised the garment upon the point of his sword, and perceived, beneath, other remains of dress, heaped high together, while even the floor below was stained with gore.

Look again at the elements of Gothic fiction on page 276. Which Gothic elements can you identify in the extract from *The Italian*?

▶ *The Woman in Black* is considered part of the Gothic novel tradition.

Below is a student's answer to the question: 'How is suspense created in the extract from *The Italian*?'

> The extract from *The Italian* creates suspense through a range of techniques. First and foremost, it tells us that the character was looking for a way out 'unsuccessfully'. So we know he must be sort of really scared because he can't find a way out. Then the writer gets us to focus on something really frightening – a bloody garment. This really brings suspense because now we are thinking, what can this be. Also the word 'bloody' gives a good visual image and creates danger and suspense.

ACTIVITY 1   **A02**   **SKILLS** REASONING

▼ STRENGTHS AND WEAKNESSES

Copy and complete the following table, listing the good and bad points of the student's answer above, then write an answer of your own.

▼ POSITIVES	▼ NEGATIVES
Points out specific techniques, such as visual imagery	Points are not developed. They are mentioned but the effect of each technique is not explained in detail.
Shows some evidence of structuring the answer with the phrase, 'First and foremost'	

EXAM-STYLE QUESTION

A01

A02

SKILLS CRITICAL THINKING, ANALYSIS, REASONING, INTERPRETATION

How does the writer of 'Whistle and I'll Come to You' create an atmosphere of fear and suspense?

In your answer, you should write about:

- the setting and the weather
- the narrator's thoughts and feelings
- the use of language and structure.

You should support your answer with close reference to the extract, including **brief** quotations.

(30 marks)

'NIGHT'
ALICE MUNRO

BACKGROUND AND CONTEXT

Alice Munro is a Canadian writer and Nobel Prize winner. She is best known for the changes that she introduced to the modern short story, particularly the way in which she moves the narrative between the past and the present. She has published several collections of short stories, including *Dance of the Happy Shades* (1968) and *Open Secrets* (1994).

Her stories are often set in Huron County, Ontario, where she was born in 1931. 'Night' appeared in the collection *Dear Life*, published in 2012 as the second of four stories in the section titled 'Finale'. Munro herself called these 'not quite stories' in view of the fact that they are autobiographical writings with fictional elements.

▲ Canadian short story writer Alice Munro won the Nobel Prize in Literature in 2013.

KEY POINT

You can draw upon your own experiences in your writing but you can also be creative with that experience, changing events to explore what might have happened.

▲ Consider the ways that the first paragraph sets up the narrative voice.

appendix A small organ in the human body

neighbors Munro uses American English spellings.

BEFORE YOU START READING

1 You may have siblings. Quite often, relationships with siblings are complicated, especially teenage siblings. Discuss the advantages and disadvantages of having siblings.

2 Good physical health is something that people often take for granted. How would you feel if you were ill, not just for a few days, but for an extended period of time?

3 Read about Huron County, Ontario in Canada. What was life like in rural Canada in the 1940s and 1950s?

▼ 'NIGHT' BY ALICE MUNRO

When I was young, there seemed to be never a childbirth, or a burst appendix, or any other drastic physical event that did not occur simultaneously with a snowstorm. The roads would be closed, there was no question of digging out a car anyway, and some horses had to be hitched up to make their way into town to the hospital. It was just lucky that there were horses still around – in the normal course of events they would have been given up, but the war and gas rationing had changed all that, at least for the time being.

When the pain in my side struck, therefore, it had to do so at about eleven o'clock at night, and a blizzard had to be blowing, and since we were not stabling any horses at the moment, the neighbors' team had to be brought into action to take me to the hospital. A trip of no more than a mile and a half but an adventure all the same. The doctor was waiting, and to nobody's surprise he prepared to take out my appendix. …

▶

nostalgia A feeling that a time in the past was good.

So I lay, minus my appendix, for some days looking out a hospital window at the snow sifting in a somber way through some evergreens. I don't suppose it ever crossed my head to wonder how my father was going to pay for this distinction. (I think he sold a woodlot that he had kept when he disposed of his father's farm. He would have hoped to use it for trapping or sugaring. Or perhaps he felt an unmentionable nostalgia.)

Then I went back to school, and enjoyed being excused from physical training for longer than necessary, and one Saturday morning when my mother and I were alone in the kitchen she told me that my appendix had been taken out in the hospital, just as I thought, but it was not the only thing removed. The doctor had seen fit to take it out while he was at it, but the main thing that concerned him was a growth. A growth, my mother said, the size of a turkey's egg.

But don't worry, she said, it's all over now.

The thought of cancer never entered my head and she never mentioned it. I don't think there could be such a revelation today without some kind of question, some probing about whether it was or it wasn't. Cancerous or benign – we would want to know at once. The only way I can explain our failure to speak of it was that there must have been a cloud around that word…

So I did not ask and wasn't told and can only suppose it was benign or was most skillfully got rid of, for here I am today. And so little do I think of it that all through my life when called upon to list my surgeries, I automatically say or write only "Appendix". …

In the heat of early June I got out of school, having made good enough marks to free me from the final examinations. I looked well, I did chores around the house, I read books as usual, nobody knew there was a thing the matter with me.

Now I have to describe the sleeping arrangements in the bedroom occupied by my sister and myself. It was a small room that could not accommodate two single beds side by side, so the solution was a pair of bunk beds, with a ladder in place to help whoever slept in the top bunk climb into bed. That was me. When I had been younger and prone to teasing, I would lift up the corner of my thin mattress and threaten to spit on my little sister lying helpless in the bunk below. Of course my sister – her name was Catherine – was not really helpless. She could hide under her covers, but my game was to watch until suffocation or curiosity drove her out, and at that moment to spit or successfully pretend to spit on her bared face, enraging her.

I was too old for such fooling, certainly too old by this time. My sister was nine when I was fourteen. The relationship between us was always unsettled. When I wasn't tormenting her, teasing her in some asinine way, I would take on the role of sophisticated counsellor or hair-raising storyteller…

asinine Stupid or silly.

I don't mean to say that I was entirely in control of her, or even that our lives were constantly intertwined. She had her own friends, her own games. …

In the month June, as I have said, I was free of school and left on my own, as I don't remember being in quite the same way in any other time of my growing-up. I did some chores in the house, but my mother must have been well enough, as yet, to handle most of that work. Or perhaps we had just enough money at the time to hire what she – my mother – would call a maid, though everyone else said hired girl. I don't remember, at any rate, having to tackle any of the jobs that piled up for me in later summers, when I fought quite willingly to maintain the decency of our house. It seems that

▶

the mysterious turkey egg must have given me some invalid status, so that I could spend part of the time wandering about like a visitor.

Though not trailing any special clouds. Nobody in our family would have got away with that. It was all inward – this uselessness and strangeness I felt. …

It must have been just that every moment of the day was not filled up with jobs, as it was in summers before and after.

So maybe that was the reason that I had begun to have trouble getting to sleep. At first, I think, that meant lying wide awake maybe till around midnight and wondering at how wide awake I was, with the rest of the household asleep. I would have read, and got tired in the usual way, and turned out my light and waited. Nobody would have called out to me earlier, telling me to put out my light and get to sleep. For the first time ever (and this too must have marked a special status) I was left to make up my own mind about such a thing.

It took a while for the house to change from the light of day and from the household lights turned on late into the evening. Leaving behind the general clatter of things to be done, hung up, finished with, it became a stranger place in which people and the work that dictated their lives fell away, their uses for everything around them fell away, all the furniture retreated into itself and no longer existed because of nobody's attention.

You might think this was a liberation. At first, perhaps it was. The freedom. The strangeness. But as my failure to fall asleep prolonged itself, and as it finally took hold all together until it changed into the dawn, I became more and more disturbed by it. I started saying rhymes, then real poetry, first to make myself go under but then hardly of my own volition. The activity seemed to mock me. I was mocking myself, as the words turned into absurdity, into the silliest random speech.

I was not myself.

I had been hearing that said of people now and then, all my life, without thinking what it could mean.

So who do you think you are, then?

I had been hearing that too, without attaching to it any real menace, just taking it as a sort of routine jeering.

Think again.

By this time it wasn't sleep I was after. I knew mere sleep wasn't likely. Maybe not even desirable. Something was taking hold of me and it was my business, my hope, to fight it off. I had the sense to do that, but only barely, as it seemed. Whatever it was was trying to tell me to do things, not exactly for any reason but just to see if such acts were possible. It was informing me that motives were not necessary.

It was only necessary to give in. How strange. Not out of revenge, or for any normal reason, but just because you had thought of something.

And I did think of it. The more I chased the thought away, the more it came back. No vengeance, no hatred – as I've said, no reason, except something like an utterly cold deep thought that was hardly an urging, more of a contemplation, could take possession of me. I must not even think of it but I did think of it.

---

liberation To be set free.

▶

▲ 'A chair was pushed under the doorknob...'

▲ What senses are mentioned in this section?

The thought was there and hanging in my mind.

The thought that I could strangle my little sister, who was asleep in the bunk below me and whom I loved more than anybody in the world.

I might do it not for jealousy, viciousness, or anger, but because of madness, which could be lying right beside me there in the night. Not a savage madness either, but something that could be almost teasing. A lazy, teasing, half-sluggish suggestion that seemed to have been waiting a long time.

It might be saying why not. Why not try the worst?

The worst. Here in the most familiar place, the room where we had lain for all our lives and thought ourselves most safe. I might do it for no reason I or anybody could understand, except that I could not help it.

The thing to do was to get up, to get myself out of that room and out of the house. I went down the rungs of the ladder and never cast a single look at my sister where she slept. Then quietly down the stairs, nobody stirring, into the kitchen where everything was so familiar to me that I could make my way without a light. The kitchen door was not really locked – I am not even sure that we possessed a key. A chair was pushed under the doorknob so that anybody trying to get in would make a great clatter. A slow careful removal of the chair could be managed without making any noise at all.

After the first night I was able to make my moves without a break, so that I could be outside, as it seemed, within a couple of smooth seconds.

Of course there were no streetlights – we were too far from town.

Everything was larger. The trees around the house were always called by their names – the beech tree, the elm tree, the oak tree, the maples always spoken of in the plural and not differentiated, because they clung together. Now they were all intensely black. So were the white lilac tree (no longer with its blooms) and the purple lilac tree – always called lilac trees not bushes because they had grown too big.

The front and back and side lawns were easy to negotiate because I had mown them myself with the idea of giving us some townlike respectability. ...

Back and forth I walked, first close to the house and then venturing here and there as I got to rely on my eyesight and could count on not bumping into the pump handle or the platform that supported the clothesline. The birds began to stir, and then to sing – as if each of them had thought of it separately, up there in the trees. They woke far earlier than I would have thought possible. But soon after those earliest starting songs, there got to be a little whitening in the sky. And suddenly I would be overwhelmed with sleepiness. I went back into the house, where there was suddenly darkness everywhere, and I very properly, carefully, silently, set the tilted chair under the doorknob, and went upstairs without a sound, managing doors and steps with the caution necessary, although I seemed already half asleep. I fell into my pillow, and I woke late – late in our house being around eight o'clock.

I would remember everything then, but it was so absurd – the bad part of it indeed was so absurd – that I could get rid of it fairly easily. My brother and sister had gone off to their classes in the public school, but their dishes were still on the table, a few bits of puffed rice floating in the excess milk.

Absurd.

▶

demons Something that makes you anxious and causes you problems.

▲ '...in those days the smell of tobacco smoke was everywhere...'

When my sister got home from school we would swing in the hammock, one of us at either end.

It was in that hammock that I spent much of the days, which possibly accounted for my not getting to sleep at night. And since I did not speak of my night difficulties, nobody came up with the simple information that I'd be better off getting more action during the day.

My troubles returned with the night, of course. The demons got hold of me again. I knew enough soon to get up and out of my bunk without pretending that things would get better and that I would in fact go to sleep if I just tried hard enough. I made my way as carefully out of the house as I had done before. I became able to find my way around more easily; even the inside of the rooms became more visible to me and yet more strange. …

The east wall of the kitchen had no windows in it but it had a door opening on a stoop where we stood to hang out the heavy wet washing, and haul it in when it was dry and smelling all fresh and congratulatory, from white sheets to dark heavy overalls.

At that stoop I sometimes halted in my night walks. I never sat down but it eased me to look towards town, maybe just to inhale the sanity of it. All the people getting up before long, having their shops to go to, their doors to unlock and milk bottles to take inside, their busyness.

One night – I can't say whether it could be the twentieth or the twelfth or only the eighth or the ninth that I had got up and walked – I got a sense, too late for me to change my pace, that there was somebody around the corner. There was somebody waiting there and I could do nothing but walk right on. I would be caught if I turned back, and it would be worse that way than to be confronted.

Who was it? Nobody but my father. He too was sitting on the stoop looking towards town and that improbable faint light. He was dressed in his day clothes – dark work pants, the next thing to overalls but not quite, and dark, rough shirt and boots. He was smoking a cigarette. One he rolled himself, of course. Maybe the cigarette smoke had alerted me to another presence, though it's possible that in those days the smell of tobacco smoke was everywhere, inside buildings and out, so there was no way to notice it.

He said good morning, in what might have seemed a natural way except that there was nothing natural about it. We weren't accustomed to giving such greetings in our family. There was nothing hostile about this – it was just thought unnecessary, I suppose, when we would see each other off and on all day.

I said good morning back. And it must have really been getting towards morning or my father would not have been dressed for a day's work in that way. The sky may have been whitening but hidden still between the heavy trees. The birds singing, too. I had taken to staying away from my bunk till later and later, even though I didn't get comfort from doing so as I had at first. The possibilities that had once inhabited only the bedroom, the bunk beds, were taking up the corners everywhere.

Now that I come to think of it, why wasn't my father in his overalls? He was dressed as if he had to go into town for something, first thing in the morning.

I could not continue walking, the whole rhythm of it had been broken.

"Having trouble sleeping?" he said.

▶

My impulse was to say no, but then I thought of the difficulties of explaining that I was just walking around, so I said yes.

He said that was often the case on summer nights.

"You go to bed tired out and then just as you think you're falling asleep you're wide awake. Isn't that the way?"

I said yes.

I knew now that he had not heard me getting up and walking around on just this one night. The person whose livestock was on the premises, whose earnings such as they were lay all close by, and who kept a handgun in his desk drawer, was certainly going to stir at the slightest creeping on the stairs and the easiest turning of the knob.

I am not sure what conversation he meant to follow then, as regards to my being awake. He seems to have declared wakefulness to be a nuisance, but was that to be all? I certainly did not intend to tell him more. If he had given the slightest intimation that he knew there was more, if he'd even hinted that he had come here intending to hear it, I don't think he'd have got anything out of me at all. I had to break the silence out of my own will, saying that I could not sleep. I had to get out of bed and walk.

Why was that?

I did not know.

Not bad dreams?

No.

"Stupid question," he said. "You wouldn't get chased out of your bed on account of good dreams."

He let me wait to go on, he didn't ask anything. I meant to back off but I kept talking. The truth was told with only the slightest modification.

When I spoke of my little sister I said that I was afraid I would hurt her. I believed that would be enough, that he would know enough of what I meant.

"Strangle her," I said then. I could not stop myself, after all.

Now I could not unsay it, I could not go back to the person I had been before.

My father had heard it. He had heard that I thought myself capable of, for no reason, strangling little Catherine in her sleep.

He said, "Well."

Then he said not to worry. He said, "People have those kinds of thoughts sometimes."

He said this quite seriously and without any sort of alarm or jumpy surprise. People have these kinds of thoughts or fears if you like, but there's no real worry about it, no more than a dream, you could say.

He did not say, specifically, that I was in no danger of doing such a thing. He seemed more to be taking it for granted that such a thing could not happen. An effect of the ether, he said. Ether they gave you in the hospital. No more sense than a dream. It could not happen, in the way that a meteor could not hit our house (of course it could, but the likelihood of its doing so put it in the category of couldn't).

ether An anaesthetic gas used in the 19th and early 20th centuries.

▶

He did not blame me, though, for thinking of it. Did not wonder at me, was what he said.

There were other things he could have said. He could have questioned me further about my attitude to my little sister or my dissatisfactions with my life in general. If this were happening today, he might have made an appointment for me to see a psychiatrist. (I think that is what I might have done for a child, a generation and an income further on.)

The fact is, what he did worked as well. It set me down, but without either mockery or alarm, in the world we were living in.

People have thoughts they'd sooner not have. It happens in life.

If you live long enough as a parent nowadays, you discover that you have made mistakes you didn't bother to know about along with the ones you do know about all too well. You are somewhat humbled at heart, sometimes disgusted with yourself. I don't think my father felt anything like this. I do know that if I had ever taxed him, with his use on me of the razor strap or his belt, he might have said something about liking or lumping it. Those strappings, then, would have stayed in his mind, if they stayed at all, as no more than the necessary and adequate curbing of a mouthy child's imagining that she should rule the roost.

 "You thought you were too smart," was what he might have given as his reason for the punishments, and indeed you heard that often in those times, with the smartness figuring as an obnoxious imp that had to have the sass beaten out of him. Otherwise there was the risk of him growing up thinking he was smart. Or her, as the case might be.

However, on that breaking morning he gave me just what I needed to hear and what I was even to forget about soon enough.

I have thought that he was maybe in his better work clothes because he had a morning appointment to go to the bank, to learn, not to his surprise, that there was no extension to his loan. He had worked as hard as he could but the market was not going to turn around and he had to find a new way of supporting us and paying off what we owed at the same time. Or he may have found out that there was a name for my mother's shakiness and that it was not going to stop. Or that he was in love with an impossible woman.

Never mind. From then on I could sleep.

▲ How does Munro bring her story to a resolution?

UNDERSTANDING THE TEXT

KEY POINT

'Night' blends elements of the autobiography and short story genres. It narrates past events but gives a present reflection upon on those events.

According to the writer, 'Night' is part of a 'separate unit, one that is autobiographical in feeling, though not, sometimes, entirely so in fact'. This means that, though it is a short story, it is not the same as others in the genre. It borrows heavily from the writer's own childhood experiences. The story, narrated from an adult's point of view, in the first person, is both a narration of events unfolding and a present reflection on those past events.

'Night' shows you the interior world of the narrator. Her thoughts about her illness and its effects, her conflicted feelings about her sister and general reflections about her family and background, are all a part of the narrative. At the same time, the reader is shown a glimpse of life in rural Canada in the 1950s and gains an understanding of the family relationships that have a significant impact on the narrator.

Some of the themes in this extract are:

■ family relationships
■ the impact of prolonged illness
■ fear for one's mental health
■ reflecting on the past.

Look at the examples from the text that illustrate these themes in the following table. Match each example with one of the themes listed above and talk about their effect.

▼ THEME	▼ EXAMPLE	▼ ANALYSIS
	'The more I chased the thought away, the more it came back... I must not even think of it but I did think of it.'	
	'I knew now that he had not heard me getting up and walking around on just this one night.'	
	'I don't remember, at any rate having to tackle any of the jobs that piled up for me in later summers, when I fought quite willingly to maintain the decency of our house.'	
	'so that I could spend part of the time wandering about like a visitor'	This shows that she was allowed to be freer, than she would have otherwise been, because of her illness. It hints at the idleness that would have contributed to the narrator's sense of unease.

AUTOBIOGRAPHY OR FICTION

The autobiographical and fictional elements of this short story are very cleverly intertwined, so it is difficult for the reader to judge where the autobiography ends and the storytelling begins. This is partly what makes the story both entertaining and effective. However, there are certain sections where the reader feels that one aspect is stronger than the other.

Two such extracts are given in the table on page 289. Complete the table by adding more points to the 'Explanation' column. The first point has been included for you.

▶ Alice Munro was inspired by her native Huron County, Ontario in Canada.

▼ ASPECT	▼ EXTRACT	▼ EXPLANATION
Fictional element is strong	'One night – I can't say whether it could be the twentieth or the twelfth or only the eighth or the ninth that I had got up and walked – I got a sense, too late for me to change my pace, that there was somebody around the corner. There was somebody waiting there and I could do nothing but walk right on'	Important for plot development
Autobiographical element is strong	'I have thought that he was maybe in his better work clothes because he had a morning appointment to go to the bank, to learn, not to his surprise, that there was no extension to his loan. He had worked as hard as he could but the market was not going to turn around and he had to find a new way of supporting us and paying off what we owed at the same time. Or he may have found out that there was a name for my mother's shakiness and that it was not going to stop. Or that he was in love with an impossible woman.'	Strong sense of family history

EXPLORING LANGUAGE

KEY POINT

Every choice a writer makes is intentional, helping them to achieve their intention: the impact they want their writing to have on the reader.

Munro tells her story using largely straightforward and sometimes informal language choices, suggesting the narrator is telling her story to a listening audience. It helps to create a sense of honesty and of intimacy between the narrator and the reader.

Although straightforward, the language Munro chooses reveals much about her characters, their relationships and their lives.

As you explore some of the aspects of the story, think about language choice, looking carefully at the writer's choice of:

- nouns, verbs, adjectives or adverbs and their connotations and implications
- emotive language
- descriptive detail to create a vivid picture in the reader's mind
- informal language and/or sentence structure to suggest hurried or troubled thoughts
- sentence structure, for example, short single clause sentences or minor sentences to create dramatic impact.

▶ **Identify quotations that you feel reveal something significant about her relationships with:**
- her mother
- her sister
- her father.

In each of the quotations you choose, identify a word, phrase or sentence structure choice that adds impact or reveals something significant about the relationship.

▶ **Identify two quotations that show the narrator's thoughts and feelings as she contemplates the murder of her sister.**

In each of the quotations you choose, identify a word, phrase or sentence structure choice that adds impact or reveals something significant about the narrator's thoughts and feelings.

▶ **Identify two or more quotations that show Munro building tension as the narrator gets up and walks around and outside the house in the night.**

In each of the quotations you choose, identify a word, phrase or sentence structure choice that helps the writer to achieve her intention of building tension.

EXPLORING SPEECH

In fictional narratives, conversation or dialogue between characters can be used to reveal character, show the relationship between characters, create conflict or tension, or convey action. Dialogue can be expressed using direct or indirect speech.

In **indirect speech**, what was said is reported by the narrative voice. For example:

Then he said not to worry.

In **direct speech**, the words are written as they were spoken between quotation marks. For example:

He said, 'People have those kinds of thoughts sometimes.'

Compare the two examples from 'Night' above, showing the narrator's father trying to comfort his daughter. Which seems more significant and has greater impact: the indirect speech, recounting what her father said, or the direct speech, directly stating what her father said?

Look closely at all the examples of direct speech in the narrator's conversation with her father at the end of the story. Which examples do you think are the most significant?

EXPLORING STRUCTURE

Short stories must have a tight structure in order to convey a complete story in relatively few words. This structure can be summed up in four stages:

- **exposition:** the setting and key characters are introduced
- **conflict:** a problem is introduced
- **climax:** the problem reaches its peak
- **resolution:** the problem is resolved.

The plot diagram below illustrates this structure. Copy and fill in the boxes with an event or reference from 'Night' that corresponds with the different stages of the plot of a short story.

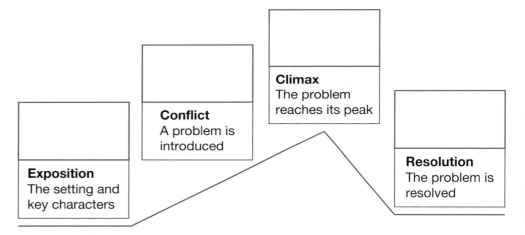

How does each of these stages in the story 'Night' engage the reader's attention and interest?

ACTIVITY 1   **A04**   **SKILLS** COLLABORATION, EMPATHY, NEGOTIATION

▼ THINKING ABOUT ADVICE

In groups, discuss the kind of advice you would give someone who is recovering from a long illness. Talk about different aspects, such as taking care of their health, building up strength and stamina as well as ways to occupy their time.

ACTIVITY 2 | **A04** | **A05** | **SKILLS** CRITICAL THINKING, ANALYSIS, INTERPRETATION, ADAPTIVE LEARNING, CREATIVITY

▼ WRITING TASK

Write a short story that begins with the words, 'I had been alone for many days…'. Try to follow the structure of the short story in the diagram that you completed.

ACTIVITY 3 | **A04** | **SKILLS** PROBLEM SOLVING, REASONING

▼ WRITING A SUCCESSFUL ANSWER

KEY POINT

Thought clouds are often useful in the initial stages of planning an answer. Once you see the ideas set out visually, you are often better able to order your thoughts.

Look at the following thought cloud that could be used to plan an answer to the question, 'How is the narrator's fear and anxiety conveyed in 'Night'?' Complete the thought cloud and number the points in the order in which you think they should appear in an answer. Find an example to support each point and write a sentence explaining why the example illustrates the point.

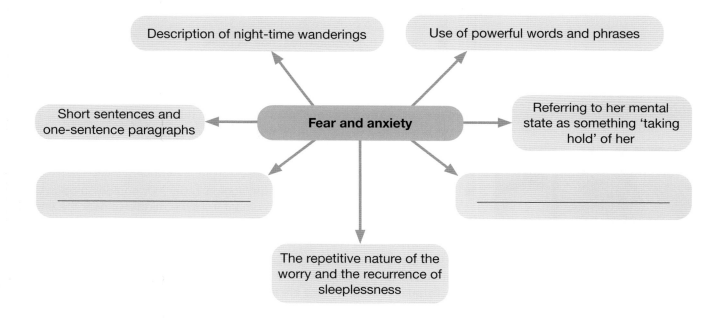

Description of night-time wanderings

Use of powerful words and phrases

Short sentences and one-sentence paragraphs

Fear and anxiety

Referring to her mental state as something 'taking hold' of her

The repetitive nature of the worry and the recurrence of sleeplessness

EXAM-STYLE QUESTION

A01

A02

SKILLS CRITICAL THINKING, ANALYSIS, REASONING, INTERPRETATION

How does the writer of 'Night' present the narrator?

In your answer you should write about:

- the narrator's family life and experiences
- the narrator's thoughts and feelings
- the writer's use of language and structure.

You should support your answer with close reference to the extract, including **brief** quotations. **(30 marks)**

LEARNING OBJECTIVES

This lesson will help you to:
- understand some of the key elements of imaginative writing.

AN INTRODUCTION TO IMAGINATIVE WRITING

You can gather ideas for your imaginative writing from your imagination, or from your own experience. There are several elements you need to think about as you turn your ideas into an effective piece of writing. Each one needs careful thought.

PLOT

The plot consists of the main events of a story. You can develop a plot by listing the events that you think will take place in your story. These events, and the order in which they occur, may well change as you write and develop your characters and setting.

ACTIVITY 1   A01   SKILLS ▶ CRITICAL THINKING, TEAMWORK

▼ WORKING ON A PLOT

Working in small groups, choose a story that you all know or that you have studied in school. Work together to list four key stages of the story:
- **exposition:** the setting and key characters are introduced
- **conflict:** a problem is introduced
- **climax:** the problem reaches its peak
- **resolution:** the problem is resolved.

STRUCTURE

▲ Emlyn Williams's *Night Must Fall* is a psychological thriller partly set in a courtroom.

Here are some key questions to ask yourself in relation to structure:
- What intention do you aim to achieve in your writing?
- How will you open your narrative?
- How will you end it? Happily, sadly, or with a surprising twist?
- Will you tell your narrative in chronological order? Or could you open your story with a tense or dramatic moment from the middle or near the end of your story?
- How could you structure your narrative to help you achieve your intention?

Works of crime fiction often follow a particular structure: a crime is shown at the start but the perpetrator is not revealed until the end. Whilst this is quite a predictable structure, there are ways in which a writer can use structure to challenge and surprise the reader.

There are many examples of stories that use unconventional or non-chronological structures. For example, Emlyn Williams's play, *Night Must Fall*, concerns the actions of a murderer. The opening scene takes place in a court where the murderer is convicted: the audience learns the identity of the murderer and one of their victims, but the identify of a second victim is not revealed. The next scene is set before the second murder, and the audience has to follow the character that they know to be the killer through scenes with other characters, unsure who his second victim will be. The effect would be very different if the murderer's identity and both their victims' identities were revealed in the opening scene.

ACTIVITY 2   A01   SKILLS ▶ CRITICAL THINKING, PROBLEM SOLVING, ADAPTIVE LEARNING

▼ THINKING ABOUT STRUCTURE

Choose a story that you know well. It could be a film, book, a short story or even a fairytale.

1 Write down the four key stages of the story's structure. Are the events of the story structured in chronological or non-chronological order?

2 Try re-structuring the four key stages of the story in a different order. What effect do you think this would have on the story and the reader's experience?

NARRATION

Who will tell your story? Will it be told in the third person by an all-knowing narrator who knows the characters' thoughts, or will it be told by one of the characters in the first person, whose knowledge and understanding of events is limited? Or could it be narrated in the first person by someone unknown, who watches the events without being involved?

ACTIVITY 3   A04   A05   SKILLS ▶ ADAPTIVE LEARNING, CREATIVITY, INNOVATION

▼ CHOOSING A NARRATOR

Working in pairs, write two versions of the first three or four sentences of a story entitled 'Runaway'. Write the first version in the first person, from the point of view of the first character you introduce. Write the second version in the third person. Which version do you prefer? Why?

CHARACTER

How much do your readers need to know about your characters? How will you reveal this information to the reader? Will you introduce the character upfront, so that the reader knows all about this character from the start, or will the reader slowly get to find out about the character as they see what the character does and hear what the character says, and learn what the character thinks?

HINT

Look back at the activities on pages 214–217 for more on creating characters.

KEY POINT

Your imaginative writing skills will develop with practice. At first, you will have to think carefully about all the different aspects of storytelling: plot, structure, narrative, character, and so on. However, the more you write, the more you will build up an understanding of the choices you could and should make to craft effective imaginative writing.

ACTIVITY 4   A04   A05   SKILLS ▶ ADAPTIVE LEARNING, CREATIVITY, INNOVATION

▼ WRITING CHARACTER

Look again at one of the story openings you wrote in Activity 3. Focus on the main character. Add two or three sentences to your story opening introducing them to the reader: their appearance, their personality, their past history.

Now try presenting this character in a different way. Write four or five sentences showing this character interacting with another character. Try to show your main character's appearance, personality and past history using only what they say and what they do.

Compare the two different ways in which you have shown this character. Which version do you prefer? Why?

LEARNING OBJECTIVES

This lesson will help you to:

- develop strategies to generate ideas for imaginative writing tasks.

GENERATING IDEAS

Any activity or exam question that asks you to write imaginatively will give you some sort of starter, even if it is simply a title. This is your starting point from which you will have to generate ideas, develop them and craft them to build an effective narrative that is written engagingly and accurately.

GENERATING IDEAS FOR DIFFERENT PURPOSES

SUBJECT VOCABULARY

plagiarise to take someone else's ideas and present them as your own

When you are asked to produce a piece of imaginative writing, focus on the title, first sentence or topic you are given. Remember, your ideas must be original – do not take or plagiarise the plot of a film or story you have seen or read. However, your ideas do not need to be true: you can set your story anywhere and make your characters do things that people might not do in real life.

ACTIVITY 1   A04   SKILLS CREATIVITY

▼ **WRITING FROM EXPERIENCE**

Look at the exam-style question below:

▶ **Write a story that begins: 'I could hardly believe my eyes.'**

One way to generate ideas for a story beginning with these words is to think about your own experience. Write a sentence summing up a time when you could hardly believe your eyes.

You can also think about the experiences of people you know that you might have heard or been told about. Write a sentence summing up a time when someone you know could hardly believe their eyes.

You can also imagine the experiences of people you do not know. What situation or event in a story might make a character say or think: 'I could hardly believe my eyes.'? Write a sentence summing up the event or situation you have imagined.

Review the three ideas you have noted. Which one do you think would make the most entertaining or engaging story?

KEY POINT

Your initial plan need not be hugely detailed. Begin by thinking about the four key stages of narrative structure:

- exposition
- conflict
- climax
- resolution.

ACTIVITY 2   A04   SKILLS CREATIVITY, TEAMWORK

▼ **WHAT IF...?**

Look at one student's ideas gathered in response to the exam-style question above.

My parents were away for the weekend. I had a few friends over. When we woke up in the morning, I couldn't believe the mess…

In groups, think about anything and everything that could happen next in the story. Note down as many ideas as you can, beginning with the words:

What if…?

Working closely with your group, select the strongest ideas and plan the story.

ACTIVITY 3   A04   SKILLS ▶ CREATIVITY

▼ ASKING QUESTIONS

Once you have a basic story structure, you can ask yourself questions to develop your ideas.

Look at one student's plan below.

- My parents were away for the weekend. I had a few friends over.
- When we woke up in the morning, I couldn't believe the mess.
- We tidied up as best we could. We decided to cook dinner for my parents.
- Our cooking made a massive mess of the kitchen. My parents came home early. They grounded me.

Note down as many questions as you can about this story plan, beginning with the words:

What...?   How..?   and   Why...?

For example:

Why did my parents go away for the weekend?   What did we break?

How did we make a mess?   Why did my parents come home early?

Choose your best ideas to develop the story plan above.

HINT

For example, five typical elements of science fiction might be:
- space flight
- new technology
- computer malfunction
- a strange new planet
- aliens.

ACTIVITY 4   A04   SKILLS ▶ CREATIVITY, TEAMWORK

▼ EXPLORING GENRE

When you write imaginatively, you can write in any genre. For example, you could choose to write a fairy tale or fantasy story, a horror story, a science fiction story, a detective story or an adventure story.

In pairs, choose three different story genres. For each one, note down five typical elements of the genre. Which would you include in the first paragraph of a story that begins, 'I could hardly believe my eyes'?

Working on your own, write three introductory paragraphs, one for each of your chosen genres.

▲ Which three genres will you choose?

LEARNING OBJECTIVES

This lesson will help you to:

- understand how to structure your ideas to create an engaging plot in your imaginative writing.

PLOT

When you are structuring your story's plot, you should always consider the questions: 'What is my intention in this story?' and 'How will this part of the story help me to achieve my intention?'

If your intention is to engage the reader's interest with a mystery, you are unlikely to achieve that intention by beginning your story with a lengthy description of your main characters. Similarly, an exciting adventure story is unlikely to succeed if the adventure is interrupted with a long explanation of your villain's family history!

FIRST STEPS OF PLOTTING

Before you plot anything, you will need a clear sense of the intention you want to achieve in your writing. Writing a short sentence stating your intention will help you keep on track throughout the planning process.

KEY POINT

In a novel or feature film, a writer may have several intentions. In your imaginative writing, aim to achieve just two or three.

ACTIVITY 1 | **AO1** | **SKILLS** CRITICAL THINKING, INTERPRETATION

▼ INDENTIFYING INTENTIONS

A writer's intention in a story, or part of a story, might be to:

- frighten the reader
- shock the reader
- create excitement
- create tension
- mislead the reader
- create mystery
- create sympathy for one or more characters
- amuse the reader
- sadden the reader
- surprise the reader.

Working in pairs, list five stories that you know. They could be books, television programmes, films or plays. Which of the above intentions did the writer aim to achieve in each story, or in one part of the story, that you have listed?

ACTIVITY 2 | **AO4** | **SKILLS** CREATIVITY, CRITICAL THINKING

▼ ACHIEVING YOUR INTENTION

Look closely at the writing task below:

Write about a time when you were in a hurry.

Firstly, choose the main intention you want to achieve in your response to this task.

Now, plan your story in four stages:

exposition → conflict → climax → resolution

Review your planning. Where in your story do you feel you can achieve your chosen intention? How? Note your ideas.

DEVELOPING A PLOT

Openings and endings are arguably the most important parts of a story. Your opening must immediately engage the reader, or they may stop reading. Similarly, a disappointing ending can ruin a good story.

You should always have a clear idea of how you will open and end your story before you start to write it.

ACTIVITY 3 | A04 | SKILLS ▸ CREATIVITY

▼ OPENINGS

Look again at the plot you planned in Activity 2. You could begin your story with:

- **a description:** for example, of the setting, or a character
- **action:** for example, one or more of your characters is doing something dramatic or is in a tricky situation
- **dialogue:** for example, two characters are having a disagreement
- **the middle of the story:** you do not have to tell your story in chronological order. You can begin with a dramatic moment before you reveal how the characters came to be in this situation.

Write three different opening sentences to the story you planned in Activity 2, using a different technique in each one.

ACTIVITY 4 | A04 | SKILLS ▸ CREATIVITY

▼ ENDINGS

Look again at the plot you planned in Activity 2. Plan three different ways in which your story could end. It could have:

- **a happy ending:** all the problems and conflicts of the story are resolved
- **an unhappy ending:** at least one of the problems of the story remains unresolved, but perhaps the main character has learnt something from the experience
- **a twist:** nothing works out as the characters, or the reader, expected them to work out.

ACTIVITY 5 | A04 | SKILLS ▸ CREATIVITY, CRITICAL THINKING

▼ REVIEWING YOUR PLOT

Review all the ideas you gathered in Activities 2, 3, and 4.

Choose your opening, your ending, and make any final adjustments to the plot.

Swap your final story plan with a partner. Can they guess the intention you aim to achieve? How successful do they think your plot will be in achieving it?

LEARNING OBJECTIVES

This lesson will help you to:

■ understand ways of engaging the reader in the opening of your imaginative writing.

OPENINGS

The opening of a piece of imaginative writing can focus on setting, character or action, but it must engage the reader. A mysterious setting, a character in a difficult situation, or a fast-moving, action-packed sequence of events can all grab the reader and keep them reading.

EXPLORING AN OPENNG PARAGRAPH

Look at the opening of Graham Greene's *Brighton Rock* and think about how this opening engages the reader's attention and interest.

Whitsun A date in the Christian calendar, seven weeks after Easter.

▼ FROM *BRIGHTON ROCK* BY GRAHAM GREENE

Hale knew they meant to murder him before he had been in Brighton three hours. With his inky fingers and his bitten nails, his manner cynical and nervous, anybody could tell he didn't belong – belong to the early summer sun, the cool Whitsun wind off the sea, the holiday crowd.

Think about how much information the writer gives you in this paragraph. The reader is given just:

■ two details of Hale's appearance, two things about his manner, and something of his thoughts and feelings

■ four details about the setting

■ one hint at what will happen next.

Now think about how much the writer reveals in this short paragraph with these few details. Note down everything you learn about:

■ character: Who is Hale? What is he like?

■ setting: Where is Hale? What is this place like?

■ action: What is happening or about to happen?

Look particularly closely at the first sentence of the paragraph. How does this grab the reader's attention?

KEY POINT

Effective writing can use a small amount of detail to convey a great deal of information and have a significant impact.

ACTIVITY 1   A04   A05   SKILLS ▶ CREATIVITY, INNOVATION

▼ WRITING AN OPENING

You are going to write the opening of a story in which a student arrives for their first day at a new school. Imagine this student walking through the school gates.

Note down:

■ two or three details about the student's appearance and manner

■ two or three details about the school setting

■ one thing that could happen next.

Use all of your ideas to write a short opening paragraph for the story.

Review the opening sentence of your paragraph. Does it grab the reader's attention as powerfully as the opening sentence of *Brighton Rock*?

KEY POINT

Nineteen Eighty-Four was first published in 1948. It imagines a world of the future.

▲ The term 'Big Brother' (along with others like 'Thought Police') were first invented by Orwell, but have now become part of everyday language usage.

Now look at the beginning of an equally famous novel. In *Nineteen Eighty-Four*, George Orwell tells the story of a dystopian world where the population is under the complete control and supervision of a powerful and mysterious government Party, headed by Big Brother. The narrative follows Winston Smith as he seeks to rebel against Big Brother and the Party.

▼ FROM *NINETEEN EIGHTY-FOUR* BY GEORGE ORWELL

It was a bright cold day in April, and the clocks were striking thirteen. Winston Smith, his chin nuzzled into his breast in an effort to escape the vile wind, slipped quickly through the glass doors of Victory Mansions, though not quickly enough to prevent a swirl of gritty dust from entering along with him.

The hallway smelt of boiled cabbage and old rag mats. At one end of it a coloured poster, too large for indoor display, had been tacked to the wall. It depicted simply an enormous face, more than a metre wide: the face of a man of about forty-five, with a heavy black moustache and ruggedly handsome features. Winston made for the stairs. It was no use trying the lift. Even at the best of times it was seldom working, and at present the electric current was cut off during daylight hours. It was part of the economy drive in preparation for Hate Week. The flat was seven flights up, and Winston, who was thirty-nine and had a varicose ulcer above his right ankle, went slowly, resting several times on the way. On each landing, opposite the lift-shaft, the poster with the enormous face gazed from the wall. It was one of those pictures which are so contrived that the eyes follow you about when you move. BIG BROTHER IS WATCHING YOU, the caption beneath it ran.

What does this opening reveal about the world that Orwell has imagined for his novel and the people that live in it? Note down everything you learn about:

■ character: Who is Winston Smith? What is he like? What is his life like?
■ setting: What is this place like?
■ action: What is happening? What could happen next?

What is the writer's focus in this opening: character, setting or action?

ACTIVITY 2 | A04 | A05 | SKILLS ▸ CREATIVITY, INNOVATION

▼ WRITING THE FUTURE

You are going to write the opening of a story set in the future. Like in *Nineteen Eighty-Four*, open your story with a character returning from work to their home. What will their home of the future be like?

Note down:

■ two or three details about the setting
■ two or three details about your character
■ one thing that could happen next.

Use all of your ideas to write a short opening paragraph for the story.

Review the opening sentence of your paragraph. Does it set the scene as powerfully as the opening sentence of *Nineteen Eighty-Four*?

LEARNING OBJECTIVES

This lesson will help you to:

- understand the impact of choosing to write in the first or third person
- understand the impact of choosing to write in the past or present tense.

NARRATIVE CHOICES

One of the choices that writers make, and many students forget to consider, is the narrative voice in which to write. Narratives are usually told in the first or third person, and in the past or present tense. Each of these choices can affect the reader's response to your writing, and some of the other choices you can make in your writing.

FIRST- AND THIRD-PERSON NARRATIVES

Compare the following two versions of the same story opening.

VERSION A

> I stood outside the school gates, anxiously staring at the sea of faces and bodies in the playground. I could hear shrieks of laughter, cries of fear and the clatter of running footsteps echoing in the cold air. My stomach churned and my heart seemed to have stopped. I knew I would have to move soon. I knew I had to walk through the gates. But I had frozen.

VERSION B

> He stood outside the school gates, anxiously staring at the sea of faces and bodies in the playground. Shrieks of laughter, cries of fear and the clatter of running footsteps echoed in the cold air. His stomach churned and his heart seemed to have stopped. He knew he would have to move soon. He knew he would have to walk through the gates. But he was frozen.

▶ **Which version is written in the first person? Which version is written in the third person?**

▶ **Which version do you find more engaging?**

▶ **Which version makes you empathise more strongly with the character in the story?**

SUBJECT VOCABULARY

empathise to understand the feelings of another person

A LIMITED POINT OF VIEW

In a first-person narrative, everything must be told or seen or heard or felt by the narrator. In a third-person narrative, the writer can show the same events from different perspectives and show events that the main character does not see or hear.

Which of these events and ideas could be shown in the first-person version of the story? Which could not?

- The student's dad sits at home wondering how he is getting on at his new school.
- Two older students secretly plot to get the new student into trouble.
- Another student feels sorry for the new student but is too shy to say anything to him.
- A teacher tells another teacher in the staffroom that she is worried about the new student.

ACTIVITY 1 · A04 · SKILLS ADAPTIVE LEARNING, CREATIVITY, INNOVATION

▼ WRITING FROM DIFFERENT PERSPECTIVES

You are going to write the opening paragraphs of a story about a character who goes for a walk in the countryside, or in a local park, and encounters danger.

Write the opening paragraph of the story in the first person, from the point of view of the character who goes for a walk.

Now, re-write the opening paragraph in the third person, focusing on:

■ the character who goes for a walk

■ the dangerous situation in the countryside or park before the character encounters it.

Will readers respond to both story openings in the same way? Write two or three sentences explaining your ideas.

EXPLORING TENSE

Narrative is most frequently written in the past tense. However, writing in the present tense can create a sense of urgency or immediacy, as though the reader is experiencing events as they happen rather than being told about events that have already happened.

KEY POINT

Once you have decided on the tense and person in which you will write, stick to it. Always check you use tense and person consistently in your narrative writing.

ACTIVITY 2 · A04 · SKILLS ADAPTIVE LEARNING, CREATIVITY, INNOVATION

▼ EXPERIMENTING WITH TENSE

Write a short paragraph from the middle of the story you began in Activity 1. In this paragraph, your main character encounters danger.

You could choose to write in the first person or the third person:

> As I reached the top of the hill, I froze. Just ahead of me, there was a…

> As he reached the top of the hill, he froze. Just ahead of him, there was a…

In which tense did you choose to write your paragraph? Try writing it again in a different tense. If your first version was in the past tense, write it again in the present tense. If, however, you wrote your first version in the present tense, write it again in the past tense.

Check both versions to be sure that you have written in the same tense and in the same person consistently throughout each one.

Which version do you prefer? What impact does each tense have on your writing?

LEARNING OBJECTIVES

This lesson will help you to:
- ■ think about how to create and use characters in your writing.

CHARACTERS

The characters in a narrative have as much impact on the reader as the actions they take and the experiences they encounter. To fully engage the reader in your writing, it is essential to create interesting characters.

Characters are not just the people in a story. They are the people the reader empathises or sympathises with, the people the reader fears or admires, the people the reader loves or hates or loves to hate. A great character can be far more memorable than the individual things they do or feel or say in a story, although each of those things helps to build an impression of a character in the reader's mind.

ACTIVITY 1   **A01**   **SKILLS**   CRITICAL THINKING

▼ LEARNING ABOUT CHARACTERS

In pairs, read the following excerpts from pieces of imaginative writing and identify how you learn about each of the characters. Do you learn about them through what they do, what they say, what the narrator tells you about them, or a combination of two or more of these?

- ■ He thought she was stunning. You could tell when he spoke about her. You could tell when he insisted on waiting for her after school, when the rest of us were going to the park. Most of all, you could tell when he found out she had been texting one of the boys in the year above.

- ■ I noticed them crawling out of the rotten woodwork onto the paving slabs. Small and black and oozing. Before they could get to my prize roses, I lifted my foot and ground them into the concrete. Mary would have screamed and told me to stop, but she was not there to see what I had done. And I was not going to tell her.

- ■ He was the biggest rabbit in the litter. Since they had arrived in the straw, under the lamp, he had quickly learnt to barge his brothers and sisters to one side so that he always got the best feed. Now that they were weaned the others simply moved aside when he wanted a drink or the best spot in the warm straw bed.

▲ 'He was the biggest rabbit in the litter.'

ACTIVITY 2 | A01 | SKILLS CRITICAL THINKING

▼ QUESTIONS TO ASK ABOUT CHARACTERS

Try answering the following questions about each of the characters in Activity 1.

- ■ Who are they?
- ■ What are they?
- ■ What are they doing?
- ■ How would you describe their personality?
- ■ What do you learn about their relationship with other characters?

CHARACTER BUILDING

In many stories, there are heroes and villains: a hero the reader can empathise with and a villain the reader can despise.

ACTIVITY 3 | A04 | A05 | SKILLS CREATIVITY, INNOVATION

▼ HERO AND VILLAIN

Create two characters: a student and a teacher. Make one a character for the reader to admire or empathise with. Make the other a character for the reader to hate.

Picture these two characters interacting in a classroom. Copy and complete the table below to create them.

	▼ STUDENT	▼ TEACHER
One word to sum up their personality		
Two details about their appearance	1 2	1 2
Something they do		
Something they say		
What others think of them		

HINT

A character's appearance can reveal a great deal about them. For example, which is more revealing: the fact that a character is wearing a suit and has a beard, or that their suit is stained and their beard is dotted with scraps of food?

ACTIVITY 4 | A04 | A05 | SKILLS CREATIVITY, INNOVATION

▼ INTRODUCING CHARACTERS

Working on your own, write an opening section for a story introducing the two characters you created in Activity 3. You can use some or all of the ideas you noted.

Ask a partner to read the opening of your story and to note their impressions of your two characters. Have your two characters created the impression you intended them to create?

LEARNING OBJECTIVES

This lesson will help you to:
- use speech to reveal character.

MONOLOGUES AND DIALOGUES

Monologues convey the thoughts or speech of a single character, whereas dialogues are exchanges between more than one character. They serve different purposes in imaginative writing: monologues can create a vivid and direct impression of the speaker's character through their thoughts and feelings, whereas dialogues are highly effective in revealing characters and the relationship between them.

MONOLOGUE

SUBJECT VOCABULARY

monologue the speech or thoughts of one person alone

▲ Can you think of a famous monologue?

The following extracts are taken from Susan Hill's novel, *I'm the King of the Castle*. When Edmund Hooper is about 11 years old, his father tells him that another boy is coming to live in their house, along with his mother who is to be their housekeeper.

> Hooper began to mould plasticine between his hands, for another layer to the geological model, standing as a board beside the window. He thought of the boy called Kingshaw, who was coming.
>
> 'It is my house,' he thought, 'it is private, I got here first. Nobody should come here.'

Hooper's thoughts are conveyed to the reader as a **monologue**.

▶ **What is revealed about his thoughts and feelings in the second paragraph of the extract above?**

▶ **The writer could have chosen to reveal these thoughts and feelings in a dialogue between Hooper and, for example, his father. Why do you think the writer chose not to do this?**

DIALOGUE

SUBJECT VOCABULARY

dialogue the speech between two or more people involved in a conversation

Soon the boys are left together.

> He walked round the table, towards the window. Kingshaw stepped back as he came.
>
> 'Scaredy!'
>
> 'No.'
>
> 'When my father dies,' Hooper said, 'this house will belong to me. I shall be master. It'll all be mine.'
>
> 'That's nothing. It's only an old house.'

In this extract, the characters of the boys and their relationship are conveyed to the reader through **dialogue**.

▶ **What does this dialogue reveal about the characters of Hooper and Kingshaw and their relationship?**

▶ **Try re-writing the extract above using two monologues: one showing Hooper's thoughts and feelings and one showing Kingshaw's. You will also need to describe what happens.**

▶ **How are your impressions of the characters and their relationship changed in the versions you have written?**

ACTIVITY 1   A04   A05   **SKILLS** ADAPTIVE LEARNING, CREATIVITY, INNOVATION, TEAMWORK

▼ WRITING MONOLOGUES

Working in a pair, discuss and note the possible thoughts and feelings of:

■ a character lying in bed, unable to sleep

■ a character about to give a speech to a crowd of strangers

■ a character with someone who refuses to speak to them.

Use your notes to write three short monologues, one for each character.

ACTIVITY 2   A04   A05   **SKILLS** ADAPTIVE LEARNING, CREATIVITY, INNOVATION, TEAMWORK

▼ WRITING DIALOGUES

Working in a pair, discuss and note the possible thoughts, feelings actions and speech of:

■ a homeowner finding a stranger in his or her back garden

■ a group of friends trying to persuade a security guard to let them into a shopping mall

■ a teacher asking a student why their homework has not been done.

Use your notes to write four short pieces of dialogue, one for each situation.

Review your writing. Can you add impact to your dialogue through your choice of **identifiers**? For example:

| …he whispered. | …she bellowed. | …he hissed. | …she giggled. |

SUBJECT VOCABULARY

identifiers phrases indicating who is speaking in dialogue

ACTIVITY 3   A04   A05   **SKILLS** ADAPTIVE LEARNING, CREATIVITY, INNOVATION

▼ CONVEYING CHARACTERS

Picture the scene: three friends, walking in the woods, have stumbled across a suitcase full of money.

Working in pairs or on your own, think about how each of the three characters might react to their find. You could decide to create:

■ an honest character

■ a character who urgently needs money for a good cause

■ a nervous character

■ any other type of character.

Use your ideas to write a short story extract using dialogue and monologue.

Do not state what your characters are like. Try instead to reveal their characters to the reader through their thoughts, conveyed in monologue, and through their dialogue with each other. Choose your identifiers carefully to show not only **what** is said, but **how** it is said.

▲ In this scenario, the suitcase is a catalyst for drama and tension.

KEY POINT

What people say and how they say it has a huge influence on our impression of them. In the same way, a character's speech can make a powerful impression on your reader.

DESCRIPTIVE WRITING

Descriptions can be used to develop and add impact to narratives, instructions, explanations and argument. Effective descriptions build a vivid picture in the reader's mind using the five senses.

USING THE SENSES

It is through your five senses that you experience the world around you: everything you know and understand is discovered through sight, sound, touch, smell and taste. The more that your descriptions engage your reader's senses, the more effective your writing will be.

Were you woken by an alarm clock or by the sound of a parent's voice this morning? Was the first thing that you saw a bright light shining in your face? Was the first thing you felt someone pulling back the blankets? Did you smell toast? Was the first thing you tasted toothpaste, some fruit juice or a boiled egg?

▲ Are your senses acute or dull in the morning?

| ACTIVITY 1 | A04 | A05 | SKILLS ▶ CREATIVITY |

▼ USING YOUR SENSES

Working on your own, try to remember and list the first things that you heard, saw, felt, smelt and tasted after waking up this morning. Use this list as the basis of a description of the first half hour of your day.

SHOW, NOT TELL

Sometimes, you can describe things more convincingly by 'showing' the reader rather than telling them.

| ACTIVITY 2 | A02 | SKILLS ▶ ANALYSIS, COLLABORATION |

▼ SHOWING OR TELLING?

Each of the sentences below has a pair: a sentence with the same meaning. Match them.

A: The sun was shining and I was boiling hot.

B: Vik frowned and wrinkled their nose.

A: My stomach churned and my heart pounded.

B: The sun scorched my skin and sweat soaked my shirt.

A: Vik did not want to do it.

B: I was terrified.

Which one in each pair **tells** the reader something and which **shows** the reader the same thing? Which one in each pair do you find more effective?

The following extract is adapted from *The War of the Worlds* by H.G. Wells. One night, Ogilvy sees what he believes to be a falling meteorite. The next day, he goes to find the meteorite. What he finds, though, is not what he expected…

▲ A still from the 1953 film adaption of *The War of the Worlds*.

incrustation A hard coating on the outside of something.

▼ FROM *THE WAR OF THE WORLDS* BY H.G. WELLS

The Thing itself lay almost entirely buried in sand, amidst the scattered splinters of a fir tree it had shivered to fragments in its descent.

The uncovered part had the appearance of a huge cylinder, caked over and its outline softened by a thick scaly dun-coloured incrustation. It had a diameter of about thirty metres. He approached the mass, surprised at the size and more so at the shape, since most meteorites are rounded more or less completely. It was, however, still so hot from its flight through the air as to forbid his near approach. A stirring noise within its cylinder he ascribed to the unequal cooling of its surface; for at that time it had not occurred to him that it might be hollow.

Suddenly he noticed with a start that some of the grey clinker, the ashy incrustation that covered the meteorite, was falling off the circular edge of the end. It was dropping off in flakes and raining down upon the sand. A large piece suddenly came off and fell with a sharp noise that brought his heart into his mouth.

And then he perceived that, very slowly, the circular top of the cylinder was rotating on its body. It was such a gradual movement that he discovered it only through noticing that a black mark that had been near him five minutes ago was now at the other side of the circumference. Even then he scarcely understood what this indicated, until he heard a muffled grating sound and saw the black mark jerk forward an inch or so. Then the thing came upon him in a flash. The cylinder was artificial – hollow – with an end that screwed out! Something within the cylinder was unscrewing the top!

ACTIVITY 3 | A02 | SKILLS ▶ CRITICAL THINKING, ANALYSIS

▼ IDENTIFYING SENSES

Working in a pair, identify all the senses that Wells uses to create a vivid picture of the 'Thing' in the reader's mind. For each sense, note any words or phrases Wells uses to engage the reader's imagination. For example:

- sight: 'a huge cylinder' creates an impression of the object's appearance
- touch: 'a thick scaly… incrustation' describes…

ACTIVITY 4 | A04 | A05 | SKILLS ▶ CREATIVITY, INNOVATION

▼ USING YOUR SENSES

1 Picture the scene: you wake one morning to find a large cardboard box at the end of your bed. You listen: is something moving inside the box? Is something trying to get out?

2 In pairs, list all the sights, sounds, smells, touches and tastes you could use to describe this scene. Then, compile nouns, adjectives, verbs and adverbs you could use to convey them.

3 Use the vocabulary you have gathered to write this scene.

KEY POINT

Choose vocabulary with care and always consider synonyms that could have greater impact than the first word that comes to mind. For example, which of these synonyms creates the most vivid visual image of the cardboard box: dirty, grubby, stained, muddy, grimy, filthy or dusty?

VOCABULARY FOR EFFECT

Almost every noun, verb, adjective and adverb in the English language has at least one synonym: a word with a similar meaning. However, not all synonyms have the same effect or impact.

CHOOSING THE RIGHT WORD

▲ '...it tasted of tomatoes...'

Read the two versions of the same account that follows.

EXTRACT A

When I was fourteen, I went to the dentist to have a tooth removed under general anaesthetic. That night, I still felt odd and dreamed I was eating a big ice cream cornet covered in strawberry sauce. To my surprise, I realised it tasted of tomatoes, which I don't like. For the next six months I couldn't look at ice cream without feeling sick.

EXTRACT B

When I was fourteen, I was sent to the dentist to have a tooth pulled out under general anaesthetic. That night, I still felt weird and dreamed I was eating a huge ice cream cornet smothered in strawberry sauce. To my horror, I realised it tasted of tomatoes, which I loathe. For the next six months I couldn't look at ice cream without my stomach doing somersaults.

SUBJECT VOCABULARY

synonyms words that share the same meaning as other words; for example, 'quick' might be a synonym for 'fast'

| ACTIVITY 1 | A02 | A05 | SKILLS | CRITICAL THINKING, INNOVATION |

▼ THE EFFECTS OF DIFFERENT WORDS

In pairs, list the words and phrases that have been changed between Extract A and Extract B. There are eight changes to find. For each one, note the effect of the change.

▼ EXTRACT A	▼ EXTRACT B	▼ EFFECT
'went'	'was sent to'	Suggests they were not willing to go

For each of the words and phrases that have changed, note another **synonym** that could have been used. Which choice would be most effective: the choice in Extract A, the choice in Extract B, or the synonym that you noted?

As you write, and when you have finished writing, you need to review your vocabulary choices. You need to look at each sentence you have written and think about the most significant words in it: the words that convey the most significant ideas.

KEY POINT

Your first choice of vocabulary may not be the best choice. Always review your vocabulary choices to see if they can be improved.

ACTIVITY 2   A02   A05   SKILLS ▶ CRITICAL THINKING INNOVATION

▼ IDENTIFYING SIGNIFICANT WORDS

Which words in these sentences are the most significant? Choose two from each sentence.

1 The tyres screeched on the tarmac as we raced around each corner.

2 The vase fell to the ground and smashed.

3 It was a big dinner plate with one small potato sitting in the middle of it.

For each word that you have chosen, note two or three synonyms. Which word would be most effective in the sentence: the original word, or one of your synonyms? Re-write each sentence using your own choice of vocabulary.

CONNOTATIONS

SUBJECT VOCABULARY

connotations ideas linked to a word; ideas that have become associated with a word

Different synonyms have different **connotations**: different ideas and associations that they conjure in readers' minds. Look at the examples below. Each word or phrase that could fill the gaps in these sentences has a similar meaning but conveys a slightly different idea in its connotations.

Dinner arrived and the _____ was overpowering

> aroma
> smell
> stench

He stared in shock for a moment, then_____

> yelped
> screamed
> cried out

What connotations does each choice have?
Note your ideas.

ACTIVITY 3   A04   A05   SKILLS ▶ CREATIVITY INNOVATION

▼ CHOOSING THE PERFECT WORD

Working on your own, describe in one paragraph a scene or event that has surprised you. Before you write, think about your intention: what impression do you want to create of this scene or event?

When you have written your paragraph, identify five significant vocabulary choices you could improve to help you achieve your intention more fully. Note three synonyms for each one, then decide which are the perfect words to use in your description.

LEARNING OBJECTIVES

This lesson will help you to:
- create effects in imaginative writing through the way in which sentences are organised.

SENTENCES FOR EFFECT

Sentences must be structured to convey meaning as clearly as possible. However, your choice of sentence structure can also add significant impact to your writing.

SENTENCE TYPES

doing wheelies Balancing a bicycle on its rear wheel while riding it.

dog collar An informal description of the white collar worn by the clergy of some Christian churches.

▲ A biker demonstrating a wheelie.

HINT

Look back at previous sections about the effect of different sentences on pages 22–23, 40–41 and 198–199.

In her novel, *The Risk of Darkness*, Susan Hill describes a young woman priest walking home. At the time of the novel's setting, the sight of a woman priest was a novelty in England.

> A boy bounced past her on a bicycle doing wheelies over the cobbles. Jane smiled at him. He did not respond but when he had gone by, turned and stared over his shoulder. She was used to it. Here she was, a girl, wearing jeans, and a dog collar. People were still surprised.

The first sentence could be reduced to just five words and it would still make sense and convey a similar meaning. What do you think is achieved by including the rest of the sentence?

▶ **In pairs, make every sentence as short as you can to convey the same series of events but in less detail. What is lost from the text's impact by reducing it in this way?**

ACTIVITY 1 | A01 | SKILLS ANALYSIS, CREATIVITY

▼ **DEVELOPING SENTENCES**

Sentences can be developed by:
- adding an additional clause, using a conjunction (such as 'and', 'when', 'although') to link it
- adding an additional clause using a non-finite *-ing* verb (such as 'running', 'smiling', 'hoping') to link it
- adding an additional clause using a relative pronoun (such as 'who', 'which', 'that')
- adding a prepositional phrase: a detail linked with a preposition (such as 'in an hour', 'on the table', 'under the duvet').

In how many different ways can you develop the sentences below?

In each case, think about your intention: will the detail you add help to create tension or add humour or simply build a more detailed image in the reader's mind?

- The door opened.
- They could see the dog.
- The road was full of traffic.

SENTENCE LENGTH

Longer sentences can build detail or convey a series of events. Shorter sentences can add emphasis or dramatic impact to your writing. Thinking carefully about sentence length can improve your writing significantly.

ACTIVITY 2   **AO5**   **SKILLS**   INNOVATION, ANALYSIS

▼ EXPERIMENTING WITH SENTENCE LENGTH

Each of the following sentences contains three clauses:

1 He remembered leaving his keys on the shelf and he had seen them just a moment ago but now they were gone.
2 He had thought the house was empty but he could hear footsteps on the bare floorboards upstairs and they were heading for the stairs.

Re-write each sentence as two sentences: one sentence should contain two clauses, the other just one. You will need to decide:

■ which two pieces of information you want to link in a longer sentence
■ which one piece of information you want to highlight in a shorter sentence.

SEQUENCING CLAUSES

Some sentences can be restructured to position key ideas or key moments at the end of the sentence to give them greater impact.

For example, these two sentences convey exactly the same meaning, but the clauses are sequenced in a different order:

■ He told them my secret before I could stop him.
■ Before I could stop him, he told them my secret.

Which sentence do you feel highlights the key moment most effectively?

ACTIVITY 3   **AO5**   **SKILLS**   INNOVATION, ANALYSIS

▼ EXPERIMENTING WITH SENTENCE STRUCTURE

Each of the sentences below contains two clauses. Re-write them, swapping the clauses around.

1 The creature lunged at me, snarling and snapping its huge yellow teeth.
2 We quickly hurried out of the door when he was looking the other way.

Which version of each sentence has the greatest impact, do you think?

ACTIVITY 4   **AO5**   **SKILLS**   CREATIVITY, INNOVATION

▼ CRAFTING SENTENCE STRUCTURES

Write the opening paragraph of a story in which a character finds someone or something in a place where they should not be. Aim to write at least five sentences.

When you have written your paragraph, review each of your sentence structures. Could you add impact to your writing by:

■ developing any of your sentences with additional detail?
■ breaking any of your multiclause sentences down into shorter sentences to add dramatic impact?
■ restructuring or resequencing any of your multiclause sentences to highlight key moments or ideas?

LEARNING OBJECTIVES

This lesson will help you to:

■ take greater control over your writing

■ think about the use of the senses when writing

■ make clear what you want to say about characters, actions and locations.

PUTTING IT INTO PRACTICE

In the exam, you will need to demonstrate the following points in your imaginative writing.

■ Ideas that are communicated effectively and imaginatively. This is what you will have to plan before you start.

■ Writing that is engaging, clear and accurate. This is what you will have to check after you finish.

EXAM-STYLE QUESTION

A04

A05

SKILLS ▶ CRITICAL THINKING, ANALYSIS, ADAPTIVE LEARNING, CREATIVITY, INNOVATION

flies burrow into their flesh A vivid image using carefully chosen vocabulary to shock the reader.

the sea crashing into the rocks at the foot of the cliffs A vivid image using dramatic language.

standing still as if hoping not to be noticed Use of humour.

the deafening blare of a fog horn Use of sensory detail to build the picture.

I was terrified Use of a short sentence – dramatic.

plummeting over the cliff edge Emotive language choice creates drama.

The conflict – the sheep dangerously close to the cliff – builds to a climax.

We, the dogs and the sheep headed home A short sentence giving a final satisfying resolution to the story.

Write about a time when you, or someone you know, had an unexpected experience. Your response could be real or imagined. **(30 marks)**

Now read the example student answer and the commentary that follows.

It was a warm summer's day when my mum and I left the farm to round up the sheep. Every summer, before the sun is too hot, we round them up and bring them in so they can be dipped, pushed one at a time through a long bath of insecticide to protect them from fly-strike. Sheep get it when flies burrow into their flesh and lay their eggs in the wound.

The sheep we were looking for had spread themselves over the moor and across to an open area of land between the road and the sea. With us we had two sheep dogs. Once we had crossed the road, we sent the dogs round in wide-sweeping paths to move the sheep together into a flock that we could move across the road and back to the farm.

Below us, to our left, we could hear the sea crashing into the rocks at the foot of the cliffs. Ahead of us we could see the dogs, their heads up as they looked from side to side for sheep that had wandered off or were standing still as if hoping not to be noticed. The dogs gathered them up and pushed the flock away from the sea and up towards the road.

From ahead of us, came the deafening blare of a fog horn. We hadn't noticed the clouds that had come up behind us. They had not yet blotted out the sun and we were busy trying to keep an eye on our flock moving slowly towards the road. Ahead of us the dogs were barking furiously now and we stepped forwards to see what was troubling them. Again the fog horn blared.

Before we knew what was happening, a cold damp fog had blown up behind us and suddenly surrounded us. We could see nothing of the dogs or sheep, but we could hear them and the sea pounding the rocks fifty metres below us.

I was terrified. I imagined the sheep plummeting over the cliff edge, and the dogs racing after them and following them over the edge. Mum, the dogs and the sheep remained perfectly calm. She made me stand still while the sheep and dogs moved carefully around us, until the breeze dropped and the fog slid away off the cliff and moved slowly, back down to the water. We, the dogs and the sheep headed home.

This is a highly effective piece of imaginative writing. A vivid scene is created through precise use of vocabulary, which shows it's not always necessary to use lots of figurative language to describe effectively. The atmosphere becomes increasingly tense, showing the student has a good grasp of how to structure a piece of writing. There is a good balance of longer, more detailed sentences and short sentences for effect.

COMMENTARY

This is an explanation of how this sample answer was written. Try following this process in your own imaginative writing.

PLANNING THE PLOT

The planning of this piece is focused on the fog surrounding the two characters who were caught unawares. The rounding up of the sheep provides exposition, explaining why the characters were on the cliffs when fog enveloped them, building a sense of danger.

The writer uses descriptive detail of the sea and cliffs to build the conflict (or problem) of the fog to a climax in which the narrator vividly describes their worst fears. Finally, the story is brought to a rapid resolution with the lifting of the fog.

CHECKING

This is where you must read the extract aloud or, under exam conditions, imagine the sound of a voice reading it aloud. This is the most effective way of checking your writing. If the punctuation is poor, you will struggle to read the extract fluently, and if there are lapses in grammar, then the sense of the writing will not be clear. If you find yourself stumbling as you read, stop and slowly re-read the sentence, looking for the error that tripped you up. If you can find no error, try re-writing the sentence using a different structure to make it easier to read and understand.

EXAM-STYLE QUESTION

A04

A05

SKILLS   CRITICAL THINKING, ANALYSIS, ADAPTIVE LEARNING, CREATIVITY

Write a story with the title, 'Left Behind'. Your response could be real or imagined.   **(30 marks)**

Allow yourself 45 minutes to respond to this question with a piece that is 300–400 words in length.

Exchange your finished piece with a partner, then read each other's work and exchange comments. Try to identify areas for possible improvement, and suggest ways in which those improvements could be made.

KEY POINT

Remember that good imaginative writing grabs the reader's interest from the start and holds it throughout. Your choice of ideas, structure, vocabulary and sentence structure all help you to achieve this. Careful checking of your writing means the reader can focus on enjoying your writing, not on making sense of it.

▲ The writer uses descriptive detail of the sea and cliffs to build the conflict.

PAPER 3: POETRY AND PROSE TEXTS AND IMAGINATIVE WRITING

Assessment Objective 1

Read and understand a variety of texts, selecting and interpreting information, ideas and perspectives

Assessment Objective 2

Understand and analyse how writers use linguistic and structural devices to achieve their effects

This chapter focuses on Paper 3: Poetry and Prose Texts and Imaginative Writing of the English Language A course. Working through these lessons and activities will help you develop the reading and writing skills that you will need for the Paper 3 non-examined assessment.

Paper 3 is worth 40% of the total marks for the course and is split into two sections:

- Assignment A: Poetry and Prose Texts
- Assignment B: Imaginative Writing.

In Assignment A of your non-examined assessment, you will need to be able to meet Assessment Objectives AO1 and AO2.

In Assignment B of your non-examined assessment, you will need to be able to meet Assessment Objectives AO4 and AO5.

Assessment Objective 4

Communicate effectively and imaginatively, adapting form, tone and register of writing for specific purposes and audiences

Assessment Objective 5

Write clearly, using a range of vocabulary and sentence structures, with appropriate paragraphing and accurate spelling, grammar and punctuation

In Paper 3, the assessment objectives are worth the following amounts:
AO1 – 8%
AO2 – 12%
AO4 – 12%
AO5 – 8%

NON-EXAMINED ASSESSMENT OVERVIEW

These two pages give those taking this option a general idea of the non-examined assessment requirements. They are followed by a section on Assignment A and another on Assignment B. The non-examined assessment option (also called Paper 3), provides an alternative to examination Paper 2 and covers the same content in different ways. It has advantages and disadvantages.

The two non-examined assessment tasks for Paper 3 are as follows:

■ Assignment A on Poetry and Prose Texts
■ Assignment B on Imaginative Writing.

UNDERSTANDING THE NON-EXAMINED ASSESSMENT OPTION

NON-EXAMINED ASSESSMENT TASKS FOR PAPER 3

Assignment A

Poetry and Prose Texts: study and analyse selections from a range of fictional poetry and prose texts, taken from Section B of the Pearson Edexcel Anthology.

In practice, this piece must focus on three texts (including at least one prose text and one poetry text).

Assignment B

Imaginative Writing: explore and develop imaginative writing skills.

The emphasis of this assignment is very much on your own ideas and ways of expressing yourself.

SUBJECT VOCABULARY

plagarise to take someone else's ideas and present them as your own

---

The written non-examined assessment that you will complete for Paper 3 is worth **40%** of your total English Language course (the same as Paper 2). You have to submit **two** assignments, (known as units). One will be based on Section B of the Pearson Edexcel Anthology, which will be assessed for your **reading** skills. The other will be a piece of personal imaginative writing, which is entirely your own work and which will be assessed for your **writing** skills.

You must work under the guidance of your teacher, who is authorised to assess your non-examined assessment and who has to authenticate it, but your non-examined assessment is something that you are in charge of. It is vital that you do not copy or borrow writing from elsewhere and then pretend it is your own: you will be required to sign a form stating that the work is your own.

ADVANTAGES AND DISADVANTAGES OF THE NON-EXAMINED ASSESSMENT

The non-examined assessment has many advantages.

■ You have more time to plan, think about and improve your assignments.

■ Work does not have to be completed under controlled conditions.

■ You have more freedom to choose what to write about and what to submit.

■ Your non-examined assessment folder is solid evidence of what you can do in your own time and to the best of your abilities.

However, there are disadvantages too.

■ The non-examined assessment may take up too much of your time. The two assignments together are worth 40% of the GCSE, whereas the exam is worth 60%, so you must prioritise your exam preparation over your non-examined assessment.

■ You may be tempted to take short-cuts. If you cheat and get found out, the penalties can be very severe. Teachers and moderators are very good at detecting plagiarism so it is simply not worth the risk to **plagarise**. Furthermore, cheating will not help you to develop your writing skills.

WORD COUNT

There is no definite requirement regarding the length of coursework pieces, except that they should be as long as they need to be. Most students' coursework units are between 1800 and 2200 words. The board advises that Assignment A should be approximately 1200 words in length and Assignment B should be approximately 700 words in length, but there is no penalty for exceeding this recommendation.

SUBMITTING ASSIGNMENTS

AUTHENTICITY

Near the end of the course, you will be asked to sign a Non-examined Assessment Authentication to confirm that you produced your non-examined assessment independently. Teachers are always warned to look out for signs of plagiarism or excessive assistance from others. You should therefore work independently, although it is a good idea to show others what you have written and ask for verbal feedback. If you are unsure, ask your teacher what level of feedback is appropriate.

PRESENTATION OF THE NON-EXAMINED ASSESSMENT

Each piece of non-examined assessment should contain your name, the date on which the work was completed, the mark awarded and a brief teacher comment justifying the mark. This comment should be based on the assessment criteria for the mark range awarded.

Non-examined assessment pieces may be handwritten or word-processed.

STANDARDISATION OF NON-EXAMINED ASSESSMENT

Towards the end of the course, Pearson Edexcel will request a sample of non-examined assessment to be sent to a Pearson Edexcel-appointed non-examined assessment moderator. The moderator will either confirm the marks awarded by the teachers in your centre or will adjust marks accordingly. English departments always standardise the marking by sharing out work from each class amongst all the teachers in the department to ensure the marking of the Pearson year group is consistent.

USING PREVIOUS CHAPTERS

ASSESSMENT OBJECTIVES FOR PAPER THREE

Reading (Assignment A):

AO1 Read and understand a variety of texts, selecting and interpreting information, ideas and perspectives

AO2 Understand and analyse how writers use linguistic and structural devices to achieve their effects

Writing (Assignment B):

AO4 Communicate effectively and imaginatively, adapting form, tone and register of writing for specific purposes and audiences

AO5 Write clearly, using a range of vocabulary and sentence structures, with appropriate paragraphing and accurate spelling, grammar and punctuation

The assessment objectives for the non-examined assessment and for Papers 1 and 2 are the same. This means that the Paper 2 chapter on the fiction Anthology texts (pages 208–291) will give you plenty of activities and information that can be used to help you with Assignment A. For example, if your assignment is to compare three Anthology texts in some way, you should work your way carefully through the activities on those texts, as they will give you ideas and quotations to use in your non-examined assessment.

Likewise, for Assignment B, all the activities for Paper 2 Section B: Imaginative writing (pages 292–313) will be very helpful for your non-examined assessment. There are sections on generating ideas, plotting, characterisation, description, using monologues and dialogues, vocabulary choice and so on, which will help you to create a good story. The fiction stories in the Anthology may also help to give you inspiration. Look at the way that they use technique and structure and handle character, situation, mood and theme.

People often write best when they can draw on their own experiences, such as a powerful memory or an eventful day. You could write to explore your feelings and thoughts, or you could use these experiences as part of an entertaining account or story. However, you can also take inspiration from the experience of friends or relatives, or a true story that has fired your imagination. Your approach to this assignment can be light-hearted or deeply serious, and you can submit imaginative responses to any of the Anthology texts.

HINT

Note that AO3 (relating to comparison) is not relevant to the non-examined assessment at all.

LEARNING OBJECTIVES

This lesson will help you to:
- understand how to approach Assignment A (reading skills).

ASSIGNMENT A: POETRY AND PROSE TEXTS

The first assignment is an analytical answer to a question on at least three of the texts in the Poetry and prose texts section of the Anthology. These must be one prose text, one poetry text, and at least one other. Your teacher will set the task but you can be involved in choosing which texts to write about.

In Assignment A, you will be assessed on:
- A01: your understanding of, and response to, the texts and your use of quotation or textual reference (12 marks)
- A02: your analysis of the writer's use of language and structure (18 marks).

This means that this assignment is worth a total of 30 marks, which corresponds to 20% of the International GCSE in English Language.

WORD COUNT

You should aim to write approximately 1200 words. You will not be penalised for writing more, but you will not be given more marks because you have written more. Your focus should be on quality, not quantity.

ANTHOLOGY POETRY AND PROSE TEXTS

For Assignment A, you will write about texts from Section B of the Anthology:
- 'Disabled' by Wilfred Owen
- 'Out, Out—' by Robert Frost
- 'An Unknown Girl' by Moniza Alvi
- 'The Bright Lights of Sarajevo' by Tony Harrison
- 'Still I Rise' by Maya Angelou
- 'The Story of an Hour' by Kate Chopin
- 'The Necklace' by Guy de Maupassant
- 'Significant Cigarettes' (from *The Road Home*) by Rose Tremain
- 'Whistle and I'll Come to You' (from *The Woman in Black*) by Susan Hill
- 'Night' by Alice Munro.

THE QUESTION

The assignment could be a detailed analysis of the writers' use of language and structure in three texts, or it could focus on a theme that three texts have in common. Whatever the assignment, you should give a detailed analysis of the writers' use of language and structure. The following questions are good examples:

▶ **Discuss how the writers use language to present the situation and characters in 'Disabled', 'Night' and 'The Story of an Hour'.**

▶ **Consider any three texts about aspects of identity. How do the writers present their ideas about identity?**

▲ Make detailed notes on your chosen texts, as this will ensure that you have read them thoroughly.

TIPS ON THE READING ASSIGNMENT

HINT

Remember that teachers and moderators are human beings and that they will respond to genuine engagement (that is, when students are doing their best to think for themselves). They will be less impressed by responses that show little individuality.

▶ **Choose two poems and one prose text. How do they use language and structure to focus on a significant moment or incident?**

All assignments for this unit must address the Assessment Objectives for reading. In simple terms, this means that you must:

■ show that you have read your chosen texts thoroughly and understand them well enough to develop an interpretation

■ show how language and structure are used to achieve effects.

For this assignment, you must **not** submit:

■ work based on Section A of the Anthology

■ imaginative or empathetic responses to Section B texts (although these could be submitted for Assignment B).

1 'Analyse, not summarise' is a useful motto to bear in mind. It is assumed that you could summarise or re-tell the 'stories' in the texts if you were asked to do so, but nobody is asking you to summarise. Instead, analyse what you have read.

2 Try to develop your own opinion on texts and think for yourself. Do not rely only on teacher notes. The most successful answers will show a detailed and perceptive understanding of language and structure.

3 A key feature of a successful answer is that it gives 'a detailed exploration of the effects of language and structure'. The word 'exploration' implies that there is a value in trying to be fresh and individual in your approach. Make your points tentatively, considering different ideas and using phrases such as 'this could be seen as…', 'on the other hand this may be…', and 'another meaning of this might be…'. This kind of writing shows that you are thinking about the texts and responding to them. Although you may misunderstand a text, it is equally true that there is no 'right answer' – only good and less good answers.

4 You must support all of your points with clearly relevant and well-explained evidence.

5 You must write about the language and structure of the texts and how this helps to convey meaning and fulfil the writer's intention. Just as in the exams, it is always better to write in some detail about a few quotations, than to quote frequently but fail to comment in detail.

6 It is best to focus closely only on the texts that you have chosen and not to bring in any other texts that you might think of.

USING ACTIVITIES FROM PREVIOUS CHAPTERS

Once you have chosen the three texts that you are going to write about, you need to work carefully through the pages on those texts that you will find in the chapter on Paper 2.

Once you have done this, work through the lesson, 'Putting it into practice', on pages 224–225. On page 225, you will find the following question:

Read the extract from *Frankenstein*. How does the author convey the narrator's thoughts and feelings? In your answer, you should write about:

■ the setting

■ the narrator's reaction to the creature he has created

■ the use of language and structure.

You should support your answer with close reference to the extract, including **brief** quotations. **(30 marks)**

This is an exam-style question, but you could adapt it to suit the three texts you have chosen to write about in your non-examined assessment assignment.

For example, you could ask the following question.

▶ Explore how the writers present the relationship between the physical environment and the feelings they create in three poems or prose texts: 'An Unknown Girl', 'The Bright Lights of Sarajevo' and 'Whistle and I'll Come to You'.

PLANNING AN ANSWER

Once you have decided on a question and chosen which texts you will write about, you should spend some time planning your answer.

You may find it useful to draw up some tables of points, quotations, evidence and their effects. You can then include these in your non-examined assessment essay.

For example, these tables refer to the question above. Copy and complete them to find more information which you would include if you were answering this question.

▼ EVIDENCE: A DETAIL ABOUT THE CITY NOTICED BY HARRISON	▼ WHAT THIS TELLS YOU ABOUT THE ENVIRONMENT
'To get the refills they wheel home in prams'	Shows how the Sarajevans improvise with whatever they have to cope with the situation.

▼ EVIDENCE: CONTRASTING WORDS OR PHRASES	▼ WHAT IS THE EFFECT OF THE CONTRAST?
'Queuing for the… grams of bread / Often dodging snipers on the way'	Queuing is an everyday activity, but the idea of being shot at as part of the routine is shocking.

SAMPLE STUDENT ANSWER

Read through the following extract from one student's response to the question.

'The Bright Lights of Sarajevo' describes how the poet is surprised to find young people from different ethnic groups strolling around war-torn Sarajevo at night, and how boys meet girls despite the danger and darkness, and how romance can grow and life goes on, despite the war.

Much of the language of the poem is straightforward and conversational: 'I see a pair…'. This helps to make the poem sound spontaneous, as though the poet is commenting on what he sees as he sees it.

What Harrison observes shows us the paradoxes of wartime: how ethnic differences disappear at night; how romance can burst into life in a terrible and fearful environment; how romantic feelings can exist in the same place where people were killed by shells earlier in the war. For example, Harrison describes 'a pair' standing on 'two shell scars' where previously a bread queue was 'massacred'. This emotive verb leaves the reader in no doubt about the violence of the war, while the metaphor of 'scars' suggests the painful wounds the violence inflicted on the city.

Throughout the poem Harrison conveys the contrast between the activities of ordinary Sarajevans and the strange and difficult conditions in which they live: a couple form a relationship amid the scars of war, people queue for bread, or to refill empty canisters of gas which they 'wheel home in prams' while 'dodging snipers'.

The threat of violence and death is powerfully contrasted with everyday, mundane activities of getting food and warmth. However, these two contrasting aspects work together to highlight the struggle to survive during wartime. Another poem in which the writer explores the impact that a physical environment has on her is 'An Unknown Girl' by Moniza Alvi...

▶ In his depiction of Sarajevo and its inhabitants, Harrison brings out the contradictions of wartime.

KEY SKILLS

This extract shows some of the key skills you will need to demonstrate in your response to the assignment:

- **Understanding:** the student quickly and briefly summarises the content of the text, showing a clear, perceptive awareness of the writer's ideas

- **Interpretation:** the student identifies and explores the writer's intention in the poem and responds to it

- **Evidence:** the student supports each of their points with clear, relevant quotations and textual reference

- **Analysis:** the student explores the writer's choice of language and of structure, and how the writer uses these choices to add impact to their ideas.

If you have worked through the relevant sections on the texts that you have chosen, and have understood how to create an effective and perceptive answer about your chosen texts, then you should now be ready to plan your own piece of non-examined assessment. Good luck!

KEY POINT

Your response to the texts and your analysis of language and structure are essential elements of a successful response.

LEARNING OBJECTIVES

This lesson will help you to:

■ understand how to approach the imaginative writing element of your non-examined assessment.

ASSIGNMENT B: IMAGINATIVE WRITING

The second assignment is a piece of personal and imaginative writing. This will be based on a topic or topics that will be given to you by your teacher.

The aim of your piece of writing is to entertain and engage the reader. In this way, it is like the imaginative writing task set in Section B of Paper 2.

The assignment is worth the same amount as Assignment A, making it worth 20% of the International GCSE in English Language.

Your teacher will set the question or choice of questions.

THE TOPIC

The topic could be suggested by a piece in the Anthology, such as the following question:

▶ **Write about a time you, or someone you know, suffered an injury.**

Alternatively, it could be an unrelated topic, perhaps relating to an image or concept such as the following suggestions:

▶ **Write a story with the title 'The End'.**

▶ **Write a story that begins 'Everything was ready.'**

▶ **Write a story that ends 'I never saw them again.'**

ELEMENTS OF STORYTELLING

Turn to the Paper 2 chapter on imaginative writing (pages 292–313) and work through as many of the activities as you can, particularly the sections on plot, structure, vocabulary for effect and sentences for effect. This will focus your mind on narrative methods and techniques.

ACTIVITY 1   **A04**   **A05**   **SKILLS** ▶ CRITICAL THINKING, ANALYSIS, ADAPTIVE LEARNING, CREATIVITY, INNOVATION

▼ GOALS IN WRITING

KEY POINT

Your goal should be to create expressive, well-structured and accurate writing.

There are three vital goals. You have to demonstrate:

■ effective selection, structure and expression of your ideas

■ effective choice of vocabulary and sentence structure

■ accurate spelling, punctuation and grammar.

Write a detailed plan for one of the suggested titles on this page and two good opening paragraphs in response to your chosen title.

TIPS ON THE WRITING ASSIGNMENT

1 Write from your own perspective. Why set your story in a small town in another country, about which you know little, when you have stories about your own (or someone else's) experience that are waiting to be told?

2 Remember that you don't have to be totally truthful, even when writing a story based on your own experience; you can imagine and embellish.

3 If you are aiming for the higher grades, you should consider structuring your work in a fresh or original way. You need to show skill in engaging and keeping your reader's interest.

4 Experiment with form. For example, try telling a story from different angles, from the points of view of different characters.

5 In stories, create characters as well as atmosphere and give them motives. Don't just focus on drama and violence: think of consequences.

Finally, remember:

■ the non-examined assessment takes careful thought and planning

■ seek advice, but write as yourself in your own words

■ use spell checkers carefully – it is allowed!

ACTIVITY 2   **A04**   **A05**   **SKILLS**   CRITICAL THINKING, ANALYSIS

▼ MARKING A RESPONSE

Before you start to plan your own story, here is an example of a piece written by an International GCSE student. Read it and then assess it using the mark scheme.

> **'Escape'**
>
> The blade glinted in the light of the moon, until dark clouds gathered and hid it. The beam of a spotlight – or was it headlights? – pierced the darkness, lighting up trees, bushes and vast muddy puddles in the track through the woods. A shadowy figure ducked into the thick bushes. He bent down and sawed at the padlock around a chain circling his leg, then, when it fell away onto the ground, he stood up, and went out into the cover of the night…
>
> His name was John O'Malley, leutenant – a sniper – the best in the regiment. During his escape from the prison camp in Germany, he had managed to keep his Lee-Enfield scope under his greatcoat. Just as he was preparing to move on swiftly, there was the roar of a vehecle. He ducked into a dark ditch, crouching in dank muddy water. Once the lorry was safely out of earshot he moved on through the trees, then clambered down the frosty slopes to a village. If anyone had been watching as he flitted from tree to tree, they would have thought it was some woodland creature: but nobody was watching.
>
> The streets were deserted, no-one observed him as he slipped along them. Then he muttered to himself: 'Damn! Just my luck,' as he came in view of a checkpoint. There was nothing else he could do, so, sweating, he

▶

▲ 'The beam of a spotlight – or was it headlights?'

approached and handed his forged papers to the obnoxsious-looking guard. He scrutenised them with a bad-tempered expression on his face. Then he handed them back. The guard shouted something and the gate lifted. He bought a ticket, for he spoke good German, and boarded the train near the massive, snorting steam engine. For the first time he felt that he might really escape. He almost dared to relax a little, as he settled into a window seat. Then suddenly there was a sound of boots and someone shouting 'Halt! Halt!' as SS soldiers poured onto the train and issued abrupt commands. The exits were blocked, one of them asked for his papers, but was not satisfied with them. He shouted out some questions and ordered him off the train. John's heart sank, he was back to square one.

He was shoved into the back of a van with a couple of dangerous-looking dogs and various bits of equipment. The door was locked. Drearily, he wondered what his chances were of escaping again on the way to the camp, or another, tougher camp. At least he was alive, and in one peice, he thought, it was something to be grateful for. At least the Germans did not exicute escaped prisoners. Not usually, in any case.

There might be another chance, he told himself, he must stay alert...

Although this response is not perfect, it has many good points.

What marks for AO4 (out of 18) and AO5 (out of 12) do you think this should be given? Use the assessment grids for Assignment B on page 329.

ACTIVITY 3   **AO4**   **AO5**   **SKILLS** ANALYSIS, REASONING, CREATIVITY

▼ THE STRUCTURE OF 'ESCAPE'

HINT

Try summarising the key events of the story in chronological order to help you.

In pairs or individually, copy and complete the following table, noting the four stages of narrative writing used in 'Escape'. You could begin by summarising the content of each paragraph, bearing in mind that a section may contain more than one paragraph.

▼ SECTION	▼ PARAGRAPH(S)	▼ SUMMARY OF CONTENT
1 Exposition	2	Introduces the situation and character
2 Conflict		
3 Climax		
4 Resolution		

Looking at the table, would you say that 'Escape' is a well-structured story?

If so, what are the things that make its planning or structure effective, given the limitation of the word count?

MAKING CHOICES ABOUT CONTENT

Answer the following questions about 'Escape':

▶ **Why is it probably best to base your story on one simple incident?**

▶ **Why is it best to have only one or two main characters?**

▶ **A lot of young people writing stories tend to include too many events and characters: why do you think this is?**

BEGINNING, MIDDLE AND END

HINT

'Escape' has one main character, two or three clear settings, a simple (though dramatic) situation, two incidents, a difficult problem and an ending that is conclusive for the time being, though it leaves a cliffhanger. In other words, it contains more than enough for 400–500 words. Don't try to include too many characters or too many events – focus on one incident or one problem.

However long or short, all stories will have a beginning, a conflict that rises to a climax, and an ending. The beginning must engage the reader's interest and make them want to read on (for example, in 'Escape', you probably wanted to know who the character was and what he was escaping from). The ending need not fully resolve all the conflicts of the story, especially in a very short story, but it should bring the main conflict to some sort of end.

| ACTIVITY 4 | A04 | A05 | SKILLS | CRITICAL THINKING, ANALYSIS, ADAPTIVE LEARNING, CREATIVITY, INNOVATION |

▼ PLANNING YOUR STORY'S BEGINNING, MIDDLE AND END

Plan your own story with the title 'Escape' using the four-part narrative structure exposition–conflict–climax–resolution.

DEVELOPING YOUR PLAN

KEY POINT

Considering how you can use these five key features of narrative writing will help you to plan and tell a story that fully engages your reader.

One way to develop your plan is to consider which types or functions of writing you are going to use.

Even though you may only write around 700 words, using several types or functions of writing will give your story a sense of variety, which will help to keep your reader interested.

These types or functions of writing are:

■ description: helping the reader to picture the scene is vital

■ narrative: it is important that the reader understands what happens and what the characters do

■ dialogue: speech can bring a story and its characters to life: it can convey their thoughts and feelings very directly and convincingly

■ thoughts and feelings: showing (not telling) a character's thoughts and feelings through their actions gives the character more depth and encourages the reader to engage and empathise with them

■ background information: it is often engaging or useful to give the reader relevant details about a character's or place's background.

When you are planning, think how you could incorporate some or all of these. Even if you decide to have only one character, you may find that having your character say something to themselves will add something to your writing.

ACTIVITY 5 **AO4** **AO5** SKILLS ▶ ADAPTIVE LEARNING, CREATIVITY, INNOVATION

▼ USING TYPES OF WRITING TO PLAN STRUCTURE

1 Using the following checklist, tick the functions of writing that you will probably use and write short notes to your plan showing where and how you might use each one.

- ☐ Description
- ☐ Narrative
- ☐ Dialogue
- ☐ Thoughts and feelings
- ☐ Background information

2 Go back to 'Escape' and read it again. Find examples of each of the five functions of writing and label them. Notice how the writer moves from one function to another, even incorporating two different functions in the same sentence.

What types of story have you found easiest, or perhaps most enjoyable, to write in the past? Choose two from the list below.

- ■ Science fiction
- ■ Fantasy
- ■ War
- ■ Romance
- ■ Comedy
- ■ Thriller
- ■ Horror
- ■ Realism.

If you are given the title of a story to write, it will normally be one or two very general words, so it is likely that you will be able to relate the title to any genre. Imagine that the title that you have been given is 'The Decision'. Choose one of the two genres that you selected from the list and jot down some ideas for a story in that genre with that title. You could do this in a list or spider diagram. Include details about:

- ■ the main character
- ■ the setting
- ■ the situation
- ■ the central incident or event
- ■ a problem to solve
- ■ the ending.

▲ Your favourite film genres may inspire you to choose the genre of your writing: horror, science fiction, fantasy?

The following spider diagram is a plan for a simple realistic story entitled 'The Decision'.

Describe: Setting near school – street

Characters: Ant is quieter than his friends; one of the new members is seen in distance – what do his old friends think of this new friend? What does Ant think of him?

Narrative: Meets one or two friends – walks with them? later on his own thinks about problem

Situation: 15-year-old boy; problem – is he going to go out with a group of friends, though he doesn't much like one or two new members, and he is worried that they will get them into trouble [how?]

Decides at end to go with them, but might leave early – he tells best friend – reaction in **dialogue**

Dialogue and thoughts or feelings

This example is based on a very simple situation that may be familiar to you. Experienced writers often advise new writers to 'write about what you know'. The ideas gathered above might suggest ways in which your response to this title could draw on your own experience, altering what actually happened as much as you like. However, a title such as 'The Decision' could work in any genre at all.

CHARACTERISATION AND PERSPECTIVE

Part of the planning process will involve thinking about your main character. It is a good idea to tell the story from this character's point of view, as this will give the reader a strong sense of their personality. One of the things you should decide quite quickly is whether to tell the story in the first or third person. First-person narrative is best if you want the reader to see everything from your main character's point of view, whereas third-person narrative is best if you want the reader to understand everything via an all-knowing narrator.

Once you have chosen your narrative perspective, copy and complete the following table, filling in details about your main character. You do not need to include all of them in your story: only the details that will show the reader something significant about your main character.

Gender	
Age	
Ethnicity	
Where from originally?	
Living where (if different)?	
Social background?	
Two words to sum up their personality, for example, outgoing or shy, rash or cautious?	
Clever or average?	
Pleased about what in life?	
Upset about what in life?	

ASSESSMENT GRIDS

▼ ASSIGNMENT A : POETRY AND PROSE TEXTS		
▼ LEVEL	**▼ MARK**	**▼ AO1 READ AND UNDERSTAND A VARIETY OF TEXTS, SELECTING AND INTERPRETING INFORMATION, IDEAS AND PERSPECTIVES (12 MARKS)**
	0	No rewardable material.
Level 1 *Limited Basic*	1–3	■ Basic selection of information/ideas. ■ Limited use of quotations/textual references. ■ Limited understanding of information/ideas, likely through retelling or paraphrasing.
Level 2 *Some Developing*	4–6	■ Some selection of valid information and ideas. ■ Some use of valid quotations/textual references. ■ Some valid interpretation demonstrating a developing understanding of information and ideas.
Level 3 *Clear Relevant*	7–9	■ Clear and relevant selection of information, ideas and/or perspectives. ■ Clear and relevant use of supporting quotations/textual references. ■ Relevant interpretation demonstrating a clear understanding of information, ideas and/or perspectives.
Level 4 *Detailed Perceptive*	10–12	■ Detailed and persuasive selection of information, ideas and perspectives. ■ Discriminating use of supporting quotations and textual references. ■ Perceptive interpretation demonstrating a convincing understanding of information, ideas and perspectives.
▼ LEVEL	**▼ MARK**	**▼ AO2 UNDERSTAND AND ANALYSE HOW WRITERS USE LINGUISTIC AND STRUCTURAL DEVICES TO ACHIEVE THEIR EFFECTS (18 MARKS)**
	0	No rewardable material.
Level 1 *Limited Basic*	1–3	■ Limited identification of language **and/or** structural devices. ■ Limited selection of textual references **and/or** examples. ■ Offers basic and simple comment on the effect of language **and/or** structure.
Level 2 *Some Developing*	4–6	■ Some identification/selection of language **and/or** structural devices. ■ Some accurate textual references **and/or** examples. ■ Offers some developing comment on the effect of language **and/or** structure.
Level 3 *Clear Relevant Explanatory*	7–10	■ Clear and relevant selection of language **and** structural devices. ■ Relevant and generally appropriate use of textual references **and** examples. ■ Makes clear explanations of the effects of language **and** structure.
Level 4 *Thorough Confident Exploratory*	11–14	■ Thorough and confident selection of language **and** structural devices. ■ Confident and detailed use of textual references **and** examples. ■ Makes a detailed exploration of the effects of language **and** structure.
Level 5 *Discriminating Perceptive Analytical*	15–18	■ Subtle and discriminating selection of language **and** structural devices. ■ Discriminating and assured use of textual references **and** examples. ■ Makes a perceptive analysis of the effects of language **and** structure.

▼ ASSIGNMENT B: IMAGINATIVE WRITING

▼ LEVEL	▼ MARK	▼ AO4 COMMUNICATE EFFECTIVELY AND IMAGINATIVELY, ADAPTING FORM, TONE AND REGISTER OF WRITING FOR SPECIFIC PURPOSES AND AUDIENCES
	0	No rewardable material.
Level 1	1–3	■ Communication is at a basic level, and limited in clarity. ■ Uses basic vocabulary, often misspelt. ■ Uses punctuation with basic control, creating undeveloped, often repetitive, sentence structures.
Level 2	4–7	■ Communicates in a broadly appropriate way. ■ Shows some grasp of the purpose and of the expectations/requirements of the intended reader. ■ Straightforward use of form, tone and register.
Level 3	8–11	■ Communicates clearly. ■ Shows a clear sense of purpose and understanding of the expectations/requirements of the intended reader. ■ Appropriate use of form, tone and register.
Level 4	12–15	■ Communicates effectively. ■ A secure realisation of the writing task according to the writer's purpose and the expectations/requirements of the intended reader is shown. ■ Effective use of form, tone and register.
Level 5	16–18	■ Communication is perceptive and subtle. ■ Task is sharply focused on purpose and the expectations/requirements of the intended reader. ■ Sophisticated use of form, tone and register.

▼ LEVEL	▼ MARK	▼ AO5 WRITE CLEARLY, USING A RANGE OF VOCABULARY AND SENTENCE STRUCTURES, WITH APPROPRIATE PARAGRAPHING AND ACCURATE SPELLING, GRAMMAR AND PUNCTUATION
	0	No rewardable material.
Level 1	1–2	■ Expresses information and ideas, with limited use of structural and grammatical features. ■ Little awareness is shown of the purpose of the writing and the intended reader. ■ Little awareness of form, tone and register.
Level 2	3–4	■ Expresses and orders information and ideas; uses paragraphs and a range of structural and grammatical features. ■ Writes with some correctly spelt vocabulary, e.g. words with regular patterns such as prefixes, suffixes, double consonants. ■ Uses punctuation with some control, creating a range of sentence structures, including coordination and subordination.
Level 3	5–7	■ Develops and connects appropriate information and ideas; structural and grammatical features and paragraphing make the meaning clear. ■ Uses a varied vocabulary and spells words containing irregular patterns correctly. ■ Uses accurate and varied punctuation, adapting sentence structure as appropriate.
Level 4	8–10	■ Manages information and ideas, with structural and grammatical features used cohesively and deliberately across the text. ■ Uses a wide, selective vocabulary with only occasional spelling errors. ■ Positions a range of punctuation for clarity, managing sentence structures for deliberate effect.
Level 5	11–12	■ Manipulates complex ideas, utilising a range of structural and grammatical features to support coherence and cohesion. ■ Uses extensive vocabulary strategically; rare spelling errors do not detract from overall meaning. ■ Punctuates writing with accuracy to aid emphasis and precision, using a range of sentence structures accurately and selectively to achieve particular effects.

EXAM PREPARATION

SUCCESSFUL REVISION

Many books offer different suggestions and advice for revision. One thing is clear: not everything works for everyone. Each person has particular ways of revising and habits of working. Look at all the advice and try out the different suggestions. Decide clearly what knowledge, skills and techniques you need to develop, consolidate or revisit.

PLAN YOUR LEARNING AND REVISION

HOW TO PLAN A SCHEDULE

- Draw up a table to show the days and weeks before the examination.
- Decide how much time to give to the subject in each week or day.
- Work out a timetable.
- Think about the need for variety and breaks.
- Make sure your schedule is building towards a 'peak' at the right time.

HOW TO IMPROVE

- Test yourself.
- Test a friend.
- Practise answering exam questions.
- Write answers to the time limits of questions in the actual exam.
- Check that you understand all texts, looking particularly at words, meaning, plot and character.
- Revise technical terms, using the glossary on pages 334–335.
- Make sure you can apply these terms properly, spell them properly, give examples, and explain how and why the techniques are used.

AIDS TO LEARNING

Write short, clear notes. Use aids such as:

- postcards
- diagrams
- flowcharts
- mnemonics (aids to memory, such as rhymes)
- computer programmes
- websites and apps.

GOOD PREPARATION

Good preparation is one of the main elements affecting how people perform in exams. This includes both attitude of mind and physical preparation.

- Check how long the exam lasts and use your time properly.
- Make sure you understand the specification and know what you have to do.

Don't be tempted to rush your initial reading. It is surprising how many exam candidates make basic mistakes because they did not carefully read through the text in front of them.

USING YOUR TIME EFFECTIVELY IN THE EXAMINATIONS

Note that the time allocation of 2 hours and 15 minutes for Paper 1 includes time to check instructions and read the paper carefully. Decide how much time you need to allocate to each question: the question paper gives suggestions. You should also aim to leave enough time for checking through at the end. An example of how to plan your time for each paper is given below.

PAPER 1: NON-FICTION TEXTS AND TRANSACTIONAL WRITING (COMPULSORY IN BOTH ROUTES)

▼ READING THE QUESTION PAPER	▼ SECTION A 80 MINUTES / 45 MARKS	▼ SECTION B 40 MINUTES / 45 MARKS	▼ FINAL CHECKING
5–10 minutes	Planning: 5 minutes Writing: 75 minutes	Planning: 10 minutes Writing: 30 minutes	5–10 minutes

Duration of exam: 135 minutes (2 hours 15 minutes) **Total marks: 90**

SPECIFICATION A: PAPER 2 (EXAM OPTION)

▼ READING THE QUESTION PAPER	▼ QUESTION 1 40 MINUTES / 30 MARKS	▼ QUESTION 2 40 MINUTES / 30 MARKS	▼ FINAL CHECKING
5–10 minutes	Planning: 5 minutes Writing: 35 minutes	Planning: 5 minutes Writing: 35 minutes	5–10 minutes

Duration of exam: 90 minutes (1 hour 30 minutes) **Total marks: 60**

CHECK YOUR WORK

Check that you are keeping to your planned timings. Keep thinking throughout about:

- relevance, presentation, accuracy and vocabulary choice.

If you manage to leave some checking time at the end:

- Make sure you have answered all questions fully and appropriately.
- Correct any errors in spelling or punctuation (particularly checking that all sentences have full stops).
- Make sure everything you have written can be read easily.

RELATIONSHIP OF ASSESSMENT OBJECTIVES TO UNITS

▼ UNIT NUMBER	▼ ASSESSMENT OBJECTIVE				
	AO1	AO2	AO3	AO4	AO5
PAPER 1	7%	8%	15%	18%	12%
PAPER 2 / PAPER 3	8%	12%	0%	12%	8%
TOTAL FOR INTERNATIONAL GCSE	15%	20%	15%	15%	20%

PLANNING YOUR ANSWERS

ANSWER THE QUESTION

Do **not** just write down everything you know or think: this is the most common mistake made by exam candidates. Planning consists of:

- reading the question carefully and deciding what the key words in it are
- deciding on the main points you wish to make, what the question is looking for and how you intend to tackle it
- making sure that the points you want to include are appropriately positioned and structured in the answer
- structuring your answer logically and clearly
- choosing examples or quotations.

THINKING ABOUT THE QUESTION

Identifying the key words in the question can help to show:

- **what** the question is looking for
- **how** to tackle it.

Key words and phrases in the question show what the examiner is expecting from an answer. For example:

- **'how does the writer'** is asking you to explain methods and techniques
- **'explain'** asks you to make clear to the examiner your understanding of the text and its methods
- **'analyse'** expects you to look in detail at the writing, its methods and techniques and its effects
- **'compare'** asks for an examination of similarities and differences, usually in two writers' ideas and perspectives and how they are presented.

KEY POINTS

Write down quickly, in note form, your immediate thoughts about the subject. You may find a diagram useful for this purpose. Do not write full sentences here, or you will waste too much time.

THE CONTENT OF THE ANSWER

The examiner **does** want to know what you think: your own personal ideas and opinions. However, a series of unsupported statements that start with the words 'I think…' is not enough, since the examiner also needs to know that these ideas are based on your analysis of the texts, your understanding of the subject matter and other evidence.

A LOGICAL STRUCTURE

- Note the points you want to make.
- Before writing your answer, sequence your points in a logical order. This will not necessarily match the order in which your chosen quotations appear in the text.

WRITING ANALYTICALLY

When writing analytically, whether for English Language or Literature, be sure to structure your paragraphs around a key point, using quotations or textual reference as evidence, then exploring in some detail how your evidence supports your point.

EVALUATIVE COMMENTS

For questions assessed on AO2 (for example, Questions 4 and 5 on Paper 1), you should always analyse the writer's use of language and structure and its impact on the reader. Do not simply identify the techniques the writer has used. You will get few marks for just pointing out that the writer uses short sentences and alliteration without analysing the effect of those choices. If you can write a few lines exploring how a writer uses language effectively in just one or two quotations, your answer will be significantly more successful.

USING QUOTATIONS AND TEXTUAL REFERENCE

When writing about texts, whether books, poems, articles or extracts, one of the most important features to include are quotations or textual reference, where this is required. Quoting is a skill that has to be practised. Overuse of quotations is as significant a mistake as not using any at all. You should use quotations and textual reference:

- to illustrate or give an example, for example, an emotive verb choice or a significant sentence structure
- to explain why you believe something, to support an opinion or argument or to prove a point.

Quotations should be relevant, effective and short: a single word to a line or two at the most. Introduce quotations fluently into your sentence structure. Avoid writing things like, 'He says…'.

LESS CAN BE MORE

If you can, practise doing Section B type questions, but never rush them. Just as you should concentrate on explaining in some detail how a writer creates effects for Section A, so in Section B, your aim should not be to show how much you can write, but to show that you can think as you write – carefully considering your ideas, paragraphing, sentence structure, vocabulary, persuasive or rhetorical techniques and so on. Try to write with care!

LAST-MINUTE REVISION

Think ahead. Revision the night or morning before an exam can be very useful, but generally only if you have done all of the work already. Last-minute revision should consist of looking at checklists, summative notes, mnemonics and any of your particular weaknesses. This can be very helpful, but make sure that you do not panic and make sure that you have done all of the actual work in the weeks before your exam.

ON THE DAY OF THE EXAM

Again, checklists and mnemonics can be useful to consult as you go into school, as might reading through a model answer or two. Always read the exam paper carefully all the way through, and look at the choices for Section B before you start Section A. Many experienced teachers would advise taking some 'mint-time' (that is, the time it would take a mint to dissolve in the mouth – and there is no reason why you should not take one just before you go into the exam room) to read and think and make some notes, before you begin the first question. This can have the effect of steadying the nerves as well as allowing you to think. (Not chewing gum, though!)

TIME WAITS FOR NO-ONE!

Your teacher may not make you practise answering exam questions against the clock, but you should do it anyway. It is invaluable practice for the real exam, which is always a race against time.

What is essential is that you divide your time up carefully in the exam: many students will find it harder to answer Section A with enough detail and accuracy than to complete a reasonable answer to Section B, so you could allow more time for Section A, and reduce the time you spend on Section B. Be careful, though, not to spend so long on Section A that you run out of time on Section B. Remember that your answer in Section B does not have to be a certain length, which means that you can gain good marks with a carefully written answer of 400 words.

Good luck!

GLOSSARY

adjective a word that describes a noun or pronoun

adverb a word that describes a verb or an adjective

alliteration the use of several words together that begin with the same sound or letter

atmosphere the feeling that an event or place gives you

bias not fair; a particular point of view influenced by one's own or someone else's opinions

chronologically organised in linear time

clause a group of words that make up part of a sentence

conjunction a word that joins parts of a sentence

connotations ideas linked to a word; ideas that have become associated with a word

contrast where two objects, people or ideas are placed next to each other to highlight their differences

denotation what something is

dialogue the speech between two or more people involved in a conversation

direct address using second person pronouns 'you' or 'your'

direct speech words spoken by a character in a novel, play or poem

dynamic verb a verb that describes actions or events that are happening, e.g. 'I go'

emotive language dramatic language that stirs emotion in the reader

empathise to understand the feelings of another person

explicit expressed in a way that is very clear and direct

first person written from the perspective of one person – that is, using 'I'; this differs from the second person, which directly addresses the reader ('you'), and the third person ('he', 'she' and 'it')

flashback when the narrator of a story jumps out of the present in order to describe an event which happened in the past (often in the form of memories)

hyperbole exaggerating for effect

identifiers phrases indicating who is speaking in dialogue

imperative verbs verbs that give an instruction or command

implications what is implied or suggested

implicit suggested or understood without being stated directly

infer read between the lines

intention the impact the author wants their writing to have on the reader

ironic using words to convey a meaning that is completely opposite to their apparent meaning

juxtaposition putting two very different things close together in order to encourage comparison between them

memoir a form of autobiography

metaphor describing something by comparing it to an image which it resembles, in a way that says the object *is* the image

mnemonic a device used to aid memory – usually in the form of a saying or rhyme

monologue the speech or thoughts of one person alone

narrative a story

narrator a character that tells the story in a novel, play, poem or film

noun a word that represents a person, place, object or quality

noun phrase a group of words built around a head noun, in which each word adds to the noun's meaning

objective based on facts, or making a decision that is based on facts rather than on your feelings or beliefs

onomatopoeia where a word sounds like the noise it makes

paradox a situation (or description) which seems contradictory and unlikely, but is actually true or accurate

personal pronoun a word used instead of a noun, such as 'I', 'you' or 'they'

personification when something which is not human is made to sound human by attributing human qualities to it

persuasive able to make other people believe something or do what you ask

plagiarise to take someone else's ideas and present them as your own

predicate the parts of a sentence that are not the subject, containing the verb and providing information about the subject

premodified a noun with a description before it, e.g. 'the big blue car'

preposition a word that is used before a noun or pronoun to show time, place or direction

prolepsis suggestions of things that will happen, before they do

pronoun a word that is used instead of a noun

protagonist the main character

quotation marks punctuation marks used to indicate where you have quoted

quotations words from a text

referend the thing or idea to which a word refers

register the type or style of vocabulary used according to the situation

repetition saying the same thing more than once to highlight its importance

retrospective written in the past tense; looking back at events that have already occurred

rhetorical device using language in a certain way to achieve an effect

rhetorical questions questions that are asked to make a point rather than to get an answer

rhyme scheme the rhyming pattern used in a poem

rhyming couplet a pair of lines that rhyme

setting the place where something is or where something happens, and the general environment

simile a description that says that an object is *like* an image

stereotypes fixed and generalised ideas about particular types of people or groups

synonyms words that share the same meaning as other words; for example, 'quick' might be a synonym for 'fast'

syntax the way in which words and phrases are arranged into sentences

third person using the third person – that is, 'he', 'she' and 'it'; this differs from the first person ('I') and the second person, which directly addresses the reader ('you')

time-shift moving between different periods of time

topic sentence the first sentence in a paragraph, often used to explain the key idea

transactional non-fiction writing for a purpose: to inform, explain, review, argue, persuade or advise

travelogue a book that describes a travel experience

triple structure where three words or ideas are linked in order to add emphasis to a key point

unbiased fair; not influenced by one's own or someone else's opinions

verb a word that describes actions

INDEX

127 Hours (film) 117

A

Abani, Chris 216–17
Adichie, Chimamanda Ngozi 96–102
adjectives 16–17
adverbials 21, 198
adverbs 22
advisory writing 85, 174, 182–3
Alagiah, George 70–1, 86–7, 103–7, 170–2
alliteration 31, 64, 89
Alvi, Moniza 234–8
analysing texts 4–15, 154–61
Angelou, Maya 247–53
apostrophes 50
arguments 84, 174–5, 180–1
assessment grids 328–9
assessment objectives
    imaginative writing 207, 315, 317
    non-examined assessment 315, 317
    non-fiction texts 57, 165–7
    poetry and prose 207, 315, 317
    reading skills 3
    transactional writing 57
    writing skills 25
assignments 316–29
assonance 89
atmosphere 217, 276–7, 279–80
attitudes 79
audience 82–3, 153, 249–50
    children and teenagers 178–9, 183
    writing for 83, 183, 184–7, 195
autobiographies 58, 59–60, 287–9
    Between a Rock and a Hard Place
        (Aron Ralston) 117–21
    *Beyond the Sky and the Earth: A Journey
        into Bhutan* (Jamie Zeppa) 95, 134–40
    blogs 192
    Chinese Cinderella (Adeline Yen Mah) 147–51
    Explorer's Daughter, The (Kari Herbert)
        108–12
    H is for Hawk (Helen Macdonald) 141–6
    memoirs 108, 134, 137, 141
    'Night' (Alice Munro) 222, 281–91
    Passage to Africa, A (George Alagiah) 70–1,
        86–7, 103–7, 170–2
    Taking on the World (Ellen MacArthur) 59–60,
        157–8
    Touching the Void (Joe Simpson) 153, 155–6,
        163–7, 168–9

B

'being' words 17
Between a Rock and a Hard Place (Aron
    Ralston) 117–21
*Beyond the Sky and the Earth: A Journey into
    Bhutan* (Jamie Zeppa) 95, 134–40
bias 12, 58
biographies 58, 59–60
blank verse 223
blogs 192
brackets 51, 53
'Bright Lights of Sarajevo, The' (Tony Harrison)
    239–46, 320–1
Brighton Rock (Graham Greene) 298
Bryson, Bill 6–7
Byrne, Jane 94–5

C

capital letters 17, 53
'Capybara' car review 161
characters 214–17, 265–6, 293, 302–5, 327
Chinese Cinderella (Adeline Yen Mah) 147–51
Chopin, Kate 254–7
Cider with Rosie (Laurie Lee) 90–1, 92–3
'Cinderella' 264
clarity 26–7, 34–5, 38–9
clauses 20–1, 22, 23, 34–7, 310–11
    separating 49
    sequencing 199, 311
CLEARER FROST 88
climax 42, 43, 292
colloquial speech 86, 250
colons 51
commands 20
commas 49, 53, 199
comparing texts 12, 67–8, 70–1, 74, 82–3,
    162–7
    evidence for 168–9
    exam preparation 170–3
    poetry and prose 246, 264
conclusions 43, 203
conflict 42, 43, 292
conjunctions 20, 21, 22, 23, 34, 36, 37, 198
connotations 7, 18–19, 28, 196, 251, 309
content 46–7, 48
contrast 31, 243
'Corpse' (Semezdin Mehmedinovic) 246
creative non-fiction 143–4
crime fiction 292

D

'Danger of a single story, The' (Chimamanda
    Ngozi Adichie) 96–102
dashes 51, 53
declarative sentence 20
denotation 18
describing words 16
descriptions 91, 111, 137, 138–9, 172
descriptive writing 30, 41, 174–5,
    193, 306–7
dialogue 271–2, 289–90, 304–5
diaries 58, 65–6
Diary of a Young Girl, The (Anne Frank) 65–6
direct address 13, 31, 186, 249–50
direct speech 8, 49, 53, 289–90
'Disabled' (Wilfred Owen) 226–9
'doing' words 17
Duffy, Carol Ann 211–12
dynamic verbs 161

E

EDINGLY openers 22
editing 54–5
ellipses 51
emotions, conveying 149–51, 256–7, 277
emotive language 12, 13, 64, 86–7, 89, 196
Encyclopaedia Britannica 76–7
endings, imaginative writing 297
evidence 8–9, 93, 107, 111, 168–9
exam preparation 94–5, 170–3, 204–5, 224–5,
    312–13, 330–3
exclamation marks 48, 53
exclamations 20
experience, writing from 279, 294

E (continued)

explanation 8–9
explanatory writing 174–5, 177–8
explicit meaning 6–7, 162
Explorer's Daughter, The (Kari Herbert) 108–12
'Explorers or boys messing about?' (Steven
    Morris) 113–16
exposition 42, 43, 292

F

facts 11, 84–5, 115–16
FANBOYS 20
feature articles 58
figurative language 210–13
film reviews 74–6, 179, 189, 190–1
first person 218, 293, 300–1
first-person narration
    fiction texts 218–19, 273–5, 287, 289
    imaginative writing 293, 300–1, 327
    non-fiction texts 119–20, 121, 152
Five Stories of an Hour (film) 254
flashbacks 5, 221
form 188–93
Frank, Anne 65–6
Frankenstein (Mary Shelley) 224–5
Frost, Robert 222–3, 230–3
full stops 48, 53

G

Game of Polo with a Headless Goat
    (Emma Levine) 129–33
genre 275–6, 295, 326
glossary 334–5
Golding, William 212–13
gothic fiction 273, 275–6, 279–80
grammar 53, 313
Greene, Graham 298

H

H is for Hawk (Helen Macdonald) 141–6
Harrison, Tony 239–46, 320–1
head noun 16
Henri, Adrian 211–12
Herbert, Kari 108–12
heroes 303
Hill, Susan
    I'm the King of the Castle 304
    Risk of Darkness, The 310
    'Whistle and I'll Come to You' (from *The
        Woman in Black*) 273–4
How the Poor Die (George Orwell) 158–60,
    170–2
hyperbole 13, 31, 89

I

'I am prepared to die' (Nelson Mandela) 62–3,
    64
iambic pentameter 223
ideas
    developing 45, 198
    generating 200, 294–5
    linking 46–7, 198, 199
    presenting 167
    separating 49
    sequencing 44–5, 47, 73, 156, 199
    structuring 47, 201
identifiers 305
I'm the King of the Castle (Susan Hill) 304
imagery 210–13, 237, 251

imaginative writing 207, 292–313
  assignments 316–17, 322–7, 329
  characters 293, 302–5, 327
  descriptions 306–7
  endings 297
  four stages 292, 296
  ideas and planning 294–5, 313, 325–7
  monologues and dialogues 304–5
  narrative choices 293, 300–1, 327
  openings 297, 298–9
  plot 292, 296–7
  sentences 310–11
  structure 292–3, 324–5, 326
  word choice 307, 308–9
imperative sentence 20
imperative verbs 13, 205
implications 251
implicit meaning 6–7, 162
'In the Middle of Dinner' (Chris Abani) 216–17
indicative content 157–8
indirect speech 289–90
inferring 6–7, 19, 70, 93, 144, 233
informative writing 174–5, 176–7, 191–3
intention 10–12, 30–1, 33, 59–60
  and audience 82–3
  autobiographies 106, 107, 111
  diaries and letters 66, 67
  imaginative writing 296
  and language choice 79–81, 106–7
  obituaries 61–2
  opinion pieces 71–2
  reviews 74
  speeches 64
  and structure 90–1
  travel writing 68
interpreting texts 66, 161, 208–9
interrogative sentence 20
introduction 43
inverted commas 49
irony 30
Italian, The (Radcliffe) 279–80

J

Johnson, Jane 218–19
journals 58
juxtaposition 213

K

Kid, Harry 68–70, 71, 78
King Lear (William Shakespeare) 43

L

language
  analysing 67–8, 70, 107, 111, 120
  autobiographies 107, 111, 119–20,
    137–40, 151
  choice 80–1, 83, 86–7, 107, 119–20,
    127, 151, 154–5, 289
  commenting on 88–9
  conveying emotion 151, 228–9, 257
  creating atmosphere 276–7
  creative non-fiction 144
  emotive 12, 13, 64, 86–7, 196
  figurative 210–13
  first-person narration 119–20, 289
  for effect 30–1, 86–9, 133, 137, 139, 144
  identifying language choices 100
  identifying writer's purpose and intention 80–1
  newspaper articles 126–7
  persuasive 13, 85
  poetry 228–9, 232–3, 238, 243–4, 250
  prose 257, 266, 271, 276–7, 289–90
  reporting events 107, 120, 126–7

  reviews 76
  style 120
  travel writing 137–40
  use of 10, 12, 13, 16–23, 79, 154–7
language features 89, 119, 127, 139, 155–6, 174
language techniques 88–9, 119, 144, 155, 232,
  249, 250
Lawrence, D. H. 66–7
layout 189
Lee, Laurie 90–1, 92–3
Let's Give It Up for Gimme Lao! (Sebastian Sim)
  214–15
letters 65, 66–7, 189, 191
Levine, Emma 129–33
linking ideas 46–7, 198, 199
literary devices 10, 31, 155, 213
Lord of the Flies (William Golding) 212–13
'Love is...' (Adrian Henri) 211–12

M

MacArthur, Ellen 59–60, 157–8
Macbeth (William Shakespeare) 231–2
Macdonald, Helen 141–6
Maddox, Lucy 13–15
magazine articles see newspaper and magazine
  articles
Mah, Adeline Yen 147–51
main body 42, 43
main clauses 21, 34–5, 49
Mandela, Nelson 61–4
Maupassant, Guy de 258–66
meaning 6–7, 18, 32–3, 162
  and punctuation 49, 50, 51
  and sentence structure 36
Mehmedinovic, Semezdin 246
memoirs 108, 134, 137, 141
metaphors 64, 210–12, 251
minor sentences 35, 89
mnemonics 52
monologues 304, 305
Morris, Steven 113–16
Mrs Dalloway (Virginia Woolf) 221
multiclause sentences 21, 22–3, 34–5, 36–41,
  89, 311
Munro, Alice 222, 281–91
'Myth of the Teenager' (Lucy Maddox) 13–15

N

naming words 16
narrative structure 42–3, 220–3, 294, 324–5, 326
narrative voice 152, 218–19, 293, 300–1, 327
narratives 44
'Necklace, The' (Guy de Maupassant) 258–66
news reports 58, 103–7
newspaper and magazine articles 46–7, 58,
  71–4, 189, 190
  'Don't demonise social media, it can be a
    blessing for teens with problems'
    (The Guardian) 73–4
  'Explorers or boys messing about?'
    (Steven Morris) 113–16
  'It's over for fossil fuels' (The Guardian) 5,
    10–11
  'Nelson Mandela obituary' (The Guardian)
    61–2
  'Week-long break from social media 'lowers
    anxiety and alleviates depression''
    (The Telegraph) 72–3, 74
  'When it's too windy for wind turbines: the
    downside of eco-power' (The Telegraph)
    11–12
  'Young and dyslexic?' (Benjamin Zephaniah)
    122–8

Nichols, Grace 208–9
'Night' (Alice Munro) 222, 281–91
Night Must Fall (Emlyn Williams) 292
Nineteen Eighty-Four (George Orwell) 299
No Time to Die (film) 75–6, 179
non-examined assessment 315–29
non-fiction texts
  analysing 154–61
  Anthology texts 96–151, 173
  comparing 12, 67–8, 70–1, 74, 82–3, 162–73
  identifying audience and intention 82–3
  identifying writer's perspective 78–81
  interpreting 66, 161
  language analysis 67, 70, 88–9
  structure 72, 73, 90–1
  types 58–77, 152, 153
  understanding 73, 92–5
  unseen texts 92–5, 152–61
non-finite -ing verbs 22, 23, 34, 36, 37
noun phrase 16, 21
nouns 16–17, 21, 161

O

obituaries 61–2
object (part of a sentence) 21
objectivity 58
Of Mice and Men (John Steinbeck) 8–9
onomatopoeia 64, 89
openings 42–3, 202–3, 271, 297, 298–9
opinion pieces 71–2
opinions 10–12, 71–2, 84–5, 115–16
Orwell, George
  How the Poor Die 158–60, 170–2
  Nineteen Eighty-Four 299
'Out, Out—' (Robert Frost) 222–3, 230–3
Owen, Wilfred 226–9

P

paradoxes 242
paragraphs 8–9, 44–5
  linking ideas 47
  opening 298
  short 125
  structure 72–3, 90–1
Passage to Africa, A (George Alagiah) 70–1,
  86–7, 103–7, 170–2
past tense 223, 301
pathetic fallacy 212
personal pronouns 60
personification 31, 64, 161, 210, 212
perspectives 78–81, 163–7, 300–1
persuasive language 13, 85
persuasive writing 101, 174–5, 181–2, 185–7
plagiarism 294
planning 291, 296–7, 313, 325–7
plot 292, 296–7
poetry 122, 208–9
  Anthology texts 226–53, 318
  assignments 316–21, 328
  characters in 216–17
  comparing texts 246
  imagery and figurative language 210–12,
    237, 251
  meaning 32–3
  rhyme and rhythm 222–3, 243, 252
  setting and atmosphere 217, 242
  structure 222–3, 252
  themes 241–2, 248–9
  word arrangement 32–3
  word choice 228–9, 237, 244
point, evidence and explanation 8–9, 107, 111
point of view 13, 78–81, 163–7, 181, 300–1, 327
possession 50

'Praise Song for my Mother' (Grace Nichols) 208–9
precision 26–7, 194
predicate (part of a sentence) 21
premodified nouns 161
prepositional phrases 22
prepositions 17, 22, 23
present tense 301
prolepsis 221
pronouns 21, 60
proof-reading 54, 55
proper nouns 17
prose 208
    Anthology texts 254–91, 318
    assignments 316–21, 328
    autobiographical fiction 287–9
    characters 214–16, 265–6
    dialogue 271–2, 289–90
    figurative language 212–13
    narrative voice 218–19
    settings 212–13, 217
    speech 289–90
    structure 220–2, 277–8
    vocabulary choice 276–7
protagonist 9, 293, 327
punctuation 8, 48–51, 53, 199
purpose 62, 64, 83, 294
    identifying 30, 59–60, 66, 67–8, 80–1, 91
    and language choice 33, 80–1, 111, 197
    primary/secondary 174, 175, 177
    unseen texts 152, 153
    writing for 174–83

Q

question marks 48, 53
questions 20, 48
quotation marks 8
quotations 8, 67, 93, 168–9, 231–2

R

Radcliffe, Ann 279–80
Ralston, Aron 117–21
reading skills 3–23
    poetry and prose 208–9, 224–5
    skimming and scanning 4–5
    unseen texts 92, 152, 154
reference writing 76–7
referends 28
register 77, 195
relative clauses 22, 35
relative pronouns 23, 37
repetition 13, 31, 89, 195, 250
reporting events 58, 103–7, 120, 126
reports 191–2
resolution 42, 43, 292
retrospective writing 223
reviews 74–6, 174, 179
    'Capybara' car review 161
    form 189, 190–1
    No Time to Die film review 75–6, 179
rhetoric 64
rhetorical devices 10, 13, 64
rhetorical questions 13, 31, 89, 249
rhyme 222–3, 243, 252
rhyme schemes 243, 252
rhyming couplets 243
rhythm 222–3, 252
Risk of Darkness, The (Susan Hill) 310
Road Home, The (Rose Tremain)
    see 'Significant Cigarettes'

S

Salt Road, The (Jane Johnson) 218–19
Sarajevo Blues see 'Corpse' (Semezdin Mehmedinovic)
scanning 4–5
science fiction 295
second-person narration 218
semi-colons 51
sense of place 137, 213, 217
senses 26, 306, 307
sentences 16–17, 20–3, 34–41
    analysing 89, 120, 156, 158, 277
    breaking down 36–7
    building 22, 34–5, 36–7, 198
    developing 198–9, 310
    effect of 22–3, 38–41, 44, 198–9, 310–11
    for clarity 38–9, 44
    how to end 48, 53
    how to open 22
    length 310–11
    linking and developing ideas 198, 199
    punctuation 48–51, 53, 199
    structure 34–7, 89, 91, 120–1, 156, 198–9, 277, 310–11
    syntax 156
    types 20–1, 34–5, 310
    word order 31
sequencing clauses 199, 311
sequencing ideas 44–5, 47, 73, 156, 199
settings 212–13, 217, 242
Shakespeare, William
    King Lear 43
    Macbeth 231–2
Shelley, Mary 224–5
short stories
    'Necklace, The' (Guy de Maupassant) 258–66
    'Night' (Alice Munro) 222, 281–91
    'Story of an Hour, The' (Kate Chopin) 254–7
    structure 222, 290–1
show, not tell 306
'Significant Cigarettes' from *The Road Home* (Rose Tremain) 267–72
significant words 309
Sim, Sebastian 214–15
similes 31, 64, 210, 211, 248, 251
Simpson, Joe 153, 155–6, 163–7, 168–9
single clause sentences 20, 21, 34, 36–7, 38, 89
skimming 4–5
Socratic circle 213
speech 35, 271–2, 289–90, 304–5
    colloquial 86, 250
    parts of 16–17
    punctuation 49, 50, 53
speeches 62–4, 96–102, 189
spelling errors 52
stages (in writing) 43
Steinbeck, John 8–9
stereotypes 14
'Still I Rise' (Maya Angelou) 247–53
'Story of an Hour, The' (Kate Chopin) 254–7
storytelling 292–3
structure
    conveying emotion 150
    exam-style question responses 101–2
    for effect 120–1, 145, 198–9, 257, 278
    identifying 46–7, 90–1
    imaginative writing 292–3, 324–5, 326
    non-fiction texts 90–1

paragraphs 72–3, 90–1, 125, 127
persuasive speech 101
poetry 220, 222–3, 252
principles of 42–3
prose 220–2, 223, 257, 277–8
purpose and intention 59–60, 62, 72–3, 90–1
sentences 20–3, 34–41, 89, 91, 120–1, 156, 198–9, 277, 310–11
sequencing and linking ideas 44–7, 73, 156, 199
short stories 222, 290–1
unseen texts 155–7, 158
in writing 9, 42–7, 90–1, 156, 220–3
style 157, 243
subject (of a sentence) 21
subordinate clauses 21, 34, 49
'Sunrise in Mozambique' (Harry Kid) 68–70, 71
suspense 273, 280
synonyms 7, 29, 93, 194, 307, 308
syntax 14, 156

T

Taking on the World (Ellen MacArthur) 59–60, 157–8
tense 301
tension 23, 90, 145, 257, 278
Tesla, Nikola 46–7
themes 99, 126, 143, 241–2, 248–9, 266
third person 218, 293, 300–1
third-person narration 152, 218, 293, 300–1, 327
'This is just to say' (William Carlos Williams) 32–3
thought clouds 291
time-shifts 220, 221, 223
TIP it 152, 153
Touching the Void (Joe Simpson) 153, 155–6, 163–7, 168–9
transactional writing 30, 42–3, 174–205
    audience 184–7
    conclusions 203
    form 188–93
    openings 202–3
    planning 200–1, 204
    sentences for effect 198–9
    types 174–83
    vocabulary for effect 194–7
travel writing 68–71
    Beyond the Sky and the Earth: A Journey into Bhutan (Jamie Zeppa) 95, 134–40
    Explorer's Daughter, The (Kari Herbert) 108–12
    Game of Polo with a Headless Goat (Emma Levine) 129–33
    'Sunrise in Mozambique' (Harry Kid) 68–70, 71
    'Travels in Albania' (Jane Byrne) 94–5
'Travels in Albania' (Jane Byrne) 94–5
Tremain, Rose 267–72
triple structure 13, 31

U

understanding the text
    autobiographies 106, 111, 119, 137, 149–50, 287–8
    creative non-fiction 143–4
    newspaper articles 73, 115–16, 125–6
    opinion vs. facts 115–16
    poetry 228, 231–2, 236–7, 241–2, 248–9

prose 256, 264, 271, 275
short stories 287–8
speeches 99
themes 143, 241–2, 248–9
travel writing 111, 131–3, 137
'Unknown Girl, An' (Moniza Alvi) 234–8
unseen texts 92–5, 152–61

V

'Valentine' (Carol Ann Duffy) 211–12
verbs 16–17, 21, 34, 35, 89
dynamic 161
imperative 13, 205
linking clauses and sentences 23, 34,
36–7, 198
non-finite *-ing* form 22, 23, 34, 36, 37
opening sentences with 22
villains 303
vocabulary 9, 26–33
choosing 26–9, 32–3, 194–7, 244, 308–9
for effect 28–9, 86–7, 194–7, 276–7, 308–9
imaginative writing 307, 308–9

non-fiction texts 62, 77, 86–7, 157
poetry and prose 244, 276–7
transactional writing 194–7

W

Walk In the Woods, A (Bill Bryson) 6–7
War of the Worlds, The (H.G. Wells) 306–7
websites 76
Wells, H.G. 306–7
'Whistle and I'll Come to You' (Susan Hill) 273–8
'White Comedy' (Benjamin Zephaniah) 122
Williams, Emlyn 292
Williams, William Carlos 32–3
Woman in Black, The (Susan Hill) 273–8
Woolf, Virginia 221
word classes 16–17
writing
from experience 279, 294
for audience 83, 183, 184–7, 195
for effect 32–3, 44–5, 194–9
for purpose 174–83
improving and correcting 53–5

openings and conclusions 202–3
planning 175, 200–1, 204
punctuation 48–51, 53, 199
sentences 34–41, 48–51, 53
sequencing and linking ideas 44–7, 198–9
spelling 52
stages of a text 42–3, 201, 202–3
structure in 9, 42–7, 90–1, 156, 220–3,
292–3
types of 132, 174–5
word choice 26–33
see also imaginative writing

Y

'Young and dyslexic?' (Benjamin Zephaniah)
122–8

Z

Zephaniah, Benjamin
'White Comedy' 122
'Young and dyslexic?' 122–8
Zeppa, Jamie 95, 134–40

NOTES